*Cracker Culture*

CRACKERS

Clockwise: from Edward King, *The Great South* . . . (Hartford, 1875), 372; *Harper's New Monthly Magazine* 11 (1855), 189; F. D. Srygley, *Seventy Years in Dixie* . . . (Nashville, 1891), 89; ibid., 194; ibid., 191; *Harper's New Monthly Magazine* 16 (1857–58), 173; Srygley, *Seventy Years in Dixie*, 23.

# GRADY McWHINEY

# *Cracker Culture*

## CELTIC WAYS

## IN THE OLD SOUTH

*With a Prologue by*

FORREST McDONALD

*The University of Alabama Press*

TUSCALOOSA AND

LONDON

Copyright © 1988 by
THE UNIVERSITY OF ALABAMA PRESS
Tuscaloosa, Alabama 35487
All rights reserved
Manufactured in the United States of America

Manufactured in the United States of America

Library of Congress Cataloging-in-Publication Data

McWhiney, Grady.
    Cracker culture.

    Bibliography: p.
    Includes index.
    1. Southern States—Civilization—Celtic influences.
    2. Southern States—Civilization—1775–1865. I. Title.
    II. Title: Celtic ways in the Old South.
F213.M38   1988   975'.03   86-16052
ISBN 0-8173-0328-6 (alk. paper)

British Library Cataloguing-in-Publication Data is available.

In memory of my "Cracker" parents—
Dad, a native Louisianian;
Mother, a Texan

# Cracker

A braggart, liar (1681). One full of conversation (Scottish). A lie (1625). A name for the "poor whites" in the southern United States (1767).—*The Oxford Universal Dictionary on Historical Principles*

One who cracks; a braggart. One of a class of low whites from the southern United States. *Crack:* To boast; to brag; that is, to utter vain, pompous, blustering words. To chat; to talk freely and familiarly (Scottish).—*Webster's New Twentieth Century Dictionary of the English Language Unabridged*

The People I refer to are really what you and I understand by *Crackers* . . . Persons who have no settled habitation, and live by hunting and plundering the industrious Settlers.—James Habersham to Governor James Wright, August 20, 1772

# Leisure

Leisure is an attitude of mind and a condition of the soul that fosters a capacity to perceive the reality of the world. . . . Culture depends for its very existence on leisure [but] . . . in our bourgeois Western world total labor has vanquished leisure. . . . [Unless] we regain the . . . ability for nonactivity, unless we substitute true leisure for our hectic amusements, we will destroy our culture—and ourselves.—Josef Pieper, *Leisure: The Basis of Culture,* translated by Alexander Dru (New York, 1963), 11, 19–21

# CONTENTS

# ILLUSTRATIONS

## Illustrations

# PREFACE

IN *Southerners and Other Americans* (1973), which emphasized various similarities between Southerners and Northerners, I also recognized that important differences have separated the South and the North throughout American history. Noting that such an authority as Thomas Jefferson "characterized Southerners as hotheaded, indolent, unstable, and unjust; Northerners as cool tempered, sober, persistent, and upright," I concluded: "Of course the South is different." But my attempt to explain why the South and North were not alike left me uncomfortable. My observations about southern "style" or "sensuality" failed to address, much less answer, the big question: How does one account for the differences between Southerners and Northerners?

Fifteen years ago I had no satisfactory answer to that question; now I believe I have. More than a decade of research and analysis done by Forrest McDonald and me, by some of our students, and by a number of other scholars has convinced me that fundamental and lasting divisions between Southerners and Northerners began in colonial America when migrants from the Celtic regions of the British Isles—Scotland, Ireland, Wales, and Cornwall—and from the English uplands managed to implant their traditional customs in the Old South. From a solid eighteenth-century base in the southern backcountry, these people and their descendants swept westward decade after decade throughout the antebellum period until they had established themselves and their anti-English values and practices across the Old South. By 1860 they far outnumbered the combined total of all other white Southerners and their culture dominated the region. The antebellum North, on the other hand, was settled and influenced principally by people who had migrated from the English lowlands. They were joined in some places, and in their movement westward, by other immigrants, especially Germans, who easily meshed with prevailing northern ways but often

xiii

suffered either cultural isolation or serious problems of adjustment when they settled in the Old South. The course of antebellum American history was shaped far more by the differences between Northerners and Southerners than by any likenesses. Their conflict in the 1860s was not as much brother against brother as culture against culture.

What is most remarkable about the Old South's predominant culture, which I call Cracker culture, is how closely it resembled traditional Celtic culture. Most of the habits, customs, and values that British Celts brought with them to the colonial South not only survived but prevailed. To be sure, some residents of the Old South were not part of Cracker culture—specifically, a few planters, some townfolk and professional people, even some slaves—but the overwhelming majority of Southerners were, whether they acknowledged it or not. Some Crackers were rich, others poor, and still others were neither; but they all more or less acted alike and shared the same values. And that is the point: Cracker does not signify an economic condition; rather, it defines a culture.

Scotch-Irish settlers, "in whose dialect a *cracker* was a person who talked boastingly," brought the term to the South, where during the colonial period it was associated mainly with herdsmen of Celtic origins. "The Cracker was typically a Scotch-Irishman," one scholar noted. In 1766 a colonial official informed the earl of Dartmouth: "I should explain to your Lordship what is meant by Crackers; a name they have got from being great boasters; they are a lawless set of rascalls on the frontiers of Virginia, Maryland, the Carolinas, and Georgia, who often change their place of abode." In 1783 a German visiting the Carolina backcountry found longhorn cattle, swine, and slovenly people whom he identified as "Crackers." In 1790 a Spanish official reported the "influx [into Florida] of rootless people called *Crackers.*" He described them as rude and nomadic, excellent hunters but indifferent farmers who planted only a few patches of corn, and as people who kept "themselves beyond the reach of all civilized law."[1]

Cracker soon became part of the American vocabulary, but it has almost always been used disparagingly to describe the mudsills of the South. Contemporaries and scholars alike usually equated

1. Delma E. Presley, "The Crackers of Georgia," *Georgia Historical Quarterly* 60 (1976), 102–16; Gary S. Dunbar, "Colonial Carolina Cowpens," *Agricultural History* 35 (1961), 130; Joe A. Akerman, Jr., *Florida Cowman, A History of Florida Cattle Raising* (Kissimmee, Fla., 1976), 59; Terry G. Jordan, *Trails to Texas: Southern Roots of Western Cattle Ranching* (Lincoln, Nebr., 1981), 34; Johann David Schopf, *Travels in the Confederation [1783–1784]* . . . , trans. and ed. Alfred J. Morrison (new ed., 2 vols., New York, 1968), II:222–23; James A. Lewis, "Cracker—Spanish Florida Style," *Florida Historical Quarterly* 63 (1984), 188, 191. On the nature of the Scotch-Irish, see Leroy V. Eid, "The Colonial Scotch-Irish: A View Accepted too Readily," *Eire-Ireland: A Journal of Irish Studies* 21 (1986), 81–105.

# Preface

Crackers with poor whites. Few writers chose, as did the historian Lewis C. Gray, to distinguish between the two: "The distinctive characteristics of the poor whites were recognized in the various special appellations by which they were contemptuously known in different parts of the South, such as, 'piney-woods people,' 'dirt-eaters,' 'clay-eaters,' 'tallow-faced gentry,' 'sand-hillers,' and 'crackers.' The term *crackers*, however, was sometimes applied also to mountaineers and other small farmers." Gray also acknowledged that many of the Old South's herdsmen were called Crackers. To most travelers in the antebellum South, especially those from England and the North, a Cracker was any Southerner whose ways differed significantly from their own, and many accounts of trips through the Old South devoted space to laughing and sneering at the rustic and lazy habits of the Crackers. Even Southerner Daniel R. Hundley listed "Crackers"—along with "Squatters," "Sandhillers," "Rag Tag and Bob Tail," and "People in the [Pine] Barrens"—as "Poor White Trash."[2]

Nor have attitudes changed much since antebellum times. Modern critics, in expressing contempt for Southerners and their ways, use Cracker synonymously for hillbilly, peckerwood, honkie, dough-face, raw-gum chewer, white trash, and redneck. Indeed, in a nation in which slurs based upon race, ethnicity, or religion have become strictly taboo, it is still acceptable to lampoon Crackers as a group. Neither actor Charlton Heston, a native of Michigan and a self-professed critic of discrimination, nor his editors bothered to delete from his published journal a candid reference to a foreign actor being cast as a Confederate officer that included the phrase: "I'll concede he makes an unlikely cracker." Consider the reaction if Heston had said the man "makes an unlikely nigger" or "an unlikely spic."[3]

Crackers have been handicapped in defending themselves for various reasons, including the traditional emphasis of their culture on oral rather than written expression. It is difficult to conceive of a Cracker jotting off an essay in defense of his ways, as a Northerner might do. Other than a check, a Cracker is unlikely to write anything more than words to a tune. But his songs—heard over hundreds of country radio stations—both defend and justify his traditions. Consider the message in Buck Owens's "I wouldn't live in New York

2. Lewis C. Gray, *History of Agriculture in the Southern United States to 1860* (2 vols., Washington, D.C., 1933), I:484, 149; Henry Benjamin Whipple, *Bishop Whipple's Southern Diary, 1843–1844*, ed. Lester B. Shippee (Minneapolis, 1937), 257; Rosalie Roos, *Travels in America, 1851–1855*, ed. Carl L. Anderson (Carbondale, Ill.,1982), 97–98; Daniel R. Hundley, *Social Relations in Our Southern States*, ed. William J.

Cooper, Jr. (1860; new ed., Baton Rouge, 1979), 257.

3. J. Wayne Flynt, *Dixie's Forgotten People: The South's Poor Whites* (Bloomington, 1979), 9; Theodore Rosengarten, *All God's Dangers: The Life of Nate Shaw* (New York, 1975), 512; Charlton Heston, *The Actor's Life: Journals, 1956–1976*, ed. Hollis Alpert (New York, 1976), 191.

City if they gave me the whole dang town," or in Hank Williams, Jr.'s "If Heaven ain't a lot like Dixie then I don't want to go." The Cracker's songs are his folk poetry; they help him maintain his pride and his culture even when he is living in Detroit, Bakersfield, or Atlanta. Compared with the numbers that hear Cracker lyrics, few people read the anguished words of such backcountry Southerners as Verna Mae Slone, who complained in her autobiography that critics "have taken our pride and our dignity and have disgraced us in the eyes of the outside world. When our children go into the cities for work or are drafted into the army, they are forced to deny their heritage, change their way of talking, and pretend to be someone else, or be made to feel ashamed, when they really have something to be proud of."[4]

That antebellum as well as postbellum observers often failed to distinguish between Crackers and poor whites, who shared the same culture, is understandable. All poor whites were Crackers even though not all Crackers were poor whites. Frederick Law Olmsted, an observant Yankee who visited the South in the 1850s, noted that some Crackers "owned a good many negroes, and were by no means so poor as their appearance indicated." Crackers and poor whites shared something else: they were Southerners. "We do not remember ever to have seen [poor whites] in the New-England States," wrote Daniel Hundley in 1860. "They are . . . found in Ohio, Pennsylvania, Indiana, and all States of the [Old] North-west, though in . . . these last they came originally from the South." The characteristics of poor whites drawn up by Hundley, which match a list compiled much later by Lewis C. Gray, credit them with being courageous, lazy, lustful, quarrelsome, violent, ignorant, superstitious, drunkards, gamblers, and livestock thieves. Both agreed that poor whites also were nonmaterialistic. "Dollars and dimes," Hundley claimed, "they never bother their brains any great deal about."[5]

4. *The Best of Buck Owens*, vol. 4, Capital ST-830; *Hank Williams, Jr., High Notes*, Elektra/Asylum, E1-60100-A; Verna Mae Slone, *What My Heart Wants to Tell* (New York, 1980), xii–xiii. On Cracker music, see Bill C. Malone, *Country Music U.S.A.: A Fifty-Year History* (Austin, 1968); idem, *Southern Music American Music* (Lexington, Ky., 1979); and Charles K. Wolfe, *Tennessee Strings: The Story of Country Music in Tennessee* (Knoxville, 1977).

5. John Hebron Moore—who notes that "the culture of cotton farmers and cotton planters of the Old Southwest were virtually identical (except for the so-called river planters of the Natchez region), and that both groups emerged

from the backcountry of South Carolina and Georgia about 1800"—is the first scholar to observe that the river planters, or "the great agriculturists," followed a totally different "system of farming." See his "Two Cotton Kingdoms" (MS in possession of the author) and his forthcoming book by the Louisiana State University Press on the cotton kingdom in Mississippi and the Old Southwest from 1793 to 1860. Frederick Law Olmsted, *The Cotton Kingdom: A Traveller's Observations on Cotton and Slavery . . .* , ed. Arthur M. Schlesinger (new ed., New York, 1953), 206; Hundley, *Social Relations*, 257, 262, 265, 266, 268, 269, 272, 276, 282; Gray, *History of Agriculture*, I:484.

Hundley's list, allowing for exaggeration, is a fair outline of Cracker traits. Southerners of English or other non-Celtic ethnic background, unless they had become Crackerized, did not practice many Cracker ways; nor did a number of sophisticated and Yankeeized Southerners, who tried to modify or to abandon their Cracker culture. Probably few Southerners fully possessed all the characteristics Hundley listed, but in combination those traits set an ideal standard; any significant deviation indicated that a Cracker had lost some of his cultural heritage.

Anyone who writes about Cracker culture owes a great debt to Frank L. Owsley, whose *Plain Folk of the Old South* (1949) was a pioneering effort to describe ordinary Southerners and to justify them historically. One of the most important books ever produced about the South, *Plain Folk* explained better than any previous work the nature of antebellum southern society and how a mass of rural plain folk—chiefly farmers and herders—shaped the Old South. Owsley stressed the distinctiveness of Southerners. "Fat or lean, blond or brunet, the Southern type could be discerned by travelers from abroad and from other parts of America," he observed. "Appearance, the indefinable qualities of personality, and their manners and customs . . . set them apart from the inhabitants of the other sections of the United States, and in this way strengthened their sense of kinship." That sense of kinship was so strong, Owsley believed, that the "Southern people . . . were a genuine folk long before the Civil War. Even the Southern aristocracy . . . were folkish in their manners and customs and shared to a marked degree in this sense of solidarity." What unified them most was the "common national origin of the bulk of the people." With unusual insight, Owsley came very close to identifying the cultural ethnicity of Southerners when he wrote: "The closely knit family with its ramified and widespreading kinship ties was a folk characteristic which the Southerners possessed to a degree second only to the Highland Scots of an earlier time." By emphasizing culture rather than economics as a primary determinant, Owsley departed from the fashionable trend in the historiography of his time. Moreover, his defense of southern and agrarian ways combined with his attempt to protect the South's history from distortion brought down upon him the full wrath of many nationalistic historians. But none of his critics has been able to refute Owsley's basic theme of an Old South culturally dominated by plain folk whose ways were quite distinctive from those of Northerners.[6]

Finally, a few words about my major sources. Soon after my research on this volume began, it became clear that I could learn only

6. Frank L. Owsley, *Plain Folk of the* 1982), 7–8, 91–94.
*Old South* (1949; new ed., Baton Rouge,

a limited amount about Cracker culture from the standard primary sources upon which much of antebellum southern history has been written—the letters, diaries, and memoirs of educated Southerners (mostly planters, townfolk, and professionals). The reason was simple enough. Those people, the most cosmopolitan and learned of Southerners, were not representative of Cracker culture; indeed, many of them were not Crackers at all. What I needed—but could rarely find—were sources written by Crackers themselves, telling what they thought and did. These proved to be extremely rare; Crackers infrequently took pen in hand, and the resulting documents seldom survived to be examined by scholars. What is abundant are the observations of contemporaries, especially travelers, who visited various parts of the South throughout the antebellum years. Travel accounts have been criticized as being of limited value because visitors tended to pass through rapidly and were unfamiliar with the local people and their traditions, but I have found this unfamiliarity of visitors with Cracker culture to be more an asset than a drawback. Because these travelers were outsiders, from a different cultural background, they often found Crackers unusual and therefore noticed and remarked upon things that Crackers themselves took for granted and would not have thought worth pointing out.

But travel accounts have been criticized on other grounds as well—that they are biased, stereotyped, and exaggerated. Some are obviously biased, but when they are they can tell us as much about the observer as they do about the observed, and when we have reciprocal accounts the evidence is mutually reinforcing. For example, when Southerners almost uniformly describe Yankees as money-grubbing and Yankees regularly describe Southerners as improvident, each is speaking contemptuously of the other but the comments are nonetheless revealing. As for stereotypes, they are often there, of course, but they are generally easy to filter out. The most obvious example is the common practice of attributing to slavery the Southerner's disdain for work; the very same travelers who do so report a similar disdain in those many parts of the South where there were few if any slaves and among the great majority of whites who owned no slaves. And as to exaggerations, sometimes the accounts are clearly so, and yet hyperbole can often capture the essence of a people's character more accurately than a bare recitation of facts can do. Tocqueville's often-quoted description of the Yankee trader with China—a man who endured eight to ten months of privation and severe hardship at sea just so "he can sell a pound of his tea for a halfpenny less than the English merchant"—is a good case in point.[7] Tocqueville's sketch is obviously overdrawn, but it

7. Alexis de Tocqueville, *The Republic of the United States of America, and Its* *Political Institutions,* trans. Henry Reeve (New York, 1858), 460.

expresses the spirit of the Yankee entrepreneur better than an entire volume of shipping statistics.

My sources also determined this book's organization. As I became familiar with the contemporary accounts, I soon realized that Cracker ways could best be explained topically rather than chronologically. What was important was continuity rather than change. Contemporaries said the same things about Cracker customs and values from the middle of the eighteenth century to the middle of the nineteenth century. By 1860 Crackers were growing more cotton and relatively fewer animals than they had in the past, but Cracker ways—aside from a few changes wrought by technology and some improved agricultural techniques—were essentially what they had been in the colonial South; indeed, they also were generally the same as those practiced by traditional Celts in Scotland and Ireland from the twelfth century through the first half of the eighteenth century.

Many people have contributed to this book. For research assistance, I thank all the helpful people at archives throughout the South as well as those at the National Library of Scotland, the National Library of Ireland, the British Library, and the Henry E. Huntington Library, where Robert Middlekauff and Martin Ridge were especially kind. For calling my attention to references or for reading and criticizing all or parts of this manuscript, I am grateful to Georgianne Bailey, John B. Boles, Jerrold Lee Brooks, Stewart J. Brown, Robert Browning, Harry M. Caudill, Kenneth Cherry, William J. Cooper, Jr., Michael Daniel, John Morgan Dederer, James F. Doster, Daniel Gillis, John D. W. Guice, Judith Lee Hallock, Stephen L. Hardin, David Edward Harrell, Robert Haws, James Michael Hill, Sam B. Hilliard, Timothy Johnson, Terry G. Jordan, J. Crawford King, Jr., Robert T. Maberry, Jr., John McCardell, Vista McCroskey, Ellen McDonald, Sue B. McWhiney, Elizabeth Shown Mills, Gary B. Mills, John Hebron Moore, Margaret Deschamps Moore, Warner O. Moore, Milton B. Newton, Jr., Chris Nordmann, Jerry C. Oldshue, Harriet C. Owsley, Daniel Pierce, Ben H. Procter, Charles P. Roland, Daniel E. Sutherland, David Weaver, Samuel J. Wells, Kenneth R. Wesson, and Lynn Wesson. For her fine work, I thank the excellent copy editor, Beverly T. Denbow. I owe special thanks to my friend Forrest McDonald, not only for his expert editorial advice and his fine Prologue to this volume, but for generously sharing with me over the past decade his ideas and research on the Celtic South.

Grady McWhiney

Texas Christian University

# PROLOGUE

THE Celtic interpretation of southern history, to which this volume is a major contribution, can be summed up in two general propositions. One is that, by virtue of historical accident, the American colonies south and west of Pennsylvania were peopled during the seventeenth and eighteenth centuries mainly by immigrants from the "Celtic fringe" of the British archipelago—the western and northern uplands of England, Wales, the Scottish Highlands and Borders, the Hebrides, and Ireland—and that the culture these people brought with them and to a large extent retained in the New World accounts in considerable measure for the differences between them and the Yankees of New England, most of whom originated in the lowland southeastern half of the island of Britain. The second is that the material culture underlying the traditional folkways, values, norms, and attitudes both in the upland areas prior to the eighteenth century and in the antebellum South was primarily related to herding, in contrast to the commercial mixed agriculture that was the norm both in southeastern Britain and in New England.

For a number of years Grady McWhiney and I have been investigating various aspects of this thesis, sometimes jointly, sometimes separately. Jointly, for example, we have studied immigration history and devised methods of estimating the ethnic makeup of the American population through name analysis (see Chapter I below). The results of such study are necessarily imprecise, but they tend to bear out the first proposition: in each of the decennial censuses from 1790 through 1860, about half of the white population of the South was of Irish, Scottish, or Welsh extraction, and about half of the remainder had originated in the western and northern English uplands. Upwards of three-quarters of the population of New England was of English lowlands extraction and continued to be so until the massive influx of Irish immigrants after the Great Famine of the 1840s.

xxi

# Prologue

Similarly, we have worked together in exploring the relevant literature from such other disciplines as cultural geography, anthropology, and historical sociology. Much of this literature, when considered in a comparative perspective, documents the persistence of Old World habits in America, often in spite of radical changes in the physical environment. Housing affords a good example. Scotch-Irish immigrants to America (who made up the largest component of the population in the southern backcountry) were inexperienced in building with wood, the most readily available material in frontier America, for the Irish woods had been stripped by the English during the seventeenth century; they learned the techniques, especially of corner timbering for log structures, from the Germans in Pennsylvania. But otherwise their dwellings were reproductions of what they had been accustomed to in Ulster and in western Scotland. The internal dimensions of the houses were sixteen feet by twenty-two feet, as compared to fifteen by twenty-one in the Ulster houses; the external dimensions were the same as in Ulster. The dimensions had originally been set by the limits on roof sizes imposed by the shortage of wood and were retained in America out of habit despite the abundance of wood. The dog-trot house that evolved later was simply a structure that comprised two of the traditional houses placed a few feet apart and enclosed under a single roof.[1]

But a great deal of the research has taken place on an individual basis. The most important direct primary sources by which one can compare Old World ways with southern ways are the recorded observations of contemporaries. Professor McWhiney has made an almost exhaustive examination of them, having studied such records in collections of manuscripts and rare books in Scotland, Ireland, and England as well as in repositories throughout the United States. It is primarily upon that study that the present work is based:

1. Data on housing are derived from E. Estyn Evans, "The Scotch-Irish: Their Cultural Adaptation and Heritage in the American Old West," in *Essays in Scotch-Irish History*, ed. E. R. R. Green (London, 1969), 78–80. For examples of other work by geographers, sociologists, and anthropologists, see Fred B. Kniffen and Henry Glassie, "Building in Wood in the Eastern United States: A Time-Place Perspective," *Geographical Review* 56 (1966), 40–66; John Fraser Hart, "Land Rotation in Appalachia," ibid. 67 (1977), 148–51; John Solomon Otto and Nain Estelle Anderson, "Slash-and-Burn Cultivation in the Highlands South: A Problem in Comparative Agricultural History," *Comparative Studies in Society and History* 24 (1982), 131–47; Duane G. Meyer, *The Highland Scots of North Carolina, 1732–1776* (Chapel Hill, 1961); Michael Hechter, *Internal Colonialism: The Celtic Fringe in British National Development, 1536–1966* (Berkeley and Los Angeles, 1977); and Given Neville, "Kinfolds and Covenant: Ethnic Community among Southern Presbyterians," in *The New Ethnicity*, ed. John Bennett (St. Paul, 1975). For a bibliography of works on the South by anthropologists, see Carole E. Hill, "Anthropological Studies in the American South: Review and Directions," *Current Anthropology* 18 (1977), 309–26.

# Prologue

McWhiney presents here extracts and summaries of the descriptions recorded by hundreds of observers of Britain, Ireland, and the South from the seventeenth through the nineteenth centuries.

My own, much more modest contribution has been to survey the scholarly literature regarding the history of the Celtic peoples from ancient times until the massive migrations of the seventeenth, eighteenth, and nineteenth centuries. This body of literature is, for a number of reasons, not entirely satisfactory. There are inherent difficulties in dealing with the history of nonliterate peoples, as the Celts were until relatively recently; and even in the nineteenth-century South, it was rare for people to set their doings down in writing. Again, much of the history of Ireland, Scotland, and Wales—especially since the sixteenth century, when written records became more available—has been the work of scholars who are not fluent in Gaelic or Welsh and who therefore have had to depend upon sources in English. Related to this problem is another. Irish, Welsh, and Scottish historians have often tended to view the past of their countries in terms of the norms of English history—concentrating on economic development and the evolution of political institutions and boundaries—which are far from central to the history of the Celts.

Despite these problems, however, it is possible to trace the course of Celtic history, at least in general terms, with some measure of confidence. It is for the purpose of placing the eyewitness accounts in historical perspective that this Prologue is intended.

\* \* \*

At the outset, it is necessary to inquire whether it is proper to refer to the inhabitants of Ireland, Scotland, Wales, and Cornwall as Celtic. Those people commonly call themselves Celts, and so august an authority as the *Encyclopedia Britannica* also calls them Celts, but that does not necessarily settle the matter. If one asks whether they are genetically descended from the ancient Celts, the answer is at most "partly," for the earliest Celts in Britain and Ireland doubtless interbred with peoples who were already there when they arrived from the Continent; and there were repeated infusions of Roman, Anglo-Saxon, Danish, Norse, and French blood in their veins over the ensuing millennia.

If, on the other hand, one asks whether the Irish, Scots, and Welsh are culturally descended from the ancient Celts, the answer must be more complex. At first blush it may seem farfetched that the culture of the primitive tribal herdsmen and warriors who pillaged Rome in the fourth century B.C., and were defeated by Caesar in Gaul during the first, could still have been a living force in Britain and Ireland during the seventeenth and eighteenth centuries A.D.

xxiii

and, with modifications, in the American South in the nineteenth. Yet no one considers it strange that legacies of the cultures of the ancient Hebrews, Greeks, Romans, and Germans continue to be living forces as the twentieth century draws to a close. The question of the perdurance of Celtic culture therefore requires careful scrutiny.

We may begin at the beginning, to the extent that the beginning is known. The ancient Celts were a people who "came out of the darkness" and appeared in central Europe between the eighth and sixth centuries B.C. Archaeological remains at Halstatt in modern Austria indicate their presence there at that time, and remains in Stuttgart, Germany, and La Tene, Switzerland, provide more information about them during the fifth century B.C. After that, descriptions of the Celts begin to appear in the writings of classical authors.[2]

The society of the Celts was tribal, rural, and pastoral. They were technologically as advanced as the Mediterranean peoples, especially in metallurgy, an art well suited to their woodland habitats and to their demand for weapons and chariots. In northern Europe they were better at raising cereal crops than were the Romans, who frequently tried to impose unsuitable Mediterranean farming techniques. Yet the Celts, like many other primitive peoples, disdained the art of farming: men were loath to work the fields, leaving tillage to women or slaves. The free males were pastoralists who held great herds of cattle and hogs in common by tribes and reckoned wealth by the numbers of their animals. "They have huge quantities . . . of meat, especially fresh and salt pork," wrote the Greek geographer Strabo. "Their pigs are allowed to run wild, and are noted for their height, and pugnacity and swiftness." The Celts enjoyed lavish feasts and heavy drinking, instrumental and vocal music, hunting and fishing, poetry and oratory. They esteemed truth and honor, but the aim of extolling themselves. . . . They are boasters and threateners, and given to bombastic self-dramatisation, and yet they are quick of mind and with good natural ability for learning." Above all, they were fierce warriors. Polybius recorded that the Celts "slept on straw, usually ate meat and did nothing other than fight." Strabo

2. The following account of the ancient Celts is based upon Gerhard Herm, *The Celts: The People Who Came out of the Darkness* (New York, 1977); Robin Place and Ann Ross, *The Celts* (London, 1977); Barry Cunliffe, *The Celtic World* (New York, 1979); Lloyd Laing, *Celtic Britain* (New York, 1979); Nora Chadwick, *The Celts* (Middlesex, England, 1970); Ann Ross, *Everyday Life* *of the Pagan Celts* (London, 1970); T. G. E. Powell, *The Celts* (New York, 1958); Jan Filip, "Early History and Evolution of the Celts: The Archaeological Evidence," in *The Celtic Consciousness*, ed. Robert O'Driscoll (New York, 1982), 33–50; and J. Markale, *Celtic Civilization* (London and New York, 1978).

CELT HUNTING A BOAR

From James Logan, *The Scottish Gael; or, Celtic Manners,
as Preserved Among the Highlanders . . .* (2 vols., Inver-
ness, 1876), II:28.

wrote: "The whole race is madly fond of war, high-spirited and quick to battle, and on whatever pretext you stir them up, you will have them ready to face danger, even if they have nothing on their side but their own strength and courage." Perhaps their courage arose in part from their belief in the immortality of the soul.

Their attacks, when they first invaded the Mediterranean world about 450 B.C., were devastating, and for more than two hundred years they terrorized and pillaged and overran a vast area of central and southern Europe, from the Iberian peninsula to the Balkans and beyond; and yet they had a crucial weakness as warriors. The Roman Livy, writing in the third century B.C., pointed it out. "This people," said he, "have no self-control." In 225 B.C. they engaged a Roman army at Telemon, north of Rome, the fate of the Roman republic being in the balance. The Romans, protected by tall shields and bearing superior arms, but most importantly well-disciplined, held against the Celts and methodically destroyed them. It is said that 40,000 Celts were slain. From then on, the Romans drove them steadily, inexorably northward and westward, and they were pressed by Germanic peoples as well. Julius Caesar, who conquered them in Gaul (modern France) in a campaign that lasted from 58 to 50 B.C., echoed Livy's description: the Celts were "reckless," given to "sudden impulsive decisions," and moved by "rash impetuosity." Though they were "quick and eager to start a war," he wrote, "they lack the strength of character and resolution necessary for enduring disasters."

Though driven from the Continent, the Celts had long since begun to invade Britain and Ireland, possibly as early as the eighth or even as early as the twelfth century B.C. By the second century they had conquered, destroyed, or become assimilated with most of the previous inhabitants of the islands. For a time they apparently flourished, their tribal-pastoral culture enriched by the arrival of a more agriculturally advanced and less nomadic group of Celts, the Belgae, and by maritime intercourse with Iberia and perhaps even the eastern Mediterranean. As they flourished, they continued to fight—in the absence of an external enemy, one another.

Then came the Romans. Caesar made brief raids on Britain from Gaul, but the real conquest of Britain did not begin until A.D. 43. When the conquerers arrived, their efforts were eased by another practice that would plague the Celts throughout their history: instead of joining together to repel the common enemy, some joined the Romans in order to wreak mayhem against their tribal Celtic enemies. Thus aided, the Romans steadily advanced, and within two decades they had established a regime that would last 350 years. Their conquest was not, however, complete: what would become Wales (except for the vale of Glamorgan), the uplands of northern

# Prologue

England, most of Scotland, and all of Ireland remained outside the area of Roman rule.[3]

In the part of Britain that they controlled, the Romans had a profound impact. They introduced centralized administration, something previously lacking in all Celtic societies, and over time they instilled the habit of obedience to an abstract government rather than to tribal chieftains. Simultaneously, by imposing order with a large standing army and by instituting a more diversified economic system—including great estates or villas that were based upon tillage agriculture—they effectively undermined the old chiefs and replaced them, as the "aristocracy," either with Romans or, as Tacitus put it, with "noble youths" of Celtic stock who were educated or reeducated in the ways of the Romans. They also introduced cities as centers of administration and commerce, and they connected them with networks of roads. In sum, Roman Britain was to a large extent de-tribalized and de-pastoralized, and to some extent commercialized and urbanized: de-Celticized. To employ one more "ize," the Romans civilized much of Britain and began the enduring division between a lowland south and east and an upland, predominantly Celtic, north and west.

*     *     *

Roman rule in Britain started to collapse during the late fourth century, and in 410 Rome withdrew the last of its troops. There ensued a long period of chaos and stagnation, during which Britain was invaded and conquered both from the west and from the east. The result was another transformation; but in a perverse way the new order, once it became somewhat stable, confirmed and solidified the old.

The western invasion emanated from Ireland. The society of Ireland lacked political unity, but by the fourth or fifth century the hundred or so *tuaths* or petty kingdoms that inhabited the island had combined into geographical groupings called the Five Fifths: Ulster, Meath, Leinster, Munster, and Connaught. The resulting cohesion, together with the weakening of the Roman position, made possible a Gaelic counterinvasion of the north and west of Britain. Irish warriors invaded Wales, the Isle of Man, and Dumnonia (later the shires of Cornwall and Devon) and in league with Brythonic (British) Celts established petty kingdoms there. Just as important, Irishmen from Ulster gained control of the inner Hebrides and the

3. Among the more important works on Roman Britain are Sheppard S. Frere, *Britannia: A History of Roman Britain* (Cambridge, Mass., 1967); A. L. F. Rivet, ed., *The Roman Villa in Britain* (New York, 1969); Anthony R. Birley, *The People of Roman Britain* (Berkeley and Los Angeles, 1980); and Eric Birley, *Roman Britain and the Roman Army* (Kendal, England, 1953).

sparsely populated southwest mainland of Scotland (Argyll), naming their new kingdom Dalriada. These men were called Scotti, that being the Latin word for the Irish, and it is from them that Scotland derives its name.[4]

The eastern invasions were those of Germanic peoples—Jutes, Angles, and Saxons—who came in a succession of waves between the middle of the fifth century and the middle of the sixth. The distinctions among the Germans progressively lessened, and though there came to be seven separate kingdoms in the area they occupied, the people could, by the seventh century, think of themselves as "the nation of the English." The territory dominated by the Anglo-Saxons was essentially the same as that which had been controlled by the Romans; the rest of the archipelago remained Celtic. There were nine Welsh (or Brythonic Celtic) kingdoms, most of which were sealed off from England during the eighth century by the great earthwork wall known as Offa's Dyke. In Ireland the Five Fifths remained intact, despite the evolution of a High Kingship that nominally ruled the whole. In what would become Scotland, political arrangements remained unresolved, four groups being locked in a struggle for dominance: the Scotti in the north and west, the ancient Picts in the northeast, a mixture of Brythonic Celts and Gaels in the extreme southwest, and Angles in the southeast.[5]

Still another round of invasions, these by Scandinavians, began near the end of the eighth century and continued intermittently until the middle of the eleventh.[6] Politically, the result of the Viking incursions was to reduce the archipelago to the rule of four kingdoms: England, Wales, Ireland, and Scotland, the Scotti prevailing in the last. Culturally, the coming of the Scandinavians resulted in

4. Charles Thomas, *Britain and Ireland in Early Christian Times: A.D. 400–800* (London, 1971); Francis J. Byrne, "Early Irish Society (1st–9th century)," in *The Course of Irish History*, ed. T.W. Moody and F. X. Martin (Cork, 1967), 44–46, 57–59. The five divisions became seven in the fifth century and then settled down to four, Meath being absorbed by the others. Ruth Dudley Edwards, *An Atlas of Irish History* (2d ed., London and New York, 1973), 13–19. See also Givyn A. Williams, *When Was Wales? A History of the Welsh* (London, 1985), 21, 28, 33, 34, 38; W. Croft Dickinson, *Scotland from the Earliest Times to 1603*, rev. and ed. Archibald A. M. Duncan (3d ed., Oxford, 1977), 25–26.

5. Peter Hunter Blair, *An Introduction to Anglo-Saxon England* (2d ed., New York, 1956); Goldwin Smith, *A History of England* (4th ed., New York, 1974), 13–69; G. R. J. Jones, "Celts, Saxons, and Scandinavians," in *An Historical Geography of England and Wales*, ed. R. A. Dodgshon and R. A. Butlin (London and New York, 1978), 57–71; Archibald A. M. Duncan, *Scotland: The Making of the Kingdom* (New York, 1975), 87–88; Prys Morgan and David Thomas, *Wales: The Shaping of a Nation* (Newton Abbot and London, 1984), 58–61.

6. The following description of the Scandinavians and of their impact is drawn in large measure from Rudolph Poertner, *The Vikings: Rise and Fall of the Norse Sea Kings*, trans. Sophie Wilkins (New York and London, 1975); Johannes Brondsted, *The Vikings* (Baltimore, 1965); and Jacqueline Simpson, *The Viking World* (New York, 1980).

a revolution by intensification of previously existing traits and tendencies.

To understand the cultural impact, it is necessary to be aware that it was Danes who subdued most of the English lowlands and Norwegians who raided and settled elsewhere. The Danes practiced mixed agriculture at home; pressed by overpopulation, they set out mainly in search of new lands to farm. In England they instituted land tenure by the payment of rents instead of services, and they established and reinvigorated cities (which had not fully recovered under the Anglo-Saxons) both as administrative and as commercial centers. Together, these complementary developments gave renewed impetus to the emergence of mixed commercial farming by individual families and to the growth of maritime trade, intranational as well as international—for which the lowlands were naturally suited by climate, soil, and access to navigable water.[7]

The raiders and invaders from Norway, while of the same stock as the Danes, had been forced by nature to develop a different kind of material culture. The extremely harsh climate and the scarcity of arable land made the Norsemen into fishermen and herdsmen, and as herdsmen they developed patterns of behavior (and even myths and legends) that were in many ways strikingly similar to those of the Celts. They were fiercely warlike; they were bombastic and boastful; they drank prodigious quantities of alcohol; they were lavish in their hospitality; they were organized into clans.

It happened that, when the Norse excursions began, the northwestern part of the area of Anglo-Saxon political dominance was a frontier region, in the American sense of the term: an almost uninhabited wilderness of woods and undeveloped uplands, much better suited to pastoralism than to tillage agriculture. It was in this region that Scandinavians mainly located. Though scholars have disagreed as to how numerous the settlers were, it seems safe to say that a majority, and possibly a large majority, of the inhabitants from the eleventh century onward were primarily of Norse or Norse-Gaelic extraction and secondarily of Danish-English extraction.[8]

Meanwhile, the Norsemen had long since infested other parts of the archipelago. By the 860s, when the first great Danish incursions into Anglo-Saxon Britain began, Norse had come to dominate the Shetland and Orkney islands, the northern and western Highlands of Scotland, and the Hebrides, and they had gained footholds in the

---

7. H. C. Darby, *An Historical Geography of England before A.D. 1800* (Cambridge, 1936), 133–63; G. Jones, "Celts, Saxons, and Scandinavians," 71–76; H. C. Darby, "The Anglo-Scandinavian Foundations," in *An Historical Geog-*

*raphy of England before 1600,* ed. H. C. Darby (Cambridge, 1976), 1–38.
8. H. C. Darby, "Anglo-Scandinavian Foundations," 22, 24–28. See also the map, Fig. 3.3, in Dodgshon and Butlin, *Historical Geography,* 72.

north of Ireland and the southwestern Scottish Highlands. In addition, they had established Ireland's first towns—Dublin, and afterward Wexford, Waterford, Limerick, and Cork—as raiding and trading posts.[9]

The Norse left a sizable legacy before leaving for good in 1266. There was considerable mixing of Scandinavians with Gaels, partly through rape and partly through intermarriage. More significant was the emergence of a Gaelic-Norse subculture, a fierce, hardy breed known in Irish as Gall-Ghaidel (Anglicized as Galloway) that for centuries would dominate the west of Britain from the Hebrides to southern Wales, irrespective of political boundaries. Still more significant, at least for the future of the American South—for this was the region from which the largest component of the southern population would originate—was a cultural by-product of the maritime skills the Norsemen brought with them. Though Viking dominance of the seas may temporarily have cut the centuries-old connections of Ulster, Argyll, and the Hebrides, in the long run the acquisition of some knowledge of seamanship made the connections far firmer. This gave "the Hebridean lord of the tenth century and later a mastery over his environment unknown to the tribe of Fergus in the sixth," writes an eminent historian. "Now the Isles were no longer appendages of an essentially land-based Dalridian kingdom, but home of a race of vigorous and independent chieftains who could choose the master they wished to serve—in Ireland, Man, Galloway, or Scotia." These emerging "Lords of the Isles," in league with kinsmen in Ulster, would, like the Galwegians, long hold sway over their region regardless of kings who claimed to rule from London, Edinburgh, or Dublin.[10]

\*        \*        \*

Such a king came in 1066 in the person of William the Conquerer. Or rather, the foundations for such kings were laid that year, for the Norman Conquest only began with the victory of the duke of Normandy over the English King Harold at the Battle of Hastings. Normanization of England, Wales, Scotland, and Ireland was a process that took a century and a half and was never completely implemented.

9. Poertner, *Vikings*, 37–40; Gordon Donaldson, *Scotland: The Shaping of a Nation* (Newton Abbot and London, 1980), 15–16; Liam de Paor, "The Age of the Viking Wars," in Moody and Martin, *Course of Irish History*, 91–106.

10. Seumas MacManus, *The Story of the Irish Race: A Popular History of Ireland* (Old Greenwich, Conn., 1931), 167–85; George Henderson, *The Norse Influence on Celtic Scotland* (Glasgow, 1910); Duncan, *Scotland*, 86; Henry L. Snyder, "From the Beginnings to the End of the Middle Ages," in *Irish History and Culture: Aspects of a People's Heritage*, ed. Harold Orel (Lawrence, Kans., 1976), 33–34; G. Williams, *When Was Wales?*, 57–58. See also G. W. S. Barrow, *The Kingdom of the Scots: Government, Church, and Society from the Eleventh to the Fourteenth Century* (New York, 1973), 365–66, 376–77.

# Prologue

British historians continue to disagree over the extent of the changes brought by the Normans, though they are now generally agreed that the changes were not so revolutionary as was long thought. The major change, at least during the reign of William and his sons (which lasted until 1135), was to subordinate England and, at least nominally, the three Celtic kingdoms to a Norman aristocracy. Almost all of Wales had fallen to the Normans before the end of the eleventh century, though most of it had been reconquered by the Welsh before the end of the twelfth and was contested thereafter for two more centuries. Most of Ireland except Ulster likewise fell fairly soon, though the Irish remained in an almost perpetual state of rebellion; under King John (1199–1216) even the Ulster chieftains were induced to swear oaths of loyalty to the English throne, but none considered the oaths especially binding. In Scotland, King Alexander I (1107–24) and King David I (1124–53) voluntarily placed themselves under Norman protection; David also brought many Norman and Flemish families to Scotland and created baronies for them.

Whatever the changes wrought by the Normans in England, the changes they effected in the Celtic kingdoms were superficial. The historical geographer R. A. Butlin has noted that the "actual percentage of the area of Wales characterized by Norman manorial systems was small, and in the greater part of Wales the social structures, and settlement and economic systems still derived, even as late as 1500, almost entirely from native institutions and traditions."[11] That judgment is confirmed by the descriptions written by Gerald of Wales, the earliest post-Norman observer whose writings have survived. Gerald, a well-educated and widely traveled cleric and sometime chaplain to Henry II, was born in Wales of a Norman father and a mother of royal Welsh blood. He lived in Wales much of his life and accompanied King John to Ireland in 1185, remaining more than a year. His depictions of the Welsh and Irish bear a remarkable resemblance to those of the Celts penned by ancient writers—and to the later observations of travelers in Wales, Ireland, Scotland, and the antebellum South reported in this book.[12]

"It must always be remembered," Gerald wrote, "that the Welsh are not being enervated by daily toil. . . . One cannot say here, as elsewhere, that the farmer's toil is one long round." "They do not have orchards or gardens. . . . most of their land is used for pasture. They cultivate very little." "They do not live in towns, villages, or castles, but lead a solitary existence, deep in the woods." "They eat

11. R. A. Butlin, "The Late Middle Ages, c. 1350–1500," in Dodgshon and Butlin, *Historical Geography*, 119–50 (quotation on 133).

12. Giraldus Cambrensis, *The Itiner-* *ary through Wales and the Description of Wales* (New York, 1978). The quotations and descriptions that follow are from 233, 236–38, 243, 245, 250, 251, 252, 256, 257, 259–60, 262–63, 265, 270.

plenty of meat, but little bread." "In times of scarcity, their absti-
nence and frugality are most remarkable, but, when they have gone
without food for a long time, their appetite becomes enormous,
especially when they are sitting at someone else's table. . . . They
lose all control of themselves, and insist on being served with vast
quantities of food and more especially intoxicating drink." Withal,
they were hospitable and gregarious. They loved music and were
skillful at it. They were an oral people, having a bardic tradition and
being "endowed with great boldness in speaking and great confi-
dence in answering. . . . They love sarcastic remarks and libellous
allusions." They were sexually of loose morals. They were "very
sharp and intelligent," but they "rarely keep their promises, for their
minds are as fickle as their bodies are agile." They also habitually
"steal anything they can lay their hands on," engaging in "plunder,
theft and robbery, not only from foreigners and people hostile to
them, but also from each other."

They had great respect for birth and genealogy, and it was through
loyalty to clans that their warlike dispositions most commonly
found outlet. "They are fierce rather than strong, and totally dedi-
cated to the practice of arms," Gerald wrote. "Not only the leaders
but the entire nation are trained in war. . . . They esteem it a disgrace
to die in bed, but an honour to be killed in battle." They are most
"ferocious when battle is first joined. They shout, glower fiercely at
the enemy, and fill the air with fearsome clamour, making a high-
pitched screech with their long trumpets. . . . They seem most
formidable opponents." But "if the enemy resists manfully and they
are repulsed, they are immediately thrown into confusion. . . . Their
sole idea of tactics is either to pursue their opponents, or else to run
away from them." Yet if they are routed and even slaughtered today,
"tomorrow they march out again, no whit dejected by their defeat
or their losses."

To summarize Gerald's description of the Irish would be virtually
to repeat the foregoing two paragraphs; instead, an additional point
about the Irish wants making. In time, Ireland absorbed invaders
and conquerers, whether Norwegian, Norman, Scots, or English.
All intermarried with the natives, and all but the English, who
arrived in the seventeenth century and afterward, ultimately aban-
doned their language for Gaelic. Some Normans even became sub-
jects of legends in Gaelic poetry.[13] In the north of Ireland, Gaelic
Scots settled in great numbers and "were merged in their surround-
ings. The connection between Ireland and Scotland by means of this
Scottish colony in Ulster became strengthened," and it led to im-
portant military cooperation against England.[14]

13. Roger Chauvire, *A Short History of* *Ulster from the Earliest Times to the*
*Ireland* (New York, 1961), 36–37. *Present Day* (4 vols., London, 1919–20),
14. Ramsay Colles, *The History of* I:83.

Robert the Bruce, the Scots king who reunited Scotland by force and then won its independence by defeating the English at Bannockburn in 1314, had at one point been forced to flee Scotland, and Ulster provided him sanctuary. After Bannockburn, Ulster appealed to Robert to send his brother Edward to become king of a united Ireland and liberate it from England. Edward did become king of Ireland, but he overreached himself and was killed in 1318. Meanwhile another significant Scottish-Irish military connection began. Fierce Scots mercenary soldiers called galloglas (from *gall oglach*— foreign warrior) began to contribute their services in Ulster; the galloglas "prolonged the life of the independent Gaelic kingdoms for more than two centuries after the defeat of Edward Bruce."[15]

As for Scotland, some modern Scots historians insist that it had ceased to be Celtic. "Certainly," writes one of the most distinguished of them, Gordon Donaldson, "any possibility that Scotland might be a predominantly Celtic country vanished in the twelfth century" because the Lowlands were transformed at that time by Norman feudalism. That oversimplifies the matter, for as T. C. Smout writes, over the course of time the clan system (which continued to prevail in the Highlands and Borders) "became imbued with some feudal characteristics of Norman origin" just as feudalism "became imbued with clannish characteristics of Celtic origin." Indeed, "thoroughly feudal landlords like Grant or Fraser of Norman or Fleming origins could in a surprisingly short time transform tenants into 'clansmen' prepared to accept an ancient family history as the true link to their 'chief.' " And, most tellingly, Donaldson himself observes (only a few pages after the passage quoted above) that by the early fourteenth century Scots of all origins had "laid aside their particular memories of the past and adopted as their heritage the history and mythology of the original Scots, who had come as Irish invaders."[16]

And if the recorded observations of travelers in Scotland are to be credited, the ordinary Scots—except for those in the Norman-created Lowland burghs—retained their primitive, pastoral, warlike Celtic ways as surely as had the Irish and the Welsh. A Frenchman (1385): The Scots are "bold, hardy, and much inured to war" but also treacherous and thieving. "In Scotland you will never find a man of worth: they are like savages.... We have never known till now what was meant by poverty and hard living." An Italian (circa 1430): "The common people are poor, and destitute of all refinement. They eat flesh and fish to repletion, and bread only as a dainty. The men are small in stature, bold and forward in temper; the women, fair in complexion, comely and pleasing, but not distinguished for their

15. Ibid., I:83–86; Edwards, *Atlas of Irish History*, 29.
16. G. Donaldson, *Scotland*, 19, 23– 24; T. C. Smout, *A History of the Scottish People, 1560–1830* (Glasgow, 1969), 20–23, 40–43 (quotation on 42).

chastity." A Spaniard (1498): "The Scotch are not industrious, and the people are poor. They spend all their time in wars, and when there is no war they fight with one another. . . . They have more meat, in great and small animals, than they want, and plenty of wool and hides. . . . The corn is very good, but they do not produce as much as they might, because they do not cultivate the land. . . . The inhabitants [of the Western Isles] speak the language and have the habits of the Irish." Another Italian (1545): "So many horses . . . , and so many oxen, and so many flocks of sheep, that wonder arises in the beholders, on account of the multitude of them. Nor in truth is there any shepherd placed over the sheep to tend them, neither indeed a herdsman near the oxen. . . . But that each man may know his own, they smear some mark on the skin with some native pitch." An Englishman (1618): "Once in the yeere, which is the whole month of August, and sometimes part of September, many of the nobility and gentry of the kingdome (for their pleasure) doe come into these high-land countries to hunt, where they do conforme themselves to the habite of the High-land-men, who for the most part, speake nothing but Irish." Another Englishman (1655): "The barrenesse of the countrey, poverty of the people, generally affected with slothe, and a lazy vagrancy of attending and followeing theyr heards up and downe in theyr pastorage, rather than any dextrous improvement of theyr time, hath quite banished all trade from the inland parts. . . . the rest of the country from [the Firth of Clyde] on the west side, with all the islands up towards the most northerne headland, being inhabited by the old Scotts and wilde Irish, and speaking theyr language, which live by feeding cattle up and downe the hills, or else fishing and fowleing, and formerly (till that of late they have been restrayned), by plaine downeright robbing and stealeing."[17]

In sum, most of the inhabitants of the upland areas—whether Gaelic, Brythonic, Norse-Gaelic, or some other form of hyphenated Celtic—remained isolated from and hostile to their English neighbors, and they remained tribal, pastoral, and warlike.

\*    \*    \*

It was upon the accession of the Tudor dynasty in 1485 that the final political subjugation of the Celtic kingdoms began. Cultural subjugation and in some instances cultural absorption followed slowly but inexorably from the political.

The Welsh part of the story can be told briefly. In Wales as in other historically Celtic areas there had been no individual "ownership"

17. Peter Hume Brown, ed., *Scotland Before 1700, from Contemporary Docu-* ments (Edinburgh, 1893), 8, 11, 12, 15, 26–27, 29, 43–44, 48, 60–61, 120, 163.

CATTLE RAID

From John Derricke, *The Image of Ireland*, edited by
J. Small (1581; reissued, Edinburgh, 1883),
unnumbered page.

of land. Rather, the land was held by the clan or kin-group as a whole. The old system broke down between the middle of the fourteenth and the middle of the fifteenth centuries—first as a result of the Black Death, then after the great Glendower Rebellion of 1400–1407, in which the Welsh struggled valiantly but vainly to regain their independence from the English Crown, and further as a result of Wales' involvement in the English Wars of the Roses. In those chaotic circumstances, and in the absence of strong clan chieftains, many individuals (both Welsh opportunists and English adventurers) began to gain control of lands formerly held jointly, and by 1500 these people constituted an emerging English-style gentry. They sought and obtained from Henry VII, first of the Tudors, charters conferring upon them the benefits of English land law. The policy was extended by Henry VIII, and in acts of 1536 and 1543 the English Parliament went the rest of the way: Wales was politically absorbed into England, was given representation in Parliament and made subject to parliamentary taxation, and was placed under English common law. It thus became the first part of the Celtic fringe in which the machinery for decelticization was set in place—though most of it remained primarily pastoral for another three centuries.[18]

The Irish part of the story is longer and more complex. At the time of the Tudor accession, Ireland had been substantially free from effective English rule for the better part of a century, but the Tudors crushed the Irish in four great waves of conquest—in the 1490s, the 1530s and 1540s, the 1570s and 1580s, and the period 1595 to 1603. Each of these except the first began as a rebellion of Irish chieftains; each resulted in the slaughter of thousands upon thousands of Irish men, women, and children. When James VI of Scotland acceded to the English Crown as James I in 1603, Ireland lay at England's mercy.[19]

Nor were James and the English disposed to be merciful. In 1609, after the greatest chieftains in Ulster had left for the Continent, taking many of their best fighting men with them, James confiscated all the land in six of Ulster's nine counties. He then regranted it to "planters," who recruited tenants from England and the Scottish Lowlands. In the 1640s Ireland rose in rebellion and supported Charles I in his unsuccessful wars with Parliament, only to be devastated by Oliver Cromwell in 1649–52. Cromwell confiscated the lands of all who had participated in the rebellion and parceled

18. G. Williams, *When Was Wales?*, 48–51, 73–74, 89–90, 91–92, 99–100, 122; R. A. Dodgshon, "The Early Middle Ages," in Dodgshon and Butlin, *Historical Geography*, 94.

19. Art Cosgrove, "The Gaelic Resurgence and the Geraldine Supremacy,"

and G. A. Hayes-McCoy, "The Tudor Conquest," in Moody and Martin, *Course of Irish History*, 158–88; James Michael Hill, *Celtic Warfare, 1595–1763* (Edinburgh, 1986); Margaret Mac-Curtain, *Tudor and Stuart Ireland* (Dublin, 1972), 1–113.

it out to his soldiers. Ireland rose once again in the 1690s in support of the dethroned James II after England's "Glorious Revolution"; this time the Irish were defeated by William III. Still more confiscations followed, until only 14 percent of the land was owned by "mere" Irish. During the following century, most of the Irish who retained a taste for fighting went abroad as "wild geese"—almost half a million fought in the armies of France alone—but even so, sporadic rebellions continued to erupt until Ireland finally won its independence in the 1920s.[20]

The story in Scotland is even longer and even more complex, but it can be encapsulated.[21] By the middle of the sixteenth century portions of the Lowlands had taken on some of the characteristics that would in time make Lowlanders more like the English than like the Celts. This transition was visible in the tendency of the gentry, the lairds, to go increasingly into mixed commercial agriculture (though some continued also to be clan chieftains) and in the growth of the burghs and their dominance by merchants, kirkmen, and lawyers; the influence of both gentry and burghers had much to do with the beginning of the Protestant Reformation in Scotland in 1559. That most of the Lowlands remained as wild as ever is attested, however, by the fact that in 1582 James VI himself was kidnapped and held in Ruthven castle by a band of Presbyterian earls/chieftains. It would be more than a century before Presbyterianism became the established Kirk of Scotland, and during that time there was turbulence and warfare in abundance. Not until the eighteenth century did the Lowlands come to be dominated by the dour, industrious, orderly, morally rigid, and frugal Presbyterian Scots of the stereotype.

The transformation of the Highlands, the Hebrides, and Ulster was even slower. During the seventeenth century clansmen in these areas rose against the English on each of the occasions when the

20. M. Perceval-Maxwell, *The Scottish Migration to Ulster in the Reign of James I* (London and New York, 1973); Colles, *History of Ulster*, III; MacCurtain, *Tudor and Stuart Ireland*, 140–60, 174–96; Edwards, *Atlas of Irish History*, 58–66, 168–79; Edward MacLysaght, *Irish Life in the Seventeenth Century* (1939; reprint, Dublin, 1979).

21. The following observations about Scotland are based on, among others, Smout, *History of the Scottish People*; G. Donaldson, *Scotland*; Jenny Wormald, *Court, Kirk, and Community: Scotland, 1470–1625* (London, 1981); idem, *Lords and Men in Scotland: Bonds of Manrent, 1442–1603* (Edinburgh, 1985); Maurice Lee, Jr., *Government by Pen: Scotland under James VI & I* (London, 1980); William Ferguson, *Scotland's Relations with England: A Survey to 1707* (Edinburgh, 1977); David Mathew, *Scotland under Charles I* (London, 1955); David Stevenson, *The Scottish Revolution, 1637–44: The Triumph of the Covenanters* (New York, 1973); F. D. Dow, *Cromwellian Scotland, 1651–1660* (Edinburgh, 1979); William Ferguson, *Scotland: 1689 to the Present* (New York, 1968); and Christopher Sinclair-Stevenson, *Inglorious Rebellion: The Jacobite Risings of 1708, 1715 and 1719* (New York, 1971).

Irish did and on at least four more besides—in 1615, 1666, 1679, and 1685. During the eighteenth century Highlanders rose again in 1715, 1719, and 1745. During the half-century following the Forty-five came the Clearances, the English effort to extirpate the Highlands of the last vestiges of traditional Gaelic culture.

\*     \*     \*

Thus at various times during the seventeenth and eighteenth centuries it became increasingly difficult for the inhabitants of Wales, Ireland, and Scotland to retain their accustomed ways of life, and ultimately it became impossible. Under such circumstances there are, broadly speaking, three courses that people can follow: they can adapt, they can resist change unto death, or they can leave. We are concerned here with those who left.

As indicated earlier, migrants from the British uplands and Ireland settled mainly in the southern colonies. The first round of southern settlement was in the Chesapeake region. More than 5,000 immigrants went there during the first two decades after 1607, but the mortality rate was so high that scarcely a quarter of them survived. By 1640 the population of Virginia had grown to about 8,000 and that of Maryland to about 1,500, mostly by additional migrations. The decisive emigration to the Chesapeake colonies began around 1642 with the outbreak of the English Civil War. Royalist strength was concentrated in the English uplands and Wales, and when the Puritan-Parliamentarian "Roundheads" triumphed, a sizable exodus from "Cavalier" country to the Chesapeake area ensued. This is not to suggest that more than a handful of the approximately 15,000 who emigrated were cavaliers in the sense of nobility or landed gentry, or even that most went for political or religious reasons. Indeed, 70 to 90 percent apparently went as indentured servants, and most apparently went to escape severe economic hardships at home. Nonetheless, it is a fact that (in striking contrast to New England) Virginia and Maryland were originally peopled mainly from the upland, pastoral portions of Britain and from Ireland.[22]

The Irish had long been in the habit of migrating from their homeland. After each of the rebellions thousands of Irishmen had followed their chieftains into exile. During the seventeenth century,

22. Edmund S. Morgan, *American Slavery, American Freedom: The Ordeal of Colonial Virginia* (New York, 1975), 136, 180, 395–410; Bureau of the Census, *Historical Statistics of the United States: Colonial Times to 1957* (Washington, D.C., 1960), 756; James Horn, "Servant Emigration to the Chesapeake in the Seventeenth Century," in *The Chesapeake in the Seventeenth Century: Essays on Anglo-American Society*, ed. Thaddeus W. Tate and David L. Ammerman (Chapel Hill, 1979), 51–95, esp. the maps on 67 and 71; John Eacott Manahan, "The Cavalier Remounted: A Study of the Origins of Virginia's Population, 1607–1700" (Ph.D. diss., University of Virginia, 1947).

even before the great rebellion of 1641, many young men and women went from Ireland to the Chesapeake area, some kidnapped or transported but most voluntarily as indentured servants. During the 1640s and 1650s thousands more fled or were deported as felons or rebels. Considerable numbers of these went to the Chesapeake, but most went to the West Indies. By the time of the Restoration, Irish constituted a large majority of the perhaps 80,000 white inhabitants of the English islands in the Caribbean. Barbados had, at that time, about 30,000 black slaves and about 20,000 indentured white felons and rebels, these being overwhelmingly Irish; St. Christopher was said to contain 20,000 Irish.[23]

Remigration to the mainland began in 1669. During the next three decades the Irish labor force in the English West Indies was substantially replaced by blacks imported from Africa, and most of the Irish moved to the new Carolina colonies. There their numbers were augmented by immigrants arriving directly from Ireland. Englishmen and Huguenots went to the Carolinas as well, of course, but in the words of an early South Carolina historian, "No country furnished the province with as many inhabitants as Ireland." The historian was Robert Mills, writing in 1826, and he added, "Scarcely a ship sailed from any of [Ireland's] ports, for Charleston, that was not crowded with men, women, and children." In addition, 25,000 to 30,000 were transported as convicts between the 1720s and the 1760s, mainly to Maryland and Virginia, and perhaps as many more immigrated as indentured servants during that period, again mainly to Maryland and Virginia.[24]

The last and greatest wave of immigration to the South was that of the Scotch-Irish. It is generally recognized that not many Scots emigrated directly from Scotland to America: a few hundred a year went from the Lowlands, mainly to the Chesapeake region, and about 20,000 went from the Highlands during the decade before the American Revolution, mainly to the Carolinas. By contrast, the number of putative "Scots" who migrated from northern Ireland during the six decades before the Revolution has been estimated

23. Moody and Martin, *Course of Irish History,* 174–203; MacLysaght, *Irish Life;* Carl Bridenbaugh and Roberta Bridenbaugh, *No Peace Beyond The Line: The English in the Caribbean, 1624–1690* (New York, 1972), 12–21, 225–28; Richard S. Dunn, *Sugar and Slaves: The Rise of the Planter Class in the English West Indies, 1624–1713* (Chapel Hill, 1972), 56–57, 69.

24. Richard S. Dunn, "The English Sugar Islands and the Founding of South Carolina," *South Carolina Historical and Genealogical Magazine* 72 (1971), 82–83; Edward McGrady, *The History of South Carolina under the Proprietary Government, 1670–1719* (New York, 1897), 73–128, 143; Robert Mills, *Statistics of South Carolina . . .* (Charleston, 1826), 175; Abbot Emerson Smith, *Colonists in Bondage: White Servitude and Convict Labor in America, 1607–1776* (Chapel Hill, 1947), 48–49, 52, 134; Carl Bridenbaugh, *Myths and Realities: Societies of the Colonial South* (Baton Rouge, 1952), 7.

variously from 130,000 to 500,000. That about a third of these landed in southern ports is well known, as is the fact that all but a handful of the rest landed in Philadelphia, from which they moved inland and thence down the interior uplands from Maryland to Georgia. After the Revolution they continued to follow that migratory pattern, but many also went down the Ohio River to Kentucky and to southern Ohio, Indiana, and Illinois.[25]

The prevailing understanding—or, rather, misunderstanding—is that the Scotch-Irish were descendants of Scots who settled on the Ulster plantations created by James I in 1610 and rarely intermingled with the "mere" or pure Irish. There are several things wrong with that view. One is that, as we have seen, Ulstermen, Hebrideans, and western Highlanders were all but indistinguishable, having for centuries been a part of a single, herding, seafaring, and warrior culture that as a practical matter had been politically autonomous under the Lordship of the Isles until the end of the fifteenth century. As importantly, the seventeenth-century migrations from Scotland to Ireland cannot be squared with the myth that the eighteenth-century Scotch-Irish were descended from the settlers on the Ulster plantations. As of the death in 1625 of James, about 14,000 new Scots had been settled in Ulster, perhaps half being Lowlanders, the rest being from the Hebrides and western Highlands. The number approximately doubled during the 1630s, but the newcomers apparently came mainly from the area between Aberdeenshire and Inverness, and they went not to the plantation areas but to Counties Antrim and Down, which were not among the six escheated counties. Many of the newly arrived Scots in Ulster fled or were killed during the turbulent 1640s, and by 1652 the total number had declined to about 20,000. Another large migration took place during the next two decades, and Sir William Petty estimated that in 1672 there were 100,000 Scots in northern Ireland. Few Scots went to Ireland during the next generation, but in 1695 a devastating famine swept the Highlands and Islands, and a mass exodus ensued. The Bishop of Baphoe estimated that no fewer than 50,000 Scots *families*—overwhelmingly western Highlanders and Hebrideans—

25. C. Bridenbaugh, *Myths and Realities*, 124–33; Ian C. C. Graham, *Colonists from Scotland: Emigration to North America, 1707–1783* (Ithaca, N.Y., 1956), 25, 38–42; Robert J. Dickson, *Ulster Emigration to Colonial America, 1718–1775* (London, 1966). Dickson takes considerable pains to disprove the claim of Michael J. O'Brien (in *A Hidden Phase of American History: Ireland's Part in America's Struggle for Liberty* [New York, 1919] and in "Shipping Statistics of the Philadelphia Customs House, 1773 to 1774, Refute the Scotch-Irish Theory," *American-Irish Historical Society Journal* [1923]) that 150,000 emigrants left Ireland for America in the early 1700s and that two-thirds of these were Catholic Irish. Dickson's argument is sometimes inconsistent and not entirely convincing, yet O'Brien's claims clearly seem extravagant.

moved to northern Ireland during the late seventeenth and early eighteenth centuries.[26]

In sum, the "Scotch-Irish" who emigrated to America during the eighteenth century were not descendants of Lowland settlers in the Ulster plantations but members of a traditionally Gaelic (or Norse-Gaelic) society who had been moving back and forth between Ulster and the Highlands and Islands for nearly a thousand years.

\* \* \*

One final matter remains to be considered, and that concerns the effects of the American environment upon these people. Three general principles, we believe, were involved in the interaction between frontier and pioneer. The first has to do with the insular quality of life on the frontier. A long succession of commentators, from Crève-coeur to Frederick Jackson Turner and his disciples, insisted that the American wilderness was a great environmental grindstone, pulverizing the cultural attributes that Europeans brought with them and transforming the immigrants into a new and homogenized species. It is difficult to imagine how a view so contrary to common sense and regard for history could have endured. A moment's reflection should be sufficient to indicate what, above all else, the essentially uninhabited American frontier provided what Europe could not: places where people could, by choice, live with like-minded people in isolation from others. What happens can be put best in the language of historical geographers. In frontier circumstances, as Robert D. Mitchell writes, tradition "is modified because of selective trait retention by the culture bearers as they negotiate and settle the new environments. The core culture undergoes trait reduction and simplification, while those traits which are retained are intensified and become the framework to which inno-

26. Regarding the Ulster-Hebrides-Highland culture in general, see Jennifer M. Brown, ed., *Scottish Society in the Fifteenth Century* (New York, 1977); Wormald, *Court, Kirk, and Community*; Colles, *History of Ulster*; G. A. Hayes-McCoy, *Scots Mercenary Forces in Ireland, 1565–1603* (Dublin and London, 1937); Donald Gregory, *The History of the Western Highlands and Isles of Scotland . . .* (Edinburgh, 1881); and Michael Sheane, *Ulster & the Lords of the North* (Stockport, England, 1980), esp. 112–22. For migrations from Scotland to Ulster, see Perceval-Maxwell, *Scottish Migration*; Colles, *History of Ulster*, III:180, 183–84; Charles Henry Hull, ed., *The Economic Writings of Sir William Petty* (2 vols., New York, 1963–64), I:149; L. M. Cullen and T. C. Smout, eds., *Comparative Aspects of Scottish and Irish Economic and Social History, 1600–1900* (Edinburgh, n.d. [ca. 1977]), 4, 24; Smout, *History of the Scottish People*, 144–45; Audrey Lockhart, *Some Aspects of Emigration from Ireland to the North American Colonies between 1660 and 1775* (New York, 1976), 19; Philip S. Robinson, *The Plantation of Ulster: British Settlement in an Irish Landscape, 1600–1670* (Dublin and New York, 1984); Raymond Gillespie, *Colonial Ulster: The Settlement of East Ulster, 1600–1641* (Cork, 1985).

# Prologue

vative or borrowed traits are added to form the configuration of a new society."[27]

Retentiveness and simplification are functions of the second principle, that of cultural conservatism or inertia.[28] Change, historians are wont to believe, is the stuff of history; but the stuff of society, if cultural anthropologists are to be credited, is resistance to change, or at least resistance to the changing of fundamental patterns of life's rhythms, rituals, and belief-structures. To be more precise, cultural conservatism is the tendency to continue to think and behave in customary, socially conditioned, and familiar ways unless wars, conquest, technology, interaction with alien groups, or other forces necessitate change; and it is the tendency to retain or revert to those norms in modified form despite the forces of change.

The principle is, of course, most readily apparent when one observes relatively primitive societies, but it can be equally operative among more advanced peoples. In eastern Europe, successions of regimes have been trying for a thousand years and more to impose a viable political hegemony over the scores of ethnic and national groups in the area, invariably in vain. Present Communist regimes, for all their ruthlessness and their modern technology, have been unable to homogenize even such small, multiethnic countries as Czechoslovakia and Yugoslavia, as were Hapsburgs, Jagiellonians, Ottomans, and Romanovs before them. As for the West, Eugen Weber has demonstrated that in France, that epitome of nineteenth-century nationalism, nearly half of the population, six decades after the Revolution, still not only read no French but did not even speak it. And modern Spain offers a striking example of the retention of identity by such groups as the Basques, Catalonians, Murcians, Andalucians, and Castilians, even though the kingdom has been politically unified for nearly five centuries. If cultural conservatism could be so potent in a Europe that had experienced absolutism, the scientific revolution, the Enlightenment, the French Revolution, and the industrial revolution, it seems likely that it would have been even stronger in an isolated colonial America.[29]

---

27. Robert D. Mitchell, *Commercialism and Frontier: Perspectives on the Early Shenandoah Valley* (Charlottesville, 1977), 14.

28. Specialists appear to be in general agreement as to the force of cultural conservatism, though they disagree about the dynamics of cultural change. See, for example, George C. Homans, *The Human Group* (New York, 1950); George P. Murdock, "How Culture Changes," in *Man, Culture, and Society,* ed. Harry L. Shapiro (New York, 1956); Raymond Firth, *Elements of Social Organization* (London, 1951); Michael

Hechter, "The Political Economy of Ethnic Change," *American Journal of Sociology* 79 (1968), 1151–78; and Ralf Dahrendorf, *Essays in the Theory of Society* (Stanford, 1968). My reading on the subject has been extensive but unsystematic and untutored.

29. Richard V. Burks, *East European History: An Ethnic Approach* (American Historical Association Pamphlets, no. 425, Washington, D.C., 1961, 1973); Eugen Joseph Weber, *Peasants into Frenchmen: the Modernization of Rural France, 1870–1914* (Stanford, 1976). See also Hechter, *Internal Colonialism.*

# Prologue

The third principle, associated with the geographers Fred Kniffen and Milton Newton, is that of cultural preadaptation or preselection. Like most other sound scientific principles, that of cultural preadaptation is obvious once someone else has thought it up. It is this. Over the course of time, a society will develop combinations of traits and habits of behavior that have survival value in a particular human or physical environment, along with other traits that may be irrelevant or even detrimental to survival. Placed in a different environment, members of a society will fare well or ill, depending less upon their adaptability to new surroundings than upon the compatibility between their previously evolved ways and those new surroundings.[30]

Conditions among the inhabitants of the English uplands, Wales, Scotland, and Ireland had long been adverse to the perpetuation of their traditional ways. In the American South migrants from those areas could preserve those ways and flourish. Indeed, in a manner of speaking, their entire history had prepared them to be Southerners.

FORREST McDONALD

30. Milton B. Newton, Jr., "Cultural Preadaptation and the Upland South," *Geoscience and Man* 5 (1974), 143–54; Fred B. Kniffen, "Folk Housing: Key to Diffusion," *Annals of the Association of American Geographers* 55 (1965), 549–77.

# I

# *Settlement*

HISTORIANS, in their much-argued efforts to determine the extent to which the antebellum North and South were similar or different,[1] have paid too little attention to the abundant observations of contemporaries. Most of the people who traveled in antebellum America—Northerners, Southerners, and Europeans—concluded that the South and the North were significantly different places with incongruous inhabitants and cultures. "Thus far all is new, all is strange," a young New Yorker wrote during a visit to the southern United States in 1843–44. His first impression—that in the South he was among foreigners—never altered. "Life here is so different from that at the north," he declared. "I felt . . . that I was indeed a stranger in a strange land." A Southerner, in turn, spoke of the northern United States as a "strange land" that he could never understand; another Southerner called the North "a totally foreign country," and a third wrote from Boston in 1854: "I long to return to the South. Kind as many persons have been to me here, I am *not at home*. I feel as an alien." An Englishman noted: "one could scarcely fail to remark how essentially the characters of the Northern and Southern people differ." Southerners, said a Scot, "are quite a distinct race from the 'Yankees.' " "The manners and habits of Northerners," insisted another foreigner, "are strikingly distinct

---

1. On this continuing dispute, see such recent works as James M. McPherson, "Antebellum Southern Exceptionalism: A New Look at An Old Question," *Civil War History* 29 (1983), 230–44; Forrest McDonald and Grady McWhiney, "The South from Self-Sufficiency to Peonage: An Interpretation," *American Historical Review* 85 (1980), 1095–1118; Edward Pessen, "How Different from Each Other Were the Antebellum North and South?" ibid. 1119–49; Thomas B. Alexander, Stanley L. Engerman, Forrest McDonald, Grady McWhiney, and Edward Pessen, "Antebellum North and South in Comparative Perspective: A Discussion," ibid. 1150–66; Forrest McDonald, Grady McWhiney, and Edward Pessen, "Communications," ibid. 86 (1981), 243–45.

from there fellow citizens to the southward."[2] The number of observers who recorded such statements is endless.

To understand why Southerners and Northerners were different from and often antagonistic toward each other—indeed, to understand the Old South—one must put aside some myths. The most important myth to recognize and to discard is the belief that southern ways were English ways.

How, one might ask, could emphasizing English influence on the South be a mistake when "everyone knows" that the vast majority of southern whites are and always have been of Anglo-Saxon origins; when a distinguished southern historian can insist that the "English influence [on the South] was powerful"; or when another can state that "the South *is* the habitat of the quintessential WASP" and call it "the biggest single WASP nest this side of the Atlantic"?[3] The answer is that both the common wisdom and the scholars are wrong.

There has been all too little understanding of the ethnic background of white Southerners. "They were mostly transplanted Englishmen with a scattering of continental Europeans," writes one author, who supports his argument with a quotation from Stephen Vincent Benét: " 'And those who came were resolved to be Englishmen, Gone to the World's End, but English every one.' "[4] A different writer claims that both the North and the South "were peopled by Englishmen,"[5] and two others emphasize "the gap between Anglo-Saxon and African in the South."[6]

Accounts of the South's past usually make such vague or sweeping references to cultural ethnicity that readers are likely to be confused over who are and who not are Anglo-Saxons. For example, the authors of a popular work praise "the German colonists of the South"

2. Henry Benjamin Whipple, *Bishop Whipple's Southern Diary, 1843–1844*, ed. Lester B. Shippee (Minneapolis, 1937), 13, 26, 15; Charles S. Sydnor, *A Gentleman of the Old Natchez Region: Benjamin L. C. Wailes* (Durham, N.C., 1938), 183; *Southern Quarterly Review* 26 (1854), 432; Paul H. Hayne to his wife, September 16, 1854, Paul Hamilton Hayne Papers, Duke University; Catherine C. Hopley, *Life in the South From the . . . Spring of 1860 to August 1862* (1863; reprint, 2 vols., New York, 1974), I:143; William Thomson, *A Tradesman's Travels, in the United States and Canada, in the Years 1840, 41 & 42* (Edinburgh, 1842), 46; Charles Joseph Latrobe, *The Rambler in North America . . .* (2 vols., London, 1835), I:60–61. See also [Sarah] Mendell and [Charlotte] Hosmer, *Notes of Travel and Life* (New York, 1854), 188, 249; Samuel Gottlieb

Ludvigh, *Licht und Schattenbilder Republikanischer Zustande . . .* (Leipzig, 1848), 311; Michel Chevalier, *Society, Manners and Politics in the United States . . .*, trans. Thomas Gamaliel Bradford (Boston, 1839), 150–57; and Stephen Davis, *Notes of a Tour of America . . .* (Edinburgh, 1833), 101.
3. Clement Eaton, "Custom and Manners," in *The Encyclopedia of Southern History,* ed. David C. Roller and Robert W. Twyman (Baton Rouge, 1979), 321; George B. Tindall, *The Ethnic Southerners* (Baton Rouge, 1976), 8.
4. Monroe Lee Billington, *The American South: A Brief History* (New York, 1971), 9.
5. I. A. Newby, *The South: A History* (New York, 1978), 39.
6. William B. Hesseltine and David L. Smiley, *The South in American History* (2d ed., Englewood Cliffs, N.J., 1960), 2.

for their "many sterling qualities" and announce that their "fore-sighted methods of farming contrasted with the wasteful methods of the Anglo-Saxons." According to these authors: "The Scotch-Irish early became Southerners. They were of the same Anglo-Saxon stock as the people of the coast regions."[7] To contend that the Scotch-Irish came from the "same Anglo-Saxon stock" as the English indicates a profound ignorance of the most important cultural conflict in the history of the British Isles. Moreover, ignoring the Germanic heritage of the Anglo-Saxons is as serious as overlooking the conquest and occupation of England by Anglo-Saxons and the significant Germanic contributions to the English language and culture.[8]

Standard histories of the South give no indication that Celts were important in the region. Some works notice the Scotch-Irish and the Scots,[9] but the *Encyclopedia of Southern History*—which devotes numerous pages to such ethnic groups and their influence as the English, the Germans, the French, the Indians, the Africans, the Spanish, and even the Acadians—ignores the Scots, the Scotch-Irish, the Irish, the Cornish, and the Welsh. The indexes of most

---

7. Francis B. Simkins and Charles P. Roland, *A History of the South* (4th ed., New York, 1972), 36–37.

8. Goldwin Smith, *A History of England* (4th ed., New York, 1974), 13–30; Warren O. Ault, *Open-Field Farming in Medieval England: A Study of Village By-Laws* (London, 1972), 16; Eric Kerridge, *Agrarian Problems in the Seventeenth Century and After* (London, 1969), 32–33, 90–91, 161–62.

9. W. J. Cash, *The Mind of the South* (paperback ed., New York, 1941), 30–34, 56, suggests that the Southerner "had much in common with the half-wild Scotch [*sic*] and Irish clansmen" for "his chief blood-strain was likely to be . . . Celtic." Scots and Scotch-Irish are mentioned in Hesseltine and Smiley, *The South in American History*, 34–35, 44, 51, 54–55, 58, 60, 62, 72, 75, 130; Billington, *American South*, 18–19; Simkins and Roland, *History of the South*, 34–36; and in many local histories. See also such specialized studies as James G. Leyburn, *The Scotch-Irish: A Social History* (Chapel Hill, 1962); Charles A. Hanna, *The Scotch-Irish: Or, the Scot in North Britain, North Ireland and North America* (2 vols., 1902; reprint, Baltimore, 1968); T. W. Moody, "Irish and Scotch-Irish in Eighteenth Century America," *Studies* 35 (1946),

84–90; W. T. Latimer, "Ulster Emigration to America," *Journal of the Royal Society of Antiquaries of Ireland* 32 (1903), 385–92; E. R. R. Green, "The 'Strange Humors' That Drove the Scotch-Irish to America, 1729," *William and Mary Quarterly* 12 (1955), 113–23; idem, "Queensborough Township: Scotch-Irish Emigration and the Expansion of Georgia, 1763–1776," *William and Mary Quarterly* 17 (1960), 183–99; Jean Stephenson, *Scotch-Irish Migration to South Carolina, 1772* (Strasburg, Va., 1971); Jack W. Weaver, ed., *Selected Proceedings of the Scotch-Irish Heritage Festival at Winthrop College* (Rock Hill, S.C., 1980); Robert L. Meriwether, *The Expansion of South Carolina* (Kingsport, Tenn., 1940), 79–88; Patricia G. Johnson, *James Patton and the Appalachian Colonies* (Verona, Va., 1973), 3–15; Robert Ramsey, *Carolina Cradle: Settlement of the Northwest Carolina Frontier, 1747–1762* (Chapel Hill, 1964); Robert J. Dickson, *Ulster Emigration to Colonial America, 1718–1775* (London, 1966); Desmond Clarke, *Arthur Dobbs, Esquire, 1689–1765; Surveyor-General of Ireland, Prospector, and Governor of North Carolina* (Chapel Hill, 1957); and Carl Bridenbaugh, *Myths and Realities: Societies of the Colonial South* (Baton Rouge, 1952).

volumes on the South do not include the words Celt or Celtic. Few general works on the Old South even mention the Irish. Those that do usually state that only a meager number of Irishmen migrated to the antebellum South and those who did were generally hired to do work that slaves were too valuable to undertake.[10]

And yet the works of some specialists indicate that in the South, in striking contrast to New England, there was a large Celtic component in the population from the beginning. In an analysis of 7,359 references to seventeenth-century Virginians, John Eacott Manahan found in 1946 that 6,647 (90 percent) came from Cornwall, Wales, Ireland, or the Celtic fringe of England. Conversely, Charles Banks, in his study of 2,885 English immigrants to New England between 1620 and 1650, showed in 1930 that only 185 originated in the Celtic fringe; 2,043 (71 percent) came from the east and southwest of England. More recent scholarship by James Horn and David Grayson Allen sharpens, elaborates, and in some respects corrects these studies but generally bears them out.[11]

Approaching the subject in a different way, Harry M. Caudill also found that many more Celts settled in the antebellum South than conventional sources acknowledge. Using a modern Welsh telephone directory and old Welsh church records, Caudill refuted Ellen Churchill Semple's contention that the settlers of eastern Kentucky were Anglo-Saxons. "The 1984 [Welsh] telephone directory," he found, "is astonishingly similar to the name listings of that portion of Kentucky which begins about thirty miles east of Lexington and continues to the Big Sandy and the Virginia line. In turning its pages a Kentuckian develops the distinct feeling that he is not in a foreign country but is back home.' " All but 6 of the 112 Kentucky counties named for persons have Celtic names. Caudill concluded that rather than *The Anglo-Saxons of the Kentucky Mountains* Semple "should have called her article *The Celts of the Kentucky Mountains.*"[12]

10. Clement Eaton, *A History of the Old South: The Emergence of a Reluctant Nation* (3d ed., New York, 1975), 14, 255; Michael V. Gannon, "Catholic Church," in Roller and Twyman, *Encyclopedia of Southern History,* 189–90.

11. John Eacott Manahan, "The Cavalier Remounted: A Study of Virginia's Population, 1607–1700" (Ph.D. diss., University of Virginia, 1947); Charles Edward Banks, *Topographical Dictionary of 2885 English Emigrants to New England, 1620–1650,* ed. and indexed by Elijah E. Brownell (3d ed., Baltimore, 1963), xii, passim; James Horn, "Servant Emigration to the Chesapeake in the Seventeenth Century," in *The Chesapeake in the Seventeenth Century: Essays on Anglo-American Society,* ed. Thaddeus

W. Tate and David L. Ammerman (Chapel Hill, 1979), 51–95, esp. the maps on 67 and 71; and David Grayson Allen, *In English Ways: The Movement of Societies and the Transferal of English Local Law and Custom to Massachusetts Bay in the Seventeenth Century* (Chapel Hill, 1981), 8–9, 17, 245–90.

12. Harry M. Caudill, "Kentucky and Wales: Was Ellen Churchill Semple Wrong?" (MS in possession of the author). See also Thomas L. Purvis, "The Ethnic Descent of Kentucky's Early Population: A Statistical Investigation of European and American Sources of Emigration, 1790–1820," *Register of the Kentucky Historical Society* 80 (1982), 253–66.

Similarly, a number of scholars have found that large numbers of Irish arrived in the South at an early time. One investigator has discovered records of "a great infusion of Irish blood" into the South throughout the colonial period.[13] Another concludes that thousands of Irish were transported to America between 1703 and 1775 and that many settled in Virginia, the Carolinas, and Georgia.[14] And yet another scholar estimates that in 1790 Irish settlers constituted 25 percent of the population of South Carolina and 27 percent of that of Georgia.[15]

The Irish presence in the South has been overlooked by historians who have assumed incorrectly that during the colonial period of American settlement all natives of Ireland outside Ulster were devout Catholics. "The passionate and exemplary attachment of the Irish nation to the Catholic faith dates from a later time," wrote a distinguished Irish historian about the seventeenth and eighteenth centuries; "the real contest was between Englishmen and Irishmen rather than Protestants and Catholics. . . . In Ireland in the seventeenth century . . . the Irish laity were still for the most part only passively and traditionally Catholic."[16] Nor had the situation changed appreciably by the first part of the nineteenth century. "The figures on church attendance in pre-famine Ireland indicate that only thirty-three per cent of the Catholic population went to mass," noted an eminent authority. "Most of the two million Irish who emigrated between 1847 and 1860 were part of the pre-famine generation of nonpracticing Catholics, if indeed they were Catholics at all." Not until the latter part of the nineteenth century, long after most of the Irish who came to the South had migrated, did the "devotional revolution" turn Ireland into a country of churchgoers who equated Irish nationalism with Catholicism.[17]

Irish settlers in the South, especially those who arrived in the seventeenth and eighteenth centuries, suffered little cultural shock; nominal Catholics at most, they mixed with the Scotch-Irish and Scots—people with whom they had shared traditions and ways for centuries—feuded and stole each other's livestock, just as they had always done, and helped to spread Celtic culture across the southern backcountry.[18]

13. Michael J. O'Brien, *Irish Settlers in America* (2 vols., Baltimore, 1976), I:10–39, 73–104, 158–78, 196–216, 250–56, 259–69, 416–26, 522–24, 539–42, 558–67, II:1–38, 56–72, 128–53, 165–244, 344–65, 397–402, 556–91; idem, *A Hidden Phase of American History: Ireland's Part in America's Struggle for Liberty* (1919; reprint, Baltimore, 1973), 241–52, 322–72.

14. Audrey Lockhart, *Some Aspects of Emigration from Ireland to the North American Colonies between 1660 and 1775* (New York, 1976), 90, 96, 134, 140.

15. David Noel Doyle, *Ireland, Irishmen and Revolutionary America, 1760–1820* (Dublin, 1981), 75.

16. Edward MacLysaght, *Irish Life in the Seventeenth Century* (1939; reprint, Dublin, 1979), 280–84.

17. Emmet Larkin, "The Devotional Revolution in Ireland, 1850–75," *American Historical Review* 77 (1972), 636–51.

18. On the cultural similarity between

Even in eighteenth-century Ireland there was more interaction and friendship between Catholics and Protestants than has generally been assumed. "There are very few families of Protestants and Catholics which are not intermarried with each other; of consequence, little or no bigotry prevails," reported the Reverend Stewart Dobbs from County Antrim at the beginning of the nineteenth century.[19] A story is told of the friendship between a local Irish priest and a Protestant minister who was in danger of being transferred because his congregation was so small. On the critical Sunday when the minister's bishop arrived for a final check on church attendance, the Catholic priest told his own congregation what would happen to his friend if the bishop found the church empty. "The whole [Catholic] congregation was moved to tears, . . . sailed down to the Protestant Church, and filled it to capacity. The old bishop was charmed and declared they were the finest congregation he ever saw. . . . Ever afterwards the people prided themselves on the work of that Sunday."[20]

The evidence indicates that in the backcountry South large numbers of Irish simply adopted the religion of their neighbors. For example, Andrew Leary O'Brien, who was born in County Cork, Ireland, in 1815, migrated to South Carolina, married a local girl, and converted to her Methodist faith.[21] Thousands of other Irish

---

Irish Catholics and Protestants, see Alan J. Gailey, "The Scotch-Irish in Northern Ireland: Aspects of their Culture," in Weaver, *Proceedings of Scotch-Irish Heritage Festival*, 44–47; Richard Ned Lebow, *White Britain and Black Ireland: The Influence of Stereotypes on Colonial Policy* (Philadelphia, 1976), 76–77. On the cultural similarity of the Scots and the Irish, especially their ways and beliefs, see John D. Sheridan, "The Irish Character," in *Ireland by the Irish*, ed. Michael Gorman (London, 1963), 34; Peter Hume Brown, ed., *Scotland Before 1700, from Contemporary Documents* (Edinburgh, 1893), 12; Thomas Crofton Croker, *Researches in the South of Ireland . . .* (1824; reprint, New York, 1969), 78–79, 116, 232, 234–35; Edmund Spenser, *A View of the Present State of Ireland*, ed. W. L. Renwick (Oxford, 1970), 38; Edward Burt, *Burt's Letters from the North of Scotland*, ed. R. Jamieson (1754; reprint, 2 vols., Edinburgh, 1974), II:86; Christopher Lowther, *Our Journall into Scotland Anno Domini 1629 . . .*, ed. W. D. (Edinburgh, 1894), 18. On the cultural similarities between the Scots, the Irish, and

the Welsh, see Sir Leonard Twiston Davies and Averyl Edwards, *Welsh Life in the Eighteenth Century* (London, 1939), v–vii, 1–47, 116–19, 124–25, 139–40, 225; Margaret Calderwood quoted in J. G. Fyfe, ed., *Scottish Diaries and Memoirs, 1746–1843* (Stirling, Scotland, 1942), 83–84.

19. William Shaw Mason, ed., *A Statistical Account or Parochial Survey of Ireland, Drawn up from the Communications of the Clergy* (3 vols., Dublin, 1814–19), III:27–28.

20. James Berry, *Tales of Old Ireland*, ed. Gertrude M. Horgan (Salem, N.H., 1984), 23–24.

21. Andrew Leary O'Brien, *The Journal of Andrew Leary O'Brien . . .* (Athens, Ga., 1946), 4, 5, 12, 38, 40. Charles S. Sydnor, "A Decade of Nationalism, 1836–1845," in *Travels in the Old South: A Bibliography*, ed. Thomas D. Clark (3 vols., Norman, Okla., 1959), III:169, notes that O'Brien, a native of Ireland who had studied for the priesthood, "fitted into the life of the South too well to leave a first-rate travel account, for he seldom wrote like a stranger looking at society from the outside."

joined the Baptist, Methodist, or Presbyterian church. A Catholic bishop, after traveling in the antebellum South, maintained "that, calculating from the names of the people, no less than forty thousand had lost the Faith in the Carolinas and Georgia."[22] Later a British Catholic observed that the South was full of people with Irish names. "No doubt," he wrote, "the Wesleyan missionaries on circuit baptised the children and grandchildren of Irish who had not brought their women or their priests. Wesleyan ministers, Methodist bishops, bear Irish names—Healy, Murphy, Connor. Their blood could only have come from Ireland. . . . One of these Irish patriarchs . . . did meet a priest after fifty years, and could only present two grownup generations of Methodists."[23]

As Forrest McDonald has shown in the Prologue, conflict between the English and the Celtic inhabitants of the British Isles marked the history of that area for well over a thousand years. Eventually the English, from their cultural stronghold in the southeastern part of what became the United Kingdom, managed to dominate the whole through persistence, orderly habits, an internalized sense of propriety, a unique system of common law, the habit of obedience to that law, literacy, a capacity for devising flexible but stable political institutions, and other cultural traits. But the peoples who occupied Cornwall, Wales, Scotland, Ireland, the Hebrides, and the western and northern English uplands resisted all the way; and as late as the latter part of the eighteenth century few of them except Scottish Lowlanders—of whom only small numbers emigrated to the South—had yet been encultured into English ways.

This cultural conflict between English and Celt not only continued in British North America, it shaped the history of the United States. British immigrants—English and Celtic—brought with them to America their habits and values as well as their old feuds, biases, and resentments. How much of their cultural baggage they managed to retain over time depended on where they settled in America; those settlement patterns, in turn, helped create a sectionalism that swayed the social, economic, and political life of the nation and ultimately exploded into the War for Southern Independence.[24]

Before examining the culture that Celts brought to America, it is

22. J. J. O'Connell, *Catholicity in the Carolinas and Georgia* (New York, 1879), 180.

23. Sir Shane Leslie, "Lost Irish in the U.S.A.: The Church in the Deep South," *Tablet* 211 (February 1, 1958), 103.

24. See, for example, Forrest McDonald and Grady McWhiney, "The Antebellum Southern Herdsman: A Reinterpretation," *Journal of Southern History* 41 (1975), 147–66; idem, "The South from Self-Sufficiency to Peonage," 1095–1118; Grady McWhiney and Perry D. Jamieson, *Attack and Die: Civil War Military Tactics and the Southern Heritage* (University, Ala., 1982), 170–91.

important to look at antebellum settlement and migration patterns and to determine as best we can who settled where. The first federal census, taken in 1790, reveals that the seven states north of the Mason-Dixon line contained approximately 1,900,000 people— about the same number as the six states south of that line—but by 1860 the North could claim a population of over 20,300,000, or some 9,100,000 more than the South.[25]

The importance of these figures in understanding settlement patterns is that they show that the Old South, relative to the Old North, was sparsely settled. Even near the end of the antebellum period, after the southern frontier (that is, the point beyond which there were fewer than two people per square mile) extended into Texas, there remained an extensive interior frontier in the South. Large areas in Georgia, western North Carolina, eastern Tennessee, Florida, Alabama, Mississippi, Louisiana, Arkansas, Missouri, and Texas contained fewer than five persons per square mile. In 1850 only six southern states had as many as twenty settlers per square mile; Alabama, Georgia, Louisiana, and Mississippi had between eleven and sixteen; Arkansas and Florida between two and four; and Texas fewer than one per square mile. Throughout the first half of the nineteenth century, despite the push of westward migration, the Old South remained a thinly populated area of untouched forests and vast grazing lands.[26]

Such a region was ideally suited for the clannish, herding, leisure-loving Celts, who relished whiskey, gambling, and combat, and who despised hard work, anything English, most government, fences, and any other restraints upon them or their free-ranging livestock. Between the early seventeenth and the late eighteenth centuries, hordes of Celts from the British Isles found their way to the southern parts of what would become the United States; indeed, a steady stream of them crossed the Atlantic before the American Revolution. In the 1770s James Boswell spoke of "the present rage for emigration" from the Highlands of Scotland, and Dr. Samuel Johnson observed that many people "have departed both from the main of *Scotland*, and from the Islands." Still another diarist noted in 1767: "The Gazette says 10,000 people a year go from the North of Ireland to America."[27]

Most of these people left their homes because conditions in the

25. Bureau of the Census, *The Statistical History of the United States from Colonial Times to the Present* (Stamford, Conn., 1965), 11–13.

26. Clifford L. Lord and Elizabeth H. Lord, *Historical Atlas of the United States* (New York, 1953), 46–51; Donald B. Dodd and Wynelle S. Dodd, *Historical Statistics of the South, 1790–1970* (University, Ala., 1973), 2–58; Thomas C. Donaldson, *The Public Domain: Its History, with Statistics* (Washington, D.C., 1884), 28–29; Bureau of the Census, *Seventh Census of the United States, 1850* . . . (Washington, D.C., 1953), Table LV, lxxxii–lxxxiii.

27. Lockhart, *Aspects of Emigration,* 90, 96, 134, 140; M. J. O'Brien, *Irish Settlers,* I:10–23; Edward McGrady, *The History of South Carolina Under the*

TWO CRACKERS

From *Harper's New Monthly Magazine* 91 (1895), 339.

Old World had become inimical to survival, at least in accordance with their traditional pastoral ways of life. A group of Scots on their way to North Carolina in 1774 gave an inquisitive official some rare testimony on their motives for migration. George Morgan, Donald McDonald, and John Catanock explained that they had left Scotland because rents had been "raised from Two to Five Pounds Sterling" while the "price of Cattle at the same time [had been] reduced full one half." William McLeod was off "to . . . North Carolina, where he has a Brother settled who wrote him to come out assuring him that he would find a better Farm for him than he possest at home." James Sinclair was migrating because "he had lost great part of his Cattle two years ago, the rearing of Cattle being his principal business, the prices of Cattle were reduced one half while the Rents were nevertheless kept up and in many places advanced." John Ross was on his way "to Carolina because the rent of his Possession was greatly Advanced, [and] the price of Cattle which must pay that Rent reduced more than one half." George Grant planned to settle in North Carolina "because Crops failed [at home], and at the same time the price of Cattle was reduced more than One Half. That his Brothers in Law already in America have assured him that from the Cheapness of Provisions . . . he may better his Circumstances in that Country." Hector McDonald was going to North Carolina "because the Rents of his possession had been raised from one pound seven shillings to Four pounds, while the price of the Cattle raised upon it fell more than One half." William McKay also intended to settle "in North Carolina, because his Stock being small, . . . and the price of Cattle low, he found he could not have bread for his Family at home." William Gordon, "having two Sons already settled in Carolina, who wrote him encouraging him to come there, and finding the Rents of Lands raised in so much, that a Possession for which his Grandfather paid only Eight Merks Scots he himself at last paid Sixty, . . . was induced to emigrate for the greater benefit of his Children." John McBeath "left [Scotland] . . . because Crops failed, he lost his Cattle, the Rent of his possession was raised, . . . [and] he was Encouraged to emigrate by the accounts received from his own and his Wife's Friends already in America, assuring him that he would procure comfortable Subsistence in that Country for his Wife and Children." Eliz. McDonald left "because several of her

*Proprietary Government, 1670–1719* (New York, 1897), 115, 556–57, 629; Robert Mills, *Statistics of South Carolina . . .* (Charleston, 1826), 175; Ian C. C. Graham, *Colonists from Scotland: Emigration to North America, 1707–1783* (Ithaca, N.Y., 1956), 9, 18; Abbot Emerson Smith, *Colonists in Bondage: White Servitude and Convict Labor in America, 1607–1776* (Chapel Hill, 1947),

52, 62–66, 134, 142, 163–65, 331; R. W. Chapman, ed., *Johnson's Journey to the Western Islands of Scotland and Boswell's Journal of a Tour to the Hebrides with Samuel Johnson, LL.D.* (Oxford, 1979), 267, 119; Sylas Neville, *The Diary of Sylas Neville, 1767–1788,* ed. Basil Cozens-Hardy (London, 1950), 3.

Friends having gone to Carolina before her, had assured her that she would get much better Service and greater Encouragement in Carolina." James Duncan was migrating "because . . . the price of Cattle [was] so much reduced that one Cows price could only buy a Boll of Meal." William McDonald planned to join "Friends already in Carolina, [who] have given him assurances of bettering his Condition"; he "left . . . because Crops failed, Bread became dear, the Rents of his possession were raised, . . . [and] the price of Cattle [became] so low . . . that he could no longer support his Family at Home." Aeneas McLeod left home "because . . . the price of Cattle was reduced one half, the Rent was nevertheless still kept up." Hugh Matheson was on his way to "Carolina because . . . the price of Cattle has been of late so low, and that of Bread so high, that the Factor who was also a Drover would give no more than a Boll of Meal for a Cow." William Sutherland planned to settle in "Carolina because he lost his Cattle in 1772, and . . . was obliged to perform with his Family and his Horses so many and so arbitrary Services to his Landlord at all times of the Year . . . that his little Stock daily decreasing, he was encouraged to go to Carolina by the assurances of the fertility of land." George McKay left because "the price of Cattle on which he chiefly depended was greatly reduced, . . . by which the Farmers in general were brought into great distress." Alexander Morison migrated because his rent had "doubled, the price of Cattle [remained] low . . . ; the Tenan[t]s were in various ways opprest by . . . Factors; And . . . Reports from America [gave him] . . . hopes of bettering his Circumstances in that Country."[28]

Similar reports were heard from Ireland. "Our Country is now in a distressed Situation," an Irishman wrote his relatives in South Carolina in 1788; "neither the farmer, tradesman, nor Beggar can live, owing [to] the number of Taxes, high price of Land, & scarcity of Provisions, which is still growing worse & worse, Whereas Your Country, by report is growing better & better; Emigration is . . . keen; numbers are going this year [including] . . . my Brothers . . . with their families [who] intend . . . taking shipping at Belfast for Charlestown, if they come across you, your advice to them would surely be necessary."[29]

28. Viola Root Cameron, comp., *Emigrants from Scotland to America, 1774–1775, Copied from a Loose Bundle of Treasury Papers in the Public Record Office London, England* (Baltimore, 1976), 8, 10, 16, 22, 19, 18, 15–16, 12, 7, 6, 10–11, 12, 13, 20, 14, 22–23, 17–18.

29. Andrew Gibson to Robert Love, June 2, 1788, Love Family Papers, Winthrop College, Rock Hill, South Carolina. On Irish and Scottish immigration to the southern colonies, see also Arthur Young, *Arthur Young's Tour in Ireland (1776–1779)*, ed. Arthur W. Hutton (2 vols., London, 1892), I:402; Andrew Gibson to Robert Love, September 22, 1790, Love Family Papers; [Janet Schaw], *Journal of a Lady of Quality . . .*, ed. Evangeline Walker Andrews, in collaboration with Charles McLean Andrews (New Haven, Conn., 1921), 257–59; Chapman, *Johnson's Journey*, 33, 88, 90, 119, 246, 295, 346, 361.

By the time of the American Revolution there were Celts through-
out the South, but the greatest concentration of them was in the
backcountry from Pennsylvania southward to Georgia. Along that
frontier they outnumbered all other settlers and dominated the
society.[30] Moreover, the southern backcountry became the base from
which Celts swept westward to settle and acculturate the entire
South. So fecund and so peripatetic were they and their descendants
that in the seventy years between the first federal census and the
Civil War they added nearly a million souls to the population of the
South every decade and helped to expand its frontiers some twelve
hundred miles west of the Atlantic seaboard.[31]

Migration was a constant in the lives of many of these antebellum
Southerners. For some it literally meant a chance to escape, as it did
for the man who recorded in his journal just before moving more
than a hundred miles from where he lived in Sumter District, South
Carolina: "Followed by Dr. Sanders to Lynchburg twice to day with
Double barrelled Gun." Other people moved because they were
restless and because they were programmed to do so by their culture.
An autobiographer admitted, "I had been reared to a belief and faith
in the pleasure of a frequent change of country." A visitor recorded
that a typical Southerner was someone who, after clearing a few
acres and "building a log-house," "sells the farm, and migrates again
to another part of the uncleared forest, repeating this operation three
or four times in the course of his life." An antebellum traveler found
southern "roads crowded with emigrants of every description. . . . I
could compare them only to the gipsy bands." "Many of our neigh-
bours are preparing to move to Texas and Louisiana," remarked an
Alabamian in 1854. "The people here [in the South]," stated still
another observer, "are given to rambling about instead of attending
to their farms."[32]

The mobility of antebellum Southerners can be illustrated by an
example. In 1850, Lowndes County, Mississippi, had somewhat over
1,600 heads of families, of whom only 103 were born in the state.
The vast majority came from other southern states; only 77 were

30. Bridenbaugh, *Myths and Realities*, 132.

31. Bureau of the Census, *Statistical History of the United States*, 27. An example of this migration can be seen in James Buckner Barry, *Buck Barry, Texas Ranger and Frontiersman*, ed. James K. Greer (Lincoln, Nebr., 1978), 1–13.

32. John D. Ashmore Plantation Journal, August 18,1854, John D. Ashmore Papers, Southern Historical Collection, University of North Carolina, Chapel Hill; Gideon Lincecum, "Autobiography of Gideon Lincecum," *Mississippi Historical Society Publications* 8 (1904), 464; Sir Charles Lyell, *A Second Visit to the United States . . .* (2 vols., London, 1849), II:89; Frederick Hall, *Letters from the East and from the West* (Washington, D.C., 1840), 310–11; James Mallory Journal, October 8, 1854 (original owned by Edgar A. Stewart of Selma, Alabama), microfilm copy, University of Alabama, Tuscaloosa; Thomas Nuttall, *A Journal of Travels into the Arkansas Territory . . .* (Philadelphia, 1821), 58.

NORTH CAROLINA CABIN

From North Carolina Collection, UNC Library at
Chapel Hill.

from the northern United States, and only 61 were foreign-born. The largest numbers came not from the adjoining states of Tennessee and Alabama, which together contributed less than a fifth of Lowndes County's families; more than half came from Virginia and the Carolinas. Judging by the different birthplaces of the children of these families, it is clear that each family had moved several times before settling in Lowndes County.[33]

Let us consider a few of these restless folk. William Love was born in Ireland in 1746. He migrated to South Carolina before 1774 and served as a second lieutenant in William Gaston's company "of the third regiment of regular troops" during the American Revolution. After the war, Love spent the rest of his life in South Carolina, but his children moved to Tennessee, Mississippi, and Missouri.[34]

George Washington Mitchell's grandparents were born in Ireland and moved to western Pennsylvania in 1752. His father was born in Hillsborough, North Carolina. He was born in Maury County, Tennessee, in 1815, and settled in Florence, Alabama, in 1834.[35]

The great-grandfather of William Wear migrated from the north of Ireland to Virginia before the American Revolution. His son Adam married Margarett Blackburn of Virginia, who was of the same Scotch-Irish stock. Adam and Margarett settled in Washington County, eastern Tennessee. Their son George Wear married Sally Rhea and moved to northern Alabama and then, in 1831, to Missouri.[36]

Columbus Morrison was born in 1808, fourteen miles east of Charlotte, North Carolina. His "parents were of old Scotch Presbyterian descent." He lived for a short time in Virginia and South Carolina and, after his marriage, settled on a small farm near Tuscaloosa, Alabama.[37]

Lorenzo Dow Lewis was born in Cherokee County, Alabama, in 1847. His father had been born in Tennessee; his great-grandfather, George Lewis, "came from Wales to Virginia and thence to Tennessee."[38]

John Davidson's great-grandfather came from Scotland to Virginia before the American Revolution. John's father was born in South

33. Betty Wood Thomas, comp., *1850 Census, Lowndes County, Mississippi* (Columbus, Miss., 1978), 5–172.

34. William Love Family Genealogy, Love Family Papers; Revolutionary War Pension and Bounty Land Warrant Application Files, M-804, Roll 1590, National Archives (copy), Love Family Papers.

35. Biographical memoranda on George Washington Mitchell, James

Blair Hall Papers, Alabama Department of Archives and History, Montgomery.

36. Biographical memoranda on William B. Wear, Hall Papers.

37. Columbus Morrison Journal, May 9, 1845, Southern Historical Collection, University of North Carolina, Chapel Hill.

38. Biographical memoranda on Lorenzo Dow Lewis, Hall Papers.

Carolina. John was born in Georgia. His children were born in Alabama.[39]

Rosanna Toland Barry left Antrim, north Ireland, for America in 1797 with her husband and children. They landed in Philadelphia, traveled overland to Pittsburgh, and went down the Ohio River to settle in Bardstown, Nelson County, Kentucky. Her husband got into trouble with the law and she moved with her children to Washington County, Kentucky, where he subsequently rejoined the family. After some time they moved again, this time to Hartford, Ohio County, Kentucky. In 1810 they moved to Montgomery County, Tennessee. In 1814 they moved to Christian County, Kentucky, where her husband died the next year. She remained on the farm until 1822, when she migrated one last time to live with her daughter. That was Rosanna's seventh move in twenty-five years.[40]

Many such family histories exist, but there simply are not enough of them to prove that most of the people who settled the Old South were of Celtic descent. If early censuses had recorded the national origins of Americans, it would be relatively easy to establish the ethnic backgrounds of Southerners; unfortunately, census takers failed to gather such information until the middle of the nineteenth century. Alternatively, the ethnic composition of the population might be reconstructed from lists of arriving immigrants, but only fragmentary records exist for the colonial and early national periods. Except for the years 1798–1800, recording the arrival of immigrants was not required by law until 1819. The resulting records are useless in analyzing the ethnic makeup of the southern population because so few migrants came to the South after 1800. Only about 4.2 percent of the white people in the South in 1850 were foreign-born; most of them were concentrated in such urban places as New Orleans, Mobile, and Charleston, and most were potato-famine Irish.[41] Some 25,000 or more Irish, a quarter of the city's population, lived in New Orleans; and even in Apalachicola, Florida, the Irish were the largest foreign-born element in the population.[42]

Because the records of early settlers are either unavailable or sketchy, it is necessary to rely upon various techniques of name analysis to determine migration and settlement patterns. Tracing

39. Biographical memoranda on John Wesley Davidson, Hall Papers.

40. Reminiscences of Mary Jane Barry Killebrew, Kinchloe-Bishop Family Papers, Mississippi Department of Archives and History, Jackson.

41. Calculations and data on the legislation concerning the recording of immigrants are from Bureau of the Census, *Statistical History of the United States*, 48, 11–12, 57.

42. Earl F. Niehaus, *The Irish in New Orleans, 1800–1860* (Baton Rouge, 1965), 110; H. P. Owen, "The Port of Apalachicola," *Florida Historical Quarterly* 43 (1964), 1–25. See also Patrick O'Sullivan, "Catholic Irish in the Deep South," *Ecumene* 8 (1981), 42–48.

ancestry through surnames is both complex and inexact, but fairly reliable approximations can be reached if the list of European names is full and accurate, if the body of American names being analyzed is large enough to absorb the invariable flukes and exceptions, and if a rigorous methodology is formulated. Wherever possible, in our attempt to determine what ethnic groups settled where, Forrest McDonald and I have relied upon the research of other scholars, but we also have developed, thus far, three methods of name analysis. None is foolproof, but each provides a useful check on the others and together they offer what we consider a reasonable approximation of the ethnic composition of the areas analyzed.

The focus here is on what our methods of name analysis reveal rather than on the techniques involved. Anyone interested in the specifics of our methodology may consult our articles in the *William and Mary Quarterly* and in *Names*.[43]

One of our methods, a projection technique developed by Forrest and Ellen McDonald, reveals that sectionalism based upon settlement patterns existed throughout the United States at the time the first federal census was taken. In 1790 well over three-quarters of the people living in New England were of English origins; New York, having originally been a Dutch colony, retained a large Dutch component in its population, but the single largest group, comprising something over two-fifths of the people, was English; Pennsylvania was heterogeneous—two-fifths of the people were of Celtic origins, a third were German, fewer than a fifth were English. Elsewhere, the farther south and west from Philadelphia, the more Celtic the population: in the upper South, Celts and Englishmen each constituted about two-fifths of the population; in the Carolinas, more than half the people were Celtic and Celts outnumbered Englishmen five to three.

Even more importantly, from Pennsylvania southward Celts dominated the frontier, where they constituted from 60 to nearly 100 percent of the total population. In the North Carolina tidewater districts, from 39 percent of the population in Edenton to 48 percent in Newbern were Celts, but in the upland interior they constituted 63 percent of the population in the Fayette district and almost 100 percent in the Hillsborough district. In the western Virginia counties of Fayette and Lincoln, Scots and Irish alone numbered nearly 80 percent of the population.[44]

43. Forrest McDonald and Ellen Shapiro McDonald, "The Ethnic Origins of the American People, 1790," *William and Mary Quarterly* 37 (1980), 179–99; Grady McWhiney and Forrest McDonald, "Celtic Names in the Antebellum Southern United States," *Names: Journal of the American Name Society* 31 (1983), 89–102.

44. McDonald and McDonald, "Ethnic Origins," 179–99. Thomas L. Purvis, "The National Origins of New Yorkers in 1790," *New York History* 67 (1986), 142–43, found ethnic population per-

Using the same projection technique developed for the 1790 census by the McDonalds, we also have analyzed the censuses of 1810, 1830, and 1850 and found that the Celtic portion of the southern white population stabilized at about 50 percent; the English stabilized at about a third of the total; the remainder were largely of German, French, or Spanish origins. Nearly 60 percent of the white Southerners of British extraction were Celtic; just over 40 percent were English. In New England and the upper Midwest, the English continued to constitute about three-quarters of the population until the 1840s, when the arrival of numerous refugees from the Irish potato famine changed the ratio to about sixty-forty English. In the lower Midwest—which is to say along the Ohio Valley in Ohio, Indiana, and Illinois—the ethnic distribution of the population tended to follow the southern pattern. Significantly, during the War for Southern Independence this area was teeming with southern sympathizers whom Yankees called Copperheads.

A second method of name analysis, an apportionment system that we have developed, also suggests that a Celtic cultural hegemony existed in the South. Some sample results: An examination of the names recorded in the early censuses of three Georgia counties reveals that fewer than a third of the families listed were English; more than half were Celtic. Of the families identified as being of British extraction, 62 percent were Celtic and 38 percent were English. A similar pattern was found in Lowndes County, Mississippi, where an examination of the 1,616 families listed in the 1850 census revealed that more than half were Celtic and only a third were English. Of the families identified as British, 61 percent were Celtic and 39 percent were English.[45]

The significance of these figures from Georgia and Mississippi becomes clear when we look at the ethnic pattern in a comparable northern area. For example, Eaton County, in central Michigan, was settled between 1834 and 1860 primarily by people from New England, New York, and Ohio. Nearly half of the first 2,175 families to acquire land in the county were of English ancestry; fewer than a third were of Celtic ancestry. Of the 1,702 families (or 78 percent) identified as British, fully 61 percent were of English extraction and only 39 percent were Celtic—the exact reverse of the southern pattern.[46]

centages in the Northeast quite similar to the McDonalds' figures.

45. Calculated from Frank Parker Hudson, comp., *An 1800 Census for Lincoln County, Georgia* (Atlanta, 1977), 51–103; Brigid S. Townsend, comp., *Indexes to Seven State Census Reports for Counties in Georgia, 1838–1845* (Atlanta, 1975), 19–25, 47–53; B.

Thomas, *1850 Census, Lowndes County,* 5–172; McWhiney and McDonald, "Celtic Names," 97–101.

46. Calculated from E. Gray Williams and Ethel W. Williams, comps., *First Land Owners of Eaton County, Michigan* (Kalamazoo, 1967), 1–64; McWhiney and McDonald, "Celtic Names," 101.

In an effort to overcome some of the biases inherent in our apportionment technique, we have experimented with yet another method of name analysis. We compiled a list of 2,468 names that are common to and peculiar to the shires of the south and east of England.[47] To see just how many of these names, presumably the most English of English names, could be found in the Deep South in the late antebellum period, we compared them with the 20,000 or so family names listed in the United States census of Alabama in 1850.[48] We also compiled a list of 1,087 different names, almost all of them Celtic, found on gravestones in Antrim and Down—the Ulster counties closest to Scotland but outside the plantation area created by James I[49]—which we compared with the Alabama census of 1850. The results: 84 percent of the Celtic names but only 43 percent of the English names were also found in Alabama.

Such ratios of Celts to Englishmen as our various name analysis methods reveal suggest that the North and the South were settled and dominated numerically during the antebellum period by different people with significantly different cultural backgrounds. This is not to suggest that either North or South was totally homogeneous: there were individuals and groups in both sections that resisted amalgamation. Some Scotch-Irish in New England, for example, refused from the outset to fit into Puritan society.[50] In the South there were individual hustlers, go-getters, eccentrics, hard workers, even literate people sprinkled about in the region. Furthermore, little islands of English culture persisted here and there throughout the antebellum period.

Moreover, there were scattered throughout the South, from the Carolina piedmont westward, Lowland Scots or Scotch-Irish Presbyterians who took their religion seriously and tended to be educated, disciplined, hardworking, pious, rigidly moralistic. Such people were often storekeepers or taverners, millers, ferry operators,

47. Henry Brougham Guppy, *Homes of Family Names in Great Britain* (1890; reprint, Baltimore, 1968), 67–68, 71–72, 76–77, 82–83, 168–69, 183–84, 194–95, 204–05, 214–15, 222, 224–26, 258–59, 268–69, 281, 283–85, 298–99, 319–20, 327–28, 344–46, 365–66, 375–76, 379–80, 387–88, 392–94; Sir William Addison, *Understanding English Surnames* (London, 1978), 143–59. The shires from which this list of peculiarly English names was compiled are Bedford, Berks, Buckingham, Cambridge, Dorset, Essex, Gloucester, Hamps, Hertford, Huntingdon, Kent, Leicester, Lincoln, Middlesex, Norfolk, Northampton, Nottingham, Oxford, Rutland, Somerset, Suffolk, Surrey, Sussex, Warwick, and Wilts.

48. Ronald Vern Jackson et al., eds., *Alabama 1850 Census Index* (Bountiful, Utah, 1976).

49. George Rutherford, comp., *Gravestone Inscriptions: County Antrim, Volume 1, Parish of Islandmagee* (Belfast, 1977), 1–101; A. C. W. Marrick, comp., *Gravestone Inscriptions: County Down, Volume 17, Barony of Ards* (Belfast, 1978), 1–203.

50. Maldwyn A. Jones, "Scotch-Irish," in *Harvard Encyclopedia of American Ethnic Groups*, ed. Stephen Thernstrom (Cambridge, Mass., 1980), 899.

and surveyors as well as planters. Even they, however, were not totally free from their Celtic heritage. Most lived in rude cabins and ate typical southern food no matter how much wealth they might accumulate; many drank heavily and were given to violence, no matter how pious they might be.[51]

Besides the English and the more pious Presbyterians—who were usually found in the larger plantation areas and were often reinforced in towns by northern and foreign-born merchants, the people who most successfully resisted to Celticization were those Germans who settled together in significant numbers. Germans gained the reputation in the colonial period of being industrious farmers; they cleared the land by cutting down trees, burning them, and pulling "out the stumps by the roots." This practice was in marked contrast to the "shiftlessness of the Scotch-Irish," who girdled trees, let them bleed to death and fall or be blown down, and simply planted around the stumps. In comparison to the Celts, Germans operated farms with "greater intensity, productivity, and locational stability." German farmers in Texas, for example, were "more active in market gardening" and "in supplying vegetables and fruit," and "they devoted more attention to wine-making and the production of white potatoes. In both western and eastern settlements, the Germans showed greater interest than southerners in cultivation of small grains. . . . By the same token, the Germans . . . operated on a higher level of commercialization than the Americans before the Civil War." In 1850, the average German farm in eastern Texas was half the size and contained livestock valued at less than a third as much as that of the average non-German farm. Although Germans frequently adopted southern ways, "the open range was an entirely new economic undertaking for the Germans, alien to their European agricultural heritage."[52] Germans were almost the only people in

51. Daniel R. Hundley, *Social Relations in Our Southern States,* ed. William J. Cooper, Jr. (1860; new ed., Baton Rouge, 1979), 80–81, 94–96, 127, 199, 202–03, 216–19, passim.

52. C. Bridenbaugh, *Myths and Realities,* 135, 140–41; Terry G. Jordan, *German Seed in Texas Soil: Immigrant Farmers in Nineteenth-Century Texas* (Austin, 1966), 192–94, 98, 100, 85. For a comparison of German and Celtic habits and comments on the superiority of German over Celtic farmers, see also Johann David Schopf, *Travels in the Confederation [1783–1784] . . .* , trans. and ed. Alfred J. Morrison (new ed., 2 vols., New York, 1968), I:339, II:23, 39, 154; William Faux, *Memorable Days in America . . .* (London, 1823), 127;

Louis Philippe, *Diary of My Travels in America [1797],* trans. Stephen Becker (New York, 1977), 41; Christian Schultz, *Travels . . . in the Years 1807 and 1808 . . .* (2 vols., New York, 1810), I:8; Eugene L. Schwaab, ed., *Travels in the Old South: Selected from Periodicals of the Times* (2 vols., Lexington, Ky., 1973), I:117; Friedrich Wilhelm Christian Gerstäcker, *Wild Sports in the Far West: The Narrative of a German Wanderer Beyond the Mississippi, 1837–1843,* trans. and ed. Edna L. Steeves and Harrison R. Steeves (new ed., Durham, N.C., 1968), 229–30, 355, 375–76; Francis Baily, *Journal of a Tour in Unsettled Parts of North America in 1796 & 1797,* ed. Jack D. L. Holmes (Carbondale, Ill., 1969), 41, 43.

the South whom Northerner Frederick Law Olmsted understood and admired; their neat houses and diligent merchants, mechanics, and farmers reminded him of New England. After enjoying a German inn, Olmsted remarked that he had found "Nothing so pleasant as that in Texas before, hardly in the South."[53]

Germans in Ireland, like Germans in the Old South but unlike most other settlers, successfully resisted assimilation. "They are different from the Irish in several particulars," noted an Englishman in the eighteenth century. "They are very industrious, . . . better fed, clothed, and lodged, than the Irish peasants." Excellent farmers, the Germans "till much more than the Irish. They drill their potatoes, . . . House their cattle, feeding them with hay. . . . They are cleaner and neater, and live much better; . . . and all of them have neat little kitchen gardens."[54]

Not many people besides the Germans managed to resist Celticization in Ireland. In order to protect themselves from amalgamation, the English prohibited intermarriage with the Irish in the statutes of Kilkenny as early as the fourteenth century, yet after awhile even Englishmen frequently "went native," as a seventeenth-century observer complained: "joining themselves with the Irish, took upon their wild fashions and their language, the English in length of time came to be so much weakened, that at last nothing remained to them [but] . . . the four Counties to whom the name of Pale was given." Another Englishman reported that his countrymen, after living among the Irish, adopted "Irish Customs, . . . after they had rejected the Civill and Honorable Lawes and Customes of *England,* whereby they became degenerate. . . . For, as they did not only forget the English Language, and scorn the use thereof, but grew to be ashamed of their very English Names, though they were noble and of great Antiquity; and took Irish *Surnames* and *Nickenames.* And this they did in contempt and hatred of the English Name and Nation; whereof these degenerate families became more mortal enemies [of the English] than the meere Irish."[55]

53. Frederick Law Olmsted, *A Journey through Texas . . . ,* (1857; reprint, New York, 1969), 140–47, 149, 167, 178–90; Ralph Waldo Emerson, *English Traits* (Boston, 1856), 61; Margaret Calderwood quoted in Fyfe, *Scottish Diaries and Memoirs,* 92; Timothy Flint, *Recollections of the Last Ten Years,* ed. C. Hartley Grattan (1826; reprint, New York, 1932), 12–14; Edouard de Montule, *Travels in America, 1816–1817,* trans. Edward D. Seeber (Bloomington, 1951), 137–38.

54. A. Young, *Tour in Ireland,* I:377–78, 386.

55. Lughaidh O'Clerigh, *Beath Aodha Ruaidh Ui Dhomnaill, the Life of Aodh Ruadh O'Dhomnaill,* ed. Paul Walsh (Dublin, 1948), 97; Great Britain, *The Statutes at Large Passed in the Parliament Held in Ireland, 1310–1736* (2 vols., Dublin, 1786), I:174; Gerard Boate, *Irelands Naturall History . . .* (London, 1652), 17–18; Sir John Davies, *A Discoverie of the State of Ireland: With the True Causes Why that Kingdom was Never Entirely Subdued . . .* (London, 1613), 80.

Similarly, it was extremely difficult for non-Celts who came to the Old South alone or with only their families and settled outside the towns and the large plantation areas to avoid being assimilated. Southerners of Celtic background tended to intermarry with and to absorb and acculturate all who remained among them. For example, fully 80 percent of the 8,243 people listed in antebellum marriage records of the two earliest settled northern Mississippi counties (Lowndes and Monroe) were of Celtic origins; only 7 percent were English (some 13 percent defied identification or were of other origins). In 91 percent of these weddings, one or more of the members of the 222 families with English surnames married a person with a Celtic surname; indeed, in 447 of the 565 marriages involving a person with an English surname the other partner was a Celt.[56] John Morgan Dederer claims that "the tribal Celtic-Southerner's culture and folk traits were so compatible with those of the Africans that it took little adaptation for slaves to fit Celtic characteristics around their African practices."[57] Many of the Indians of the Old South also practiced lifestyles quite similar to those of their Celtic neighbors. "The Creeks," an observer noted, "have the greatest possible repugnance to regular labour; they [delight in] . . . war or hunting; but the labour of agriculture, as a regular employment, is intolerable to them." They also shared with the Celts a "fondness for whiskey." So did the Choctaws, who enjoyed warfare, "periodical migrations," and "hunting." A visitor stated: "their living is scanty, for they use their money to buy whiskey rather than more necessary things."[58] Numerous writers reported on the Louisiana Acadians' leisurely and sensual lifestyle, which corresponded to traditional Celtic ways, as well it might, because the Cajuns originally came from Brittany and Normandy—Celtic areas of France.[59] Nor, ac-

56. Calculated from Betty Wood Thomas, comp., *Mississippi Marriages: Lowndes County, 1830–1868; Monroe County, 1821–1858* (Columbus, Miss., 1979), 5–279. For sources on the origins of surnames, see the Appendix.

57. John Morgan Dederer, "Afro-Southern and Celtic-Southern Cultural Adaptation in the Old South" (MS in possession of the author).

58. Anon., *The English Party's Excursion to Paris, . . . to which is Added, a Trip to America . . .* (London, 1850), 337–38; Victor Tixier, *Tixier's Travels . . . [1839–1840],* ed. John Francis McDermott (Norman, Okla., 1940), 56–58. On the leisurely lifestyle of southern Indians, see also Carl David Arfwedson, *The United States and Canada, in 1832,* 

*1833, and 1834 . . .* (2 vols., London, 1834), II:33–34; Philippe, *Diary of My Travels,* 108; G. P. Whittington, "Rapides Parish, Louisiana—A History," *Louisiana Historical Quarterly* 15 (1932), 576.

59. Marietta M. LeBreton, "Acadians," in Thernstrom, *Harvard Encyclopedia of . . . Ethnic Groups,* 1–3; Flint, *Recollections,* 209–310; J. W. Dorr, "A Tourist's Description of Louisiana in 1860," ed. Walter Prichard, *Louisiana Historical Quarterly* 20 (1937), 1038; Charles Sealsfield, *America: Glorious and Chaotic Land . . . ,* trans. E. L. Jordan (Englewood Cliffs, N.J., 1969), 94, 137; Tixier, *Travels,* 52–55; Frederick Law Olmsted, *A Journey in the Seaboard Slave States* (New York, 1856), 673, 682.

cording to many observers, were Celts or Cajuns more sensual and indolent than the French and the Spanish Creoles.[60]

Antebellum Southerners, despite various shared cultural traits, were no more identical than were antebellum Northerners. But the tendency, by and large, was for Celts and other non-English people in the North to become Anglicized and for Englishmen and other non-Celtic people in the South to become Celticized. Thus, more than anything else, settlement patterns determined the cultures of both sections.

60. William Kingsford, *Impressions of the West and South during a Six Weeks' Holiday* (Toronto, 1858), 53; Henry Anthony Murray, *Lands of the Slave and the Free* . . . (2 vols., London, 1855), I:248, 257–59, 261–63; Sealsfield, *America*, 24–25, 95; Lyell, *Second Visit,* II:94, 125; François Marie Perrin du Lac, *Travels Through the Two Loui-* *sianas* . . . (London, 1807), 90; Matilda Charlotte (Jesse) Fraser Houstoun, *Texas and the Gulf* . . . (Philadelphia, 1845), 77; George A. McCall, *Letters from the Frontiers* . . . (Philadelphia, 1868), 14–15; Whipple, *Southern Diary,* 110; Olmsted, *Journey through Texas,* 63, 78–79.

# II
# *Heritage*

THOSE Celts who migrated to the southern part of what became the United States brought with them from the British Isles a host of habits and traditions that distinguished them both from the Englishmen who stayed at home and from the Englishmen who settled New England. American textbooks often give the impression that the people of the British Isles were more alike than different, but contemporary observers reported Celtic culture to be quite unlike English culture. "Their customs how different from ours," wrote an Englishman of eighteenth-century Scots. "[After crossing the border between England and Scotland] the first Scotch village you enter . . . the change of manners, dress, and character, strike most forcibly. . . . Their faces . . . were different from their [English] neighbours. . . . Edinburgh must strike with the most forcible impression every Englishman: its buildings are so dissimilar to ours, [and] . . . old High Street . . . resembles no street in England."[1]

Many travelers noted the divergence between Scottish and English looks and ways, and they frequently observed that the border country between England and Scotland appeared to be far more Scottish than English. "I had entered a considerable way into England [from Scotland] ere I was struck by the peculiarities of the English face and figure," confessed a nineteenth-century visitor. "There is no . . . palpable difference between the borderers of Northumberland [in England] and those of Roxburghshire [in Scotland]. . . . But, as the traveller advances on the midland counties, the English cast of person and countenance becomes very apparent. The harder frame and thinner face of the northern tribes disappear shortly after one leaves Newcastle; and one meets, instead, with ruddy, fleshy, compactly-built Englishmen, of the true national type." An eighteenth-

1. R. L. Willis, *Journal of a Tour from London to Elgin made about 1790* . . .    (Edinburgh, 1897), 73, 43, 47.

century observer insisted "that on entering the borders of Scotland, the first town you reach is almost as perfectly Scot, as if you were a hundred miles north of Edinburgh; and there is very little appearance of any thing English, either in the customs or habits of the people, or their ways of living, eating, or behaviour: nor are there many English families to be found among them. On the contrary, in the towns of Northumberland and Cumberland, next to Scotland, there are abundance of Scotsmen, Scots customs, words, and habits." Still another traveler claimed that Kendal, in Westmoreland, appeared no more English than would "a Turkish town."[2]

Observers also agreed that Irish and Welsh customs were un-English. Early in the nineteenth century an Englishman admitted that "in political feeling, in language, in manners, and almost every particular which stamps a national character," the Irish and the English "differ essentially." More recent writers have noted that to "the majority of Englishmen, Ireland is . . . a foreign country," and that the "crowds in the Dublin streets are vastly different from English crowds. You can not see the haggard money look which is . . . characteristic of all large English cities. There is more laughter. There is no painful rushing about. There is a cheerful ease about Dublin, a casual good temper." Of the Welsh, an eighteenth-century visitor affirmed: "This People still retain their ancient Language, and differ also very much from the *English* in their Manners and Customs."[3]

The English, in general, found Celtic ways barbarous and disgusting; they spoke of Scotland, Ireland, and Wales as "frightful" places

2. Hugh Miller, *First Impressions of England and Its People* (Boston, 1852), 260–61; Henry Boswell, *Historical Description of . . . the Antiquities of England and Wales . . . and Other Curiosities in Scotland and Ireland . . .* (London, 1786), unnumbered pages; Willis, *Journal of a Tour,* 29. On the similarities between Scottish and North Country ways, see also Thomas Kirk and Ralph Thoresby, *Tours in Scotland, 1677 & 1681,* ed. Peter Hume Brown (Edinburgh, 1892), 28; Alexander Campbell, *A Journey from Edinburgh through Parts of North Britain . . .* (2 vols., London, 1802), I:164–65; Thomas Fuller, *The Worthies of England,* ed. John Freeman (1662; reprint, London, 1952), 99–100; James Dugdale, *The New British Traveller; or, Modern Panorama of England and Wales . . .* (4 vols., London, 1819), I:621, IV:430; Edward Hughes, *North Country Life in the Eighteenth Century: the North-East, 1700–1750* (London, 1952), xiii–xix, 13–17, 31–35, 113–43, 380–95.

3. Thomas Crofton Croker, *Researches in the South of Ireland . . .* (1824; reprint, New York, 1969), 2; Ella B. Day, *Mr. Justice Day of Kerry, 1745–1841: A Discursive Memoir* (Exeter, 1938), 11; H. V. Morton, *In Search of Ireland* (London, 1930), 7; Henri Misson, *M. Misson's Memoirs and Observations in His Travels over England, With some Account of Scotland and Ireland,* trans. Mr. Ozell (London, 1719), 333. See also Sir John Davies, *A Discoverie of the State of Ireland: With the True Causes Why that Kingdom was Never Entirely Subdued . . .* (London, 1613), 80; Gerard Boate, *Irelands Naturall History . . .* (London, 1652), 17–18; Anon., *Letters from an Armenian in Ireland, to His Friends at Trebisond, &c.,* trans. Edmond S. Pery (London, 1757), 11.

and of the Celtic people as being "wicked," "savage," and "indolent drunkards."[4] In the seventeenth century several distinguished Englishmen concluded that "the *English* do plainly foresee it can never be safe for them to cohabit with [the Irish, who] . . . likely [will never] . . . digest into a People good to themselves, or profitable to their King and Country." An English lord asserted at the end of the eighteenth century that England would never be able to "effect a union of sentiment, and opinions, and general manners [with the Irish, who] . . . appear to be as distinct a race from the Britons as a Mexican from a Parisian, who have nothing alike but the feathers they wear in their caps—hot, hasty and inconsiderate: they are governed by no principle of right and wrong, lazy as savages, but more ferocious and cruel in their resentments. Even education does not eradicate this disposition, it only checks its impulse and slightly veils a mischief which is innate. Twenty Irishmen in a ship give more trouble than five hundred English. They seldom ever become seamen and I believe only are good in battle, because it is so much like that mischief which is innate. If they are here twenty years their manners change no more than the colour of an Ethiopian would by looking on snow." "I find 'tis natural enough," wrote a foreigner, "for the English to despise all the rest of Mankind, and to count those miserable that Border upon them [the Scots, Irish, and Welsh]." Yet another foreigner noted the great dislike of the English for the Irish and Scots, but he concluded: "The inhabitants of this province [Wales] are the least esteemed of all others in England, insomuch that it is an affront to any man to call him Welshman." An Englishwoman acknowledged "that general prejudice which the majority of the English have against the Irish," and an Englishman stated: "I verily believe there is not an Englishman, when he knew the Country [of Scotland], but would think of a Settlement there

4. John Stevens, *The Journal of John Stevens, Containing a Brief Account of the War in Ireland, 1689–1691*, ed. Robert H. Murray (Oxford, 1912), 140; Daniel Defoe, *A Tour through the Whole Island of Great Britain [1724–1726]*, ed. Pat Rogers (New York, 1971), 382, 661; Willis, *Journal of a Tour*, 44; Anon., *The Comical Pilgrim; or, Travels of a Cynick Philosopher, Thro' the Most Wicked Parts of the World, Namely England, Wales, Scotland, Ireland, and Holland* (London, 1723), 54, 84; Croker, *Researches*, 7–8; Joseph Taylor, *Journey to Edenborough in Scotland [in the Eighteenth Century]*, ed. William Cowan (Edinburgh, 1903), 94–95; Rowland Hill, *Journal of a Tour through the North of England and Parts of Scotland . . .* (London, 1799), 9–10; John Barrow, *A Tour Round Ireland* (London, 1836), 35; James Johnson, *A Tour in Ireland; With Meditations and Reflections* (London, 1844), 144; Thomas Walford, *The Scientific Tourist through Ireland . . .* (London, 1818), 443. See also Sir John Sinclair, ed., *The Statistical Account of Scotland, 1791–1799* (reprint, 20 vols., East Ardsley, England, 1981), XVII:572; Taylor Downing, ed., *The Troubles* (London, 1980), 45; Richard Ned Lebow, *White Britain and Black Ireland: The Influence of Stereotypes on Colonial Policy* (Philadelphia, 1976), 48; idem, "British Historians and Irish History," *Eire-Ireland* 8 (1973), 3–38.

ENGLISH VIEWS OF VARIOUS CELTS

From *Punch, or the London Charivari* 5 (1843), 199; ibid. 6
(1844), 147; ibid. 11 (1846), 245.

with more Horror than any Russian would do of Banishment to Siberia."[5]

The New England Transcendentalist Ralph Waldo Emerson summed up English as well as Yankee views on the subject when he explained that "what we think of when we talk of English traits really narrows itself to a small district. It excludes Ireland, and Scotland, and Wales. . . . As you go north into . . . Yorkshire, or you enter Scotland, there is a rapid loss of all grandeur of mien and manners; a provincial eagerness and acuteness appear; the poverty of the country makes itself remarked, and a coarseness of manners [prevails]. . . . In Ireland, are the same climate and soil as in England, but less food, no right relation to the land, . . . and an inferior or misplaced race."[6]

Celts, in turn, despised the English. They resented English self-glorification, English attempts to outlaw and to abolish Celtic culture and traditions, and English claims that they were responsible for what civilization existed in Ireland, Scotland, and Wales.[7] "In Wales," wrote an Englishman, "many inconveniences are suffered from the people being disinclined to hold intercourse with the English and when able to answer questions & to give information they will avoid it by affecting not to speak English." Another Englishman reported that Welsh musicians refused to play for their English

5. Letter from ten English Lords, Justices, and Council of Ireland to King Charles I, March 16, 1642, quoted in Richard Cox, *Hibernia Anglicana: or, the History of Ireland* . . . (2 vols., London, 1689), II: App. IV, 12; Lord Collingwood quoted in Oliver Warner, *The Life and Letters of Vice-Admiral Lord Collingwood* (London, 1968), 98; Samuel Sorbiere, *A Voyage to England, Containing Many Things Relating to that . . . Kingdom* (London, 1709), 46; Jorevin de Rocheford, "Description of England and Ireland in the 17th Century," in *The Antiquarian Repertory: A Miscellaneous Assemblage of Topography, History, Biography, Customs, and Manners,* comp. Francis Grose (4 vols., London, 1807–09), IV:574; Ellen Weeton, *Miss Weeton's Journal of a Governess [1807–1825]* (1936; reprint, 2 vols., New York, 1969), II:317; Edward Burt, *Burt's Letters from the North of Scotland,* ed. R. Jamieson (1754; reprint, 2 vols., Edinburgh, 1974), II:340. See also Sorbiere, *Voyage to England,* 55.

6. Ralph Waldo Emerson, *English Traits* (Boston, 1856), 58–59.

7. Richard Stanihurst, "A Treatise

Conteining a Plaine and Perfect Description of Ireland," in *Holinshed's Chronicles of England, Scotland, and Ireland,* comp. Raphaell Holinshed (6 vols., London, 1807–08), VI:66–67; Peter Hume Brown, ed., *Scotland Before 1700, from Contemporary Documents* (Edinburgh, 1893), 52; Constantia Maxwell, ed., *Irish History from Contemporary Sources (1509–1610)* (London, 1923), 166–67, 223, 290–91; Donald McNichol, *Remarks on Dr. Samuel Johnson's Journey to the Hebrides . . .* (London, 1779), 72–73; Fynes Moryson, *Shakespeare's Europe: Unpublished Chapters of Fynes Moryson's Itinerary, Being a Survey of the Conditions of Europe at the End of the 16th Century,* ed. Charles Hughes (London, 1903), 481; Anon., *Scotland Delineated, or a Geographical Description of Every Shire in Scotland . . .* (2d ed., Edinburgh, 1799), 16. On English efforts to destroy Celtic culture in the British Isles, see Michael Hechter, *Internal Colonialism: The Celtic Fringe in British National Development, 1536–1966* (Berkeley and Los Angeles, 1977), 47–123.

visitors because they considered them "deceitful." About the same time, an Englishman observed that the Scots "have a dreadful Notion of the English," to whom, according to one Scotsman, "God had not given . . . over-much wit or sense." English customs, concluded a Scotswoman, were not suitable for Scotland. "It is surprizing," she wrote, "how much nonsense I have heard spoken by folks who would introduce English customs into Scotland, without considering the difference of the two countrys." Yet another Scotswoman noted at the end of the eighteenth century that Englishmen and Scots who tried to imitate them were called "Whigs . . . [which] was used to designate a character made up of negatives: One who had neither ear for music, nor taste for poetry; no pride of ancestry; no heart for attachment; no soul for honour. . . . A Whig, in short, was what all highlanders cordially hated,—a cold, selfish, formal character."[8]

Most of the Celtic migrants to various parts of America during the seventeenth and eighteenth centuries were smart enough or lucky enough to settle where both the physical environment and the local society suited and would tolerate their traditional culture, but some were less fortunate. Those who landed in New England, for example, faced special hostility from the earlier settlers whose ways were "fundamentally English."[9] One authority noted that "from the first" New Englanders had serious "misgivings" about Celts who settled among them. "In 1718 several hundred newly arrived Scotch-Irish immigrants were sent from Boston to the frontier." The purpose was both to isolate and to make use of them by placing them between the Indians and the earlier settlers, for "New England in the early 18th century was as ethnically homogeneous as its name implied and was disposed to look suspiciously on strangers." At first New England's clergymen thought that no doctrinal barrier would prevent the meshing of Scotch-Irish Presbyterians into the Puritan Congregational church; both, after all, were Calvinist. "But the Scotch-Irish brought with them their own distinctive brand of Calvinism. . . . To the surprise and irritation of the spiritual leaders of the Bay Colony, Scotch-Irish ministers wasted no time in denouncing New England churches for theological

8. Joseph Farington, *The Farington Diary,* ed. James Grieg (3d ed., 2 vols., New York, 1923), I:330; John Loveday, *Diary of a Tour in 1732 Through Parts of England, Wales, Ireland and Scotland* (Edinburgh, 1890), 40; Burt, *Letters,* II:76, 250–53; John Ramsay quoted in J. G. Fyfe, ed., *Scottish Diaries and Memoirs, 1746–1843* (Stirling, Scotland, 1942), 179; Margaret Calderwood quoted in Fyfe, *Scottish Diaries and Memoirs,* 84; Anne Grant, *Essays on the Superstitions of the Highlanders of Scotland* (2 vols., London, 1811), I:138–39.

9. David Grayson Allen, *In English Ways: The Movement of Societies and the Transferal of English Local Law and Custom to Massachusetts Bay in the Seventeenth Century* (Chapel Hill, 1981), xv, xvi, 4–8, 26–28, 30–36, 221–22.

error. . . . Besides religious antipathy there were other reasons for Puritan dislike of the Scotch-Irish. Although many settled on the frontier, the poor remained in Boston, adding to what was already a considerable burden of pauperism. Hence the fear expressed by the Surveyor General of the Customs at Boston in 1719 that 'these confounded Irish will eat us all up.' " Consequently, when several vessels arrived in Boston in July 1719 full of immigrants from Belfast and Derry, a mob of New Englanders prevented the passengers from landing. "Even so, the Boston town records reveal that between 1729 and 1742, two-thirds of the inmates of the almshouse were Scotch-Irish. In addition to being a burden, the Scotch-Irish seemed to Bostonians to be a barbarous crew. There were frequent complaints of their drinking, blasphemy, and violence that revealed itself most graphically in the practice of biting off ears in the course of fights." Court records also confirm "that the Scotch-Irish committed more than their share of crimes."[10]

Yankee prejudice against Celts, like English prejudice against Celts, continued throughout the antebellum period. The early settlers of Northampton, Massachusetts, recorded in "a single vote" their feelings towards Celts. "In 1663, three acres of land were granted to Cornelius the Irishman, providing, however, that he should not 'be capable of acting in any town affairs.' " The president of Yale College, Timothy Dwight, exemplified the strong prejudices of New Englanders against the Irish, even before the great wave of nineteenth-century Irish immigrants arrived; he described them as "almost absolutely uneducated, . . . bad managers, poor, and vicious."[11]

The English, on the other hand, received such praise as Yankees could heap only upon their own kind; the New Englander's admiration of the English almost equaled the admiration Englishmen bestowed upon themselves. "England is the best of actual nations," announced Ralph Waldo Emerson, who concluded that Yankees and Englishmen looked alike, dined alike, and that the Yankee "is only the continuation of the English genius into new conditions, more

10. Maldwyn A. Jones, "Scotch-Irish," in *Harvard Encyclopedia of American Ethnic Groups*, ed. Stephen Thernstrom (Cambridge, Mass., 1980), 899. On the difficulties of integrating Celts into New England culture, see Waldo F. Glover, "Old Scotland in Vermont," *Vermont History* 23 (1955), 92–103; Eugene R. Fingerhut, "From Scots to Americans: Ryegate's Immigrants in the 1770's," *Vermont History* 35 (1967), 186–207.

11. Timothy Dwight, *Travels in New*

*England and New York*, ed. Barbara Miller Solomon (4 vols., Cambridge, Mass., 1969), I:254, xxxvi. On the treatment of the Irish in New England, see Oscar Handlin, *Boston's Immigrants* (1941; rev., Cambridge, Mass., 1959); Stephen Thernstrom, *Poverty and Progress* (1964; reprint, New York, 1969); idem, *The Other Bostonians* (Cambridge, Mass., 1973); Patrick J. Blessing, "Irish," in Thernstrom, *Harvard Encyclopedia of . . . Ethnic Groups*, 524–45.

YANKEE LAMPOON OF IRISH AMERICANS

From *Harper's New Monthly Magazine* 23 (1861), 573.

or less propitious." Benjamin Silliman, another Yankee, echoed Emerson's views; an Englishman reported that New Englanders in general were "well disposed towards the English"; and a New England woman, who admitted, "I am so partial to the English character," claimed that "purely English children, as soon as they can talk, exhibit all the dignity and nobleness of character, so natural to the English people, as well as those strong powers of the mind which have made that nation a mistress over so many others." Another Yankee woman, who "was proud" of what she called her "pure Anglo-Saxon Pilgrim descent," noted that English manners, dinners, social forms, and style of dress were quite similar to those of New England but were unlike those in the American South.[12]

Not only were Yankees proud of their English heritage, but they thought and acted so much like Englishmen that visitors and immigrants from England frequently compared England to New England. During the American Civil War Englishman Anthony Trollope observed from Boston that it "was impossible not to feel that all that was said [by Yankees] was complimentary to England. It is her sympathy that the Northern men desire, to her co-operation that they would willingly trust, on her honesty that they would choose to depend." Earlier in the nineteenth century an English visitor heard a "communicative Yankee" boast that he "was proud to trace his genealogy to the 'Pilgrim Fathers,' and, through them, to the Normans. Intercourse, he said, had been maintained for the last two centuries between the English and American branches of the family. He also took care to inform me that the head of the English branch was a baronet." A French traveler noted that Yankee "customs are too genuinely English to admit of any sincere hatred for the people who introduce them; I assure you . . . that an Englishman can disembark here [in Boston or in New York] with the most extraordinary fashions without exciting laughter, and that the case is quite different with Frenchmen or any other [than Englishmen]." One Englishman stated that there "are so many English people here [in the North] that it seems much like home," while another quoted a Yankee as saying that in the North "Englishmen are esteemed far above all other Europeans."[13]

12. Emerson, *English Traits*, 298, 60, 117, 42; [Benjamin Silliman], *A Journal of Travels in England, Holland and Scotland* . . . (2 vols., New York, 1810), I:56, 70–71, 86; Farington, *Diary*, I:116; Emily P. Burke, *Reminiscences of Georgia* (Oberlin, Ohio, 1850), 38–39; Elizabeth Davis Bancroft, *Letters from England, 1846–1849* (New York, 1904), 193, 24, 42, 173, 213, 215, 23, 38, 50, 31–32.

13. Anthony Trollope, *North America*,

ed. Donald Smalley and Bradford Allen Booth (New York, 1951), 44; Ebenezer Davies, *American Scenes—and Christian Slavery: A Recent Tour of Four Thousand Miles in the United States* (London, 1849), 208; Edouard de Montule, *Travels in America, 1816–1817*, trans. Edward D. Seeber (Bloomington, 1951), 182; an English immigrant quoted in Charlotte Erickson, *Invisible Immigrants: The Adaptation of English and Scottish Immigrants in Nineteenth-*

English travelers, in turn, seldom failed to praise Yankees and New England.[14] "[The] manners, customs, and character of the people [of New England]," wrote an English visitor, "are, generally speaking, the same as those of the people of England." Another English traveler called New England "the best society in the country." "I confess [that New England] . . . is, and always has been, the dearest [part of the United States]," admitted still another Englishman. "I know of no place at which an Englishman may drop down suddenly among a pleasanter circle of acquaintance, or find himself with a more clever set of men, than he can do at Boston." An Englishwoman, who spent a winter in Boston, enjoyed herself thoroughly and felt completely at home. "Left the good Yankee town of Boston, this morning, full of blessings on it," lamented an English traveler, "but scarcely hoping to find another Boston, where I wished a longer stay." Yet another Englishman concluded that "Boston is the city of America that Englishmen like most." "We left Massachusetts to the last because we wished to have the best impression of America before leaving," exclaimed an Englishwoman. "I have a love for New England—a very strong affection—and shall be quite sorry to leave." "One could live here [in New England] absolutely as if in an English castle," wrote a Russian visitor, who explained that "the English style of life, with all its comforts and luxuries and all its distinctions and liveries prevails here, far from the public's censure of this violation of democratic equality in social life."[15]

What the English found so appealing in New England was that visiting there was almost like being at home; the manners and customs were remarkably like those in England. New Englanders had continued their English traditions of hard work, discipline, ambition, and orderliness. Timothy Dwight admitted that "things [in New England] are chiefly the same with those in Great Britain, or very similar. You will say that our government is the same . . . , except some slight shades of difference, that our religion is the same in all its varieties, that our manners are the same, and that this is

*Century America* (Worcester, England, 1972), 70; William Faux, *Memorable Days in America* . . . (London, 1823), 33.

14. Robert Fussell, *North America, Its Agriculture and Climate* (Edinburgh, 1857), 2; Anon., *The English Party's Excursion to Paris . . . to which is Added, a Trip to America* . . . (London, 1850), 410; Patrick Shirreff, *A Tour through North America . . . as Adapted for Agricultural Emigration* (Edinburgh, 1835), 14–15.

15. William Cobbett, *A Years Residence in the United States of America [1818–1819]* (reprint, New York, 1969), 344; Adam Hodgson, *Letters from North*

*America* . . . (2 vols., London, 1824), II:17; Trollope, *North America*, 31, 19; Marianne Finch, *An Englishwoman's Experience in America* (1853; reprint, New York, 1969), 183; Faux, *Memorable Days*, 35–36; Thomas Low Nichols, *Forty Years of American Life* (2 vols., London, 1864), I:98; Barbara Leigh Smith Bodichon, *An American Diary, 1857–8*, ed. Joseph W. Reed, Jr. (London, 1972), 117–18; Aleksandr Borisovich Lakier, *A Russian Looks at America: The Journey of Aleksandr Borisovich Lakier in 1857*, ed. Arnold Schrier and Joyce Story (Chicago, 1979), 105.

true of our whole state of society. What I mean is, that you will consider all these things copies, imperfect indeed, but still copies of the same things in Great Britain." Dwight argued that there were a few differences between New England and Old England, but he admitted that "these differences are very small." An Englishman reported that "in the New England States, the people are as clean and as neat as they are in England"; another stated that the "Arts and Sciences seem to have made a greater progress here than in any other part of America."[16]

Englishmen also found much to praise in areas outside New England where significant numbers of New Englanders had settled. A visitor reported favorably on the "high state of culture" in New York, which he described as similar to "a farm-yard view in England." Other visitors spoke of New Yorkers as having a "cockney bearing and general stiffness of demeanor," compared life on Long Island to "the happy state of the English," and noted that eastern Pennsylvania "looks like *ease* and *plenty*" with its "fine barns, fine farms," and "very clean" towns. On the Illinois frontier, an Englishman stayed overnight "under the roof of a New Englander," where he found "Every thing in the house was particularly clean and neat. The manners of the inmates were calm and dignified, a smile never playing on their countenances, or an emphatic sound proceeding from their lips."[17]

Englishmen generally were no fonder of the South than were Yankees and usually agreed that the southern states were unsuited for English settlers.[18] "To the English farmer [who intended to settle in America] I would say, for personal comfort and successful farming combined, do not go . . . south," advised an Englishman. Another native of England insisted that all of the American West "would not [be] . . . in healthful and progressive motion, were it not for the Yankees of New England." He argued that the "free states" were "not only the most populous, the most wealthy, and the most energetic in the Union; but by the activity of their intellect, the

16. Hodgson, *Letters*, II:5; Alice Morse Earle, *Home Life in Colonial Days* (reprint, Middle Village, N.Y., 1975), 188; Robert Hunter, Jr., *Quebec to Carolina in 1785–1786 . . .*, ed. Louis B. Wright and Marion Tinling (San Marino, Calif., 1943), 226; Dwight, *Travels in New England*, IV:243; Cobbett, *A Years Residence*, 58; James Franklin, *The Philosophical & Political History of . . . America* (London, 1784), 50.

17. John Benwell, *An Englishman's Travels in America . . .* (London, 1853), 9; Daniel R. Hundley, *Social Relations in Our Southern States*, ed. William J. Cooper, Jr. (1860; new ed., Baton Rouge, 1979), 214–15; Cobbett, *A Years Residence*, 348–49, 58; Shirreff, *Tour through America*, 235.

18. On Yankee attitudes toward Southerners, see David W. Mitchell, *Ten Years in the United States . . .* (London, 1862), 185; Oscar Handlin, "Yankees," in Thernstrom, *Harvard Encyclopedia of . . . Ethnic Groups*, 1028–29; John Hope Franklin, *A Southern Odyssey: Travelers in the Antebellum North* (Baton Rouge, 1976), 163–66.

exuberance of their literature, and the general vigor—public and social, as well as private and commercial—of their citizens, they give the law and tone to the whole Union." Another Englishman advised any English farmers to settle in the North, especially New York or Pennsylvania, but not in "any of the southern states," while other Englishmen spoke of the South's "evils" and how white Southerners "filled [them] with disgust."[19]

Southerners, conversely, often found little to admire in the English. In 1845 Jefferson Davis of Mississippi called "England the robber nation of the earth, whose history is a long succession of wrongs and oppressions, whose tracks are marked by the crushed rights of individuals—to England," he concluded, "I cannot go for lessons of morality and justice." In 1861 Mary B. Chesnut of South Carolina wrote: "The British is the most conceited nation in the world, the most self-sufficient, self-satisfied, and arrogant."[20]

Nor were Southerners unaware of their Celtic heritage (a Yankee once told me that Southerners could not have been of Celtic descent because they never claimed Celtic ancestry). Some Southerners, brainwashed by Yankee-written history and propaganda, may have been ignorant of their heritage, but there have always been those who appreciated their past. Antebellum Virginian John Pendleton Kennedy filled his novels with Southerners of Scotch-Irish ancestry; Mary Chesnut remarked in 1861 that "so many [Southerners] are descendants of Irishmen"; and a postbellum writer insisted that "the Southern people . . . were nearly entirely of Scotch-Irish . . . Cavalier, and Huguenot blood."[21] The heroine of *Gone With the Wind* was of Irish descent, and Andrew Jackson, who despised the English, was as aware of his Celtic ancestry as the man who eulogized him, Jefferson Davis. "Andrew Jackson was descended from an Irish family of obscure history but as far as I can learn distinguished by a love of liberty, a hatred of tyranny, and defiance of oppression," said Davis. "His grandfather fell at the siege of Carrickfergus, a victim to the progress of British aggression. His Father unable to brook the insolence of the petty tyrants—that English confiscations

19. D. R. Thomason, *Hints to Emigrants; or to those Who May Contemplate Emigrating to the United States of America* (London, 1849), 27; Charles Mackay, *Life and Liberty in America . . .* (New York, 1859), 233, 237; Faux, *Memorable Days,* 131; Isaac Holmes, *An Account of the United States . . .* (London, 1823), 142; Benwell, *An Englishman's Travels,* 111.

20. Jefferson Davis to John Jenkins, July 5, 1845, in *The Papers of Jefferson Davis,* ed. Haskell M. Monroe, Jr., James T. McIntosh, and Lynda L. Crist (5 vols. to date, Baton Rouge, 1971–), II:287; Mary B. Chesnut, *Mary Chesnut's Civil War,* ed. C. Vann Woodward (New Haven, Conn., 1981), 194.

21. John Pendleton Kennedy, *Swallow Barn* (New York, 1851), 268, 272; William R. Taylor, *Cavalier and Yankee: The Old South and American National Character* (New York, 1961), 318; Chesnut, *Mary Chesnut's Civil War,* 56. See also Anon., *English Party's Excursion,* 335–36.

set over the estates of Ireland, sought an asylum in the wilds of America."[22]

Various local studies and articles in state journals also recount the Celtic heritage of many Southerners.[23] Irvin S. Cobb, for example, pointed out in 1931 that the South's heritage was not Anglo-Saxon. "No," he wrote, "the lost Irish tribes of the South are not lost; . . . for their Irish blood is of the strain that cannot be extinguished, and it lives today, thank God, in the attributes and the habits and the customs and the traditions of the Southern people."[24]

Antebellum travelers found Celts all over the South. In 1785 a foreigner insisted that most white South Carolinians were the "ignorant, drunken descendants of the wild Irish"—"poor as rats, proud as dons, . . . lazy, . . . [and with] no morals"—who reportedly cared more about their horses than their wives. Nineteenth-century English visitors discovered "so many Highlanders settled" in parts of North Carolina "that they are obliged to have a clerk in the Post Office who can speak Gaelic." A traveler who heard a local stage driver singing "the well-known Scotch song, 'Should auld acquaintance be forgot?' " thought the man must be a native of Scotland.

22. Oliver P. Temple, *East Tennessee and the Civil War* (1899; reprint, Freeport, N.Y., 1972), 459; Jefferson Davis, "Eulogy on the Life and Character of Andrew Jackson," July 1, 1845, in Monroe, McIntosh, and Crist, *Papers of Jefferson Davis*, II:266. See also Horace Kephart, *Our Southern Highlanders* (New York, 1913), 277–99; Ben Robertson, *Red Hills and Cotton, an Upcountry Memoir* (New York, 1942); Shirley Abbott, *Womenfolks: Growing Up Down South* (New York, 1983), 23, 30–32, 35, 53.

23. See, for example, Samuel C. Williams, "Tennessee Scotch-Irish Ancestry," *Tennessee Historical Magazine* 5 (1920), 201–15; Lily Doyle Dunlap, "Old Waxhaw," *North Carolina Booklet* 19 (1920), 139–44; Orville A. Park, "The Georgia Scotch-Irish," *Georgia Historical Quarterly* 12 (1928), 115–35; A. R. Newsome, "Records of Emigrants from England and Scotland to North Carolina, 1774–1775," *North Carolina Historical Review* 11 (1934), 39–54, 129–43; Alexander R. MacDonell, "The Settlement of the Scotch Highlanders at Darien," *Georgia Historical Quarterly* 20 (1936), 250–62; G. Arthur Gordon, "The Arrival of the Scotch Highlanders at Darien,"

*Georgia Historical Quarterly* 20 (1936), 199–209; E. R. R. Green, "The 'Strange Humors' That Drove the Scotch-Irish to America, 1729," *William and Mary Quarterly* 12 (1955), 113–23; idem, "Queensborough Township: Scotch-Irish Emigration and the Expansion of Georgia, 1763–1776," *William and Mary Quarterly* 17 (1960), 183–99; George Shepperson, "Writings in Scottish-American History: A Brief Survey," *William and Mary Quarterly* 11 (1954), 163–78; Duane G. Meyer, *The Highland Scots of North Carolina, 1732–1776* (Chapel Hill, 1961); Harry Roy Merrens, *Colonial North Carolina in the Eighteenth Century: A Study in Historical Geography* (Chapel Hill, 1964), 19–31, 53–81; Fussell M. Chalker, "Highland Scots in the Georgia Lowlands," *Georgia Historical Quarterly* 60 (1976), 35–42; Delma E. Presley, "The Crackers of Georgia," *Georgia Historical Quarterly* 60 (1976), 102–16; Robert A. Fowkes, "Welsh Naming Practices, with a Comparative Look at Cornish," *Names: Journal of the American Name Society* 29 (1981), 265–72.

24. Irvin S. Cobb, "The Lost Irish Tribes in the South," *Tennessee Historical Magazine*, 2d ser., 1 (1931), 115–24.

"But, to my surprise," wrote the Englishman, "I found he had not been out of North Carolina, though his feelings appeared nearly as true to the land of his forefathers, as if they had never left it." John Claiborne, in just a few pages of his account of his trip through southern Mississippi in the 1840s, made four references to the Celtic background of the settlers. "Spent the night with our old friend, Esquire Hathorn, of Covington County—a type of old Ireland, generous, ardent, enthusiastic, hospitable and a true-blue Republican," recalled Claiborne, who noted that the region was full of "the Old Scotch families that originally settled this country." He also remarked that "there are yet living in Greene [County] some of the original immigrants who speak nothing but the Gallic." A few pages later, Claiborne referred to the descendants of what he called "an ancient and honored race of Scotch Presbyterians"; he then mentioned, in discussing the "numerous herds of cattle" found in the area, a "worthy friend of ours, for many years a Senator in the Legislature, and universally known as *Long Johnny McCleod*, [who] owns, we were told, some two thousand head [of cattle]."[25]

Visitors found aspects of the Celtic heritage in various parts of the Old South. Some observers claimed that Southerners tended to sympathize and identify with the British Celts in their struggles against their English oppressors.[26] The speech of upcountry southern "crackers" reminded one traveler of the "dialect of your genuine" Scottish border-country man. Another visitor concluded that the "population [of western Maryland] seems to have come from Wales or the West of England, and to possess, legitimately, a slow-going propensity." Kentuckians, said another traveler, were "sort of genteel Irish." The historian of Sullivan's Hollow, Mississippi, noted that "Tom Sullivan and a goodly number of the other piney woods settlers [of central Mississippi] termed themselves Scotch-Irish." When the Walton Guards, of West Florida, organized to fight for the Confederacy in 1861, three of their four elected company officers bore the obviously Celtic names of McPherson, McKinnon, and McLeod.

25. Joseph Salvador, "A Description of America, 1785," ed. Cecil Roth, *American Jewish Archives* 17 (1965), 27–33; Captain Basil Hall, *Travels in North America in the Years 1827 and 1828* (3 vols., Edinburgh and London, 1829), III:121; Margaret (Hunter) Hall, *The Aristocratic Journey; Being the Outspoken Letters of Mrs. Basil Hall Written During a Fourteen Months' Sojourn in America, 1827–1828*, ed. Una Pope-Hennessy (New York, 1931), 205, 206; B. Hall, *Travels*, III:122; John F. H. Claiborne, "A Trip through the Piney Woods [1841]," *Mississippi Historical Society Publications* 9 (1906), 515, 521, 527, 530.

26. Amelia Matilda Murray, *Letters from the United States, Cuba and Canada* (New York, 1856), 210; Trollope, *North America*, 182–84; *Richmond Dispatch* quoted in *Metropolitan Record and New York Vindicator*, March 4, 1865; Juan Papista Y Exe-Rebelde to Editor, December 31, 1865, *Metropolitan Record and New York Vindicator*, January 3, 1866.

And the names of cattlemen found in a book on Florida cattle raising could have been taken from the Belfast telephone directory.[27]

The Celtic surnames of many Southerners as well as a consciousness among some of them of their Celtic roots are important in establishing cultural links, but the most conclusive evidence comes from the pens of contemporaries. Observers of premodern British Celts and observers of antebellum Southerners, apparently without any awareness of each other's observations, found the two cultures to be astonishingly similar; indeed, a comparison of these various works indicates that the Celts brought their traditional ways and values with them to the Old South and that they not only continued to practice them but were so successful in imposing their ways upon most of the ethnic minorities they settled among that a list of southern traits most observed by contemporaries reads like an inventory of traditional Scottish, Irish, and Welsh cultural characteristics.

As we examine these characteristics, it is important to recognize that only those cultural traits associated with British Celts up to the eighteenth century are relevant. There are two reasons for this: first, all significant migration from Scotland, Ireland, and Wales to the American South ended before 1800; and second, English efforts to acculturize the Celts, which had been ongoing for centuries, began to force a number of important changes in Celtic ways during the later part of the eighteenth century.[28]

The Celts brought with them to the Old South leisurely ways that fostered idleness and gaiety, a society in which people favored the spoken word over the written and enjoyed such sensual pleasures as drinking, smoking, fighting, gambling, fishing, hunting, and loafing. In Celtic Britain and in the antebellum South family ties were much stronger than in England and in the antebellum North; Celts and Southerners, whose values were more agrarian than those of Englishmen and Northerners, wasted more time and consumed more liquor and tobacco and were less concerned with the useful and the material. Englishmen and Northerners, who favored urban villages and nuclear families, were just the opposite; imbued with a work ethic and commercial values, they were neater, cleaner, read

27. Henry Benjamin Whipple, *Bishop Whipple's Southern Diary, 1843–1844*, ed. Lester B. Shippee (Minneapolis, 1937), 77; Frederick Law Olmsted, *A Journey through Texas* . . . (1857; reprint, New York, 1969), 3; Frederick James Jobson, *America, and American Methodism* (London, 1857), 104; Chester Sullivan, *Sullivan's Hollow* (Jackson, Miss., 1978), 13; William James Wells, *Pioneering in the Panhandle: A Look at Selected Events and Families as Part of the History of South Santa Rosa County, Florida* (Fort Walton Beach, Fla., 1976), 43; Joe A. Akerman, Jr., *Florida Cowman, A History of Florida Cattle Raising* (Kissimmee, Fla., 1976), 281–87.

28. See Chapter I.

and wrote more, worked harder, and considered themselves more progressive and advanced than Celts and Southerners.[29]

During the seventeenth and eighteenth centuries the English became ever more orderly, disciplined, and hardworking; indeed, as Keith Wrightson pointed out, they molded a national society in which they integrated their capitalistic values with the "interests of the individual nuclear family." Eighteenth-century England, stated Roy Porter, was a land not of "lovable paternalistic eccentrics" but of "profit-hungry capitalists." The English rural economy—

29. See, for example, William Thomson, *A Tradesman's Travels, in the United States and Canada, in the Years 1840, 41 & 42* (Edinburgh, 1842), 20–25; Lakier, *A Russian Looks at America*, 13, 29, 237; Maxwell, *Irish History*, 314–16, 376–77; Cox, *Hibernia Anglicana*, II:App. IV, 11; Edmund Hogan, ed., *The Description of Ireland, and the State Thereof as It is at this Present in Anno 1598 . . .* (Dublin, 1878), 246; George Berkeley, *A Word to the Wise: or, An Exhortation to the Roman Catholic Clergy* (Dublin, 1752), 6–10, 12–16, 19; William Shaw Mason, ed., *A Statistical Account or Parochial Survey of Ireland, Drawn up from the Communications of the Clergy* (3 vols., Dublin, 1814–19), I:419, 536–37, III:175; J. Davies, *Discoverie of . . . Ireland*, 73–77; Leitch Ritchie, *Ireland Picturesque and Romantic* (London, 1838), 259; Weeton, *Journal*, II:22; Sinclair, *Statistical Account of Scotland*, XVII:133, 177, 198–99, 547; P. Brown, *Scotland Before 1700*, 45; *Edinburgh Review* 66 (1820), 445; Louis Simond, *Journal of a Tour and Residence in Great Britain, During the Years 1810 and 1811* (2 vols., Edinburgh, 1817), II:391–94; [Beat Louis Muralt], *Letters Describing the Character and Customs of the English and French Nations . . .* (London, 1726), 12–13, 15–17; James M. Hoppin, *Old England; Its Scenery, Art, and People* (1867; reprint, Boston, 1900), 100–104; William D. Robson-Scott, *German Travellers in England, 1400–1800* (Oxford, 1953), 236, lists some twenty distinctive English characteristics observed by various German travelers; [John Shebbeare], *Letters on the English Nation: By . . . a Jesuit, who Resided Many Years in London* (2 vols., London, 1755), I:42; Cesar de Saussure, *A Foreign View of England in the Reigns of George I & George II: The Letters of Monsieur Cesar de Saussure to His Family*, trans. and ed. Madame Van Muyden (London, 1902), 177; Paul Hentzner, *A Journey into England in the Year MDXCVIII*, ed. Horace Walpole (Edinburgh, 1881), 53–54; Thomas Platter, *Thomas Platter's Travels in England, 1599*, trans. Clare Williams (London, 1937), 183; William Cole, *The Blecheley Diary of the Rev. William Cole, M.A., F.S.A., 1765–67*, ed. Francis Griffin Stokes (London, 1931), 128; Edward Smith, *Foreign Visitors in England, and What They Have Thought of Us . . .* (London, 1889), 40, 147–48; [Lorenzo Magalotti], *Travels of Cosmo the Third, Grand Duke of Tuscany, through England, During the Reign of King Charles the Second (1669)* (London, 1821), 484–85; [Herman Ludwig Heinrich], *Tour in England, Ireland, and France in the Years 1826, 1827, 1828, and 1829* (Philadelphia, 1833), 16; Percy E. Matheson, *German Visitors to England, 1770–1795, and their Impressions* (Oxford, 1930), 2–31; Margaret Hoby, *Diary of Lady Margaret Hoby, 1599–1605*, ed. Dorothy M. Meads (London, 1930), 166, 168; Bodichon, *American Diary*, 64; Henry Arthur Bright, *Happy Country This America: The Travel Diary of Henry Arthur Bright [1852]*, ed. Anne Henry Ehrenpreis (Columbus, Ohio, 1978), 375; John Henry Vessey, *Mr. Vessey of England: Being the Incidents and Reminiscences of Travel in a Twelve Weeks' Tour through the United States and Canada in the Year 1859*, ed. Brian Waters (New York, 1956), 43; Montule, *Travels in America*, 26; Lorenzo de Zavala, *Journey to the United States of North America [1829]*, trans. Wallace Woolsey (Austin, 1980), 191–92; Henri Herz, *My Travels in America [1846–1851]*, trans. Henry Bertram Hill (Madison, 1963), 47–49.

which was "capitalistic, materialistic, [and] market-oriented"—was "far better capitalized, and more businesslike and productive, than almost any on the Continent." Regulated by laws, codes of basic values, proverbs, and wise sayings—"keep a stiff upper lip" and "keep steadily at your work"—Englishmen centered their lives on the work ethic. "Life within the [eighteenth-century English] household and community," observed Porter, "followed tightly organized, highly regulated, businesslike rounds of routine drills, plotted from the cradle to the grave."[30]

In no other part of the world, from the 1600s through the 1800s, was the work ethic more revered than in England and in the northern United States. "In England, you must before all things be successful," observed a Frenchman. "No one pities the man who is down, he is shunned and ridiculed. He is called a lazy fellow or a fool. . . . Poverty is no vice in France. It is in England. This thirst for wealth . . . has made the English nation a nation of bees. Everyone works. The heir of a millionaire does not dream of a life of idleness." "It is by industry, toil, perseverance, economy, prudence, by self-denial, and self-dependence, that a state becomes mighty and its people happy," explained an English editor. "English people are naturally industrious—they prefer a life of honest labour to one of idleness," boasted another English journalist. "An Englishman, while he eats and drinks no more, or not much more than another man, labors three times as many hours in the course of a year, as any other European," contended a New Englander. "He works fast. Everything in England is at a quick pace [performed by] . . . this laborious race." Sylvester Douglas, an English "fortune hunter" and officeholder in Ireland who in 1800 was "created Lord Glenbervie of the Irish peerage," wrote in 1793: "If this journal shall prove . . . useful . . . to myself, or to my wife and my son, . . . it may be considered as a conquest of some value made upon indolence, for I write it in general during an hour which for the greatest part of my life has been wasted in sleep or indolence. This is perhaps an advantage derived from a little essay I composed, last year, on the subject of indolence, which, together with several others only projected, I intend as lessons to our little Frederick, drawn in part from my experience and partly from reading."[31]

New Englanders, of course, brought the English work ethic to America. "God sent you not into this world as into a Play-house,

30. Keith Wrightson, *English Society, 1580–1680* (New Brunswick, N.J., 1982), 155, 156, 166, 167, 171, 181–82, 222–23, 227–28; Roy Porter, *English Society in the Eighteenth Century* (London, 1982), 16, 17, 26, 33, 53–54, 160, 161–62, 333–34, 345, 372–73.

31. [Raul Blouet], *John Bull and His Island* (New York, 1884), 52; *Times* (London), August 4, 1843; *Fraser's Magazine* 36 (1847), 373; Emerson, *English Traits*, 160, 162; [Sylvester Douglas], *The Glenbervie Journals [1793–1814]*, ed. Walter Sichel (London, 1910), 1, 6, 84–85.

but a Work-house," New England Puritans reminded each other. "Abhor . . . one hour of idleness as you would be ashamed of one hour of drunkenness," a Yankee admonished his son. An Austrian, after living ten years in Boston, said of New Englanders that there were "no people on earth with whom business constitutes pleasure, and industry amusement, in an equal degree. . . . Active occupation is not only the principal source of their happiness, . . . but they are absolutely wretched without it, and . . . know but the *horrors* of idleness." Alexis de Tocqueville observed that in the North even a wealthy man believed that he must devote his time "to some kind of industrial or commercial pursuit or to public business. He would think himself in bad repute if he employed his life solely in living." "Idleness & inactivity are the worst of miseries for a human being to endure," stated Yankee Bishop Henry Whipple in 1844. That same year another New England preacher, Henry Ward Beecher, proclaimed: "The indolent mind is not empty, but full of vermin." The Yankee hero of one of Sarah Hale's antebellum short stories concluded that "trifling away of time when there is so much to be done, so many improvements necessary in our country, is inconsistent with that principle of being useful, which every republican ought to cherish." "Labor," William Evarts announced in 1856, "we of the free States acknowledge to be the source of all our wealth, of all our progress, of all our dignity and value." Daniel T. Rodgers concluded that during the antebellum period "it was among the middling classes of the North—the Yankee bourgeoisie—that the work ethic was most firmly rooted."[32]

Celts and Southerners were quite different, believing it foolish to engage in work unnecessarily; they much preferred to enjoy life while their animals, their women, or their slaves made a living for them. Various observers from the twelfth through the eighteenth centuries emphasized that Celts were a lazy, herding people who preferred their pastoral ways to tillage agriculture, towns, and business. "The Irish are a rude people, subsisting on the produce of their

32. Perry Miller, *The New England Mind: The Seventeenth Century* (Cambridge, Mass., 1954), 44; Louis B. Wright, *The Cultural Life of the American Colonies, 1607–1763* (New York, 1957), 25; Francis J. Grund, *The Americans in Their Moral, Social and Political Relations* (2 vols., London, 1837), II:1–2; Alexis de Tocqueville, *Democracy in America . . .* , ed. Phillips Bradley (2 vols., New York, 1945), II:152; Whipple, *Southern Diary*, 121; Henry Ward Beecher, *Seven Lectures to Young Men* (Indianapolis, 1844), 21; Daniel T. Rodgers, *The Work Ethic in Industrial America, 1850–1920* (Chicago, 1978), 10, 6, xiii–xiv. On New England industriousness, see also Hodgson, *Letters*, II:138; Charles G. Parsons, *Inside View of Slavery: or, a Tour Among the Planters* (Cleveland, 1855), 40; Frederick Hall, *Letters from the East and from the West* (Washington, D.C., 1840), 239–40; François Jean, Marquis de Chastellux, *Travels in North-America . . .* (2 vols., Dublin, 1787), II:436; Faux, *Memorable Days*, 38; Earle, *Home Life*, 180, 335, 407; Lucy Larcom, "Among Lowell Mill-Girls: A Reminiscence," *Atlantic Monthly* 48 (1881), 596; Washington Gladden, *Working People and their Employers* (Boston, 1876), 62–63.

cattle, only, and living themselves like beasts—a people that has not yet departed from the primitive habits of pastoral life," wrote Giraldus Cambrensis in 1185. "In the common course of things, mankind progresses from the forest to the field, from the field to the town, ... but this nation, holding agricultural labour in contempt, and little coveting the wealth of towns, ... lead the same life their fathers did in the woods and open pastures, neither willing to abandon their old habits or learn anything new."[33] As was indicated in the Prologue, Giraldus said the same about the Welsh— who lived "upon the produce of their herds" and paid "no attention to commerce, shipping, or manufactures"—and so did observers of the early Scots: one noted that they were "given to sports and hunting, and to ease rather than toil"; another stated, "these people delight in the chase and a life of indolence." The pastoral Highlanders spent their time from May until October in the hills. During the shielings, as these summer camps were called—while the cattle grazed and the women sang, talked, and did their usual chores— the men hunted, fished, drank, played music, gambled, and occasionally made cattle raids on other clans. "As they have no manufactures among them, and their country is not fit for tillage," explained a Scot, "the common people [of the Highlands] have little to do, a few being sufficient for the care of their cattle, which are the chief produce of their lands."[34]

Later travelers described the Irish as "slothful," "the most improvident people in the whole world," "lazy to an excess"; a people "strangely given to idleness, thinking it the greater wealth to want business and the greatest happiness to have liberty"; "indolent" and willing to "dissipate the hard earnings of to-day regardless of tomorrow."[35] The Irish have "a remarkable antipathy to labour," insisted one observer; another stated that an Irishman "will submit

33. Giraldus Cambrensis, *The Historical Works of Giraldus Cambrensis [ca. 1146–1220]*, ed. Thomas Wright (1863; reprint, New York, 1968), 124. A slightly different translation of these observations on the Irish is found in idem, *The First Version of the Topography of Ireland*, trans. John J. O'Meara (Dundalk, Ireland, 1951), 85–86: "They are a wild ... people. They live on beasts only, and live like beasts. They have not progressed at all from the primitive habits of pastoral living. While men usually progress from the woods to the fields, and from the fields to the towns and communities of citizens, this people despises agriculture, has little use for the money-making of towns, ... and desires neither to abandon, nor lose respect for, the life which it has been accustomed to lead in the woods and countryside."

34. Cambrensis, *Historical Works*, 490; P. Brown, *Scotland Before 1700*, 13; Gordon Donaldson, ed., *Scottish Historical Documents* (New York, 1970), 101; James Maxwell, *Narrative of Charles Prince of Wales' Expedition to Scotland in the Year 1745* (Edinburgh, 1841), 27.

35. Edward MacLysaght, *Irish Life in the Seventeenth Century* (1939; reprint, Dublin, 1979), 40, 37, 39; Arthur Young, *Arthur Young's Tour in Ireland (1776–1779)*, ed. Arthur W. Hutton (2 vols., London, 1892), I:429, II:872; Berkeley, *Word to the Wise*, 7, 9–10, 12–16, 19; Mason, *Statistical Account ... of Ireland*, I:419; Croker, *Researches*, 13, 129.

to any fatigue provided you do not call it work." The typical Irishman, instead of "idly leaning against the jamb of his door, or striving to get heat from his fire of straws," scolded an Anglican clergyman, "could keep his blood in circulation by cleaning up the front of his cabin; by picking up his spade or fork out of the mud, and removing the refuse of the house a little farther from the door. . . . But from settled habits exertions are much neglected, and indolence becomes inveterate."[36]

Observers employed almost the exact terms and phrases in depicting the Scots, especially the Highlanders, that were used in describing the Irish. Called by contemporaries up until nearly the end of the eighteenth century "indolent," "dilatory," and noted "for their remarkable Laziness," Scots were "averse to industry, never working but from necessity."[37] They were, like the Irish, neither thrifty nor prudent. The writer who claimed the Irish "feared work more than danger" could just as well have been describing the Scots. An eighteenth-century observer said that a Scot habitually rested or went "to sleep until roused by the recollection that he must have some means of keeping warm during the winter. During the winter, unless a good opportunity for smuggling occurs, a Highland farmer has nothing to do but keep himself warm. He never thinks about labouring his fields during mild weather or collecting manure . . . ; nothing rouses him but the genial warmth of spring. I can not reckon how often I have seen Highland farmers basking in the sun on a fine summer's day, in all the comforts of idleness." As one Highland minister reported at the end of the eighteenth century: "The people being, from their infancy, principally employed in attending cattle, are generally disposed to be idle, and, though able-bodied, continued at hard work with reluctance." Scottish migrants in Canada often "sat around in the fields and told stories rather than working. On Cape Breton Island much of the work is still done by women; one man frequently played his fiddle while his wife worked in the field."[38]

36. Berkeley, *Word to the Wise*, 6; Ritchie, *Ireland Picturesque*, 259; Mason, *Statistical Account . . . of Ireland*, III:175.

37. Defoe, *Tour*, 590, 596; Burt, *Letters*, I:162, 110; Francis J. Shaw, "Landownership in the Western Isles in the Seventeenth Century," *Scottish Historical Review* 56 (1977), 48; John MacCulloch, "A Description of the Western Islands of Scotland," *Edinburgh Review* 66 (1820), 446; Sinclair, *Statistical Account of Scotland*, XVII:64, 155, 200, 238, 334, 396–97, 551. Up through most of the eighteenth century, observers usually complained about the indolence of both Highland and Lowland Scots or rarely made any distinction between them in criticizing Scottish ways.

38. Moray McLaren, *Understanding the Scots: A Guide for South Britons and Other Foreigners* (New York, 1972), 28–30; Thomas B. Macaulay, *The History of England from the Accession of James II* (5 vols., London, 1884), III:146–47; a contemporary observer quoted in James E. Handley, *Scottish Farming in the Eighteenth Century* (London, 1953), 95; Sinclair, *Statistical Account of Scotland*, XVII:551; John Shaw, "A Cape Breton Gaelic Storyteller" (Ph.D. diss., Harvard University, 1982); interview with John Shaw, August 17–18, 1983.

Southerners were just as leisure-oriented as their Celtic ancestors. In the eighteenth century Charles Woodmason described backcountry Southerners as ignorant and "very Poor—owing to their extreme Indolence." "They delight," he claimed, "in their present low, lazy, sluttish, heathenish, hellish Life, and seem not desirous of changing it. Both Men and Women will do any thing to come at Liquor, Cloaths, furniture, &c. &c. rather than work for it." Early in the nineteenth century Henry C. Knight reported that in the South "the Canaan richness of the land is productive, among better fruits, of much indolence. . . . Too many [Southerners], instead of resting on one day in seven, work only on one day in six; and therefore ever remain poor." John Shaw claimed that in the 1850s many Southerners were "so indolent that they only work two days in the week, . . . and keep holiday the other days by every possible method of dissipation." Another observer referred to the typical white Southerners as "the hardy descendants, many of them, of the early Scotch and Irish settlers. . . . Their learning is seldom such as is seen inside of school-houses; it may not even include an ability to read and write." They were, of course, "good horsemen, marksmen, and hunters," he noted, "but the men, at least, are not remarkable for agricultural industry, for the patient thrift and intelligent skill that make the successful farmer. They are squatters rather than farmers." Moreover, he concluded, "they will not work." The wife of one Southerner insisted that her husband " 'would not take a house or live in one, lest he should have to work.' "[39]

An English traveler reported that in the North there was everywhere "bustle, and all sorts of industry—men riding about, chopping down forests, building up houses, ploughing, planting, and reaping,—but . . . [in the South] all mankind appeared comparatively idle. The whites . . . consider it discreditable to work, and the blacks, as a matter of course, work as little as they can. The free population prefers hunting, and occupy themselves also very much with the machinery of electioneering." A Yankee noted that in the North one servant did the work that it took five to accomplish in the South.[40]

Observers reported that Southerners simply had a leisurely attitude toward life. In 1789, for example, a visitor described Virginians as "indolent, unindustrious, poor credit risks, . . . [and] spoiled by the abundance of Negroes," who also "prefer idleness to work."

39. Charles Woodmason, *The Carolina Backcountry on the Eve of the Revolution: The Journal and Other Writings of Charles Woodmason, Anglican Itinerant*, ed. Richard J. Hooker (Chapel Hill, 1953), 52; [Henry C. Knight], *Letters from the South and West* (Boston, 1824), 93; John Shaw, *A Ramble Through the United States . . .* (London, 1856), 221–22; Anon., " 'Movers' in the South-West," *Dollar Magazine* 7 (1851), 21–22.

40. B. Hall, *Travels*, II:117; Whipple, *Southern Diary*, 61.

Other contemporaries mentioned the "sloth and Indolence" of Southerners, especially the lazy ways of the "crackers," but most travelers claimed that being unhurried was typical of all sorts of Southerners. "The planter takes his time," noted a visitor to the South. "Leisure and ease are inmates of his roof. He takes no note of time. . . . A clock, almanac, and a good fire, are hard things to find in a planter's house. . . . The word, haste, is not in a Southron's vocabulary."[41]

Crackers were as opposed to schedules and to hard work as planters were. "Our poor white men will not . . . work if they can very well help it," explained a native Southerner; "they will do no more of it than they are obliged to. They will do a few day's work when it is necessary to provide themselves with the necessaries of life, but they are not used to steady labor; they work reluctantly, and will not bear driving."[42]

After living in the South, a Northerner concluded that all Southerners, white and black, resisted toil. "A neighbour of hers owned fifty cows, she supposed, but very rarely had any milk and scarcely ever any butter, simply because his people were too lazy to milk or churn, and he wouldn't take the trouble to make them." Slaves, she said, were as lazy as their masters: "Folks up North talked about how badly the negroes were treated; she wished they could see how much work her girls did. She had four of them, and she knew they didn't do half so much work as one good Dutch girl such as she used to have at the North. Oh! the negroes were the laziest things in creation." Such views were widespread. "Laziness is one of the great characteristics of the negro," insisted a contemporary; and even a pious Yankee visitor noted that the "lazy laughing, singing negroes about the [Mobile] wharves make you laugh in spite of yourself."[43]

The labor of slaves, which allowed some whites to enjoy opulence and leisure, tended to discredit the value of work. "If I could get

41. François Xavier Dupont, "A Letter from Petersburg, Virginia, January 10, 1789," ed. Charles T. Nall, *Virginia Magazine of History and Biography* 82 (1974), 146; J. B. Dunlop, "The Grand Fabric of Republicanism: A Scotsman Describes South Carolina—1810–1811," ed. Raymond A. Mohl, *South Carolina Historical and Genealogical Magazine* 71 (1970), 179; Lachlan McIntosh to George Washington, April 28, 1776, "Letterbook of Lachlan McIntosh, 1776–1777," ed. Lilla M. Hawes, *Georgia Historical Quarterly* 38 (1954), 153; James W. Patton, "Glimpses of North Carolina in the Writings of Northern and Foreign Travelers, 1782–

1860," *North Carolina Historical Review* 45 (1968), 298–323; J. B. Dunlop, "A Scotsman Visits Georgia in 1811," ed. Raymond A. Mohl, *Georgia Historical Quarterly* 55 (1971), 259–74; A. De Puy Van Buren, *Jottings of a Year's Sojourn in the South . . .* (Battle Creek, Mich., 1859), 88–89.

42. Frederick Law Olmsted, *The Cotton Kingdom: A Traveller's Observations on Cotton and Slavery . . .* , ed. Arthur M. Schlesinger (new ed., New York, 1953), 87.

43. Ibid., 302–03; *Southern Agriculturist* 12 (1839), 293; Whipple, *Southern Diary,* 87.

such hired men as you can in New York," a Southerner told a Yankee, "I'd never have another nigger on my place; but the white men here who will labor, are not a bit better than negroes. You have got to stand right over them all the time, . . . and then, if I should ask, now, one of my white men to go and take care of your horse, he'd be very apt to tell me to do it myself, or, if he obeyed, he would take pains to do so in some way that would make me sorry I asked him; then if I should scold him, he would ask me if I thought he was a nigger, and refuse to work for me any more."[44]

A major and often overlooked reason why Southerners—even non–slave owners—condoned slavery was their commitment to leisure; they frequently said disdainfully that only slaves and Yankees worked. "No Southern man," claimed John C. Calhoun, "not even the poorest or the lowest, will, under any circumstances, . . . perform menial labor. . . . He has too much pride for that." Though Calhoun's words were a considerable exaggeration, the Southerner's attitude toward work differed markedly from the Northerner's. "The Southerner has no pleasure in labor," wrote New Yorker Frederick Law Olmsted. "He enjoys life itself. He is content with being. Here is the grand distinction between him and the Northerner; for the Northerner enjoys progress in itself. He finds his happiness in doing. Rest, in itself, is irksome and offensive to him. . . . Heaven itself will be dull and stupid to him, if there is no work to be done in it." Even Confederate General Robert E. Lee admitted: "Our people are opposed to work. . . . Our troops[,] officers[,] community & press. All ridicule & resist it." "Industry, in the sense in which we understand that term, as implying a love of active bodily exertion, is rarely seen among the white inhabitants of the South," announced an Englishman.[45]

The South's leisurely ways were remarkably seductive. Even Yankees sometimes lost their ambition after living for a time in the South, and slaves learned to move slowly. One Northerner claimed that slaves frequently sought to be sold for less than their true value so they would not have to work "up to their strength"; another

44. Frederick Law Olmsted, *A Journey in the Back Country* . . . (1856; reprint, New York, 1970), 228.

45. E. Merton Coulter, "The Movement for Agricultural Reorganization in the Cotton South during the Civil War," *Agricultural History* 1 (1927), 11; Olmsted, *Cotton Kingdom*, 616; Robert E. Lee, *Lee's Dispatches: Unpublished Letters of General Robert E. Lee, C.S.A., to Jefferson Davis and the War Department of the Confederate States of America, 1862–65*, ed. Douglas S. Freeman

and Grady McWhiney (New York, 1957), 8; James Silk Buckingham, *The Slave States of America* (2 vols., London, 1842), II:198. See also Louis Philippe, *Diary of My Travels in America [1797]*, trans. Stephen Becker (New York, 1977), 100; Alexander Mackay, *The Western World* . . . (3 vols., London, 1849), II:134; George W. F. H. Carlisle, *Travels in America* . . . (New York, 1851), 76; Daniel J. Fox to John Fox, May 30, 1852, John Fox Papers, Duke University; A. Murray, *Letters from the United States*, 188–89.

believed that almost any Yankee worked harder than slaves. An Englishman insisted that the blacks in South Carolina "certainly dont do much work, the servants dont get thru half as much work as a white man would." And a woman in Alabama wrote relatives in Massachusetts: "You don't know how you are blessed in New England without slaves—they are a perfect torment and I wish Mrs. Beecher Stowe had about fifty to sympathize with and take care of—to feed, clothe, and bear all their impudence and laziness—it seems to me they work slower and do less than they ever did before and if I could take relations with me I would gladly exchange Massachusetts for Alabama."[46]

Nobody seems to have worked very hard in the Old South. In 1850, for example, *all* of the South's agricultural staples (cotton, corn, tobacco, rice, sugar cane, and hemp) could have been produced by fewer than half of the region's black field hands; even if one takes Calhoun literally and assumes that *only* slaves worked in the Old South, and that no white person ever lifted a finger, then each black field hand would have had to labor about 147 ten-hour days a year in Alabama and 136 ten-hour days a year in Mississippi to have produced all the cotton and corn grown in those two states in 1850. If we relieved the slaves of the burden of raising the entire corn crop and assumed that it was grown by the white plain folk, and that only half these whites tilled the fields, then the work load soars to 337 hours of labor—five or six weeks of work per year—to produce Alabama's entire corn crop in 1850. Indeed, samples of the actual work done by southern plain white folk indicate that four randomly selected families labored a total of perhaps 423 hours, or approximately eleven forty-hour weeks, per year.[47]

Celts, of course, had historically been as loath to engage in hard labor as Southerners were. "They are by nature extreamely given to Idlenes," insisted an Englishman, who claimed that the "Sea Coasts [of Ireland] . . . abounde with fish, but the fishermen must be beaten out, before they will goe to their Boats." Highland Scots were equally notorious "for their remarkable Laziness." Indeed, the wives of Scots fishermen followed what an observer called the "peculiar custom" of carrying their husbands on their backs to and from their

46. Eugene L. Schwaab, ed., *Travels in the Old South: Selected from Periodicals of the Times* (2 vols., Lexington, Ky., 1973), I:23, II:324; Nehemiah Adams, *A South-Side View of Slavery; or, Three Months at the South, in 1854* (1854; reprint, Port Washington, N.Y., 1969), 34; George Townsend Fox American Journal, November 5, 1831, Public Library, South Shields, Durham, England; Caroline Snow to Abigale Snow, January 21, 1853, Dr. Peter Snow Letters, Anderson Collection, University of Alabama, Tuscaloosa.

47. Forrest McDonald and Grady McWhiney, "The South from Self-Sufficiency to Peonage: An Interpretation," *American Historical Review* 85 (1980), 1096–1102.

SCOTSWOMEN CARRYING FISHERMEN

From Edward Burt, *Burt's Letters from the North of Scotland* (2 vols., London, 1754), I:facing 113.

boats, which were anchored off shore, " 'to keep their men's feet dry,' as they say." An authority concluded that the "Celts, holding that bodily labour of all sorts was mean and disgraceful, devoted themselves mainly to the chase."[48]

In other words, contemporaries were correct when they said that premodern Celts and antebellum Southerners loved their leisure. Commenting on just how lazy Southerners were, one man noted that "no Northern farmer" would neglect to build a bridge over a stream that crossed his property; indeed, two "live Yankees" would complete the work in a single day, but "the Southern planter will ford the creek lying between his house & stable a whole life time." The same complaint was made about Highland Scots, whose roads were equally as bad as those of Ireland and the Old South. In the 1790s a minister, noting that fords rather than bridges crossed streams on one of the most heavily traveled roads in the Highlands, wrote: "From a desire to save labour or time, the ford is often attempted, when the . . . river [is] too high, and the consequence is frequently fatal."[49]

The importance that both premodern British Celts and antebellum Southerners placed upon leisure rather than work was perhaps the single most important cultural trait that separated them from Englishmen and antebellum Northerners. Numerous observers emphasized this significant difference. "The inertness of the South affords . . . a painful contrast to the . . . activity of the North," wrote an Englishman. The producer of the Midwest, contended a visitor, was "the Yankee rather than the Kentuckian. . . . Indeed, the mechanical regularity, the neatness, and the enterprise of New-England characterize the people of Ohio generally, and constitute a marked difference between them and their neighbors over the river." Other observers contrasted the "intelligent, industrious, and thriving" Yankee settlers living north of the Ohio River with the "ignorant, lazy, and poor" settlers from Virginia and Kentucky; praised the people of the upper Midwest as being "from New England, the region of industry, economy, and steady habits"; and denounced those from south of the Ohio for scorning "not only labour, but all the undertakings which labour promotes." "[The] tastes [of a Kentuckian] are those of an idle man," insisted Tocqueville. Another Frenchman, who described Northerners as "enterprising" and Southerners as "lazy," concluded: "A Bostonian would go in search of his fortune

48. Moryson, *Shakespeare's Europe*, 483; Burt, *Letters*, I:113; Sinclair, *Statistical Account of Scotland*, XVII:325; Charles Rogers, *Social Life in Scotland: From Early to Recent Times* (1884; reprint, 2 vols., Port Washington, N.Y., 1971), II:256.

49. Parsons, *Inside View*, 99; Sinclair, *Statistical Account of Scotland*, XVII:81, 154, 410–11; W. R. Kermack, *Historical Geography of Scotland* (Edinburgh, 1926), 108–09; A. Young, *Tour in Ireland*, II:869; Sinclair, *Statistical Account of Scotland*, XVII:366.

to the bottom of Hell; a Virginian would not go across the road to seek it."[50]

The Celtic and southern commitment to leisure was summed up by a rustic Southerner, who—when admonished for his lack of ambition by a visitor—replied that if he and his neighbors "did not live up to other people's ideas, they lived as well as they wanted to. They didn't want to make slaves of themselves; they were contented with living as their fathers lived before them."[51]

50. A. Mackay, *Western World*, II:143; Charles Fenno Hoffman, *A Winter in the West* (2 vols., New York, 1835), II:139; Thaddeus Mason Harris, *Journal of a Tour* . . . (Boston, 1805), 357–58; Alexis de Tocqueville, *Democracy in America* . . . , trans. Henry Reeve (2 vols., New Rochelle, N.Y., n.d.), I:356; Felix de Beaujour, *Sketch of the United States* . . . , trans. William Walton (London, 1814), 133–34. For other contrasts between industrious Northerners and indolent Southerners, see Michel Chevalier, *Society, Manners and Politics in the United States* . . . , trans. Thomas Gam- aliel Bradford (Boston, 1839), 149–50; Thomas Hamilton, *Men and Manners in America* (2 vols., Philadelphia, 1833), I:167; F. Hall, *Letters from the East and West*, 8; D. Mitchell, *Ten Years in the United States*, 180; Thomas Nuttall, *A Journal of Travels into the Arkansas Territory* . . . (Philadelphia, 1821), 60; Timothy Flint, *Recollections of the Last Ten Years*, ed. C. Hartley Grattan (1826; reprint, New York, 1932), 29; Parsons, *Inside View*, 164.

51. Hoffman, *Winter in the West*, II:226.

# III

# Herding

TWO dominant institutions—black slavery and the open-range system of grazing livestock—made it possible for most white Southerners to practice a leisurely lifestyle. At the middle of the nineteenth century fewer than 40 percent of the nation's twenty-three million inhabitants lived in the 900,000 square miles of mostly uncleared forest that constituted the Old South, but 37 percent (three million) of these Southerners were blacks and 90 percent of those were slaves. The South produced nearly all of the nation's cotton, rice, and sugar cane, three-fourths of its tobacco, and more than half of its corn. Much of this production was done on plantations by slave labor, but in 1850 only 101,335 (18 percent) of the South's 569,201 farms produced enough agricultural staples to be classified as plantations by the Census Bureau. Fewer than 5 percent of the South's whites owned any slaves, and fewer than a third of the free southern population were even members of slave-owning families.[1]

In other words, some white Southerners managed to avoid excessive labor by owning slaves, but the vast majority did so by depending

---

1. According to the Census Bureau, a "plantation" was a farm that produced 2,000 pounds of cotton, or 3,000 pounds of tobacco, or 20,000 pounds of rice, or any amount of sugar cane or hemp. Of the roughly 170,000 southern farms with slaves, only 101,000 qualified as plantations. In 1850 the South contained the following plantations classified by principal crop: 74,000 in cotton, 15,700 in tobacco, 8,300 in hemp, 2,700 in sugar cane, and 550 in rice. Bureau of the Census, *Statistical View: A Compendium of the Seventh Census, 1850* (Washington, D.C., 1854), 178; Lewis C. Gray, *History of Agriculture in the Southern United States to 1860* (2 vols., Washington, D.C., 1933), I:529; Donald B. Dodd and Wynelle S. Dodd, *Historical Statistics of the South, 1790–1970* (University, Ala., 1973), 2–61; Bureau of the Census, *The Statistical History of the United States* (Washington, D.C., 1957), 4–13; Kenneth M. Stampp, *The Peculiar Institution: Slavery in the Ante-Bellum South* (New York, 1956), 29–33; Otto H. Olsen, "Historians and the Extent of Slave Ownership in the Southern United States," *Civil War History* 18 (1972), 101–16.

on animals for their livelihood. Neither slavery nor the plantation system was as widespread or as distinctively southern as the raising of livestock, especially hogs and cattle, on the open range. In 1860 two-thirds of the nation's hogs were grown in the Old South, and hogs and other southern livestock were worth half a billion dollars— more than twice the value of that year's cotton crop and approximately equal to the value of all southern crops combined. At first the comparison may seem inappropriate, inasmuch as only about one-fifth of the animals were slaughtered for market; however, another three-fifths of the hogs were slaughtered for home consumption, which means that the value of the annual swine "crop" was 80 percent of the total value. Furthermore, virtually all of the gross sales of livestock were net profit, whereas the profit margin in crops was relatively slender and uncertain.[2] In addition, southern animals doubtless were worth considerably more than the government records indicate because there was every reason for owners to undercount the actual number of livestock they reported to tax collectors and census takers.[3]

Practically all Southerners kept livestock for their own use, including most townsfolk, and a surprisingly large number of people whom historians have regarded only as plant growers derived as much or more of their livelihood from the animals they raised as

2. Bureau of the Census, *Agriculture of the United States in 1860 . . . Compiled from . . . the Eighth Census . . .* (Washington, D.C., 1864), 184–87. The average price for middling upland cotton between 1856 and 1860 was 11.5 cents on the New York market and 6.7 cents on the Liverpool market. The weighted average price in 1860 on the New Orleans market was 11.1 cents per pound. M. B. Hammond, *The Cotton Industry: An Essay in American Economic History* (New York, 1897), app. I; Gray, *History of Agriculture*, II:1027. For this study an average price of 10 cents per pound was used. It should be noted that cotton prices fluctuated "as much as 5 cents per pound—and more—throughout the season in every market." Harold D. Woodman, *King Cotton & His Retainers: Financing & Marketing the Cotton Crop of the South, 1800–1925* (Lexington, Ky., 1968), 19–20. On the production of hogs, see Forrest McDonald and Grady McWhiney, "The Antebellum Southern Herdsman: A Reinterpretation," *Journal of Southern History* 41 (1975), 147–66; Sam B. Hilliard, *Hog Meat and Hoecake: Food Supply in the Old South, 1840–*

*1860* (Carbondale, Ill., 1972), 129. Robert L. Ransom and Richard Sutch, *One Kind of Freedom: The Economic Consequences of Emancipation* (Cambridge, Mass., 1977), 151, 346–47 n. 12, have estimated the slaughter rate of hogs at 80 percent. See also Richard Sutch, "The Treatment Received by American Slaves: A Critical Review of the Evidence Presented in *Time on the Cross,*" *Explorations in Economic History* 12 (1975), 369–79. Because the rate of slaughter for market was about 20 percent, it follows that about one-fourth of the hogs slaughtered were killed for market.

3. For example, the 1850 federal census reports significantly fewer animals owned by James Mallory of Talladega County, Alabama, than he claimed in his carefully kept manuscript journal. Bureau of the Census, Manuscript Census Returns, Seventh Census; James Mallory Journal, 1843–77 (original owned by Edgar A. Stewart of Selma, Alabama); microfilm copies of the census returns and of Mallory's journal, University of Alabama, Tuscaloosa.

from their crops. Those who raised substantial numbers of livestock included planters, who frequently tried to produce their own meat supply; small farmers, who almost universally kept some hogs and cattle and often raised sizable herds; and herdsmen, whose main or sole occupation was herding, and who, when they raised any crops at all, did so mainly for fattening their stock or for distilling into whiskey.[4]

Throughout the antebellum period Southerners drove enormous herds of livestock over long distances to market. Thousands of swine went east, north, and south each year along established routes. "Our progress was much impeded by droves of hogs, grunting their obstinate way towards Cincinnati and a market," wrote a traveler in Kentucky. "Many of the droves were very extensive, filling the road from side to side for a long distance. . . . Though the country was well wooded, . . . I venture to say we met as many hogs as trees." In 1849 alone some 124,000 hogs passed through Cumberland Gap and Asheville, North Carolina, on their way to market.[5] The magnitude of the industry may be seen by comparing drives in the Old South with the more celebrated later drives during the heyday of the cowboy. Walter Prescott Webb's classic *The Great Plains* provides a table that shows the number of Texas cattle driven to market in each of the fifteen years from 1866 to 1880. The average annual number was about 280,000, the total during the period 4,223,497. By contrast, during the last fifteen years of the antebellum period, Southerners drove or otherwise marketed an average of 4,468,400 hogs

4. For a more detailed treatment of this topic, see McDonald and McWhiney, "Antebellum Southern Herdsman," 147–66; Forrest McDonald and Grady McWhiney, "The South from Self-Sufficiency to Peonage: An Interpretation," *American Historical Review* 85 (1980), 1095–1118.

5. Frederick Law Olmsted, *A Journey through Texas* . . . (1857; reprint, New York, 1969), 11–12; U.S. Patent Office, *Report of the Commissioner of Patents, for the Year 1850,* pt. 2: *Agriculture* (Washington, D.C., 1851), 563. See also Robert Hunter, Jr., *Quebec to Carolina in 1785–1786* . . . , ed. Louis B. Wright and Marion Tinling (San Marino, Calif., 1943), 270, 275; *Richmond Enquirer,* February 26, 1850; *Eutaw Alabama Whig,* June 30, 1859; Moritz Busch, *Travels Between the Hudson & the Mississippi, 1851–1852,* trans. and ed. Norman H. Binger (Lexington, Ky., 1971), 147–49; J. W. Wells, *History of Cumberland County* (Louisville, Ky.,

1947), 166; L. F. Johnson, *The History of Franklin County, Ky.* (Frankfort, Ky., 1912), 118; Tom Jones to his mother, October 1, 1830, MS in the Tennessee State Library and Archives, Nashville; Eugene L. Schwaab, ed., *Travels in the Old South: Selected from Periodicals of the Times* (2 vols., Lexington, Ky., 1973), I:140; William James Wells, *Pioneering in the Panhandle: A Look at Selected Events and Families as Part of the History of South Santa Rosa County, Florida* (Fort Walton Beach, Fla., 1976), 264; J. W. Dorr, "A Tourist's Description of Louisiana in 1860," ed. Walter Prichard, *Louisiana Historical Quarterly* 21 (1938), 1160; R. C. Beckett, "Antebellum Times in Monroe County," *Mississippi Historical Society Publications* 11 (1910), 92; Robert Dabney Calhoun, "A History of Concordia Parish, Louisiana," *Louisiana Historical Quarterly* 15 (1932), 63; Anon., *A Visit to Texas: Being the Journal of a Traveller* . . . (New York, 1834), 91–92.

HOG DROVERS

From *Harper's New Monthly Magazine* 15 (1857), 595.

per year; the total during the period was 67,026,000. The marketing of cattle in the antebellum South is more difficult to estimate, but in 1850 a federal agency reported that during the preceding twenty years one small area of the South—some two hundred miles square of piney woods in southern Mississippi, eastern Louisiana, and western Alabama—had raised for market 1,000,000 cows annually.[6]

It is important to understand that open-range herding and the leisure associated with it were not merely by-products of slavery, as many contemporary travelers thought, nor were they adaptations made by Europeans to the peculiar climatological and geographical conditions of the region. Nor, for that matter, were they products of a "frontier process." Open-range herding and the leisurely ways of the southern plain folk were simply the continuation in the Old South of traditions practiced for centuries by Celtic peoples. That the Celts who left the British Isles in the seventeenth and eighteenth centuries were so easily able to plant their customs and values in the antebellum South was largely a matter of timing. The traditional ways of the Celts were becoming obsolete in the modern Great Britain that was aborning in the eighteenth century, and the Celts were in fact being forced to change their ways during that so-called age of improvement. But traditional Celtic modes of behavior were marvelously adapted to life on the southern American frontier.[7] On the other hand, had the South been peopled by nineteenth-century Scots, Welshmen, and Ulstermen, the course of southern history would doubtless have been radically different. Nineteenth-century Scottish and Scotch-Irish immigrants did in fact fit quite comfortably into northern American society.[8] (Significantly the Irish, who retained their Celtic ways, did not.) But only a trickle of the flood of nineteenth-century immigrants came to the South; the ancestors

6. Walter P. Webb, *The Great Plains* (Boston, 1931), 223; Dodd and Dodd, *Historical Statistics*, 2–61; U.S. Patent Office, *Report . . . 1850*, pt. 2, 160. On southern cattle raising, also see John D. W. Guice, "Cattle Raisers of the Old Southwest: A Reinterpretation," *Western Historical Quarterly* 8 (1977), 167–87; Terry G. Jordan, *Trails to Texas: Southern Roots of Western Cattle Ranching* (Lincoln, Nebr., 1981); Kenneth D. Israel, "A Geographical Analysis of the Cattle Industry in Southeastern Mississippi from Its Beginnings to 1860" (Ph.D. diss., University of Southern Mississippi, 1970); Joe A. Akerman, Jr., *Florida Cowman, A History of Florida Cattle Raising* (Kissimmee, Fla., 1976).

7. Milton B. Newton, Jr., "Cultural

Preadaptation and the Upland South," *Geoscience and Man* 5 (1974), 143–54; John Solomon Otto and Nain Estelle Anderson, "The Diffusion of Upland South Folk Culture, 1790–1840," *Southeastern Geographer* 22 (1982), 89–98; John Solomon Otto, "The Migration of the Southern Plain Folk: An Interdisciplinary Synthesis," *Journal of Southern History* 51 (1985), 183–200.

8. See, for example, Charlotte Erickson, *Invisible Immigrants: The Adaptation of English and Scottish Immigrants in Nineteenth-Century America* (Worcester, England, 1972); Rowland T. Berthoff, *British Immigrants in Industrial America* (1953; reprint, New York, 1960).

of the vast majority of antebellum Southerners had arrived in America before the Anglicization of Scotland, Wales, and Ulster had advanced very far. Had those Celts who immigrated to the southern colonies in the seventeenth and eighteenth centuries stayed at home, most of them would have been forced to change—to become more Anglicized[9]—but by migrating to such a relatively unsettled wilderness as the Old South, they managed to remain pretty much what they and their ancestors had always been.

Celts had been open-range pastoralists since antiquity, and they continued to be open-range pastoralists in the American South. Indeed, it was their devotion to the leisurely life of herding animals on unfenced land that shaped the foremost division in the British Isles—the cultural and agricultural differences between lowland English crop growers and the upland English and Celtic animal grazers.

Since Roman times, crop production had been the most important aspect of western European agriculture in the south and east of England as well as in most places on the Continent. Under the medieval manorial system, organized to clear land and to cultivate cereal crops, animals were raised, but they were not allowed to run free; tillage predominated and shaped the culture accordingly. Fernand Braudel, in his monumental study of everyday life in Europe from 1400 to 1800, emphasizes the interrelationship between tillage, crop rotation, and fertilizer and how the manure from penned livestock was essential to "rich harvests."[10]

Long before the beginning of English settlement in America, most

9. On what happened to the Highland Scots who stayed at home, see Sir John Sinclair, ed., *The Statistical Account of Scotland, 1791–1799* (reprint, 20 vols., East Ardsley, England, 1981), XVII:20–21, 72, 215–16, 273, 523; Alexander Mackenzie, *The History of the Highland Clearances . . .* (1883; reprint, Perth, Scotland, 1979); Donald MacLeod, *Donald M'Leod's Gloomy Memoirs in the Highlands of Scotland: Versus Mrs. Harriet Beecher Stowe's Sunny Memoires In (England) a Foreign Land: Or a Faithful Picture of the Extirpation of the Celtic Race from the Highlands of Scotland* (Glasgow, 1892); John Prebble, *The Highland Clearances* (Harmondsworth, England, 1969); Elizabeth Mure quoted in J. G. Fyfe, ed., *Scottish Diaries and Memoirs, 1746–1843* (Stirling, Scotland, 1942), 72; John Knox, *A Tour through the Highlands of Scotland and the Hebride Isles in 1786* (1787; reprint, Edinburgh, 1975); R. W. Chapman, ed., *Johnson's Journey to the Western Islands of Scotland and Boswell's Journal of a Tour to the Hebrides with Samuel Johnson, LL.D* (Oxford, 1970); Rosalind Mitchison, *Life in Scotland* (London, 1978), 56–137; on what happened to the Irish who stayed at home, see Thomas Crofton Croker, *Researches in the South of Ireland . . .* (1824; reprint, New York, 1969); Daniel O'Connell, *A Memoir on Ireland Native and Saxon* (1843; reprint, Port Washington, N.Y., 1970); Humphrey O'Sullivan, *The Diary of Humphrey O'Sullivan, 1827–1835*, trans. Tomás de Bhaldraithe (Dublin, 1970); L. M. Cullen, *Life in Ireland* (London, 1979), 118–42.

10. Fernand Braudel, *The Structures of Everyday Life: The Limits of the Possible*, trans. Sian Reynolds (New York, 1981), 114–20.

# Herding

English farmland was "hedged or fenced," and farm animals were either penned or restrained in various ways. For example, fourteenth- and fifteenth-century village bylaws allowed no person to "put his beasts . . . on the pastures or the uncultivated lands of another without the leave of him to whom the pasture belongs"; these regulations also specified that "animals of every kind shall be kept [at night] . . . securely in a house or close to the end that they commit no damage in the fields," required that pigs have iron rings in their noses as well as that animals be tethered when grazing, and that every "man shall kepe his hoggs in his stye untyll such tyme as the hoggerd shall goe."[11]

By the sixteenth century "mixed farming" characterized the south and east of England and the enclosure movement was making headway all over the country. Eric Kerridge, who has demonstrated that the agricultural revolution which previous writers located between 1750 and 1850 actually began two hundred years earlier, noted that even in some of the less productive English shires "a third or half [of the land] was enclosed in the period 1550–1650" and that in many others "most of the field land was enclosed." And Joan Thirsk, writing about the sixteenth and early seventeenth centuries, observed: "The most obvious distinction between the highlands and the lowlands of England at this period, . . . lay in these two contrasted kinds of farming. In the grass-growing uplands, where the principal asset was stock, men either specialized in rearing sheep and cattle, or . . . pig-keeping, or horse-breeding or did a little of each. In the lowlands, the farmer could grow both corn and grass and vary the proportions of arable and pasture, according to the condition of his land, the place of stock in his system of husbandry, and the state of the market. He might grow corn for the town and keep animals chiefly for the sake of maintaining fertility in the corn fields . . . ; he might grow much the same acreage of arable crops but use most of them for feeding animals for the butcher . . . ; or he might fatten for the butcher, but feed his animals mostly on grass, growing a smaller amount of corn." Several combinations or variations within the system were possible, but the "mixed farming" that prevailed on the Continent and in lowland England still required orderly and usually extensive tillage as well as close control over animals.[12]

11. Warren O. Ault, *Open-Field Farming in Medieval England: A Study of Village By-Laws* (London, 1972), 46–52, 90, 102–20, 123–27, 130, 133, 135, 138, 141–42, 145–46, 149–51.
    12. Eric Kerridge, *The Agricultural Revolution* (New York, 1968), 19–22, 25, 39, 45–46, 66, 68, 78, 83, 87–88, 106, 108, 123, 144–45, 157, 175, 195, 213–14, 216–17, 219, 292, 301, 346–48; Joan Thirsk, ed., *The Agrarian History of England and Wales, IV, 1500–1640* (Cambridge, 1967), 2–6.

Just the opposite was true in Scotland, Ireland, Wales, Cornwall, and the north and west of England, where tillage was minimal and open-range herding was customary. Raymond D. Crotty, explaining the historic "concentration of European agriculture on tillage and of Irish agriculture on pasture," noted that even in "recent years while tillage accounted for half the farm land of western Europe it has accounted for less than 15 per cent of the farmland of Ireland; on the other hand, permanent pasture accounted for 70 per cent of the Irish farm land but only 30 per cent of the European farm land." P. W. Joyce reported that in early Ireland: "Forests abounded everywhere, and the animals were simply turned out and fed on mast and whatever else they could pick up." Fences were few even in the seventeenth century; indeed, "fences were altogether unknown" in County Donegal until the nineteenth century. In what sounds exactly like a description of conditions in the antebellum American South, Edward MacLysaght said of seventeenth-century Ireland: "every cornfield had to be specially fenced off in such a way as to keep cattle from entering."[13]

Throughout the eighteenth century much of Scotland was still open range. A visitor reported that Highlanders opposed enclosures as "a much more expensive Way of grazing their Cattle than letting them run as they do in the Hills." The testimony of local Highlanders confirms this observation. "The people are averse to inclosures, as they wish to have all kinds of pasture in common," wrote the Reverend Roderick Mackenzie. "The farmers have no inclosures," explained the Reverend David Dunoon, "and of course consider the vicinity of any as an intolerable grievance, so that their fields from autumn, until the briar appears in April, are one undistinguished common." In Inverness-shire, even at the end of the eighteenth century, there were "scarcely any inclosures," complained an Anglicized Scot. "The common people are inimical to them, as they are almost to every proper method of cultivating their land." "During the winter and spring," another observer reported, "the whole pasturage of the country was a common, and a poind-fold [a cattle

13. W. R. Kermack, *Historical Geography of Scotland* (Edinburgh, 1926), 71–72; Peter Hume Brown, ed., *Scotland Before 1700, from Contemporary Documents* (Edinburgh, 1893), 7, 10; Thirsk, *Agrarian History,* 15–28, 71–89, 124–42; Raymond D. Crotty, *Irish Agricultural Production: Its Volume and Structure* (Cork, 1966), 2–6; Eileen McCracken, *The Irish Woods Since Tudor Times: Distribution and Exploitation* (Newton Abbot, England, 1971), 15–32; P. W. Joyce, *A Social History of Ancient Ireland . . .* (2 vols., London, 1903), II:278–79; Arthur Young, *Arthur Young's Tour in Ireland (1776–1779),* ed. Arthur W. Hutton (2 vols., London, 1892), I:345, 461–62; E. Estyn Evans, *Irish Folk Ways* (London, 1957), 20, 24; Edward MacLysaght, *Irish Life in the Seventeenth Century* (1939; reprint, Dublin, 1979), 88, 171–72, 243–44.

enclosure] was a thing totally unknown." Highlanders typically let their animals, in the words of the Reverend John Fraser, "range at large through their neighbours fields and enclosures, and consider it as a great hardship, and a species of oppression, to have them poinded [impounded] after breaking through enclosures."[14]

Livestock still run free in parts of Scotland and Ireland. In 1981 and 1983 I observed free-ranging cattle and sheep in the Scottish Highlands and in the north and west of Ireland, and an Irish scholar reported that he could never cultivate a garden because his "neighbours have a lingering habit of ignoring the fences."[15]

"Ignoring the fences" certainly was not the practice in colonial New England. "Good fences make good neighbours," proclaimed one of Robert Frost's Yankees,[16] and David Grayson Allen as well as other scholars have pointed out that the "English puritans who came to settle in New England gave up as little of their former ways of doing things as possible. [They] . . . continued to practice the kind of agriculture with which they had been familiar in England." In New England, just as in England, animals were yoked or otherwise restrained in ways totally foreign to open-range herding. Every day animal keepers would "gather at each man's gate his stinted number of cattle, goats, or sheep, drive them as a single herd or flock to pasture, and return them. Each morning the cowherd blew his horn for the householders to bring their creatures to their gates. He watched the animals through the day in the woods and meadows, and returned them at sundown to their owners."[17] In 1760 a traveler noted that livestock in New England still grazed in "neat inclosures, surrounded with stone walls." And in the 1850s a native of Massachusetts who had settled in Kansas complained that traditional New England farming methods had ill prepared him to handle "razor-

14. Ian Whyte, *Agriculture and Society in Seventeenth-Century Scotland* (Edinburgh, 1979), 19–24; Edward Burt, *Burt's Letters from the North of Scotland*, ed. R. Jamieson (1754; reprint, 2 vols., Edinburgh, 1974), II:154; Sinclair, *Statistical Account of Scotland*, XVII:334, 414, 12, 20, 195.

15. Evans, *Irish Folk Ways*, 33. See also Allan C. Fisher, Jr., "Where the River Shannon Flows," *National Geographic* 154, no. 5 (November 1978), 656, 665; Derek A. C. Davies, *Ireland* (New York, 1972), 48.

16. Quoted in James Crawford King, Jr., "The Closing of the Southern Range: An Exploratory Study," *Journal of Southern History* 48 (1982), 53.

17. David Grayson Allen, *In English Ways: The Movement of Societies and the Transferal of English Local Law and Custom to Massachusetts Bay in the Seventeenth Century* (Chapel Hill, 1981), xvi, 4–6, 16, 21–23, 26–28, 33–35, 49–50, 221–22; Ault, *Open-Field Farming*, 77–78; Sumner C. Powell, *Puritan Village: the Formation of a New England Town* (1963; reprint, New York, 1965), 14, 19, 122, 141–42, 184–85; Alice Morse Earle, *Home Life in Colonial Days* (reprint, Middle Village, N.Y., 1975), 25, 311, 401–03; Howard S. Russell, *A Long, Deep Furrow: Three Centuries of Farming in New England* (Hanover, N.H., 1976), 35–37, 40–43, 73–74, 79, 126–27, 155.

backs" from the South. "These hogs in their native state roamed the woods at will," he explained, "and it was with difficulty that they could be kept within any inclosure."[18]

Several examples illustrate how Celtic Southerners imposed their traditional herding practices upon the environment. During the 1850s various English travelers remarked that the railroad rights-of-way in the South were unfenced, unlike those in England, and that trains often killed livestock that ventured on the tracks.[19] Their observations plus a Mississippi Supreme Court decision confirm that the Celtic tradition of free-ranging livestock prevailed in the antebellum South, in contrast to the English tradition of restraining livestock that was practiced in much of the antebellum North. In 1856 a railroad company appealed to the Mississippi high court a lower court's ruling that it must pay damage to a Mr. Patton, obviously a man of Scottish descent (a Thomas Patton died fighting the English at Pinkie in 1547), whose livestock had wandered on the tracks and had been killed by one of the company's trains.

The railroad people argued "that by their charter, they had the absolute and exclusive right to the land covered by their track, with the privilege of running their engines and cars at whatever times and at whatever speed they saw proper, without obstruction; that they were not required by their charter nor by any other law, to fence their track; that the exclusive property in it being in the company, it was a wrong on the part of the owner of these animals to suffer them to be upon the track; that it was his duty to keep them within his own enclosure, or upon his own premises, and that if injury occurred to them, in consequence of being suffered to go at large, and where they might be upon the railroad track, and thereby interfere with the legal and proper business of the railroad, it was by the plaintiff's own wrong, for which he is entitled to no redress."[20]

The court noted that "by the rule of [English] common law, the owner of cattle was bound to keep them within his own enclosures;

18. Andrew Burnaby, *Travels through the Middle Settlements in North America . . . in the Years 1759 and 1760* (1775; reprint, Ithaca, N.Y., 1960), 93; Stephen Jackson Spear, "Reminiscences of the Early Settlement of Dragoon Creek, Wabannsee County," *Collections of the Kansas State Historical Society* 13 (1913–14), 353. On fencing in the North, see also Paul G. Bourcier, " 'In Excellent Order': The Gentleman Farmer Views His Fences, 1790–1860," *Agricultural History* 58 (1984), 546–64; Earle, *Home Life*, 25, 399, 401; William Cobbett, *A Years Residence in the United States of America [1818–1819]* (reprint, New York, 1969), 71; U.S. Patent Office,

Report . . . 1850, pt. 2, 180, 191, 203, 208, 276, 303, 312.

19. John Henry Vessey, *Mr. Vessey of England: Being the Incidents and Reminiscences of Travel in a Twelve Weeks' Tour through the United States and Canada in the Year 1859,* ed. Brian Waters (New York, 1956), 53; Barbara Leigh Smith Bodichon, *An American Diary, 1857–8,* ed. Joseph W. Reed, Jr. (London, 1972), 74; Amelia Matilda Murray, *Letters from the United States, Cuba and Canada* (New York, 1856), 188.

20. *Vicksburg and Jackson Railroad Company* v. *Patton,* 31 Miss. 156 (1856).

that the owner of lands was not required to guard against their intrusion upon his premises, but that the owner of cattle was bound to prevent them from entering upon the premises of others, whether fenced or not"; and that such an argument had been "sustained by decisions of the Supreme Courts of New York, Vermont, Pennsylvania, and Michigan."[21]

But the court observed that English common law, in reference to herding, did not apply in the Old South and that rulings on the subject of enclosing animals made by the supreme courts of South Carolina and Alabama were contrary to those of the northern courts. Judge Alexander H. Handy explained, in delivering the opinion of the Mississippi court, "that the common law of England is the law of this State only so far as it is adapted to our institutions and the circumstances of the people, and is not repealed by statutes, or varied by usages which, by long custom, have superseded it; and that where the reason of it ceases, the rule itself is inapplicable."

In Mississippi and elsewhere in the South, the Celtic open-range tradition determined both law and policy. Judge Handy pointed out that there were "large bodies of woodlands and prairies, which have never been enclosed, lying in the neighborhoods of the plantations of our citizens, and which, by common consent, have been understood, from the early settlement of the State, to be a common of pasture, or, in the phrase of the people, the '*range*,' to which large numbers of cattle, hogs, and other animals in the neighborhood . . . have been permitted to resort. These large numbers of cattle and other animals are necessary to the wants and business of the people, . . . and the large and extensive tracts of land suitable for the pasture of stock, are most generally not required by the owner for his exclusive use. If so required, no one questions his right to fence them in. . . . But until he does so, by the universal understanding and usage of the people they are regarded as commons of pasture, for the range of cattle and other stock of the neighborhood."

In explaining why English common law was unsuited to conditions in the South, Judge Handy observed that "by custom a large amount of pasture, which would otherwise be lost, becomes useful and valuable, in rearing great numbers of cattle and stock of various kinds, contributing greatly to the convenience and emolument of our people. It is also highly convenient in rendering a man safe in pasturing his own cattle on his own unenclosed lands, which he could not do with safety if the common law prevailed; because his cattle, when pasturing upon his own unfenced lands, would be liable to intrude upon his neighbor, and be subjected to the common law rule arising from the trespass. He would, therefore, be compelled to enclose his own pasture-lands before he could safely use them as

21. Ibid.

such; and such a necessity in the condition of the lands of this State, would be a great public grievance."

Therefore, insisted the court, it was "the custom . . . among the people and is well settled by universal acceptation, that a man is entitled to permit his cattle and other stock to go at large in the neighborhood range, and is not liable as a trespasser for the damage done by them to the premises of his neighbor, which are not enclosed by a lawful fence. This being the condition of the people from the first settlement of the State, and the same reasons of convenience still prevailing, it is manifest that the rule of the common law is wholly unsuited to our circumstances, and, upon well settled doctrine, cannot be held to be applicable here. If there could be a reasonable doubt upon this point, it must be removed by the provisions of our statutes. These provisions are utterly irreconcilable with the rule of the common law."[22]

A comparative analysis of basic practices indicate that the open-range method of herding and the leisure ethic were integral parts of both premodern Celtic and antebellum southern culture. The Old South, it must be understood, was not one big plantation; it was, for the most part, a vast wilderness, with relatively few cleared and planted acres and with relatively few inhabitants, where cows and hogs and other livestock roamed the woods unattended. Of the antebellum South's nearly 557 million total acres, fewer than 10 percent were improved in 1850—that is, cleared and under cultivation. Only in Maryland, Virginia, Delaware, and Kentucky was more than 20 percent of the land under cultivation. In the other states of the Old South improved acreage ranged from less than 1 percent in Texas and Florida to nearly 19 percent in South Carolina. Comparative figures show that more than twice as much land was cleared and under cultivation in the North as in the South.[23]

22. Ibid. On traditional Celtic fencing laws, see W. Neilson Hancock, Thaddeus O'Mahony, and Alexander George Richey, eds., *Ancient Laws of Ireland* (4 vols., Dublin, 1865–79), I:123, 127, 163, 167, 169, 217, III:243, 291, IV:73, 85, 103, 125–27, 139, 141. For some examples of southern fencing laws, see *Statutes of the Mississippi Territory* . . . (Natchez, 1816), 214–15, 392–96, 424–26; *Acts of Alabama* . . . (Cahawba, 1820), 27, 78; *Acts of Alabama* . . . (Cahawba, 1824), 53; *Acts of Alabama* . . . (Cahawba, 1826), 14–15; *Acts of Alabama* . . . (Tuscaloosa, 1829), 32; *The Code of Alabama* . . . (Montgomery, 1852), 245–51.

23. Dodd and Dodd, *Historical Statistics*, 2–58; Thomas C. Donaldson, *The Public Domain: Its History, with Statistics* (Washington, D.C., 1884), 28–29; Bureau of the Census, *Seventh Census of the United States, 1850* . . . (Washington, D.C., 1853), Table LV, lxxxii–lxxxiii; Robert Baird, *Impressions and Experiences of the West Indies and North America in 1849* (Philadelphia, 1850), 204; Bureau of the Census, *Statistical View of the United States, . . . Being a Compendium of the Seventh Census* (Washington, D.C., 1854), 170; U.S. Patent Office, *Annual Report of the Commissioner of Patents for the Year 1848* (Washington, D.C., 1849), 360, 390, 447, 475, 495, 521–22, 664–66.

RANGE HOGS HUNTING RATTLESNAKES
From *Harper's New Monthly Magazine* 10 (1854–55), 476.

Most of the antebellum South appeared to be "one interminable forest . . . only here and there relieved by some few patches being got into cultivation," as John Henry Vessey described the seaboard South from Virginia to South Carolina in the 1850s. And he was traveling through the longest settled and most densely populated part of the region. Observers referred to other parts of the South as being "covered with heavy timber, and thinly inhabited" or as "almost an uninterrupted forest."[24]

In no place during the antebellum period was it easier for Celts to maintain their traditional pastoral ways than in these great forests that covered much of the Old South. How people lived in these wooded areas was fairly typical of the vast majority of white Southerners throughout the antebellum years. Some people planted few or no staple crops at all; some owned no land, but almost every white family owned livestock. Many of the inhabitants raised cattle and hogs as their principal occupation. "The vast number of wild cattle which range about this quarter of North America, are almost incredible," wrote a visitor. Another sojourner referred to the backcountry South as being "peculiarly adapted to the rearing of hogs and cattle; . . . no where in the United States are they raised in greater number." "The principle revenue of the people [of much of the Carolinas and Georgia] is derived from the business of raising cattle, which is practiced to a considerable extent," claimed Charles Lanman. Simon P. Richardson insisted that "most of the people [of northern Florida and southern Georgia] lived by raising stock." "The only business here [in backcountry Virginia and North Carolina]," wrote William Byrd, "is raising hogs, which is managed with the least trouble, and affords the diet they are most fond of." Kentucky and Tennessee were teeming with livestock; indeed, Robert Everest asserted, "the Indian corn and the pig appear to be the two principal articles raised."[25] Other antebellum observers described similar conditions in parts of Virginia, the Carolinas, Georgia, Florida, Mississippi, Alabama, Arkansas, Louisiana, and Texas; they noted how easily livestock subsisted and multiplied in the southern forests and

24. Vessey, *Mr. Vessey of England*, 56, 83–84, 94, 104–07; Anne Newport Royall, *Letters from Alabama, 1817–1822*, ed. Lucille Griffith (University, Ala., 1969), 81–82; Robert Everest, *A Journey Through the United States and Part of Canada* (London, 1855), 100; Anon., *The English Party's Excursion to Paris, . . . to which is Added, a Trip to America* . . . (London, 1850), 345.

25. James Sharan, *The Adventures of James Sharan: Compiled from the Journal Written During His Voyages and Travels* . . . (Baltimore, 1808), 99; Samuel R. Brown, *The Western Gazetteer; or, Emigrant's Directory* . . . (Auburn, N.Y., 1817), 126, 133, 230; Charles Lanman, *Adventures in the Wilds* . . . (2 vols., Philadelphia, 1856), I:456; Simon P. Richardson, *Lights and Shadows of Itinerant Life: An Autobiography* (Nashville, 1900), 26–27; William Byrd, *William Byrd's Histories of the Dividing Line Betwixt Virginia and North Carolina* (reprint, Raleigh, 1929), 54; Everest, *Journey*, 89.

A CRACKER COWBOY

From *Harper's New Monthly Magazine* 91 (1895), 340.

canebrakes, and they concluded that because the inhabitants were so committed to a pastoral lifestyle the southern backcountry would "probably forever remain an excellent range for hogs, cattle and horses."[26] Animals multiplied so rapidly in Texas, one writer claimed, that a man could increase his herd at the rate of a thousand a year.[27]

In their adherence to customary Celtic agricultural practices, Southerners differed significantly from Northerners in their work habits and land use. There was nothing in the South comparable to the movable sheep fence that was changed every day in New England "so that each commoner's cropland eventually had the benefit of a night's manuring." Northern farms generally were smaller, more intensely cultivated, and worth more per acre than those in the South. In 1850 southern farms averaged 384 acres each, compared to the national average of 203 acres, but Southerners rarely planted

26. See, for example, John F. D. Smyth, *A Tour in the United States of America* (2 vols., London, 1784), I:161, 291; François André Michaux, *Travels to the West of the Alleghany Mountains . . .* (London, 1805), 135, 236–37, 239, 257; Isaac Holmes, *An Account of the United States . . .* (London, 1823), 168; Charles Lanman, *Letters from the Allegheny Mountains* (New York, 1849), 153; [J. Goldsmith?], *The Present State of the British Empire in Europe, America, Africa and Asia* (London, 1765), 305, 323, 329, 330, 361, 373; Friedrich Wilhelm Christian Gerstäcker, *Wild Sports in the Far West* (London, 1854), 161, 166, 214–15, 217, 284, 293; William Faux, *Memorable Days in America . . .* (London, 1823), 134, 136, 143, 145, 189, 437; Hunter, *Quebec to Carolina*, 266, 275; [Charles A. Clinton?], *A Winter from Home* (New York, 1852), 32, 34, 35; Philo Tower, *Slavery Unmasked: Being a Truthful Narrative of Three Years' Residence and Journeying in Eleven Southern States . . .* (Rochester, N.Y., 1856), 72; A. Murray, *Letters from the United States*, 195; Johann David Schopf, *Travels in the Confederation [1783–1784]*, trans. and ed. Alfred J. Morrison (new ed., 2 vols., New York, 1968), II:246; Timothy Flint, *Recollections of the Last Ten Years*, ed. C. Hartley Grattan (1826; reprint, New York, 1932), 255–56, 305–07; Olmsted, *Journey through Texas*, 65, 93, 98; Gilbert Hathaway, *Travels in the Two Hemispheres . . .* (Detroit, 1858), 478; Matilda Char-

lotte (Jesse) Fraser Houstoun, *Texas and the Gulf . . .* (2 vols., London, 1844), II:195–96, 226; Charles Fenno Hoffman, *A Winter in the West* (2 vols., New York, 1835), II:158; Schwaab, *Travels in the Old South*, I:55–56, 166; William Darby, *The Emigrant's Guide to the Western and Southwestern States and Territories . . .* (New York, 1818), 35; [Daniel Blowe], *A Geographical, Historical, Commercial, and Agricultural View of the United States of America . . .* (London, 1820), 714; John F. H. Claiborne, "A Trip through the Piney Woods [1841]," *Mississippi Historical Society Publications* 9 (1906), 515, 523; H[arry] Toulmin, "A Geographical and Statistical Sketch of the District of Mobile," *American Register* 6 (1810), 332–33; Edward G. Stewart [of Tangipahoa Parish, Louisiana] to John W. Gurley, January 27, 1859, John W. Gurley Papers, Louisiana State University; S. Brown, *Western Gazetteer*, 230; Thomas Nuttall, *A Journal of Travels into the Arkansas Territory During the Year 1819*, ed. Savoie Lottinville (1821; new ed., Norman, Okla., 1979), 89; Vessey, *Mr. Vessey of England*, 53; John Pope, *A Tour through the Southern and Western Territories of the United States of North America . . .* (Richmond, 1792), 43; David B. Warden, *A Statistical, Political, and Historical Account of the United States of North America* (Philadelphia, 1819), 18.

27. Anon., *Visit to Texas*, 122. See also 47, 91–92, 120–21, 177–78, 211.

crops on more than a fraction of their land—herds of hogs and cattle usually roved the remainder. Less than 30 percent of the land in use was under cultivation in the South, compared to more than 50 percent in the North; the average value of southern farms was only $4.35 per acre, while that of northern farms was $19.91. From New England through New York, Michigan, and Wisconsin farmers generally produced their own food as well as a variety of such salable items as grains, hay, wool, maple sugar, fruit, dairy products, eggs, potatoes, and meat. This mixed farming, which seemed to suit the Yankee character, was hard work; it required the year-round effort of the whole family and left them little free time from their labors. Their animals had to be sheltered, fed, and cared for during the cold winter months.[28]

By contrast, the southern system of raising livestock on the open range was simple and easy. Aside from marking or branding their animals, Southerners had little more to do than round them up in the fall and either sell them to a local buyer or drive them to market. One could even raise livestock without owning land. An analysis of Covington County, Alabama, reveals that of the 497 heads of household listed in the 1850 census, 42 percent were landowners and 58 percent were tenants. None of the tenants owned land, of course, and only 6 percent of them owned any slaves, compared to 29 percent of the landowners. But fully 95 percent of the tenants and 96 percent of the landowners owned animals. As might be expected, a higher percentage of landowners than tenants possessed livestock worth

28. Thomas Ashe, *Travels in America* . . . (3 vols., London, 1808), I:61; Felix de Beaujour, *Sketch of the United States* . . . , trans. William Walton (London, 1814), 84–85; Burnaby, *Travels through the Middle Settlements*, 57; William Bartram, *Travels of William Bartram*, ed. Mark Van Doren (1791; reprint, New York, 1928), 256; Royall, *Letters from Alabama*, 115; Henry B. Whipple, *Bishop Whipple's Southern Diary, 1843–1844*, ed. Lester B. Shippee (Minneapolis, 1937), 80, 146, 189; Vessey, *Mr. Vessey of England*, 74–75; Hoffman, *Winter in the West*, II:248–49; Charles G. Parsons, *Inside View of Slavery: or, a Tour Among the Planters* (Cleveland, 1855), 4; Timothy Dwight, *Travels in New England and New York*, ed. Barbara Miller Solomon (4 vols., Cambridge, Mass., 1969), I:75–77; Cobbett, *A Years Residence*, 12, 79, 183; Anon., *Visit to Texas*, 42; Olmsted, *Journey through Texas*, 25; Henry Watson, Jr., to his relatives in New England, March 3, August 7, October 30, 1834, Henry Watson, Jr., Papers, Duke University; Faux, *Memorable Days*, 105; John Benwell, *An Englishman's Travels in America* . . . (London, 1853), 40; Robert Russell, *North America, Its Agriculture and Climate* (Edinburgh, 1857), 161; Aleksandr Borisovich Lakier, *A Russian Looks at America: The Journey of Aleksandr Borisovich Lakier in 1857*, ed. Arnold Schrier and Joyce Story (Chicago, 1979), 131; Claiborne, "Trip through the Piney Woods," 532–34; U.S. Patent Office, *Report* . . . *1848*, 361–63, 490, 491, 502–03, 537, 552, 686–91; idem, *Report* . . . *1850*, pt. 2, 228–30, 266, 270–71, 273, 275, 279–80, 282–83, 289, 322; Paul W. Gates, *The Farmer's Age: Agriculture, 1815–1860* (New York, 1960), 146, 214–17, 247–48; Dodd and Dodd, *Historical Statistics*, 2–61; H. Russell, *Long, Deep Furrow*, 25–27, 152–53, 155, 325–414, 497; Bureau of the Census, *Statistical View* . . . *of the Seventh Census*, 170.

67

CATTLE DROVERS

From *Harper's New Monthly Magazine* 10 (1854–55), 303.

more than $500—24 percent to 5 percent—but there was little difference between the percentage of landowners and tenants who owned animals worth between $100 and $500—58 percent compared to 60 percent. The census material also reveals that 60 percent of the landowners and 46 percent of the tenants slaughtered livestock valued at $50 or more in 1850. These figures show that in one year alone more than half of Covington County's heads of household butchered or sold more than 6 cows each. Covington was predominately cattle country; in 1850 it produced some 3,192 more cows and 10,253 more hogs than were needed to feed its population.[29] Many of these animals were raised by people who owned no land. One man who owned no land nonetheless possessed 160 beef cattle and 250 swine valued at $2,104; another held 200 cows and 70 hogs worth $1,390; still another owned 15 cows and 300 hogs valued at $808.[30]

Various data support the observations of contemporaries that herding prevailed throughout the southern backcountry. In 1840, for example, no fewer than twenty-five of the thirty-two counties of southern Mississippi (those south of the thirty-third parallel) contained more than four times as many beef cattle and hogs as people. Greene and Perry counties had thirteen times as many cows and pigs as people; Jones and Smith counties had nearly eleven times as many. In 1850, although more people had moved into southern Mississippi, twenty-three of its thirty-two counties still contained more than four times as many beef cattle and hogs as people.[31] Nor were these counties exceptions; local studies, census reports, wills, and estate inventories show that a Southerner's livestock often was more valuable than his crops or even his farm.[32]

29. One authority has estimated that each person living in the Deep South during the nineteenth century consumed approximately 150 pounds of pork and 50 pounds of beef per year and that these amounts convert into an individual yearly consumption of about 2.2 hogs and .17 of a cow. Hilliard, *Hog Meat and Hoecake*, 124–30.

30. This information was computed from the published census returns and from notes taken by Professor Frank L. Owsley and his students that are on deposit at The University of Alabama, Tuscaloosa.

31. Bureau of the Census, *Compendium of the . . . Inhabitants and Statistics of the United States . . . From the Returns of the Sixth Census . . .* (Washington, D.C., 1841), 56–57, 226–27; idem, *Statistical View . . . of the Seventh Census*, 261–63.

32. John Solomon Otto, "Florida's Cattle-Ranching Frontier: Hillsborough County (1860)," *Florida Historical Quarterly* 63 (1984), 71–83; inventory of the William Love estate, November 13, 1826, and will of William Love, August 28, 1826 (copies), Love Family Papers, Winthrop College, Rock Hill, South Carolina; wills of John A. Byrum, February 24, 1836, John O. D. Hill, December 27, 1835, Richard Giddeon, October 25, 1834, John H. Henry, September 1, 1838, Nathan Turner, June 21, 1842, Joseph Taylor, October 15, 1843, Mary Ann Standefer, August 2, 1842, and Nancy Holliday, November 6, 1844 (copies), Bertie (Shaw) Rollins Papers, Mississippi Department of Archives and History, Jackson; U.S. Patent Office, *Report . . . 1848*, 561–62; Chris Nordmann, "A Commitment to Leisure: The Agricultural Economy of St. Landry

The herding of cows and hogs on the same range was typically southern; indeed, it was one of the seventeen traits that Terry Jordan shows, in his excellent study of the southern roots of western cattle ranching, to have been characteristic of herding practices throughout the antebellum South. Also included in Jordan's list of southern herding traits are such practices as "the use of open range, unrestricted by fences or natural barriers"; "the accumulation by individual owners of very large herds, amounting to hundreds or even thousands of cattle"; "the neglect of livestock"; "the marking and branding of cattle"; "overland cattle drives to feeder areas or markets along regularly used trails"; "and the raising of some field and garden crops, though livestock were the principal products of the system."[33]

The traits that Jordan said characterized southern herding were traditional in Scotland, Ireland, and Wales long before they were practiced in the American South.[34] Unlike the English, the Celtic peoples of the British Isles disdained tillage agriculture, preferred instead to let their livestock make their living, and worked little except to mark or to drive their animals to market. In these and other ways their herding practices were almost exactly those that prevailed throughout the Old South, including open-range herding, overland trail drives, and the neglect of their animals.[35]

---

Parish, La., 1850," *Louisiana History* 26 (1985), 301–12; and the following unpublished seminar papers written by graduate students at The University of Alabama: Linda T. Mason, "Barn Creek, Marion County, Alabama, 1850"; Ferdinand Haslinger, "The Squatter in Pike County, Alabama, in 1850"; Aubrey Reeves, "Agricultural Changes in Dale County, Alabama, from 1860 to 1880"; Boyd Childress, "Farming and Self-Sufficiency in Knoxville, Greene County, Alabama, in 1850"; Guy R. Swanson, "Population, Agriculture, and Self-Sufficiency in Union Precinct, Greene County, Alabama, 1850"; and Katherine A. Cullen, "The Fall of Prosperity in Pleasant Ridge, Greene County, Alabama, 1860–1870."

33. T. Jordan, *Trails to Texas*, 25–26.

34. Grady McWhiney and Forrest McDonald, "Celtic Origins of Southern Herding Practices," *Journal of Southern History* 51 (1985), 165–82.

35. Ault, *Open-Field Farming*, 46–52, 90, 102–51; Thirsk, *Agrarian History*, 2–6; Archibald A. M. Duncan, *Scotland: The Making of the Kingdom* (New York, 1975), 357; E. Estyn Evans, *Irish Heritage . . .* (Dundalk, Ireland, 1977), 48–

49, 51–52, 55; Mary Corbett Harris, *Crafts, Customs and Legends of Wales* (Newton Abbot, England, 1980), 10–11, 19–20; Eugene O'Curry, *On the Manners and Customs of the Ancient Irish*, ed. W. K. Sullivan (1873; reprint, 3 vols., New York, 1971), I:ccclxx; Whyte, *Agriculture and Society*, 85; Henry Boswell, *Historical Description of . . . the Antiquities of England and Wales . . . and Other Curiosities in Scotland and Ireland . . .* (London, 1786), unnumbered pages; Crotty, *Irish Agricultural Production*, 2–6; Bruce Lenman, *An Economic History of Modern Scotland, 1660–1976* (Hamden, Conn., 1977), 23–24, 39, 57, 63, 67–68, 70–71, 87–89; R. Ian Jack, *Medieval Wales* (Ithaca, N.Y., 1972), 196–97; Sir Leonard Twiston Davies and Averyl Edwards, *Welsh Life in the Eighteenth Century* (London, 1939), 1–2, 6, 8–9, 10, 20, 225; C. A. J. Skeel, "The Cattle Trade between Wales and England from the Fifteenth to the Nineteenth Centuries," *Transactions of the Royal Historical Society*, 4th ser., 9 (1926), 135–58; Christopher Lowther, *Our Journall into Scotland Anno Domini 1629 . . .* , ed. W. D. (Edinburgh, 1894), 13–14; Robert Forbes, *Journals of the Episcopal Visita-*

Scottish Highlanders "trusted for winter provender solely to pasture grass," recalled a native. "Having little straw, and no hay, many cattle, in severe winters, perished for want."[36] An eighteenth-century visitor to the Western Islands of Scotland found no barns and reported that "common Work-Horses are expos'd . . . during the Winter and . . . have neither Corn, Hay, or but seldom Straw. . . . The Cows are likewise expos'd to the Rigour of the coldest Seasons, and become mere Skeletons in the Spring, many of them not being able to rise from the ground without help; but they recover as the Season becomes more favourable, and the Grass grows up."[37]

Livestock was no better cared for in Ireland or in Wales. Barns were rare items in Ireland, where livestock "wintered on withered grass left ungrazed and uncut during the summer. The mild Irish winters made this possible," explained a scholar, "though on farms where no hay was available during periods of hard frost or snow, many cattle, especially in the north, actually perished from starvation, and all normally lost condition to such an extent that it took until the month of June each year before they began to thrive again." "Even today," admitted an authority, "Irish farmers . . . tend to be rather haphazard in their arrangements for stock wintering." In Wales the native cattle grew tough from neglect.[38]

The settlers of Kentucky, rather than adjusting to the colder climate, simply followed their Celtic tradition of neglecting livestock. A traveler was amazed that few Kentuckians provided barns for their livestock even though the Kentucky winters were as cold as those in Pennsylvania and New Jersey, where barns were common. "Their cattle [in Kentucky]," he wrote, "are . . . exposed during the winter

tions of the Right Rev. Robert Forbes, M.A., of the Dioceses of Ross and Caithness, . . . 1762 & 1770 . . . , ed. J. B. Craven (London, 1886), 144; John Loveday, Diary of a Tour in 1732 Through Parts of England, Wales, Ireland and Scotland (Edinburgh, 1890), 111, 162; William Gilpin, Observations . . . Made in the Year 1776, on Several Parts of Great Britain . . . (2 vols., London, 1789), II:135–36; Burt, Letters, II:132–33, 151–54; Martin Martin, A Description of the Western Islands of Scotland (1716; reprint, Edinburgh, 1981), 85–86, 205–06; David W. Howell, "The Economy of the Landed Estates of Rembrokeshire, c. 1680–1830," Welsh History Review 3 (1966), 165–83; Sinclair, Statistical Account of Scotland, XVII:19–20, 27, 234, 287, 408, 672; Fyfe, Scottish Diaries and Memoirs, 260–61; P. Brown, Scotland Before 1700, 7, 10; Kermack, His-

torical Geography, 62, 71–72; Daniel Defoe, A Tour through the Whole Island of Great Britain [1724–1726], ed. Pat Rogers (New York, 1971), 377, 599, 664; A. Young, Tour in Ireland, I:150–51, 345; MacLysaght, Irish Life, 167–68, 171–72, 181, 243–44; Evans, Irish Folk Ways, 20, 33; Maire de Paor and Liam de Paor, Early Christian Ireland (London, 1978), 77, 79, 88, 92.

36. Sinclair, Statistical Account of Scotland, XVII:547.

37. Martin, Description of the Western Islands, 154–55.

38. MacLysaght, Irish Life, 170; A. Young, Tour in Ireland, II:107–08; Michael Dillon, "Farmers and Fishermen," in Ireland By the Irish, ed. Michael Gorman (London, 1963), 42; Thirsk, Agrarian History, 116–17; M. Harris, Crafts, Customs and Legends, 16; Davies and Edwards, Welsh Life, 3.

to subsist in the woods, but the consequence is, that many of them die, and all suffer extremely." Another observer noted that even though "the cold [in Kentucky] is so intense that the Ohio [River] is frozen over in winter, the cattle are not stabled." This same writer contended that "cattle throughout the cotton regions fare poorly, and have a starved appearance [in winter]."[39]

To have built barns would have impinged upon what most Celts and Southerners considered their leisurely heritage. "The men are generally idle, devoted to hunting, and the attention of their numerous herds," wrote a Northerner who lived for a time in the South. There was no pressing need for most Southerners, at least the white menfolk, to do much work, inasmuch as most of them made their living from their livestock. They had abundant free time, for they neither built barns nor grew special feed for their animals. "One great advantage this country [most of the South] has over the northern states," a contemporary observed, "is that the men are not obliged to work for the beasts, the winter being so mild, that the cattle are fat in the woods all the year; this prevents a great deal of hard labour, which must be done in the hottest season, in the northern states."[40]

Neither Southerners, especially those in the backcountry, nor their Celtic forebears devoted much time to tillage agriculture. Unlike Englishmen and Yankees, who were dedicated plowers and often obsessed with agricultural improvements,[41] Celts and most Southerners cultivated crops reluctantly and haphazardly. There were exceptions, of course, such as James Mallory, who in 1850 owned twenty-two slaves and two hundred improved acres in Talladega County, Alabama, and produced 17,600 pounds of cotton, 2,200 bushels of corn, and small quantities of wheat, rye, oats,

39. Schwaab, *Travels in the Old South*, I:56; R. Russell, *North America*, 92, 270. The southern habit of "wintering out" stock may have accounted for the poor condition of the Army of Tennessee's artillery horses. See Larry J. Daniel, *Cannoneers in Gray: The Field Artillery of the Army of Tennessee, 1861–1865* (University, Ala., 1985), 56, 71, 124, 126–27, 163, 171, 183.

40. James Pearse, *A Narrative of the Life of James Pearse . . .* (Rutland, Vt., 1825), 52; Claiborne, "Trip through the Piney Woods," 515, 521, 522, 530; Flint, *Recollections*, 305, 306–07; S. Brown, *Western Gazetteer*, 126; Dorr, "Tourist's Description," 1160; W. Wells, *Pioneering in the Panhandle*, 43; Schwaab, *Travels in the Old South*, I:21.

41. John Yeoman, *The Diary of the Visits of John Yeoman to London in the Years 1774 and 1777*, ed. MacLeod Yearsley (London, 1934), 20; Henri Misson, *M. Misson's Memoirs and Observations in His Travels over England, With some Account of Scotland and Ireland*, trans. Mr. Ozell (London, 1719), 43; Fredericka Bremer, *England in 1851; or, Sketches of a Tour in England*, trans. L. A. H. (Boulogne, 1853), 124; Thirsk, *Agrarian History*, 2–15; Kerridge, *Agricultural Revolution*, 161–64; Faux, *Memorable Days*, 409–11; Beaujour, *Sketch of the United States*, 84; Cobbett, *A Years Residence*, 12, 79, 163, 183; Dwight, *Travels*, I:75–77, 272–73, II:165, III:100, 212–13, IV:216–17; various letters from northern farmers, in U.S. Patent Office, *Report . . . 1850*, 276, 282–83, 303, 312–15.

tobacco, peas, and potatoes. But the Mallorys of the Old South, who kept detailed agricultural records and were work-oriented and profit-oriented, were atypical. Mallory's production in 1850 of four bales of cotton per field hand was nearly twice the average for the best cotton lands in southern Alabama and Georgia.[42]

More typical of the leisurely Southerner was Columbus Morrison, who was born in North Carolina in 1808 and was, in his own words, "of the old Scotch presbyterian descent." In the diary that he kept during 1845 and 1846, while living in Alabama, he advised his children to stay "constantly and energetically occupied with something useful," but Morrison failed to practice what he preached. His diary suggests that he was an unsuccessful farmer who disliked both work and supervision. He apparently left his slaves and crops unattended and spent much of his time in leisurely activities. For example, his journal entries in May and June 1845 include: "Hunted squirrels." "Read history." "Engaged as usual with gun." "Went into town this morning & fishing this afternoon." "Staid at home all day, reading." "Reading history & newspapers most all day." "Went to Browns Mill." "Mr. Goodman called—trying to make up 4th July dinner. . . . Visited Mother Johnston." "Went to town this morning. Mother Johnston spent the day with me." "Took morning ride to town." "Staid at home—employed with history." "Took children to town. Called on Mrs. Sink and Mrs. Caldwell." "Took Children to town." "Called on Mother Johnston. Took morning ride to town. . . . Reading through the heat of the day." "At home all day—lonesome." "Took morning ride to town. Wrote a letter to Rev. J. Morrison." "Took ride to town this morning." "Visited Father Johnston with children. J. Caldwell and family spent the day there." "Went to town this morning." "Went to town." "Went to town—took children to see Mrs Graham." "Mr. Skelton, Father Johnston & family, Mrs C. Johnston & family and Mrs M. Mitchell all spent the day with me." "Mr S. Skelton spent the day with me. Tried to trade his house & lot in town for my farm [but] could not agree." "At home—reading—thinking. . . . What may be the effect of town life on my health &c &c?" "Took morning ride to town. R. Porter & Slade called. Reading most of day." "Visited Father Johnston with children. . . . Mr B. McGhee took supper & spent the evening with me." "Visited Mr E. Skelton—he has a fine nursery—showed his great yield of Onions." "Went to town this morning." "Took the children to town on visit. . . . Spent the after noon with Mrs Mary

42. Mallory Journal, 1850. Average figures for southern Georgia have been calculated from Roland M. Harper, "Development of Agriculture in Lower Georgia from 1850 to 1880," *Georgia Historical Quarterly* 6 (1922), 111; Alabama averages have been calculated from the Bureau of the Census, Manuscript Census Returns, Seventh Census.

Mitchell—Lewis McGhee & Lady and Mrs Douthette were there—good company." "Went to town. . . . " "Father Johnston paid us a visit this morning. Thermometer stood 93 at 5 oclock p.m. Went to town late this evening to cool off with ice and Soda water." "Took children to see Mrs Graham. Called on Mrs Mitchell—found Mother Johnston there. Weather still hot. Beans burning up." "Lost my favourite Dog—hunted through town & found him." "Staid at home all day. Very hot & dusty. Saml Johnston called." "Took children to town. Visited Mrs Sink and Mrs Perkins. Met with my old friend Mrs Harriet Coxe. She has a fine daughter 5 years old. Came home to dinner through hot sun & a cloud of dust. Wm Johnston and B. McGhee spent the afternoon with me." Morrison's routine of visits and leisurely activities continued through the remainder of the year.[43]

Most Southerners were careless farmers. They rarely used manure or other fertilizers, and their primitive techniques appalled outsiders.[44] "You will perceive that little improvement is made at the South in agricultural pursuits generally," a Southerner admitted in 1850. Corn production in the southern piney woods, for example, averaged only "15 or 20 bushels per acre," compared to 50 to 60 bushels per acre in New York, 35 to 40 in Ohio and Indiana, and 30 to 40 in Maine and Massachusetts. In 1849 near Augusta, Maine, where corn was heavily manured and carefully cultivated, one man raised "95 bushels of shelled corn, to the acre"; another "72 bushels"; and a third "71 bushels." Besides their lackadaisically grown corn, Southerners usually planted field peas and sweet potatoes; indeed, John Claiborne reported that in many counties "the main crop is the *sweet potato*." It would grow "with little culture on soils that were too thin to produce corn." Claiborne claimed that a single acre would "yield from three to five hundred bushels," but another

43. Columbus Morrison Journal, 1845–46, Southern Historical Collection, University of North Carolina, Chapel Hill.

44. Everest, *Journey,* 84–85, 100; Hoffman, *Winter in the West,* II:248–49; Whipple, *Southern Diary,* 80, 189; Parsons, *Inside View,* 53–66; Schwaab, *Travels in the Old South,* I:142; Farmers' *Register* 1 (1833), 167; *Tennessee Farmer* 2 (1837), 41, 115; Chester Sullivan, *Sullivan's Hollow* (Jackson, Miss., 1978), 9; J. F. H. Claiborne, *Rough Riding Down South* (1862; reprint, Hattiesburg, Miss., 1984), 29. It is significant that seventeen of some twenty-four antebellum southern agricultural journals devoted to the improvement of farming techniques failed before they had published for five years. These statistics were compiled from Albert L. Demaree, *The American Agricultural Press, 1819–1860* (New York, 1940), 367, 373–74, 393–98. On traditional Celtic farming techniques see Sir William Brereton, *Travels in Holland the United Provinces, England, Scotland, and Ireland, 1634–1635,* ed. Edward Hawkins (Manchester, 1844), 132; Knox, *Tour through the Highlands,* 122; Sinclair, *Statistical Account of Scotland,* XVII:231, 305, 414, 562; Defoe, *Tour,* 660; Burt, *Letters,* II:145–48; A. Young, *Tour in Ireland,* I:211, 237, 249, II:21–22; Evans, *Irish Heritage,* 87–88; MacLysaght, *Irish Life,* 173–74.

writer considered 150 bushels of sweet potatoes per acre, at a production cost of twenty cents per bushel, an average yield.[45]

The typical southern white seemed to most observers to be an impoverished farmer, at least in comparison with hardworking Yankees, for Southerners tended to live in squalor. Frederick Law Olmsted, in a passage that can be found with variations in the accounts of numerous other travelers, wrote of an East Texas house that "was more comfortless than nine-tenths of the stables of the North," a judgment that his graphic description verified. "There were several windows, some of which were boarded over, some had wooden shutters, and some were entirely open. There was not a pane of glass. The doors were closed with difficulty. We could see the stars, as we lay in bed, through the openings of the roof; and on all sides, in the walls of the room, one's arm might be thrust out." That description sounds for all the world like the direst poverty, and it is an entirely characteristic representation of the appearance of most antebellum southern homes. But appearances were deceptive. The "farmer" that Olmsted was describing happened to own a thousand acres of land—none of which he tilled—and more hogs and cattle than he could count. His place was teeming with deer and other game, but "he never shot any; 'twas too much trouble. When he wanted 'fresh,' 'twas easier to go out and stick a hog."[46]

That was the key to how the plain folk lived: in the literal sense of the phrase, they lived "high off the hog." When the larder got low, they simply stuck another hog. For vegetables, almost no tillage was necessary, since green gardens in the southern soil and climate, once planted, grew wild, reseeding themselves year after year if they were appropriately neglected, as was also the case with "pumpkins, sweet potatoes, and several other vegetables." In 1854 a startled German, who found the South far different from his own culture, wrote to friends back home: "There are such fine fruits and plants

45. U.S. Patent Office, *Report . . . 1850*, 259–60; Flint, *Recollections*, 316; various letters from Northerners, in U.S. Patent Office, *Report . . . 1850*, 251, 269, 296, 374, 396, 434; Claiborne, "Trip through the Piney Woods," 533.

46. Frederick Law Olmsted, *The Cotton Kingdom: A Traveller's Observations on Cotton and Slavery . . .* , ed. Arthur M. Schlesinger (new ed., New York, 1953), 304–05. On the simplicity of southern architecture, see James C. Bonner, "Plantation Architecture of the Lower South on the Eve of the Civil War," *Journal of Southern History* 11 (1945), 370–88; Fred B. Kniffen and

Henry Glassie, "Building in Wood in the Eastern United States: A Time-Place Perspective," *Geographical Review* 56 (1966), 40–66; Fred B. Kniffen, *Folk Houses of Louisiana* (Baton Rouge, 1942); Henry Glassie, *Pattern in the Material Folk Culture of the Eastern United States* (Philadelphia, 1968); idem, *Folk Housing in Middle Virginia: A Structural Analysis of Historic Artifacts* (Knoxville, 1975); Eugene M. Wilson, *Alabama Folk Houses* (Montgomery, 1975); and Terry G. Jordan, *Texas Log Buildings: A Folk Architecture* (Austin, 1978).

here. The forest is a veritable vineyard, for grapes of all kinds grow in the wild forest as well as such things as are planted in the fine gardens of Germany. All such things grow in the woods here. . . . You can also keep as many cows here as you wish, for feed does not cost a penny. Cattle feed itself in the woods in winter and summer, no cattle here is fed in the barn. Grass grows six to eight feet high in the woods and one person has as much right there as the other. Similarly you can keep as many pigs as you wish, and you need not feed them. The same is true of chickens. . . . We do not want to go on, for we can live here like lords."[47]

Open-range herding, together with their laissez-faire plant growing, made Southerners lavishly self-sufficient[48]—lavishly, that is, by the plain folk's own preferred standards, which required only an abundance of leisure, tobacco, liquor, and food. Virtually every travel account indicated that Southerners enjoyed three of the four; as for the fourth, food, Sam B. Hilliard has estimated that antebellum Southerners consumed approximately 150 pounds of *lean* pork and 50 pounds of *lean* beef per capita per year, which is one-third again as much animal protein per capita as was consumed by Americans in 1977. This amounts to 248 grams of *animal* protein per man, woman, and child per day—nearly five times the amount of *total* protein intake recommended for adult males by the Food and Nutrition Board of the National Research Council in 1978.[49]

Traditionally, Celts had also consumed great quantities of protein—mostly hogs and cattle—and little bread. For vegetables, they usually "relied on those that they could gather in the wild rather than growing them themselves." Only after the English had taken their land and most of their animals did the Irish learn to raise and eat potatoes. The modern Irish so love food that their "per capita intake of calories exceeds that of any other nation in the world."[50]

But it also was traditional among the Scots, Irish, and Welsh to devote no more of their energy to tillage than did Southerners. At the end of the eighteenth century one Highland minister estimated that the average farm in his parish consisted of 27 acres devoted to

47. Anon., *Visit to Texas*, 23–24; [Joseph Eder], "A Bavarian's Journey to New Orleans and Nacogdoches in 1853–1854," ed. Karl J. R. Arndt, *Louisiana Historical Quarterly* 23 (1940), 496–97.

48. On antebellum southern self-sufficiency, see McDonald and McWhiney, "The South from Self-Sufficiency to Peonage," 1095–1118.

49. Hilliard, *Hog Meat and Hoecake*, 105. For modern consumption, real and recommended, see Anon., *The World*

*Almanac & Book of Facts, 1979* (New York, 1979), 161.

50. Agnes McMahon, ed., *The Celtic Way of Life* (Dublin, 1976), 38–46; Anon., *The Holiday Guide to Ireland* (New York, 1979), 37. Irish families were so fond of pork that they often depicted on their coats of arms the head or body of one or more fighting boars. See Brian de Breffny, *Irish Family Names: Arms, Origins, and Locations* (New York, 1982), 57–185.

IRISHMAN RESTING; SCOT DREAMING

From *Punch, or the London Charivari* 6 (1844) 238;
ibid. 7 (1844), 81.

tillage and 34,973 acres devoted to open range; another minister confessed that most of his parishioners preferred fishing to working and that "their mode of farming required little of their attention."[51]

A scholar noted that "Ireland is a country of grass and pasturage" and that it had depended "less upon tillage than any other European land." "Tillage, though ample to supply the limited needs of the country, was not extensive," observed an authority on seventeenth-century Ireland. "Tillage does not thrive in this country," bemoaned an eighteenth-century visitor to Ireland; another traveler stated: "agriculture is at a very low ebb in this country; . . . you may ride for miles, in the most fertile part of it, without seeing an acre of ploughed ground." Critics claimed that the Irish would plant only cabbages and potatoes, which they grew appropriately enough in "lazy beds."[52]

Nor were the Welsh different. "From very early times the rearing of cattle rather than crops has been the chief occupation of Welsh farmers," noted an authority. Another scholar concluded that the Welsh clung to their old agricultural ways well into the nineteenth century. "Agriculture remained medieval in simplicity until about 1760," insisted still another authority, who stated that as "late as 1812, 1,700,000 acres, out of the entire area of Wales [approximately 5,000,000 acres], were left uncultivated, though nearly half of this was capable of development."[53]

The open-range system of herding encouraged more than indifferent farming and a leisurely lifestyle. From the Celtic pastoral tradition emanated a whole network of interrelated customs and beliefs that separated Celts and Southerners from Englishmen and Yankees. Laziness and a lack of ambition were only part of that Celtic-southern tradition, which good Englishmen and Yankees deplored. Being lazy to Celts and Southerners did not mean being indolent, shiftless, slothful, and worthless; it meant being free from work, having spare time to do as they pleased, being at liberty, and enjoying their leisure. When a Celt or a Southerner said that he was being lazy he was not reproaching himself but merely describing his state of comfort. He suffered no guilt when he spent his time pleas-

51. P. Brown, *Scotland Before 1700,* 45; Chapman, *Johnson's Journey,* 144; Sinclair, *Statistical Account of Scotland,* XVII:198–99, 177, 133, 547.

52. Conrad M. Arensberg, *The Irish Countryman: An Anthropological Study* (1937; reprint, Gloucester, Mass., 1959), 38; A. Young, *Tour in Ireland,* I:400; Thomas Campbell, *A Philosophical Survey of the South of Ireland, in a Series*

*of Letters to John Walkinson, M.D.* (London, 1777), 151; MacLysaght, *Irish Life,* 171, 110; Taylor Downing, ed., *The Troubles* (London, 1980), 38.

53. Leslie Alcock, "Some Reflections on Early Welsh Society and Economy," *Welsh History Review* 2 (1964), 3; M. Harris, *Crafts, Customs and Legends,* 15; Davies and Edwards, *Welsh Life,* 1.

antly—hunting, fishing, dancing, drinking, gambling, fighting, or just loafing and talking. He could not understand why anyone would work when livestock could make a living for him; indeed, he doubted the sanity of people who labored when they could avoid it. Nor did he see any good reason to have more than he could eat, or drink, or wear, or ride.

# IV

# *Hospitality*

SOME years ago a professor at a northern university claimed that the experiences of certain travelers "do not support all that has been asserted about southern hospitality." He argued that often visitors had to pay for what hospitality they received in the Old South; "that it was not always extended in good grace and sometimes was withheld altogether."[1]

Certain Southerners doubtless were more hospitable than others, just as some people were more likely to be hospitable at certain times and under certain circumstances—when, for example, they had extra food, or beds, or a desire for company and news. One writer asserted that the southern plain folk "are hospitable to strangers, *because they are seldom troubled with them,* and because they have plenty of *maize and smoked ham.*"[2]

More often than not it was the kind of food and how it was cooked and served that caused visitors to question the hospitality of antebellum Southerners and premodern Celts. Theirs was not the fare to which most outsiders, especially Northerners and Englishmen, were accustomed, and few travelers were as tolerant as the man who wrote: "we were happy at discovering a house, at which we were hospitably received by an old woman, who had little but the barest necessities to offer us. She soon set before us a meal . . . which . . . consisted only of pork fried with onions, tops and all. Her simple house and table furniture were worse for wear, and one of our forks had but one prong."[3]

Most antebellum southern meals, as a traveler noted, were "designed for tough backwoods stomachs"; typically, Southerners "ate

1. Paton Yoder, "Private Hospitality in the South, 1775–1850," *Mississippi Valley Historical Review* 47 (1960), 432.

2. Frederick Hall, *Letters from the East and from the West* (Washington,

D.C., 1840), 118.

3. Anon., *A Visit to Texas: Being the Journal of a Traveller . . .* (New York, 1834), 247.

like wolves and used their fingers rather than their forks." Meals almost always included some form of pork, cornbread, and sour milk. Sometimes wild game, beef, chicken, sweet potatoes, field peas, rice, and greens either substituted for or supplemented the usual fare. "Nobody ever heard of dinners being served in courses," recalled a planter's daughter; "the soups, meats, and vegetables were all served on the table at once." New England native Lucius Bierce wrote: "Salt dried pork fried . . . [and] Johnny cake . . . for breakfast— pork . . . boiled with sweet potatoes, Johnny cake, and sour milk for dinner—the same cold . . . for supper. This, with little variation is [for Southerners] the round of diet, as bread, apples, or cakes would be as much a rarity as fig trees on the Green mountains. Their mode of preparing milk for use is to keep a quantity of sour, or bonny clabber on hand, and when wanted for use to put it in a churn with the same quantity of sweet milk, and churn it till it is all the same consistency, then . . . set [it] on the table in tumblers and bit and sup is the order of the day."[4]

Northerners rarely could find much in the South that they enjoyed eating. "At this dinner I made the first practical acquaintance with what shortly was to be the bane of my life, viz., corn-bread and bacon," announced a visitor in the South. "I partook innocent and unsuspicious of these dishes, as they seemed to be the staple of the meal, without a thought that for the next six months I should actually see *nothing else*. . . . Taken alone, with vile coffee, I may ask, with deep feeling, who is sufficient for these things?"[5]

Many travelers in the South must have asked themselves the same question. "We were provided with a breakfast of coarse pork and bread made of Indian corn," reported a New Yorker. "I confess that in all the various tables I have sat down to, none required more of the Spartan's seasoning than this. I was really glad to wash down the coarse and greasy mixture with a bowl of sour milk, and betake myself once more to the saddle." An Englishman observed that in the southern backcountry "the provisions are generally miserable & there is seldom a piece of [wheat] bread in the house. The most

4. Charles Sealsfield, *America: Glorious and Chaotic Land . . .* , trans. E. L. Jordan (Englewood Cliffs, N.J., 1969), 130; Robert Russell, *North America, Its Agriculture and Climate* (Edinburgh, 1857), 271; Frederick Law Olmsted, *A Journey through Texas . . .* (1857; reprint, New York, 1969), 93; John Henry Vessey, *Mr. Vessey of England: Being the Incidents and Reminiscences of Travel in a Twelve Weeks' Tour through the United States and Canada in the Year 1859*, ed. Brian Waters (New York, 1956), 68;

George W. Bagby, *The Old Virginia Gentleman and Other Sketches*, ed. Ellen M. Bagby (Richmond, 1943), 180; Marion Alexander Boggs, ed., *The Alexander Letters, 1787–1900* (Athens, Ga., 1980), 124–25; Lucius Verus Bierce, *Travels in the Southland, 1822–1823: The Journal of Lucius Verus Bierce*, ed. George W. Knepper (Columbus, Ohio, 1966), 81.

5. Olmsted, *Journey through Texas*, 15–16, 95.

ludicrous dinner I ever sat down to was at a house in the woods, where a few ribs . . . were all that greeted hungry travelers." Another foreigner declared: "The food . . . generally amounts to no more than fried fatback and cornbread." And a Northerner noted "that dyspepsia was a common complaint in Kentucky, as God knows it ought to be."[6]

Many visitors became angry because the foods they enjoyed at home were absent from southern tables. "For several days at a time we could not get a drop of milk, even for the child," complained an Englishman traveling in the South; "and though we saw hundreds of cows, they were all let loose in the woods, and not tied up for domestic purposes." Such strange behavior was beyond his comprehension; it was not the way things were done in England. He also complained that he could find no bread made of wheat, "only some lumps of paste, resembling in colour, weight, and flavour, so many knobs of pipe-clay, but got up expressly by these obliging people as wheaten cakes. Their own Indian corn bread was probably very good of its kind, and for those who like it, I dare say excellent." It was, of course, unfit for English tastes. Another Englishman agreed. After being served what he called "an infamous breakfast which you almost turn away from with loathing, & nothing but necessity would induce you to touch," he wrote in his diary: "I have . . . already had frequent cause to remark the inferiority of the South in activity & enterprize when contrasted with the North. At the same time . . . you are treated with neglect & the worst of fare."[7]

Northerners traveling in the South missed their accustomed diet as much as Englishmen did. One searched in vain for food items that were readily available in the North. "We inquired at seven stores, and at the two inns, for butter, flour, or wheat-bread, and fresh meat," he recalled. "There was none in town. One inn-keeper offered us salt-beef, the only meat except pork, in town. At the stores we found crackers, worth in New York 6 cents a pound, sold here at 20 cents. . . . When butter was to be had it came in firkins

6. Charles Fenno Hoffman, *A Winter in the West* (2 vols., New York, 1835), II:185; George Townsend Fox American Journal, November 29, 1834, Public Library, South Shields, Durham, England; Louis Philippe, *Diary of My Travels in America [1797]*, trans. Stephen Becker (New York, 1977), 60; Olmsted, *Journey through Texas*, 14. See also William Faux, *Memorable Days in America* . . . (London, 1823), 189; Andrew Burnaby, *Travels through the Middle Settlements in North America* . . . *in the Years 1759 and 1760* (1775; reprint, Ithaca, N.Y., 1960), 30–31;

Margaret (Hunter) Hall, *The Aristocratic Journey; Being the Outspoken Letters of Mrs. Basil Hall Written During a Fourteen Months' Sojourn in America, 1827–1828*, ed. Una Pope-Hennessy (New York, 1931), 271; Bierce, *Travels in the Southland*, 53; Johann David Schopf, *Travels in the Confederation [1783–1784]* . . . , trans. and ed. Alfred J. Morrison (new ed., 2 vols., New York, 1968), II:46.

7. Captain Basil Hall, *Travels in North America in the Years 1827 and 1828* (3 vols., Edinburgh and London, 1829), III:270, 115–16; Fox Journal, December 4, 1834.

from New York, although an excellent grazing country is near the town." The problem was that milking and making butter required more work than most Southerners wanted to engage in, especially on a scale necessary to supply more than a family. Another Northerner noted that Southerners "commonly make some butter and cheese, at least enough for their own families, . . . but these things engross but few of their thoughts." They liked buttermilk and sour milk and delighted in offering it to visitors. This man admitted that "in the endeavor to like it I had to overcome a strong prejudice."[8]

Wheat bread, fresh meat, butter, cheese, and what Southerners called "sweet milk" were just some of the things that were scarce in the South but abundant in the North. A New Yorker mentioned the "indifferent bread and strong butter" of the South that "contrasted unfavorably with the products of the mills of Rochester, and the dairies of Orange County [New York]." Another Northerner reported: "It is remarked that north of the Potomac, one may find good beef, and bad bacon; and south of the Potomac, good bacon and bad beef." New Englanders liked their chickens stewed or broiled; Southerners preferred them fried.[9]

Englishmen had been just as offended by the culinary habits of premodern Celts as Northerners were by those of Southerners, and for good reason—the dietary ways of Celts and Southerners were quite similar. Traditionally, both the Irish and the Scots were great meat eaters, especially pork and beef. "Celts were above all stock raisers," wrote Lloyd Laing. "The bones found at Dunadd and Dinas Powys, Glamorgan, showed the most popular meat was pork." A visitor wrote of the sixteenth-century Irish: "Flesh they devoure without bread, and that halfe raw; [they drink] . . . *Aqua Vitae* [whiskey], which they swill in after such a surfet by quarts. . . . No meat they fansie so much as porke, and the fatter the better." Thomas Dineley noted in the seventeenth century that the Irish were quite fond of "swine's flesh, . . . which differs from ye custome of England." In the seventeenth century an English officer observed that the Irish had "plenty of meat . . . and milk, . . . and what is strangest for the most part love it best when sourest. They keep it in sour vessels. . . . The meaner people content themselves with little bread but instead thereof eat potatoes, which with sour milk is the chief part of their diet." Another visitor to Ireland in the seventeenth century reported: "*Bonny-Clabber* and *Mulahaan,*

8. Olmsted, *Journey through Texas*, 84; Anon., *Visit to Texas*, 117–18.

9. Alice Morse Earle, *Home Life in Colonial Days* (reprint, Middle Village, N.Y., 1975), 148–50; [Charles A. Clinton?], *A Winter from Home* (New York, 1852), 15; [Henry C. Knight], *Letters from the South and West* (Boston, 1852), 45; Charles Lanman, *Adventures in the Wilds . . .* (2 vols., Philadelphia, 1856), II:137.

alias *Sower Milk*, and . . . a Dish of *Potatoes* boiled, is their general Entertainment. . . . And for a close to all this Treat . . . the Mistress shall produce her *Moornaun* of *Sower Milk*, and having stript up her sleeve to the Shoulder, she thrusts up to the Arm-pits, and stirring the Curds at the bottom with her Hands, she then presents you with the Liquor, and if you like it, you may fill your Belly with her Kindness till you are satisfied." Cleanliness, this man observed, was not an Irish virtue: "let me not forget their *Butter*, made up with so much Filth and *Hair*, it looks like the *Lime* we prepare to Plaister our *Walls*. . . . If they had the Wit to put the Hair in one Dish, and the Butter in another part it might be in a Man's Choice to take or leave as he pleased; but they are so order'd, you must eat both at once."[10]

Even in the eighteenth century English travelers found much to complain about in Scotland and Ireland. Richard Pococke wrote of the Irish: "their food [is] chiefly oat cakes baked on the griddle and potatoes with their butter milk." Scots, another observer noted, rarely grew vegetables other than potatoes and never kept a garden. Neither the Scots nor the Irish ate as much meat as their forefathers had; as British Celts increasingly were reduced to poverty by their English masters, meat became too expensive for most families to enjoy regularly. But there was no decrease in English willingness to denounce the dietary habits of Celts, who ate at irregular times, prepared too many "coarse" dishes, and were generally "Bad Cooks." English Captain Edward Burt explained to a friend: "I believe you would willing know (being an Englishman) what I had to Eat [in Scotland]. My Fare was a Couple of roasted Hens (as they call them);

10. Fynes Moryson, *An Itinerary: Containing His Ten Yeeres Travell* . . . (4 vols., Glasgow, 1617–18), III:162–63; Lloyd Laing, *Celtic Britain* (New York, 1979), 145; Ian Whyte, *Agriculture and Society in Seventeenth-Century Scotland* (Edinburgh, 1979), 21, 60; Richard Stanihurst, "A Treatise Conteining a Plaine and Perfect Description of Ireland," in *Holinshed's Chronicles of England, Scotland, and Ireland*, comp. Raphaell Holinshed (6 vols., London, 1807–08), VI:67; Thomas Dineley, *Observations in a Voyage through the Kingdom of Ireland . . . in the Year 1681* (Dublin, 1870), 23; John Stevens, *The Journal of John Stevens, Containing a Brief Account of the War in Ireland, 1689–1691*, ed. Robert H. Murray (Oxford, 1912), 138–39; Anon., *A Trip to Ireland, Being a Description of the Coun-* *try, People, and Manners* . . . (London, 1699), 7–8. The Scottish veterinarian James Herriot noted that as late as the 1930s the small farmers of the border-lands between England and Scotland ate little meat other than pork: "they killed a pig or two each year and cured it themselves for home consumption. On the poorer places it seemed to me that they ate little else; whatever meal I happened to stumble in on, the cooking smell was always the same—roasting fat bacon" (James Herriot, *All Creatures Great and Small* [New York, 1972], 446). "Fat bacon" became the mainstay of poor Southerners, white and black, after the antebellum period. See Forrest McDonald and Grady McWhiney, "The South from Self-Sufficiency to Peonage: An Interpretation," *American Historical Review* 85 (1980), 1095–1118.

very poor, new killed, the Skins much broken with plucking; black with Smoke, and greased with bad Butter."[11]

Most Northerners were as prejudiced against southern food as Englishmen were against Celtic food. At home their meals were prepared differently and they were accustomed to eating puddings, soups, lamb, mutton, butter, cheese, fruits, vegetables, and more wheat and other grains besides corn. Carefully tended gardens, rare indeed among Celts and Southerners, appealed strongly to Englishmen and Yankees. At the beginning of the seventeenth century, a visitor reported that in England "meats, milk, butter and cheese adorn even the poor man's table." Breads made from barley, rye, and buckwheat were special favorites; English "close bread" remained "a popular meal" in New England. Antebellum New Englanders generally consumed for "breakfast . . . bread and butter [which they often supplemented with] . . . smoke-dried beef, cheese, or some species of fish or flesh broiled or otherwise fitted to the taste of the family," explained Timothy Dwight, president of Yale College. "Supper . . . is like breakfast, except that it is made up partially of preserved fruits, different kinds of cake, pies, tarts, etc. The meats used at breakfast and supper are generally intended to be dainties. Puddings . . . very frequently constitute a part of the dinner."[12]

11. Richard Pococke, *Pococke's Tour in Ireland in 1752*, ed. George T. Stokes (Dublin, 1891), 87; Edward MacLysaght, *Irish Life in the Seventeenth Century* (1939; reprint, Dublin, 1979), 253–56; L. M. Cullen, *Life in Ireland* (London, 1979), 122–23; Richard Pococke, *Tours in Scotland 1747, 1750, 1760*, ed. Daniel William Kemp (Edinburgh, 1887), 127; Anon., *The Comical Pilgrim; or, Travels of a Cynick Philosopher, Thro' the Most Wicked Parts of the World, Namely England, Wales, Scotland, Ireland, and Holland* (London, 1723), 55; Thomas Somerville quoted in J. G. Fyfe, ed., *Scottish Diaries and Memoirs, 1746–1843* (Stirling, Scotland, 1942), 226–28; James Russell quoted in Fyfe, *Scottish Diaries and Memoirs*, 553; Edward Burt, *Burt's Letters from the North of Scotland*, ed. R. Jamieson (1754; reprint, 2 vols., Edinburgh, 1974), II:64.

12. Thomas Platter, *Thomas Platter's Travels in England, 1599*, trans. Clare Williams (London, 1937), 20, 25, 189; John Chamberlain, *The Chamberlain Letters: A Selection of Letters of John Chamberlain Concerning Life in England from 1597 to 1626*, ed. Elizabeth McClure Thomson (New York, 1965), 61; [Lorenzo Magalotti], *Travels of Cosmo the Third, Grand Duke of Tuscany, through England, During the Reign of King Charles the Second (1669)* (London, 1821), 141–42; Nicholas Blundell, *Blundell's Diary and Letters Book, 1702–1728*, ed. Margaret Blundell (Liverpool, 1952), 55, 183, 216, 237; Samuel Sorbiere, *A Voyage to England, Containing Many Things Relating to that . . . Kingdom* (London, 1709), 9; Henry Purefoy, *Purefoy Letters, 1735–1753*, ed. G. Eland (2 vols., London, 1931), 55; [John Shebbeare], *Letters on the English Nation: By . . . a Jesuit, who Resided Many Years in London* (2 vols., London, 1755), I:266; William Cole, *The Blecheley Diary of the Rev. William Cole, M.A., F.S.A., 1765–67*, ed. Francis Griffin Stokes (London, 1931), 200, 332–35; John Yeoman, *The Diary of the Visits of John Yeoman to London in the Years 1774 and 1777*, ed. MacLeod Yearsley (London, 1934), 20; Dorothy Hartley, *Lost Country Life* (New York, 1979), 52, 173, 231, 274–76; J. C. Drummond and Anne Wilbraham, *The Englishman's Food: A History of Five Centuries of English Diet*

Yankees retained their fondness for wheat as they moved west-ward. In 1851 a man in western New York announced, "*Wheat* is the great staple." Three years earlier a Michigan farmer explained, "the wheat crop [is] our staple"; another farmer estimated that "each individual consumes on the average eight bushels of wheat. . . . The consumption of corn for breadstuff in Michigan does not amount to much, as the people make use of wheat flour for their breadstuff generally."[13]

Celts and Southerners were not nearly as fond of wheat or baked bread as Englishmen and Northerners were. An English officer sta-tioned in seventeenth-century Ireland complained: "None but the best sort [of people] or the inhabitants of the great towns eat wheat, or bread baked in an oven"; indeed, a traveler reported that the Irish "seldom eat . . . bread." "Wheaten bread was scarcely known," re-called an eighteenth-century Scot. And the northern traveler Fred-erick Law Olmsted bewailed the absence of wheat flour throughout much of the South, but he discovered to his delight that the Germans in Texas not only kept clean and comfortable houses but served vegetables and wheat bread to guests rather than bacon and corn pone. In 1849 a visitor to East Tennessee claimed that on the average "a family consisting of six persons of all ages" would consume "forty bushels of Indian corn, twelve of wheat, thirty of Irish and sweet potatoes and turnips, twelve hundred pounds of pork, four hundred pounds of beef, and eight dozen of poultry, besides game and fish, per annum." Even Southerners admitted that they rarely bothered to plant orchards or gardens and paid "but little attention . . . to the making of butter and cheese."[14]

Figures computed from a report of the United States Patent Office in 1848 reveal a sectional difference between the average amount as well as the type of food consumed annually by individuals in ten counties located in New Hampshire, New York, New Jersey, Penn-

---

(London, 1959), 103–17, 185–221; MacLysaght, *Irish Life*, 109; Thomas Crofton Croker, *Researches in the South of Ireland* . . . (1824; reprint, New York, 1969), 103; Earle, *Home Life*, 56, 87, 124, 135, 148, 150, 160, 432–33; William Byrd, *William Byrd's Histories of the Dividing Line Betwixt Virginia and North Carolina* (reprint, Raleigh, 1929), 110; Philippe, *Diary of My Travels*, 110; Timothy Dwight, *Travels in New England and New York*, ed. Barbara Miller Solomon (4 vols., Cambridge, Mass., 1969), IV:249; Edouard de Mon-tule, *Travels in America, 1816–1817*, trans. Edward D. Seeber (Bloomington, 1951), 138.

13. U.S. Patent Office, *Report of the Commissioner of Patents, for the Year 1850*, pt. 2: *Agriculture* (Washington, D.C., 1851), 313; idem, *Annual Report of the Commissioner of Patents for the Year 1848* (Washington, D.C., 1849), 544, 547.

14. Stevens, *Journal*, 139; Moryson, *Itinerary*, III:162; James Russell quoted in Fyfe, *Scottish Diaries and Memoirs*, 553; Olmsted, *Journey through Texas*, 80, 140–47, 149, 167, 178–90, 235–37; J. Balestier to Edmund Burke, January 5, 1849, and S. W. Kellogg to Edmund Burke, November 14, 1848, in U.S. Patent Office, *Report . . . 1848*, 522, 560–61.

IRISH PIGS

From *Punch, or the London Charivari* 10 (1846), 171.

sylvania, Michigan, Ohio, Illinois, and Indiana, and by people in ten counties located in South Carolina, Georgia, Mississippi, Tennessee, and Kentucky. The Southerners who lived in half of these particular counties ate on an average less than a bushel of wheat each per year compared with six bushels eaten by Northerners who lived in the other counties, but Southerners devoured ten bushels of corn per year compared with only two bushels by Northerners. Moreover, Southerners ate an average of six bushels of potatoes (mostly sweet potatoes); Northerners ate fewer than four bushels. Southerners also consumed more beef and pork than Northerners: 120 compared with 108 pounds of beef per person; 173 compared with 51 pounds of pork per person.[15]

While visiting in Celtic areas, Englishmen and Northerners frequently had trouble finding another mainstay of their diet—mutton. A traveler reported that at the beginning of the eighteenth century the English ate ten times as much mutton as beef. Such an estimate seems somewhat excessive, but archaeological digs confirm a traditional English preference for beef and mutton over pork: bones found in one medieval English village were 60 percent mutton, 30 percent beef, and 8 percent pork; bones found in another were 53 percent beef, 31 percent mutton, 13 percent horse meat, and only 3 percent pork. An English officer stationed in seventeenth-century Ireland complained that he could obtain mutton only "very rarely ..., nor was there any bread, except biscuits, even in the Governor's house."[16]

Yankees shared with the English a taste for sheep, which they raised for profit and ate with pleasure. Early in the nineteenth century an Englishman described a typical Yankee farmer, who owned "only one hundred and fifty four acres of land" and lived "in the same house that his English-born grandfather" had built. This man slaughtered for his family's yearly meat supply *"four beeves,"* *"fourteen* fat hogs," and *"forty-six fat sheep!"* Other data confirm the popularity in the North of mutton and beef over pork. In 1860 Alabama contained twenty-three times as many hogs in proportion

15. U.S. Patent Office, *Report . . . 1848*, 660–63.

16. James Beeverell, *The Pleasures of London*, trans. and ed. W. H. Quarrell (1707; reprint, London, 1940), 16; P. L. Drewett, "Excavations at Hadleigh Castle, Essex, 1971–1972," *Journal of the British Archaeological Association*, 3d ser., 38 (1975), 148–50; M. L. Ryder, "Animal Remains from Wharram Percy," *Yorkshire Archaeological Journal* 46 (1974), 50; R. H. Hilton and P. A. Rahty, "Upton, Gloucestershire, 1959–1964," *Transactions of the Bristol and Gloucestershire Archaeological Association* 85 (1966), 139–43; Colin Platt, *Medieval England: A Social History and Archaeology from the Conquest to 1600 A.D.* (New York, 1978), 186–87; Sir Josias Bodley, "A Visit to Lecale, in the County of Down, in the Year 1602–3," in *Illustrations of Irish History and Topography, Mainly of the Seventeenth Century*, comp. C. Litton Falkiner (London, 1904), 330.

to the population as there were in Maine and thirty-six times as many as in Massachusetts. Diners at Boston's Revere House consumed each week seven times as much beef and five times as much mutton as pork. Between 1854 and 1860 a million more sheep than swine were brought into the New York livestock market, and most of the hogs slaughtered and packed there were "sent to other places for consumption."[17]

Even when Northerners ate pork, they prepared it differently than Southerners. "Pork . . . is never converted into bacon," explained a New Englander. "I do not know that I ever saw a flitch of bacon cured in New England in my life. The sides of the hog are here always pickled, and by the New England people are esteemed much superior to bacon."[18]

Traditionally neither Celts nor Southerners liked sheep; in fact, the herding of sheep was forced upon the Irish and the Scots by their English conquerors. A seventeenth-century traveler reported that the Irish "eat common swine's flesh, [but] seldom mutton." As late as the end of the eighteenth century, the Reverend John Graham reported from County Londonderry: "There are few sheep here, [yet] . . . every man . . . keeps a pig, many two or three." Some eighteenth-century Scots despised sheep so much that they designated them "as the property of the wives, being beneath the attention of their husbands; and the lowest fellow would have thought himself dishonored by entering a lyre or assisting at a sheep-shearing." Sheep were equally unpopular in the Old South. "No flocks of sheep . . . appear through all this route," reported a traveler through the South. "The most familiar animal is the swine, which are everywhere present in the forests, by the way side, and rooting around every cabin." In 1850 a South Carolinian informed the commissioner of patents: "My neighbors . . . will not eat mutton." Nor would a slave touch mutton, claimed an Englishman. "Give him his customary rations of bacon and corn meal—mutton he will reject—and he will perform his day's labor cheerfully," insisted John Henry Vessey.[19]

17. Burnaby, *Travels through the Middle Settlements*, 97–98; Earle, *Home Life*, 188–89; Faux, *Memorable Days*, 275; William Cobbett, *A Years Residence in the United States of America [1818–1819]* (reprint, New York, 1969), 70, 347; Paul W. Gates, *The Farmer's Age: Agriculture, 1815–1860* (New York, 1960), 146, 214–17, 247–48; Donald B. Dodd and Wynelle S. Dodd, *Historical Statistics of the South, 1790–1970* (University, Ala., 1973), 2–61; Howard S. Russell, *A Long, Deep Furrow: Three Centuries of Farming in New England* (Hanover, N.H., 1976), 25–27, 152–53, 155, 325–414, 497.

18. Dwight, *Travels*, IV:249.

19. Moryson, *Itinerary*, III:163; William Shaw Mason, ed., *A Statistical Account or Parochial Survey of Ireland, Drawn up from the Communications of the Clergy* (3 vols., Dublin, 1814–19), I:604–05; John Ramsay, *Scotland and Scotsmen in the Eighteenth Century, from the MSS. of John Ramsay, Esq. of Ochteryre,* ed. Alexander Allardyce (2 vols., Edinburgh, 1888), II:408; George Lewis, *Impressions of America . . .* (Edin-

If Englishmen and Northerners dining in Celtic regions missed their usual fare of wheat bread and mutton, they were even more likely to be disappointed when offered something to drink. They were by tradition drinkers of beer and cider. New Englanders were especially fond of cider. President John Adams reportedly "drank a large tankard of hard cider every morning."[20]

Travelers in premodern Ireland, Scotland, and the Old South were much more likely to be served whiskey. Early in the seventeenth century a traveler stated that the Irish "Neither have . . . any beer made of malt and hops; nor yet any ale." Some years later an English officer claimed that the Irish "seldom taste" beer or ale. About the only sure place of finding beer in the Old South was in a German inn or settlement. One German complained that in the South "little beer is drunk." Whiskey was "the region's favorite beverage," a traveler in the South remarked, and it had been the standard drink in Celtic Britain since antiquity. But whiskey was still quite a foreign beverage in eighteenth-century England, uncommon if not unknown to most Englishmen. Of his first taste of whiskey, an English visitor to Ireland in the late eighteenth century wrote: "After supper, I for the first time drank whisky . . . , the taste of which is harsh and austere, and the smell worse than the taste." Also during the eighteenth century an English officer in Scotland reported that he had tasted whiskey for the first time and did not like it.[21]

Englishmen and Northerners who visited Celtic Britain and the Old South usually denounced whiskey and those who drank it. "In all these parts [of Ireland] the drinking of whiskey very much prevails," wrote an Englishman; "they have a notion here that it is the

---

burgh, 1845), 147–48; Wilmot S. Gibbs to Thomas Ewbank, December 16, 1850, in U.S. Patent Office, *Report . . . 1850*, 233; Vessey, *Mr. Vessey of England*, 89. See also [Clinton?], *Winter from Home*, 36; Melville J. Herskovits, *The Myth of the Negro Past* (New York, 1941), 158. Professor Stewart J. Brown of the University of Georgia suggests: "Perhaps the Scottish and Irish hatred of sheep in the American South was a hold-over from the clearances of tenant farmers in Ireland and Scotland to make room for sheep pasture."

20. Moray McLaren, *Understanding the Scots: A Guide for South Britons and Other Foreigners* (New York, 1972), 51; Earle, *Home Life*, 161. See also Platter, *Travels in England*, 20; Timothy Flint, *Recollections of the Last Ten Years*, ed. C. Hartley Grattan (1826; reprint, New

York, 1932), 323; Dwight, *Travels*, IV:249; Montule, *Travels in America*, 180.

21. Moryson, *Itinerary*, III:163; Laing, *Celtic Britain*, 151; Stevens, *Journal*, 139; Stanley Baron, *Brewed in America: A History of Beer and Ale in the United States* (Boston, 1962), 31–87; Philippe, *Diary of My Travels*, 41, 59; Thomas Pennant, *A Tour in Scotland and Voyage to the Hebrides; MDCCLXXII* (London, 1790), 221; McLaren, *Understanding the Scots*, 51; Arthur Young, *Arthur Young's Tour in Ireland (1776–1779)*, ed. Arthur W. Hutton (2 vols., London, 1892), II:147, 152–53; Croker, *Researches*, 228, 229; Thomas Campbell, *A Philosophical Survey of the South of Ireland, in a Series of Letters to John Walkinson, M.D.* (London, 1777), 141–42; Burt, *Letters*, I:163, II:261–62.

"HERE'S TO YOU COLONEL"

From Mrs. Frances M. Trollope, *Domestic Manners of Americans* (London, 1832), facing 151.

wholsomest of spirits; tho' I have reason to think it is the worst of that kind; and has tended very much to debauch and corrupt the common people." In eighteenth-century Scotland "whisky was a bad habit," claimed a contemporary. "At every house it was offered, at every house it must be tasted or offence would be given." Highlanders drank whiskey "like Water," insisted a shocked Englishman. Nor were Southerners different. "I am afraid my brave Tennesseeans indulge too great a fondness for whiskey," wrote a woman from the North. "When I was in Virginia, it was too much whiskey [now] . . . in Tennessee, it is too, too much whiskey!" Earlier an observer reported that backcountry Southerners drank to excess—one Sunday morning a church group consumed two barrels of whiskey before ten o'clock in the morning; "we could hear them firing, hooping, and hollowing like Indians," he wrote. In 1848 a newspaper editor told the commissioner of patents that Cincinnati was "the greatest market in the world for . . . whiskey" and that most of it was sent to the South.[22]

Southerners, like their Celtic ancestors, probably made as much whiskey as they bought; indeed, the illegal manufacturing of whiskey, called moonshining both in Ireland and in the South, has always been a respected activity where Celtic culture prevailed. "Drinking moonshine . . . wasn't thought of as a sin back then," recalled a backcountry southern woman. "I have been told that even the preachers would take a drink now and then. My stepmother said her parents always kept a large barrel of moonshine sitting inside their cabin door, with a cup on a nail above, so anyone, even the small children, could take some whenever they desired. Moonshine whiskey was used a lot for medicine." It was part of their Celtic heritage for Southerners to consider moonshine "both wholesome and harmless." In the eighteenth century Englishman Edward Burt reported that Scots considered whiskey "a very good Remedy in a Fever." They also let children drink whiskey. A Scotswoman recalled seeing a guest take a drink and then give "a little to each of the babies. 'My goodness, child,' said my mother to the wee thing that was trotting by the mother's side, 'doesn't it *bite* you?' 'Ay, but I like the bite,' replied the creature." When Irish writer Brendan Behan was a child his grandmother often let him get drunk. "Whiskey is their favourite beverage," said an observer of the Irish; "they

22. Pococke, *Tour in Ireland*, 63; Elizabeth Grant quoted in Fyfe, *Scottish Diaries and Memoirs*, 491; Burt, *Letters*, II:62; Anne Newport Royall, *Letters from Alabama, 1817–1822*, ed. Lucille Griffith (University, Ala., 1969), 93; Charles Woodmason, *The Carolina Backcountry on the Eve of the Revolution: The Journal and Other Writings of Charles Woodmason, Anglican Itinerant*, ed. Richard J. Hooker (Chapel Hill, 1953), 30 (see also 53, 54, 98–99); Charles Cist to Edmund Burke, n.d., in U.S. Patent Office, *Report . . . 1848*, 643–44.

look on it as wholesome, and some esteem it medicinal: hence, old women administer it to the sick."[23]

The faults that Englishmen and Yankees found in Celtic eating and drinking habits were just part of a long list of complaints they had against Southerners and other Celts.[24] For example, visitors frequently commented unfavorably on what they considered the "barbarous" eating habits of Southerners. These included people "unhesitatingly using the same glass without rinsing it, and often even without throwing away what the preceding drinker had left in the glass," and using a pocket knife to cut food and then, "in public

23. Mason, *Statistical Account . . . of Ireland*, I:121–22; Verna Mae Slone, *What My Heart Wants to Tell* (New York, 1980), 41; Daniel R. Hundley, *Social Relations in Our Southern States*, ed. William J. Cooper, Jr. (1860; new ed., Baton Rouge, 1979), 203; Burt, *Letters*, II:88; Ulick O'Connor, *Brendan Behan* (London, 1979), 19. In 1556 the Englishmen who controlled the Irish Parliament declared it a crime for the native Irish to make whiskey. Great Britain, *The Statutes at Large Passed in the Parliaments Held in Ireland, 1310–1786* (2 vols., Dublin, 1786), I:251. On whiskey making and drinking in Ireland, Scotland, and the Old South, see also Mason, *Statistical Account . . . of Ireland*, I:157, II:324, III:374; Anon., *Ireland in 1804*, ed. Seamus Grimes (1806; reprint, Dublin, 1980), 40–41; Cullen, *Life in Ireland*, 87; Sir John Sinclair, ed., *The Statistical Account of Scotland, 1791–1799* (reprint, 20 vols., East Ardsley, England, 1981), XVII:133–34, 323, 681–82; Martin Martin, *A Description of the Western Islands of Scotland* (1716; reprint, Edinburgh, 1981), 106; Louis Simond, *Journal of a Tour and Residence in Great Britain, During the Years 1810 and 1811* (2 vols., Edinburgh, 1817), II:406; McLaren, *Understanding the Scots*, 50; Declaration of Robert Love, October 8, 1806, Love Family Papers, Winthrop College, Rock Hill, South Carolina; Hundley, *Social Relations*, 226–29; Flint, *Recollections*, 37.

24. Paul Hentzner, *A Journey into England in the Year MDXCVIII*, ed. Horace Walpole (Edinburgh, 1881), 53–54; Cesar de Saussure, *A Foreign View of England in the Reigns of George I & George II: The Letters of Monsieur Cesar de Saussure to His Family*, trans. and ed. Madame Van Muyden (London, 1902), 177; Platter, *Travels in England*, 183; [Magalotti], *Travels of Cosmo the Third*, 484–85; [Shebbeare], *Letters on the English Nation*, I:42; Edward Smith, *Foreign Visitors in England, and What They Have Thought of Us . . .* (London, 1889), 40, 147–48; James Gairdner, ed., *The Paston Letters, A.D. 1422–1509* (6 vols., London, 1904), IV:60; Bodley, "Visit to Lecale," 329; Edmund Hogan, ed., *The Description of Ireland, and the State Thereof as It is at this Present in Anno 1598 . . .* (Dublin, 1878), 246; Mason, *Statistical Account . . . of Ireland*, I:536–37; Leitch Ritchie, *Ireland Picturesque and Romantic* (London, 1838), 30–31; Charles Topham Bowden, *A Tour through Ireland* (Dublin, 1791), 161–62; Constantia Maxwell, ed., *Irish History from Contemporary Sources (1509–1610)* (London, 1923), 376–77; Bierce, *Travels in the Southland*, 51; Barbara Leigh Smith Bodichon, *An American Diary, 1857–8*, ed. Joseph W. Reed, Jr. (London, 1972), 183. See also R. Russell, *North America*, 92–93; John Beste, *The Wabash . . .* (2 vols., London, 1855), I:231–32; Flint, *Recollections*, 45; Philo Tower, *Slavery Unmasked: Being a Truthful Narrative of Three Years' Residence and Journeying in Eleven Southern States . . .* (Rochester, N.Y., 1856), 230; Anne Newport Royall, *Mrs. Royall's Southern Tour . . .* (3 vols., Washington, D.C., 1830–31), I:4; Olmsted, *Journey through Texas*, 18–19, 110; John Hope Franklin, *A Southern Odyssey: Travelers in the Antebellum North* (Baton Rouge, 1976), 163–66; Oscar Handlin, "Yankees," in *Harvard Encyclopedia of American Ethnic Groups*, ed. Stephen Thernstrom (Cambridge, Mass., 1980), 1028.

and without embarassment, cleaning the fingernails and teeth with the same knife."[25]

What seemed to upset many other visitors was not so much what Southerners ate, or how they ate it, but that they somehow acquired an abundance of it with a minimum of effort. One Yankee claimed to have encountered a Southerner who did all his planting on the side of a hill so that "when his pumpkins are ripe and his potatoes dug, all he had to do is to start them and they roll right down into his kitchen." Visitors often seemed amazed that the "lazy" Southerners were not starving. "Took a stroll down through the market," wrote a Northerner visiting Charleston, South Carolina, in January, "and there saw almost all the green vegetables of a northern July." Another Northerner wrote from rural Georgia: "No time in the year but the gardens produce some vegetables; . . . things come up and look as green and flourishing as in New England in the months of May and June." Still another traveler in the South, who found "green vegetables of various kinds and excellent quality . . . abundantly supplied," was surprised to discover that Southerners "generally pay but little attention to such articles, or at best content themselves with securing a supply for their families, though a little care would ensure them almost any supposable quantity, such is the favorable nature of the soil and climate."[26]

The unwillingness of plain Southerners to work hard to produce large surpluses of foodstuffs made them appear strange indeed to such ambitious people as Englishmen and Yankees. They could not understand people who ate poke salad rather than garden-cultivated lettuce, who let their hogs and cattle and chickens find their own food, who saw no reason to toil when trot-lines tended once a day would yield more fish than families could eat. Southerners, exclaimed a foreigner, were too lazy to grow many vegetables; "their indolence makes them prefer what herbs they find growing wild to those that require the least attention to propagate." Life in the Old South was so easy, admitted a disapproving Yankee, that "one could live here forever and dream away his existence as if he were indeed in Mohommed's . . . paradise."[27]

25. Olmsted, *Journey through Texas,* 44, 26; Victor Tixier, *Tixier's Travels . . . [1839–1840],* ed. John Francis McDermott (Norman, Okla., 1940), 43, 38; Matilda Charlotte (Jesse) Fraser Houstoun, *Texas and the Gulf . . .* (Philadelphia, 1845), 129.

26. Lanman, *Adventures in the Wilds,* I:478; Fox Journal, November 1834; [Clinton?], *Winter from Home,* 15; Schopf, *Travels in the Confederation,* II:139; Henry Benjamin Whipple, *Bishop*

*Whipple's Southern Diary, 1843–1844,* ed. Lester B. Shippee (Minneapolis, 1937), 24, 91, 122, 188; Houstoun, *Texas and the Gulf,* 88; Tower, *Slavery Unmasked,* 106; Boggs, *Alexander Letters,* 16; Anon., *Visit to Texas,* 249.

27. [Janet Schaw], *Journal of a Lady of Quality . . . ,* ed. Evangeline Walker Andrews, in collaboration with Charles McLean Andrews (New Haven, Conn., 1921), 174; Whipple, *Southern Diary,* 185.

# Hospitality

Condescension from strangers sometimes riled Southerners enough to make them forget to be hospitable. Anne Royall tells of a visitor in Tennessee who chided the old lady owner of a modest eatery for having no tea, coffee, or wheat bread and who accused the people of being "savages in this country." The lady maintained her "good humour," but a native diner "colored deep" and "asked, with great spirit, 'what country may you call yours, sir?' " The critic replied that he was from the East where people knew how to live and to eat and that he had not, in his own words, " 'seen a bit of victuals fit to eat since I left.' " " 'That is a great pity, sir,' said the other. 'But we, of this country, do not rate ourselves by eating: we rate ourselves by fighting. Would you like to take a shot?' "[28]

That some visitors soon wore out their welcome or otherwise received less than an enthusiastic reception in the Old South, however, in no way refutes the claim of numerous contemporary observers that Southerners were hospitable. In the South the "doors of citizens were open to all decent travellers, and shut to none," insisted a writer. From South Carolina a visitor wrote: "The people here are very hospitable, which is indeed the character of all the Southern States." "Virginians are . . . a lively and ingenuous people, full of kind attentions to those who go among them," declared an Englishman. "The people [in the South] are extremely hospitable," stated a teacher from the North. A traveler in Mississippi discovered that "hospitality is a primitive and cardinal virtue. It is handed down in its old fashioned kindness and profusion, from father to son—and the good old customs of Virginia and Carolina still prevail." A traveler in Florida found that "the society, though comparatively isolated, is distinguished for its refinement and warmhearted hospitality." Even the most ignorant backwoodsmen (people who "had never seen a canal, a railroad, or a steamboat; and all they knew of the North was that Northerners wanted to free all the slaves") "were uniformly kind and obliging."[29]

Various travelers singled out individuals, groups, and places for special praise. "It is said to be a difficult art to make strangers feel perfectly at home," wrote a foreigner, "but to our generous friend at Mobile, . . . nothing seemed to be more easy. I hope it will be some small return for his kindness, to know, that we look back to that

28. Royall, *Letters from Alabama*, 112.

29. Earle, *Home Life*, 396; M. Hall, *Aristocratic Journey*, 208; George William Featherstonhaugh, *Excursion through the Slave States . . .* (2 vols., London, 1844), II:35; Philip Vickers Fithian, *Journal & Letters of Philip Vickers Fithian, 1773–1774: A Planta-* tion *Tutor of the Old Dominion*, ed. Hunter Dickinson Farish (1943; reprint, Charlottesville, 1968), 39; John F. H. Claiborne, "A Trip through the Piney Woods [1841]," *Mississippi Historical Society Publications* 9 (1906), 488; Lanman, *Adventures in the Wilds*, II:107, 129.

period as the most comfortable of any which we passed in the United States." One foreigner spoke of the "great deal of hospitality" bestowed upon him in Charleston; another said it "would be difficult to find in the United States or elsewhere a more agreeable or hospitable people than those of Charleston." Similar views were expressed by a traveler about the people of Huntsville, Alabama. "I entered Huntsville a stranger," he noted, "and took lodgings at its best hotel, which was comfortable, but by no means luxurious. Its reputation was not good, however, and this circumstance, in spite of my earnest excuses, caused me to become the guest of one of the leading families of the town, under whose roof I have been made to feel perfectly at home, and where I have been treated more like an old friend than a stranger. This is the way they treat pilgrims in Alabama."[30]

Planters, of course, were renowned for their hospitality. "Much has been said in praise of the hospitality of the southern planter," proclaimed an Englishman, "but they alone who have traveled in the southern states, can appreciate the perfect ease and politeness with which a stranger is made to feel himself at home. Horses, carriages, boats, servants, are all at his disposal. Even his little comforts are thought of, and every thing is done as heartily and naturally as if no obligation were conferred." Another visitor wrote that "with regard to the much-talked-of hospitality of the wealthier classes in the South, I can only say that my own experience ought to make me very eloquent in their praise. Not only does the genuine feeling exist here, but a Southern gentleman gives you such expression to his feeling by his home-like treatment of you, that to be truly hospitable you might imagine had been the principal study of his life."[31]

Planters often gave the impression that nothing meant more to them than having visitors to entertain. One account claimed that frequently "Negroes were stationed at the planter's gate where it opened on the post-road or turnpike, to hail travellers and assure them of a hearty welcome at the 'big house up younder.' " A tutor on a southern plantation recalled: "Seldom a day passed that some one did not call, and frequently a carriage-load would arrive to spend the day; for Southern people have not much idea of driving ten or fifteen miles for a twenty-minutes' call. Perhaps they came for 'a few days,' but were always welcome, however unexpected." In the rural South, observed a contemporary, a visitor "will ever find a

30. B. Hall, *Travels*, III:317; Fox Journal, November 1834; Alexander Mackay, *The Western World* . . . (3 vols., London, 1849), II:183; Lanman, *Adventures in the Wilds*, II:154.

31. Sir Charles Lyell, *A Second Visit to the United States* . . . (2 vols., New York, 1849), I:245; Lanman, *Adventures in the Wilds*, I:458–59.

much heartier welcome, a warmer shake of the hand, a greater desire to please, and less frigidity of deportment, than will be found in any walled town upon the earth's circumference." And an Englishman acknowledged: "there is a warm and generous openness of character in the southerners, which mere wealth and a retinue of servants cannot give; and they have often a dignity of manner without stiffness, which is most agreeable."[32]

Visitors related numerous examples of southern hospitality. "I have reason to speak gratefully of the courtesy and civility of the Texans," wrote an Englishwoman; "they are, moreover, so genuinely kind." She claimed that "every house . . . is open to the traveller, and no one is ever turned from the door of a dweller in the wilderness without a shelter and a meal." A foreigner told of how kindly Southerners treated a sick farmer who had caught "the bilious fever, and then the jaundice and ague" while returning on foot from New Orleans to his home in Ohio: "This sick moneyless stranger is, it appears, on his way back to Chillicothe, and is very humanely sent on by the stage, free of all expense, and is received and fed at every tavern with gratuitous kindness. Even my driver gave him, this day, a dollar." A Northerner and his traveling companion stopped at the "log-hut" of a backcountry Southerner who treated them "very hospitably; . . . he set before us a most acceptable repast of fish, ham, eggs, and coffee, for which he would not hear of receiving compensation." An Englishman observed that the "treatment in the southern states of governesses, who usually come from the North or from England, is very kind and considerate. They are placed on a much greater footing of equality with the family in which they live, than in England. Occasionally we find that the mother of the children has staid at home, in order that the teacher may take her turn, and go out to a party." A Northerner stated that in the South, "a man of decent appearance and civil deportment will always be kindly and respectfully received. So long as he behaves like a gentleman, he will receive the treatment due his character; his privacy will not be interrupted, his feelings hurt, or his peace disturbed."[33]

All this, of course, was in keeping with Celtic tradition; indeed, descriptions of entertainment of friends and visitors in the Old South are virtually interchangeable with those of how guests were

32. Earle, *Home Life*, 396; Catherine C. Hopley, *Life in the South From the . . . Spring of 1860 to August 1862* (1863; reprint, 2 vols., New York, 1974), I:82–83; Hundley, *Social Relations*, 57–58; Lyell, *Second Visit*, I:245. See also Robert Hunter, Jr., *Quebec to Carolina in 1785–1786 . . .* , ed. Louis B. Wright and Marion Tinling (San Marino, Calif., 1943), 229.

33. Houstoun, *Texas and the Gulf*, 127, 226; Matilda Charlotte (Jesse) Fraser Houstoun, *Hesperos: or, Travels in the West* (2 vols., London, 1850), II:138; Faux, *Memorable Days*, 189; Hoffman, *Winter in the West*, II:171; Lyell, *Second Visit*, I:223–24; F. Hall, *Letters from the East and West*, 113–14.

treated in premodern Ireland, Scotland, and Wales. Consider this account of a week's entertainment: "Coverlets being prepared, morn and even, . . . Wines, newly-opened, being drunk, . . . [hogs and beefs] on spits, . . . tables [full of food]; . . . Companies [of guests] coming to the . . . mansion . . . [people] discoursing uproariously. A fragrant odour issuing in strength. . . . Airs being played harmoniously. . . . The doors wide open. . . . Waxlights blazing from every wall and chamber, Every moment fresh casks being opened for the multitude, With no ebb in the . . . feast. . . . Strong steeds . . . racing. . . . The loud cry of the chase on the sides of the misty hills." This might well be a report on the party of any antebellum southern planter, but it is the account by the Irish poet Egan O'Rahilly of how Daniel O'Callaghen of County Cork, one of Ireland's "big house" gentry, entertained in the eighteenth century.[34]

Most of the Irish "gentlemen live in the country in a very hospitable way," wrote an Englishman in the 1760s; any gentleman considered it "a disgrace to a man to have a lock or key to his outward door or anything more than a latch to his buttery or cellar," and it was "the fashion in Ireland to keep near double the number of servants for what gentlemen of the same rank and fortune keep in England." A visitor explained that there were "no hotels or lodging houses" outside Ireland's main towns: "Every traveller sets up in the first house he meets, and there is provided with whatever he desires, gratuitously. Table is not usually laid until evening, but in the meantime drink is not denied travellers."[35]

Hospitality simply was a way of life in premodern Ireland. "The lady of the house meets you with her trayne," recalled a visitor at an Irish country home in the seventeenth century. "Salutations paste, you shall be presented with all the drinkes in the house, . . . you must not refuse. . . . The fyre is prepared in the middle of the hall, where you may sollace yourselfe till supper time, you shall not want sacke and tobacco. By that time the table is spread and plentifully furnished with variety of meates, but ill cooked, and without sauce. . . . Towards the middle of supper, the harper beginns to tune and singeth Irish rymes of auncient making. If he be a good rymer, he will make one song to the present occasion. Supper being ended, it is at your liberty to sit up, or to depart to your lodgeing, you shall have company in both kind. When you come to your chamber, do not expect canopy and curtaynes. It is very well if your bedd content you, and if the company be greate, you may happen to be bodkin in the middle. In the morning there will be brought unto you a cupp

34. Daniel Corkery, *The Hidden Ireland: A Study of Gaelic Munster in the Eighteenth Century* (1924; reprint, Dublin, 1979), 51–52. See also Mac-Lysaght, *Irish Life*, 81–127.

35. Edward Willes to the Earl of Warwick, ca. 1764, in *Aspects of Irish Social History, 1750–1800*, ed. W. H. Crawford and B. Trainor (Belfast, 1969), 2; Maxwell, *Irish History*, 320.

AN IRISH GENTRY "BIG HOUSE"

From J. N. Brewer, *The Beauties of Ireland* (London, 1825),
unnumbered page.

of aquavitae [whiskey]. The aquavitae or usquebath of Ireland is not such an extraction, as is made in England, but farre more qualifyed. . . . It is a very wholesome drink, and naturall to digest the crudityes of the Irish feeding. You may drink a knaggin without offence, that is the fourth parte of a pynte. Breakfast is but the repetitions of supper. When you are disposing of yourself to depart, they call for Dogh or dores, that is, to drink at the doore, there you are presented agayne with all the drinkes in the house."[36]

Nor were the Irish common folk less gracious than the gentry. "Every unprejudiced traveller who visits them will be as much pleased with their cheerfulness [and] . . . their hospitality," wrote a visitor in the 1770s. "The people [of Ireland appear] . . . very kind, according to their ability, to the distressed and wandering poor," concluded a contemporary observer, "hardly ever refusing to such, food of whatever kind they have themselves, or a night's lodging in their houses." Another contemporary noted that the Irish "peasant who volunteers to open a gate, break down a ditch, and perhaps go three miles out of his way to oblige a stranger, can hardly be suspected of any design in taking so much trouble for one whom he never saw before, nor ever expects to see again, particularly as he parts him with as much civility, when he gets nothing but thanks, as when half-a-crown is put into his hand. Neither can they be suspected of insincerity in keeping open houses for all strangers, dividing their potatoes and milk with the wanderer, and taking him to sleep under the same blanket with themselves and their children." More than one writer noted that the "poorest peasant will freely offer to share his cabin and divide his potatoes with you"; in fact, Thomas Croker spoke of the "national spirit of hospitality" in Ireland. Any visitor to the most "miserable and destitute" of Irish hovels, he insisted, "is confident of receiving shelter and every rite of hospitality as far as it is in the power of the inmates to bestow them. He is welcomed to the best seat the cabin affords, the largest potatoe is selected from the dish and placed before him, and that 'reserve towards strangers which alike characterize the Englishman and his mastiff,' is unknown. This hospitality is not confined solely to the cottage, but seems a national trait, which those who have visited the country, whatever may be their condition, are bound in gratitude to acknowledge."[37]

36. Luke Gernon, "A Discourse of Ireland, Anno 1620," in Falkiner, *Illustrations of Irish History*, 360–61.

37. A. Young, *Tour in Ireland*, II:156; Mason, *Statistical Account . . . of Ireland*, II:324, 457; Croker, *Researches*, 30, 327, 226. See also [Herman Ludwig Heinrich], *Tour in England, Ireland, and France in the Years 1826, 1827, 1828,* *and 1829* (Philadelphia, 1833), 326; Anon., *Letters from an Armenian in Ireland, to His Friends at Trebisond, &c.*, trans. Edmond S. Pery (London, 1757), 247; Bowden, *Tour through Ireland*, 250; Mason, *Statistical Account . . . of Ireland*, I:318, II:131–32, 363, III:25, 244, 271, 321–22.

# Hospitality

The premodern Welsh and Scots enjoyed a reputation equal to the Irish for hospitality. In Wales, noted an authority, "when guests came to stay they took up their residence for months at a time." A visitor described how a Welshman "most courteously desired us to walk in, and partake of such fare as his humble roof could afford, entreating us not to feel embarrassed, as he had a spare room double-beded, and could accommodate our guide and the horses." An eighteenth-century visitor to western Scotland wrote: "The people are in general extremely hospitable." Daniel Defoe reported in the 1720s that "the Highland chiefs" welcomed travelers "with good treatment, and great hospitality." A Frenchman insisted that the hospitality of Scotland far surpassed that of England. "For myself, as a traveller," he wrote, "I infinitely prefer the wild huts of the Highlands, where the stranger is always welcome, to those farms [of England] which are so *comfortable*, that we can hardly see any thing but the outside." John Ramsay claimed that up through the eighteenth century any traveler in Scotland, and especially in the Highlands, was greeted "with hospitality worthy of the patriarchal or heroic kind"; just "being a stranger entitles him to a kind reception, provided he comes not to molest or disposses the old inhabitants. . . . He will hardly pass a cottage without being offered something to eat or drink."[38]

While visiting in Scotland Washington Irving heard an apocryphal yet marvelous story that illustrates Scottish hospitality. A family, "famous for good living," maintained a continuous "open house" and a "punch bowl of mighty dimensions [that] was never suffered to be empty and all comers were welcome—the family relieved each other and there was a perpetual session." One day a stranger rode up, gave his horse to a servant, and went in to "refresh himself." He "liked the cheer" so much that "there he sat—day after day, month after month—year after year—until taking umbrage at something that occurred—he called a servant & ordered his horse." "Your honor," replied the servant, "your steed has been dead these three years."[39]

Rustic Southerners were no less hospitable than their Irish and

38. Sir Leonard Twiston Davies and Averyl Edwards, *Welsh Life in the Eighteenth Century* (London, 1939), 25; [Richard Fenton], *A Tour in Quest of Genealogy, through Several Parts of Wales, Somersetshire, and Wiltshire . . .* (London, 1811), 330; Pococke, *Tours in Scotland*, 128; Daniel Defoe, *A Tour through the Whole Island of Great Britain [1724–1726]*, ed. Pat Rogers (New York, 1971), 669; L. A. Necker de Saussure, *Travels in Scotland: Descriptive of the State of Manners, Literature, and Science* (London, 1821), 57; Ramsay, *Scotland and Scotsmen*, II:397, 399. See also Joseph Farington, *The Farington Diary,* ed. James Grieg (3d ed., 2 vols., New York, 1923), I:330; [Benjamin Silliman], *A Journal of Travels in England, Holland and Scotland . . .* (2 vols., New York, 1810), II:338, 341; Burt, *Letters*, II:268–69; Pococke, *Tours in Scotland*, 117; Ramsay, *Scotland and Scotsmen*, II:398.

39. Washington Irving, *Tour in Scotland, 1817, and Other Manuscript Notes,* ed. Stanley T. Williams (New Haven, Conn., 1927), 35–36.

Scottish ancestors had been. A visitor called hospitality in the South "a universal virtue"; another insisted that the "frankness, generosity, . . . [and] hospitality" of Southerners were in "perfect contrast to the Yankee character"; and still another claimed that all Southerners "enjoy themselves, and like to see their friends do so." "That the [southern] mountaineers are poor," noted a traveler, "is a matter of course, and the majority of their cabins are cheerless places indeed to harbor the human frame for life; but the people are distinguished for their hospitality, and always place before the stranger the choicest of their store." "During my jaunt [in the South]," wrote another sojourner, "I have entered freely the meanest habitations, and conversed familiarly with the most indigent of the people; but never have I received a rude nor an indecorous reply. When I approached the door of the rudest hut, I was invited to enter, a seat was handed me, and if the family was eating, I was pressed to partake of their meal. However homely their fare might be, they neither seemed ashamed to offer nor unwiling to share it." A traveler who spent a night in a humble Kentucky cabin reported: "The lad to whom we had been indebted for a night's shelter made every possible apology, the next morning, for our meager entertainment, by pleading extreme poverty; notwithstanding which, we found it very difficult to force any remuneration upon him."[40]

The refusal of a Southerner to take money for doing a favor was typical. A French traveler, who mistook the hospitality of a Southerner for the obsequiousness of an entrepreneur, explained: "We were planning to stock up there, but next morning he informed us that he was by no means an innkeeper, that he never accepted money, and that he insisted nevertheless on furnishing us with supplies. We accepted only a flitch of bacon, and he guaranteed that we would find none so good on our journey." Another sojourner in the South described being ferried across a river by a "half-naked, ill-looking" Southerner: "His Cabin was of the meanest kind, consisting of a single apartment, constructed of logs, which contained a family of seven or eight souls, and every thing seemed to designate him as a new and unthrifty settler. After drinking a bowl of milk, which I really called for by way of excuse for paying him a little for ferrying me over the water, to which he good humouredly replied, that he 'never took money for helping a traveller on his way.' 'Then let me

40. Lyell, *Second Visit*, II:73; James Silk Buckingham, *The Slave States of America* (2 vols., London, 1842), I:288; G. Lewis, *Impressions of America*, 184; A. Mackay, *Western World*, II:74; Philip Henry Gosse, *Letters from Alabama . . .* (London, 1859), 250; Sir Richard George Augustus, *Echoes from the Backwoods . . .* (2 vols., London, 1846), II:61–62; Lanman, *Adventures in the Wilds*, I:457; F. Hall, *Letters from the East and West*, 123; Hoffman, *Winter in the West*, II:182–84.

pay you for your milk.' 'I never sell milk.' 'But,' said I, urging him, 'I would rather pay you, I have money enough.' 'Well,' said he, 'I have milk enough, so we're even; I have as good a right to give you milk, as you have to give me money.' "[41]

Celtic hospitality was more spontaneous than planned. It was easy enough for British Celts and Southerners to share what they had with their guests because that was what their forefathers had done; one part of their tradition, an eighteenth-century Scotswoman explained, was "to please your company." "The people of the southern states are generally much more hospitable than northerners," declared a Yankee, "and this difference must be attributed mainly to the fact that they are not such a money loving people. You do not see that low mean cupidity, that base selfishness so striking a characteristic of one portion of our restless Yankee brethren." A typical Southerner was the man who "all but forced us to come home with him," explained a traveler, "assuring us that we would find no tolerable inn. . . . He lives . . . in a setting that would be lovely if the land were cleared; but, although he has six sons and several Negroes, he settles for what he cleared when he first arrived. And yet he has 3,000 acres here. I do not know what he and his sons do all day." Probably they did little more than enjoy themselves and tend to their guests. That seemed to many observers to be the way Southerners—planters and plain folk—occupied their time. John Claiborne found backcountry Southerners "ever ready to welcome the wayfarer to their hospitable firesides"; "if you are disposed to be convivial," he declared, "you may dine with some one . . . every day." Rosalie Roos, a Swedish tutor in the household of a rice planter, described a party she attended along with the planter and his family. The hosts were a family of local "Crackers," yet all the neighbors, rich and poor alike, were there and they ate and danced throughout "the whole night."[42]

At the end of the eighteenth century Alexander Campbell offered an explanation for the Celtic commitment to hospitality. This Scot believed that Celts would remain hospitable just as long as they remained Celts—that is, only so long as there was a recognizable Celtic personality: "A natural warmth of temper, a strong tincture of family pride, a love of shew and pleasure, and a thirst almost insatiable for distinction. . . . Inflexible, and ever in extremes, his soul glows fervently in friendship, or rages in unextinguishable

41. Philippe, *Diary of My Travels*, 99; F. Hall, *Letters from the East and West*, 123–24.

42. Elizabeth Mure quoted in Fyfe, *Scottish Diaries and Memoirs*, 75; Whipple, *Southern Diary*, 30; Philippe, *Diary of My Travels*, 52; Claiborne, "Trip through the Piney Woods," 509, 520, 529, 532–35; Rosalie Roos, *Travels in America, 1851–1855*, ed. Carl L. Anderson (Carbondale, Ill., 1982), 97–98.

hatred. A perfect savage in his desires and aversions, he knows no bounds to his resentment, no limits to his love; and he rarely turns his back either on a friend or a foe." Campbell claimed that such people still could be found—"in the woods of America," in the "mountains of Wales," in "the highlands of Scotland"—but not in many other places. "The more remote from the busy world, and the more ignorant of the comforts of civil society as established in great cities, and other parts that have imbibed the spirit of trade or commerce, the more do the affections which indicate innocent hilarity, equanimity, and all the amiable qualities of uncontaminated respect for sincerity, truth, strict honour, and a due observance of whatever is fit, just, and right, diffuse their influence over even the most trivial occurrence of domestic intercourse. Hence, the hospitality we so much admire among a rude and simple people, such as the Welsh peasantry, or those of the highlands of Scotland [is rapidly vanishing]."[43]

43. Alexander Campbell, *A Journey from Edinburgh through Parts of North* *Britain* . . . (2 vols., London, 1802), I:258–59.

# V

# *Pleasures*

"THE slave States are proverbial for their amusements," noted a disapproving Yankee, who stated that Southerners "are seldom taught to labor, or to engage in any kind of business. Life is to them but a play-day, and the question of every morning is—how to kill time?" In the antebellum South, insisted a foreigner, "man's love of pleasure is the equal of that in any part of the world." Other travelers contrasted the different attitudes toward diversion in the North and the South. "The southerner very often prosecutes his amusements as actively as the northerner engages in sterner occupations," stated a European. "In one section the people are in the habit of curbing their passions," another man observed, "and refraining from those pleasures which are inconvenient or expensive; in the other, they are more accustomed to indulge the propensities of their nature." Frederick Law Olmsted put it more bluntly. "The people of the Northern States, as a whole, probably enjoy life less than any other civilized people," he contended. "Perhaps it would be equally true to add—or than any uncivilized people." Southern lavishness appalled good Yankees. One wrote from the South: "A most sinful feast again!" Another said of a ball in Mobile that cost $3,000: "Money poorly spent & worse than wasted."[1]

Wherever visitors went in the Old South they commented on the prominence of entertainment in social life. A traveler claimed that

1. Charles G. Parsons, *Inside View of Slavery: or, a Tour Among the Planters* (Cleveland, 1855), 98; Edouard de Montule, *Travels in America, 1816–1817,* trans. Edward D. Seeber (Bloomington, 1951), 85; Frederick Hall, *Letters from the East and from the West* (Washington, D.C., 1840), 244; Alexander Mackay, *The Western World . . .* (3 vols., London, 1849), II:134; Frederick Law Olmsted, *The Cotton Kingdom: A Traveller's Observations on Cotton and Slavery . . . ,* ed. Arthur M. Schlesinger (new ed., New York, 1953), 560; Alice Morse Earle, *Home Life in Colonial Days* (reprint, Middle Village, N.Y., 1975), 160; Henry Benjamin Whipple, *Bishop Whipple's Southern Diary, 1843–1844,* ed. Lester B. Shippee (Minneapolis, 1937), 93.

Mobile society was "very gay and to a certain extent dissipated. . . . Many young men come here every winter . . . and leaving behind them the restraints of home they become dissipated & rush madly to destruction." Another visitor pointed out that the "people of Charleston live rapidly, not willingly letting go untasted any of the pleasure of this life. Few of them therefore reach a great age." Observers found the citizens of New Orleans devoted to "pleasure,"[2] those of Savannah "very dissipated," and sections in nearly every southern town that offered liquor, sporting women, and—as one man said of Natchez—"wonderful games of brag and poker."[3]

Even so, Southerners sometimes complained. "I was in Raleigh last week and spent some time with Frank," wrote a North Carolinian in 1829; "he is at nothing scarcely there. . . . He is as lounging as ever and as indifferent to the ladies as usual, seems he will never marry, for fear of having *forty children* and rails at Raleighs being so ill provided with ladies of another stamp, viz of pleasure."[4]

Backcountry Crackers were just as committed to amusements as townsfolk. A traveler stated that in western Virginia "drunkeness, horse-racing, and cock-fighting" were the popular "pursuits"; another man reported that "drinking [is] . . . more openly practised and encouraged in the . . . South than at the North." A Southerner discovered much less interest in horse racing and similar amusements in the North than in the South, and hardly a fourth as much "tippling." It distressed a northern woman to find so many "*Doggeries*" in the South—places "where spirituous liquors are sold; and where men get drunk, quarrel, and fight, as often as they choose." A visitor in Arkansas wrote: "The love of amusements . . . is carried to extravagance, particularly gambling, and dancing parties or balls." Of Mississippians, a traveler observed: "The men are generally idle, devoted to hunting, and the attention of their numerous herds, while their slaves till the ground. The poorer sort . . . are fond of drinking, gambling, and horse racing. From these sports quarrels often arise, which are sometimes ended by the dirk or pistol. The rich are fond of the same sports, and frequently when their imaginary honour is insulted, a duel ends the strife." One Yankee believed that "gambling and fighting" were two of the South's favorite amusements

2. Whipple, *Southern Diary,* 90; Johann David Schopf, *Travels in the Confederation [1783–1784]* . . . , trans. and ed. Alfred J. Morrison (new ed., 2 vols., New York, 1968), II:216; Charles Lanman, *Adventures in the Wilds* . . . (2 vols., Philadelphia, 1856), II:201.

3. Whipple, *Southern Diary,* 73; William Kingsford, *Impressions of the West and South during a Six Weeks' Holiday* (Toronto, 1858), 46.

4. George Little to William G. Harding, April 23, 1829, Harding and Jackson Family Papers, Southern Historical Collection, University of North Carolina, Chapel Hill.

(fighting, which is treated in Chapter VI, was certainly as popular with Southerners as drinking, gambling, and other diversions).[5]

Many Southerners were accused of having an unrestrained appetite for pleasure. A Georgian acknowledged that "pleasure & dissipation seem . . . entirely to have engrossed the minds of the young. . . . Music, painting, dancing are almost the sole studies—& even these they acquire in such a very superficial way as to be of no service." Another Southerner described the "whiskey-swilling snobs and bullies"; such an individual indulged "in cards, and wine, and loose women," and cared for nothing "but his daily drams, his cocktails, and brandy-straights, his pistols and his cards, his dogs and his sooty mistress." If rich, the bully first "collects his stock of liquors" and then "proceeds immediately to gather about him a set of boon companions like himself—idle loafers . . . ; and now he devotes his nights to gaming, drinking, and coarse libertinism, and his days to fox-hunting, horse-racing, and the like." He believed that it was "*distingue* to get drunk. He reads how that the old Cavaliers were wont in ancient times never to rise from the dinner-table sober, and damme, Sir, he intends to live like the *bloods* did in the good ole times. Egad, he would hang your temperance folks, Sir, and send all your cold-water fools to the devil!"[6]

Not all Southerners overindulged their taste for pleasure, but the temptation was strong. "Young men & young women have nothing to do," asserted a Yankee visitor to the South, "& the theater, the billiard table, the drinking saloon, the horse race, the cock fight, are but so many ways devised to . . . prevent life from becoming a burden." Another man claimed that "the Southern Gentleman had little else to do than fox-hunt, drink, attend the races, fight chicken-cocks, and grievously lament that he was owner of a large horde of

---

5. David W. Mitchell, *Ten Years in the United States* . . . (London, 1862), 195; Paul Ravesies, *Scenes and Settlers of Alabama* (Mobile, 1885), 19; Thomas C. DeLeon, *Four Years in Rebel Capitals* . . . , ed. E. B. Long (new ed., New York, 1962), 40–44; William Charles Macready, *The Diaries of William Charles Macready, 1833–1851*, ed. William Toynbee (2 vols., London, 1912), II:265–66; John O'Connor, *Wanderings of a Vagabond* . . . , ed. John Morris (New York, 1873), 460–62; Whipple, *Southern Diary*, 87; James Silk Buckingham, *The Slave States of America* (2 vols., London, 1842), I:286–87; John Hope Franklin, *A Southern Odyssey: Travelers in the Antebellum North* (Baton Rouge, 1976), 197; Anne Newport Royall, *Letters from Alabama, 1817–1822*, ed. Lucille Griffith (University, Ala., 1969), 228; Thomas Ashe, *Travels in America* . . . (London, 1809), 95; Thomas Nuttall, *A Journal of Travels into the Arkansas Territory* . . . (Philadelphia, 1821), 111; James Pearse, *A Narrative of the Life of James Pearse* . . . (Rutland, Vt., 1825), 52; Parsons, *Inside View*, 98.

6. Marion Alexander Boggs, ed., *The Alexander Letters, 1787–1900* (Athens, Ga., 1980), 41; Daniel R. Hundley, *Social Relations in Our Southern States*, ed. William J. Cooper, Jr. (1860; new ed., Baton Rouge, 1979), 44, 243, 244, 166.

savages whom he knew not how to dispose of." A diarist described what seems to have been a typical evening in some southern homes: "Company here last night. . . . Mr. Frazer & Myself played Whist and danced untill 12 oClock, Mr. Heely playing the Fidle & dancing. We drank one bottle of rum in time. Mr. Frazer verry sick after they went home." Another diarist, who traveled through Tennessee early in the nineteenth century as an Indian agent and later represented Alabama in Congress, left a clear record of his enjoyment. He spent days "eating and drinking with . . . friends" and attended all sorts of gatherings—a "Green Corn dance," a "Ball play," a "Hop," a "Ball . . . graced with the presence of Col. [Aaron] Burr"—where the diarist frequently drank or danced or did both. He seemed especially fond of celebrations including "a Barbacue at the Folly—which wound up in the evening with something like a quarrel."[7]

Southerners always appeared ready to entertain or to be entertained. "We have been so much in a constant flutter among the butterflys of Savannah, that I begin to feel like one myself," declared a woman from rural Georgia. "The ladies in Savannah seem at a loss how to kill time. . . . They therefore overload us with civilities, and draw us into parties which they justly think will excite our astonishment. Luxury and extravagance is carried to a greater excess than I ever expected. . . . We hear ladies with families of small children boasting of having been out to parties 10 nights in succession until after midnight, and sometimes until 3 o'clock in the morning; and that they had not seen their husbands for a week." At one party, which some three hundred guests attended, "every room in a large house was newly furnished for the occasion, the beds etc. sent out; refreshments handed round from garret to cellar through the night to guests, who were mostly standing and 'delightfully squeezed to death.' How delightful!" The numerous "grand dinners" followed by "balls, where all the beauty of the country was assembled," amazed some visitors. A Southerner recalled that "dinners & balls were the bright events, . . . but more characteristic of the hospitality . . . was the practically ceaseless entertainment of neighbors who came in unannounced beforehand, to spend the day & dine, or to spend the night & the forenoon of the next day. Nobody was in a hurry."[8]

How different was life in the North where the pace was so much

7. Parsons, *Inside View,* 135; Hundley, *Social Relations,* 30; John Harrower, *The Journal of John Harrower, An Indentured Servant in the Colony of Virginia, 1773-1776,* ed. Edward Miles Riley (Williamsburg, Va., 1963), 120; John McKee Diary, April 1, 25, May 1, 25, July 4, August 23, 26, December 28, 1804, February 23, May 28, July 4, 27, 1805, Southern Historical Collection, University of North Carolina, Chapel Hill.

8. Boggs, *Alexander Letters,* 49, 51; George A. McCall, *Letters from the Frontiers* . . . (Philadelphia, 1868), 275; John Witherspoon DuBois, "Recollections of the Plantation," *Alabama Historical Quarterly* 1 (1930), 112.

faster and time was reckoned as money. After visiting a New England factory, a Southerner concluded that Yankees overworked, and this produced a certain "degradation" throughout the North. A foreign observer agreed. He insisted that the "expression on faces in the North as contrasted with those of the South tell a strange, and to me an unexpected story, as regards the greatest happiness principle of the greatest number! Of course, it must be borne in mind that no rules are without exception; but, oh, the haggard faces I have seen in the Northern States. . . . Nothing like simplicity, even among children after ten years of age—hot-house, forced impetuous beings, the almighty dollars, the incentive and only guide to activity and appreciation."[9]

Observers also noted a striking contrast between the activities and manners of Southerners and those of Northerners. "Proceeding towards the South," wrote a European traveler in 1855, "I find the manners soften as well as the voice, more frankness and cheerfulness: the rather stiff formality of the Northern States is replaced by ease, and at the same time the young people are merry without being boisterous, and no one objects to those games and amusements which the spirit of the puritanical times has handed down as crimes to . . . their New England descendants." Of all Americans, claimed another observer, "the Southerners appear to the most advantage, & the New-Englanders to the least; the ease & frank courtesy of the gentry of the South (with an occasional touch of arrogance, however) contrasting favourably with the cautious, somewhat gauche, & too deferential air of the . . . [people] from the North." Many travelers testified to what one man called the Southerner's "easy but unobtrusive and manly manner." A Yankee confessed that Southerners possessed "a kind of courtliness of behavior which is not seen in the free communities of the Northern States." And a Southerner, visiting in Connecticut, noted that "the inhabitants possess neither the refinements of hypocritical politeness, nor the warm feelings of country hospitality."[10]

Observers claimed that Southerners and Northerners were easily distinguishable by what they did with their time. Southerners loved their sensual pleasures; Northerners disdained amusements for more practical pastimes. A New Yorker reported that on a boat trip southern men and women played cards, took tobacco, rocked in their chairs, and talked, while northern men and women read. An Englishwoman compared two groups of women kept indoors by bad

9. A Virginian, "One Day of a Foot Tour in Connecticut," *Southern Literary Messenger* 14 (1848), 384; Amelia Matilda Murray, *Letters from the United States, Cuba and Canada* (New York, 1856), 199–200.

10. Charles Fenno Hoffman, *A Winter in the West* (2 vols., New York, 1835), II:295; Thomas Low Nichols, *Forty Years of American Life* (2 vols., London, 1864), I:223; W. C. Cummings quoted in J. H. Franklin, *Southern Odyssey*, 187.

weather: "the weary listless manner of the Southern ladies, who were lounging about, taking snuff, and scolding their unfortunate children," contrasted sharply with "some Northern ladies, also saloon bound, for nearly two weeks, but ever busy with their books and pencils." In the opinion of a Yankee, "the education of the southern female is greatly deficient" because it only trained her "to shine in fashionable life. But . . . a young man who has nothing in the world to depend on except his industry & energy had better select for himself a partner who is a 'help meet' & not a 'help eat.' "[11]

Southerners were too impractical for such advice; neither economic recessions nor distance deterred them from their amusements. "The holidays have been very gay," reported a Southerner in 1857, "hard times do not affect the people's spir[i]ts." Backcountry North Carolinians regularly traveled thirty miles or more to attend parties, announced a visitor; "the entertainments are great, and the whole scene pleasant and diverting; but if they can get musick to indulge this mirth, it greatly adds to the pleasure of the feast." An Alabamian traveled two hundred miles round trip in 1855 to attend a fair in Montgomery, which he proclaimed "quite successful, going beyond the most sanguine expectations." And a visitor in colonial North Carolina claimed that it was "common for people to come and go from this province to Virginia, to . . . publick diversions."[12]

Like their Celtic forebears, Southerners enjoyed seeing and being seen as well as hearing and being heard; the visual, oral, and aural pleasures delighted them. What one observer said of the eighteenth-century Irish—"Ostentation is certainly a prominent feature in the Irish character. . . . Nor is this ostentation confined to the higher walks of life; every where may be traced marks of a desire to make an appearance"—another noted in the elaborate dress of southern slaves aping their masters: "saw seven gentlemen lounging about, clad in gawdy coats of pea-green, mulberry brown, and sky blue. All had smart walking-canes in their hands, 'prodigious ties' of white neckcloths, and white gloves, but their faces were black. These were no other than the slaves enjoying a holiday. So great is their love of finery that I was told they are to be seen in New Orleans with white kid gloves on."[13]

11. Carl David Arfwedson, *The United States and Canada, in 1832, 1833, and 1834* . . . (2 vols., London, 1834), II:181; Frederick Law Olmsted, *A Journey through Texas* . . . (1857; reprint, New York, 1969), 28, 39; Catherine C. Hopley, *Life in the South From the . . . Spring of 1860 to August 1862* (1863; reprint, 2 vols., New York, 1974), I:123; Whipple, *Southern Diary,* 114–15.

12. James Mallory Journal, December 31, 1857, November 19, 24–25, 1855 (original owned by Edgar A. Stewart of Selma, Alabama), microfilm copy, University of Alabama, Tuscaloosa; John Brickell, *The Natural History of North-Carolina* (Dublin, 1737), 41–42.

13. Anon., *Ireland in 1804,* ed. Seamus Grimes (1806; reprint, Dublin, 1980), 65–66; Robert Everest, *A Journey Through the United States and Part of Canada* (London, 1855), 96.

BOSTON GIRL READING

From *Harper's New Monthly Magazine* 22 (1860–61), 725.

Celts loved to talk, preach, orate, tell stories, and to listen to others do the same. Southerners displayed "a love, amounting almost to a passion, for discussion, oratory, and public speaking," insisted a visitor. "The Irish talk a lot more than we do in England: they spend words like sailors on a spree while we English are said to hoard them like misers," confessed a traveler; indeed, "the Irish do very little but talk." A critic believed that Irish bards "make the ignorant men . . . to believe they be descended of . . . some . . . notable prince; which makes the ignorant people to run mad, and caring not what they do, . . . is very hurtful to the Realm." "The *Bard*," explained an eighteenth-century visitor in Scotland, "is skilled in the Genealogy of all the Highland families; . . . celebrates, in Irish Verse, the Origins of the Tribe, [and] the famous warlike Actions of the successive Heads." One famous Scottish bard, John MacRae, migrated to the Old South and composed a poem in English about "a great loss of cattle" that an eighteenth-century Scot claimed was "little short of any thing in Gaelic composition." Even in 1974, a Scot insisted, Highlanders revered tales that "hold the knowledge of the old ways and the old days." Folklorist Irvin S. Cobb observed that the American South is the "story-telling belt in this country."[14]

Much of the talking by Celts took place while they were seated. A sixteenth-century traveler noted that the Irish liked to sit in soft places: "They freely seat themselves on hay, or straw or grass; but they avoid the hard ground."[15] Antebellum Southerners liked to sit in swings or rocking chairs on breezy porches, at the dining table, or in the "sitting room." Males also conversed regularly from chairs or benches that they occupied inside or in front of stores, courthouses, and other convenient gathering places. They preferred to do their talking in comfort, often with their feet propped up and something cool to drink at hand.

A good preacher, a political speaker, or a group of traveling players

14. John Alonzo Clark, *Gleanings by the Way* . . . (Philadelphia, 1842), 70; Derek A. C. Davies, *Ireland* (New York, 1972), 9, 49; Luke Gernon, "A Discourse of Ireland, Anno 1620," in *Illustrations of Irish History and Topography, Mainly of the Seventeenth Century*, comp. C. Litton Falkiner (London, 1904), 356; L. M. Cullen, *Life in Ireland* (London, 1979), 18; Edward MacLysaght, *Irish Life in the Seventeenth Century* (1939; reprint, Dublin, 1979), 158; Thomas Smith, "Information for Ireland," *Ulster Journal of Archaeology* 6 (1850), 166–67; John Ramsay, *Scotland and Scotsmen in the Eighteenth Century, from the MSS. of John Ramsay, Esq. of Ochteryre*, ed. Alexander Allardyce (2 vols., Edinburgh, 1888), II:414–15; Edward Burt, *Burt's Letters from the North of Scotland*, ed. R. Jamieson (1754; reprint, 2 vols., Edinburgh, 1974), II:165; Sir John Sinclair, ed., *The Statistical Account of Scotland, 1791–1799* (reprint, 20 vols., East Ardsley, England, 1981), XVII:531; Kenneth MacLeish, "Scotland's Inner Hebrides: Isles of the Western Sea," *National Geographic* 146, no. 5 (November 1974), 690; B. A. Botkin, ed., *A Treasury of Southern Folklore* . . . (reprint, New York, 1980), 417.

15. Constantia Maxwell, ed., *Irish History from Contemporary Sources (1509–1610)* (London, 1923), 320.

could always draw a crowd. Southerners not only enjoyed plays, they also liked to act. The Old South, thanks in part to its Celtic heritage, escaped the Puritan and Quaker tradition that in the North denounced theaters as ungodly and insisted that every right-minded citizen avoid plays as a matter of public duty. The Scots and the Irish always enjoyed plays, and from the opening of the first theater in Williamsburg, Virginia, in 1716, Southerners patronized playhouses—frequently on Sunday. In 1797 all the citizens of Beardstown, Kentucky, "large and small," and many people "from miles around" turned out to see a "marionette show." A visitor wrote: "Our host and hostess were present with their whole family, and on her return the lady told me that she was well pleased that her children had been there, because at least *in their old age* they would be able to say that they had seen it."[16]

Southerners, though devoted to theatricals, often favored their own productions to those poorly performed by outsiders. "Saturday night we went over to hear the Hungarian minstrels," wrote one southern woman, "but they proved to be Yankee humbugs, and their ball music was much nearer the ridiculous than the melodious." A traveler in Virginia noted that the local theater, "a neat, convenient tobacco-house," was "well fitted up for the purpose." Amateurs frequently entertained themselves and each other with plays and masquerades. "I spent this evening at Mrs. Peck's, where a small party of 25 or 30 persons were invited and was much entertained," wrote a Yankee visitor to the South. "We had two masquing parties there & the parts were capitally acted." This same man, after watching another group "of masquers at Mrs. Reid's," stated that the "disguises and acting were said to be excellent altho' it is very doubtful whether this kind of amusement well suited the dignity and standing of some of the parties concerned. It is certain it would be deemed a letting down of dignity among our northern people."[17]

Equally undignified, in the opinion of various observers, was the way Southerners danced. A Georgian recalled dances in the county courthouse that began: "Gentlemen, lead your partners. Them that's got on shoes and stockings will dance the cotillion; them that's got on shoes and no stockings will dance the Virginy reel; them that's got on nairy shoes nor stockings will dance the scamper-down." A

16. MacLysaght, *Irish Life*, 214; Eve Begley, *Of Scottish Ways* (New York, 1977), 140–41; Leonard W. Labaree, *Conservatism in Early American History* (Ithaca, N.Y., 1959), 102; Whipple, *Southern Diary*, 119–20; Sir Charles Lyell, *A Second Visit to the United States . . .* (2 vols., New York, 1849), II:95; Boggs, *Alexander Letters*, 56; Louis Philippe, *Diary of My Travels in America [1797]*, trans. Stephen Becker (New York, 1977), 119.

17. Boggs, *Alexander Letters*, 155; Andrew Burnaby, *Travels through the Middle Settlements in North America . . . in the Years 1759 and 1760* (1775; reprint, Ithaca, N.Y., 1960), 46; Whipple, *Southern Diary*, 63, 58.

curiously dressed Arkansas girl astonished a Yankee visitor with the proposal: "Well, hos, let's take a trot." Her intention, he explained, was for him to "dance a jig" with her. These Arkansas girls were said to be free enough in their ways to make Henry Clay blush. Another traveler wrote of Mississippi women: "They are fond of dancing and all the other gay amusements, and though chaste as the Virgin Queen before the Gordian Knot is tied, yet indulgent as the Cyprian goddess for ever after." At the St. Charles Hotel in New Orleans, reported a visitor, the "evenings are occupied by music and dancing: The latter is a favorite amusement here. . . . The ladies invite such gentlemen as they think agreeable, to take part in their amusements; and every evening till long after midnight, I was kept awake by the stirring and animated sounds occasioned by a 'carpet dance,' with its accompanying gigling, fiddling, and floor-shaking."[18]

Southerners of every social class danced. Dancing was so admired that people often paid to learn how to move their feet to music, just as their ancestors had in Scotland and Ireland. A Scot told some visitors "that in the Highlands there are itinerant dancing-masters, who, from time to time, make the tour of the isles and mountains, in order to give lessons to the inhabitants, even of the lowest order"; and Arthur Young described the same pattern in eighteenth-century Ireland: "Dancing is very general among the poor people, almost universal in every cabbin. Dancing-masters of their own rank travel through the country from cabbin to cabbin, with a piper or blind fiddler; and the pay is six pence a quarter. It is an absolute system of education." Like other Celts, Southerners improved their dancing skills by frequent practice. Those too old or infirm to participate usually watched. A woman reported that one of her household slaves "is to give a cotillion party tomorrow night with some of his companions, so I can see some dancing." Hardly any social event omitted dancing. A guest at a wedding "danced with the ladies" from morning until the middle of the afternoon, "when they retired to dress." But by five in the afternoon, he explained, "the ladies began dancing again. Tonight I had the honor of Mrs. Hopper for a partner in country dances. The reels, cotillion, etc. you dance with anybody you please, by which means you have an opportunity of making love to any lady you please. I danced with all the belles in the room at different times, and admire the reels amazingly, especially the six-handed ones." The dancing at this party continued until long after midnight. A traveler wrote of backcountry North Carolinians:

18. Boggs, *Alexander Letters*, 121; Whipple, *Southern Diary*, 130; Christian Schultz, *Travels . . . in the Years 1807 and 1808 . . .* (2 vols., New York, 1810), II:134; Matilda Charlotte (Jesse) Fraser Houstoun, *Texas and the Gulf . . .* (Philadelphia, 1845), 83.

"Dancing they are all fond of, especially when they can get a fiddle, or bagpipe; at this they will continue hours together, . . . so attach'd are they to this darling amusement, that if they can't procure musick, they will sing for themselves."[19]

Other Celts were as fond of dancing as Southerners were. "The enthusiasm of Scotch dancers is proverbial," noted an Englishman in 1790. Scots loved music and "appear to be natural dancers," observed a Yankee, "but even the most polished among them are less distinguished by an adherence to the rules of art, than by a certain native ease, gracefulness and spirit." Celts favored "jigs and reels and wondrously fast fiddling." In eighteenth-century Ulster dances usually lasted "from eight or nine in the evening till daybreak." The Irish were "passionately fond" of dancing, observed a spectator. Another visitor noted that the Irish "dance with that enthusiasm which manifests itself in all their actions, except the action of working." "Weddings [in Ireland] are always celebrated with much dancing," reported Arthur Young, "and a Sunday rarely passes without a dance; there are very few among them who will not, after a hard day's work, gladly walk seven miles to have a dance. [England's] John [Bull] is not so lively; but then a hard day's work with him is certainly a different affair from what it is with *Paddy.*" Dancing was no less popular in Wales and in other parts of the Celtic fringe. A traveler wrote of the Celtic region of Cumberland: "In their dances, which are jigs and reels, exertion and agility are more regarded than ease and grace. But little order is observed in these rustic assemblies: disputes frequently arise, and are generally terminated by blows."[20]

19. L. A. Necker de Saussure, *Travels in Scotland: Descriptive of the State of Manners, Literature, and Science* (London, 1821), 67; Arthur Young, *Arthur Young's Tour in Ireland (1776–1779),* ed. Arthur W. Hutton (2 vols., London, 1892), I:446; Boggs, *Alexander Letters,* 136, 115, 156; Whipple, *Southern Diary,* 58–59; Robert Hunter, Jr., *Quebec to Carolina in 1785–1786 . . . ,* ed. Louis B. Wright and Marion Tinling (San Marino, Calif., 1943), 207–08; Brickell, *Natural History,* 32.

20. R. L. Willis, *Journal of a Tour from London to Elgin made About 1790 . . .* (Edinburgh, 1897), 54; [Benjamin Silliman], *A Journal of Travels in England, Holland and Scotland . . .* (2 vols., New York, 1810), II:296; John Stevenson, ed., *Two Centuries of Life in Down, 1600–1800* (Belfast, 1920), 277; Thomas Campbell, *A Philosophical Survey of the South of Ireland, in a Series of Letters*

to *John Walkinson, M.D.* (London, 1777), 46, 141; Leitch Ritchie, *Ireland Picturesque and Romantic* (London, 1838), 190; A. Young, *Tour in Ireland,* I:446 (see also 366); Sir Leonard Twiston Davies and Averyl Edwards, *Welsh Life in the Eighteenth Century* (London, 1939), 7; James Dugdale, *The New British Traveller; or, Modern Panorama of England and Wales . . .* (4 vols., London, 1819), I:621. On the Celtic love of music and dancing, see also Alexander Campbell, *A Journey from Edinburgh through Parts of North Britain . . .* (2 vols., London, 1802), I:262; Joseph Farington, *The Farington Diary,* ed. James Greig (3d ed., 2 vols., New York, 1923), I:335; Thomas Dineley, *Observations in a Voyage through the Kingdom of Ireland . . . in the Year 1681* (Dublin, 1870), 19; Charles Topham Bowden, *A Tour through Ireland* (Dublin, 1791), 165; L. Saussure, *Travels in Scotland,* 27; [Herman Ludwig Heinrich],

IRISH MUSIC AND DANCING

From National Library of Ireland [top]; woodcut by the
School of Thomas Berwick [bottom].

# Pleasures

Southerners, like other Celts, would dance anywhere. "Dancing is the universal amusement," reported an Englishwoman visiting the South. "The scraping of the fiddles attracted us to the sugar house," wrote a visitor to Louisiana. "In a space of the floor unoccupied by machinery some fifteen women and as many men were assembled, and . . . were dancing a kind of Irish jig to the music of the negro musicians." The insistence of a Virginia innkeeper that every guest dance seemed "very odd" to a traveling Englishman, "but the Virginians are accustomed to these manners." Among backcountry Crackers a wayfarer wrote that "the company . . . dance[d] in the wide hall that here divides the larger cabins into two halves." Slaves, "decked . . . out in their best finery," danced as often and with as much enthusiasm as anyone; indeed, one onlooker claimed that with blacks and whites alike "fights as well as flirtations invariably finish with a dance." From Virginia another visitor wrote: "After dinner we danced cotillions, minuets, Virginia and Scotch reels, country dances, jigs, etc., till ten o'clock. I had the pleasure of Miss McCall for a partner. She is a fine, sensible, accomplished young girl, and by far the best dancer in the room. Her elegant figure commands attention wherever she moves." She and the other dancers apparently moved quite a bit, for the diarist exclaimed: "Miss McCall was telling me the ladies wore out a pair of satin shoes every night dancing—pretty good work for the shoemaker." One southern matron, away from home and ill, asked her daughter "what will [your] father say if I tell that I had entertained serious thought of going [to a dance]. You will all think me demented surely, but many old ladies are going, and I have been so urged, and then I have some curiosity to see . . . the gay world, . . . and last not least, they have most delightful music . . . , which is a great attraction to me, and Mr. Sorrel was to be my gallant if I went,—a safe one surely, is he not?"[21]

Tour in England, Ireland, and France in the Years 1826, 1827, 1828, and 1829 (Philadelphia, 1833), 326; Thomas Keightley, The Fairy Mythology (London, 1878), 419; Breandan Breathnach, "Traditional Music," in Encyclopaedia of Ireland (Dublin, 1968), 389; Begley, Of Scottish Ways, 133–34; Moray McLaren, Understanding the Scots: A Guide for South Britons and Other Foreigners (New York, 1972), 56–58; D. Davies, Ireland, 87; Burt, Letters, II:149–51, 167–68; Cullen, Life in Ireland, 43, 64, 70–71; MacLysaght, Irish Life, 35, 162, 164; Whipple, Southern Diary, 8, 10.

21. Margaret (Hunter) Hall, The Aristocratic Journey; Being the Outspoken Letters of Mrs. Basil Hall Written During a Fourteen Months' Sojourn in America,

1827–1828, ed. Una Pope-Hennessy (New York, 1931), 168; William Howard Russell, My Diary North and South (2 vols., London, 1863), I:374; George William Featherstonhaugh, Excursion through the Slave States . . . (2 vols., London, 1844), II:18; Moritz Busch, Travels Between the Hudson & the Mississippi, 1851–1852, trans. and ed. Norman H. Binger (Lexington, Ky., 1971), 190; Henri Herz, My Travels in America [1846–1851], trans. Henry Bertram Hill (Madison, 1963), 75; Hunter, Quebec to Carolina, 207, 209; Boggs, Alexander Letters, 94. See also Rosalie Roos, Travels in America, 1851–1855, ed. Carl L. Anderson (Carbondale, Ill., 1982), 70, 74.

The music that this woman—as well as most Southerners and other Celts—found "most delightful" was produced by string instruments played by ear. Observers most often mentioned hearing two instruments: the fiddle and the banjo. One man wrote: "do you not hear those sounds of revelry and mirth? the ceaseless tum tum of de ole banjo, and the merry twang of de fiddle and de bow?" Englishman William H. Russell watched Southerners dance an "Irish jig" as "a fiddler, and also a banjo-player . . . played uncouth music." Charles Lanman claimed that nearly every Southerner could play the fiddle, and Henri Herz insisted that the "banjo is the favorite instrument of the blacks in the United States, just as the marimba [a primitive xylophone of Africa and South America with resonators beneath each bar] is of the blacks in Brazil." (It is generally believed that blacks were familiar with the banjo before they left Africa; that may well be, but if so one wonders why the banjo was not introduced by blacks in Brazil.) "Old Pap," who "joked and fiddled" and "would sit for hours scraping upon his violin, singing catches, or relating merry and marvellous tales," was just one of numerous southern fiddlers—black and white—described by witnesses.[22]

The songs these Southerners played and sang and danced to were part of their Celtic heritage. The fiddle had become the favorite instrument in Scotland and Ireland under pressure from the English conquerors against harps and bagpipes. The harp was proscribed in Ireland in the seventeenth century; harpers could be sentenced to death, and anyone harboring a harper was liable to severe penalties. The bagpipe, although technically not officially banned along with the clan system and much of Celtic culture after the English defeated the Highland Scots at Culloden in 1746, nevertheless fell into disfavor for a time together with most other Highland ways. Dr. Samuel Johnson wrote, after visiting the Highlands in 1773: "among other changes, which the last Revolution introduced, the use of the bagpipe begins to be forgotten." Later interest in the bagpipe revived, but observers from the seventeenth through the eighteenth centuries emphasized the importance of the fiddle in the music and the dances of British Celts.[23]

22. Hundley, *Social Relations*, 60–61; W. Russell, *Diary North and South*, I:273; Lanman, *Adventures in the Wilds*, II:192; Herz, *Travels in America*, 75; F. Hall, *Letters from the East and West*, 182–83; Barbara Leigh Smith Bodichon, *An American Diary, 1857–8*, ed. Joseph W. Reed, Jr. (London, 1972), 113; Timothy Flint, *Recollections of the Last Ten Years*, ed. C. Hartley Grattan (1826; reprint, New York, 1932), 17; John F. H. Claiborne, "A Trip through the Piney Woods [1841]," *Mississippi Historical Society Publications* 9 (1906), 535, 537; Hundley, *Social Relations*, 197; Whipple, *Southern Diary*, 63–64; Olmsted, *Journey through Texas*, 79; Harrower, *Journal*, 89.

23. Allen Feldman and Eamoun O'Doherty, *The Northern Fiddler* (Bel-

"VIRGINIA HOE-DOWN"

From *Harper's New Monthly Magazine* 12 (1855–56), 38.

Even in the late twentieth century the continuity between the country music of Celts and Southerners is startling. In 1981, after hearing tapes of traditional Irish and Scottish fiddling, James Brock, an outstanding country fiddler from Aliceville, Alabama, said that he recognized many of the tunes, which were similar to southern ones, and that he was certain that much of traditional southern music originated in Ireland and Scotland. Arlin Moon, a skilled instrument maker and old-time musician from Holly Pond, Alabama, who heard the same tapes, remarked that the tunes and the fiddling styles were like those he learned from his father and were still played in the rural South. He fiddled some of the same tunes himself and then, to show that he was not simply copying what he had heard, played a tape made earlier in which J. T. Perkins, a traditional fiddler from Arab, Alabama, fiddled a number of tunes that sounded quite Celtic. "They ought to sound Irish and Scottish," said Moon; "most old time southern fiddle music came from Ireland and Scotland." A folk authority noted in 1944 that the Celtic musical tradition persisted where James Houston (Jimmie) Davis, Louisiana's singing governor, was born and reared. "Many traces of this ancient music can be found today among the rural folk that inhabit the hills of North Louisiana," explained Floy Case. "They have preserved the old Irish jigs and the Scottish ballads, although they are now generously altered by their own interpretations and arrangements. This music has been classed as 'hillbilly,' but . . . it is really 'folk' music." Southern string and bluegrass bands still play such old Irish tunes as "A Black Velvet Band," which is often called "The Girl in the Blue Velvet Band," and "The Battle of the Boyne," which evolved into "Buffalo Gal" (fiddler Benny Martin calls his version "Nashville Gal"). While touring Texas, Paddy Moloney of the traditional Irish musical group the Chieftains heard "Cotton Eyed Joe" and immediately recognized it as "The Mountain Top," an old Irish melody. Various other people have noticed the similarities between Irish and southern music. In a television documentary entitled "Irish Country," Bobby Lord observed that old-time southern and bluegrass music have their roots in the reels and jigs of Ireland; moreover, during the Grand Old Opry's sixtieth anniversary celebration, Ricky

fast, 1980), 5; MacLysaght, *Irish Life*, 35–36; R. W. Chapman, ed., *Johnson's Journey to the Western Islands of Scotland and Boswell's Journal of a Tour to the Hebrides with Samuel Johnson, LL.D.* (Oxford, 1970), 93; Thomas Kirk and Ralph Thoresby, *Tours in Scotland, 1677 & 1681*, ed. Peter Hume Brown (Edinburgh, 1892), 33–34; L. Saussure, *Travels in Scotland*, 67; Sir John Sinclair, ed., *The Statistical Account of Scotland, 1791–1799* (reprint, 20 vols., East Ardsley, England, 1981), XVII:324; A. Young, *Tour in Ireland*, I:446; George Holmes, *Sketches of Some of the Southern Counties of Ireland, Collected During a Tour in the Autumn, 1797* (London, 1801), 36; Begley, *Of Scottish Ways*, 133; Davies and Edwards, *Welsh Life*, 25.

"PASTIME"

From *Harper's New Monthly Magazine* 16 (1857–58), 174.

Skaggs stated that while on a recent tour of Europe he discovered the close parallel between the South's traditional country music and Ireland's traditional music. He recognized no such similarities elsewhere. The fiddle is the mainstay of both Irish and southern music, and Southerners, like their Celtic forebears, play their instruments by ear. "We play everything by ear and the sound is what you got to go by. I think it's something you've got to have a feel for," said bluegrass musician Jim McReynolds. "Back in them [early] years," recalled bluegrass fiddler Kenny Baker, "all a man had to do was just play it one time and I could remember it." Ralph Stanley, another famous bluegrass performer, explained: "I think a lot of this talent is borned in you."[24]

Celtic music was not English music, nor was Celtic dancing. The English liked chamber music and concerts. "Every [English] woman . . . without exception, plays the piano," claimed a nineteenth-century critic; "but in a private room I have never heard a lady or a young girl play well enough to afford pleasure. . . . They play without the least expression." Pianos in Celtic regions were rare, so much so that in antebellum Mississippi one caused "great wonderment to the denizens of the surrounding pine woods. One man, when he first saw it, thought it an ironing table; another took the pedals for pistols, and another mistook it for a fancy chest for keeping nice clothes," reported an eyewitness. In England, besides the piano, members of the viol family, especially the lute, were popular. From the sixteenth century on, substantial households owned "some keyboard instrument—the spinet or the virginals, and perhaps the regal (a portable reed-organ)." English gentlemen sometimes played an instrument for their own amusement, but never for an audience. The two major complaints expressed against music in England were the same as those expressed against dancing. First, music and dancing encouraged idleness, or as a good Englishman told his son, "let not your Legges fling away your witte, in wasting your wealth." Second, music and dancing were "too alluring and wanton for a gentleman." Philip Stubbes insisted that if anyone wanted his son "transnatured into a woman, or worse, and inclined to all kind of

24. Interview with James Brock, September 15, 1981; interview with Arlin Moon, September 19, 1981; Floy Case, "Jimmie Davis: The Singing Governor," *Mountain Broadcast and Prairie Recorder*, n.s., no. 2 (December 1944), 1; *Fort Worth Star-Telegram*, March 17, 1986, C3; "Ireland Country," Nashville Network TV, March 16, 1986; Ricky Skaggs on "Grand Old Opry 60th Anniversary," CBS-TV, January 14, 1986; Jim McReynolds quoted on the album cover of *The Jim & Jesse Story*, CMH 9022; Kenny Baker quoted on the album cover of *Kenny Baker: Portrait of a Bluegrass Fiddler*, Country Records, 719; Peter Wernick, *Bluegrass Songbook* (New York, 1976), 104, 12. See also Grady McWhiney and Gary B. Mills, "Jimmie Davis and His Music: An Interpretation," *Journal of American Culture* 6 (1983), 54–57.

Whoredome, and abhomination, sett hym to Dauncying schoole, and to learne Musicke." John Northbrooke concluded: "Dauncing is the vilest vice [o]f all. . . . They daunce with disordinate gestures, and with monstrous thumping of the feete. . . . Maidens and matrones are groped and handled with unchaste hands, and kissed & dishonestly embraced." A nineteenth-century visitor in the Scottish Highlands offered a similar complaint of what he considered a vulgar, "bare-footed" dance in a style "native of this savage isle" in which the fiddler "was not content with scraping with all his might on his violin, he stamped with his feet, hallooed, and made a frightful noise."[25]

What outsiders thought of their music—an Englishwoman called it "most defective"—made little difference to Southerners and other Celts. To amuse themselves and their friends they sang and played their traditional songs and instruments. "We passed our time most agreeably today in the charms of conversation and music," announced a guest in a southern home. "Late on Christmas eve," noted another visitor to the South, "we were invited to the window by our landlady, to see the pleasant local custom of the Christmas Serenade." The "Christmas Serenade" was more than a "local custom"; it was a Welsh tradition.[26]

Besides their addiction to music and dancing, Southerners enjoyed habits that fastidious observers described as "nasty" and "dirty-looking." One of these was the use of tobacco. "Everyone uses tobacco, chewing as well as smoking," noted a traveler in the South. "Tobacco was used by almost all the men, young and old, some lads of fifteen or sixteen chewing and spitting as much as their elders, and nearly all smoking as well as chewing, so that we were the only persons . . . who did neither the one nor the other," wrote a disgusted Englishman. "The use of tobacco is almost universal among the men, and not uncommon with the other sex," remarked a European visitor in the South; "the former devoting themselves to it in the shape of cigars and fine-cut, and the women, hailing generally from the country, in the form of snuff. 'Dipping for snuff,' as they express it, is a prevailing practice with ladies in several of the Southern States." "Both in New England & in New York tobacco chewing is a habit by far too prevalent," pronounced an observer, "but to the

25. [Raul Blouet], *John Bull and His Island* (New York, 1884), 144–45; Dorothy Hartley, *Lost Country Life* (New York, 1979), 124; Lanman, *Adventures in the Wilds*, II:195; Marcia Valle, *The Gentleman's Recreations: Accomplishments and Pastimes of the English Gentleman, 1580–1630* (Cambridge, 1977), 94, 96–97, 89; John Northbrooke, *A Treatise Wherein Dicing, Dauncing, Vaine Plaies . . . are Reproved* (London, 1579), 66–67; L. Saussure, *Travels in Scotland*, 67.

26. M. Hall, *Aristocratic Journey*, 168; Hunter, *Quebec to Carolina*, 219, 210; Olmsted, *Journey through Texas*, 68–69; Davies and Edwards, *Welsh Life*, 25.

SMOKERS—THE OLD SOUTH AND IRELAND

From *Harper's New Monthly Magazine* 12 (1855–56), 35.
William M. Thackeray, *The Irish Sketch Book of 1842*
(London, 1886), 22.

stranger, this plague in American life only begins to show itself in its detestable universality . . . in the South." German passengers on an Alabama riverboat complained of excessive smoking, drinking, chewing, and spitting. A visitor in Louisiana noticed that many of the passengers on a steamboat "were chewing . . . tobacco, [while] others were veiling the platform with a strong-smelling cloud of smoke." An Englishman reported a train ride between Atlanta and Memphis "unpleasant for although smoking is not allowed chewing is, which is infinitely more disgusting." Another Englishman asserted that tobacco chewing was "so disgustingly prevalent in the Southern and Western States" that "spittoons are in all the reading rooms, bars, lobbies, and offices of the hotels; spittoons in every railway-car; and in the halls of every State Legislature which I visited."[27]

Such criticism failed to deter Southerners. They chewed and smoked with a total disdain for the comfort of those around them. An Englishman described being "crammed" into a southern stagecoach with eight other passengers, five of whom chewed tobacco. He admitted that "during the night . . . they aimed at the windows with great accuracy, and didn't *splash* me," but by the next "afternoon tobacco-chewing became universal, and the spitting was sometimes a little wild." Another Englishman called the constant "spitting and chewing" by Southerners "a most unpleasant way of using tobacco. . . . I was rather worried to see a fine young man, talking very familiarly with [an] . . . English lady . . . , turn away now and then and discharge the brown saliva from his mouth over the porch railing." This same traveler encountered on a stagecoach a Southerner whom he considered "a great chewer and spitter. I calculated that he must have emitted the nauseus fluid from his mouth through the wash window at the rate of half a pint per hour. How his system could stand such a drain, he still looking robust, fat, and muscular, I could not understand." When some travelers joined an "old cracker" who was seated on a bench "smoking lustily" at a railroad rest stop, this Southerner said to one of them: "Stranger, I reckon my smoke ain't nohow agreeable." "No, it is not," answered the traveler. "Well move then," declared the Cracker.[28]

27. George Lewis, *Impressions of America* . . . (Edinburgh, 1845), 151; Buckingham, *Slave States*, I:270; Lanman, *Adventures in the Wilds*, II:166; M. Hall, *Aristocratic Journey*, 168; A. Mackay, *Western World*, I:151; Dr. Moritz Wagner and Dr. Karl Scherzer, *Reisen in Nordamerika in den Jahren 1852 und 1853* (3 vols., Leipzig, 1854), III:298; Victor Tixier, *Tixier's Travels* . . . *[1839–1840]*, ed. John Francis McDermott (Norman, Okla., 1940), 38; John Henry Vessey, Mr. *Vessey of England: Being the Incidents and Reminiscences of Travel in a Twelve Weeks' Tour through the United States and Canada in the Year 1859*, ed. Brian Waters (New York, 1956), 93; Charles Mackay, *Life and Liberty in America* . . . (New York, 1859), 218–19.

28. Arthur James L. Fremantle, *The Fremantle Diary* . . . , ed. Walter Lord (new ed., Boston, 1954), 45–46; D. Mitchell, *Ten Years in the United States*, 47–48; Whipple, *Southern Diary*, 75.

One traveler compared the "spitting and chewing" of Southerners with that of Irishmen, and well he might, for British Celts were as notorious in their use of tobacco as were the inhabitants of the Old South. Seventeenth-century observers in Ireland noted that "men, weomen, and children are addicted to tobacco in an abundant manner" and that "excessive Smoaking" was so widespread "an *Infant* . . . shall take more delight in handling a *Tobacco-Pipe* than a *Rattler*, and will sooner learn to make use of it, than . . . its *Sucking-bottle*." At the end of the eighteenth century witnesses complained about the "immoderate use of tobacco in various ways by both sexes, old and young." The Irish, it was charged, often spent money on "that abominable weed" rather than improving their diet; "there are many who would sooner fast the whole day than be without their tobacco." In the eighteenth century a visitor remarked that Scots "consume vast quantities of Tobacco, for there are none from ye richest to ye poorest but Who take Snuff at a most immoderate rate," and a native admitted that Scots consumed "Tobacco in all its forms. . . . Many young ladies, and perhaps the greater number of married men and women, carried snuff-boxes. The habit prevailed so generaly, that it was not uncommon for lovers to present their sweethearts with snuff-boxes."[29]

Observers frequently claimed that Southerners, unlike Northerners, often were addicted to both tobacco and liquor. "The further we have come South the more universal have we found that disgusting practice of chewing tobacco," wrote an Englishwoman, who considered Southerners to have filthy habits compared to Northerners. "Every man we meet has constantly an immense lump in his mouth, which he keeps munching at as if it were a bit of bread, and the spitting that ensues is beyond what I can describe. It makes the *gentlemen*, as they style themselves, so very offensive. Really, between tobacco and brandy they are intolerable." One traveler reported that it "is now very rare, in the free States, to see a drunken person even in the most populous cities. At the large [northern] hotels, . . . it is the exception, not the rule, to take any spiritous or fermented beverage at or after dinner; and no case of inebriety came under my notice in any of these establishments." The situation was quite different in the South. "The habitual use of ardent spirits . . .

29. D. Mitchell, *Ten Years in the United States*, 47; Dineley, *Observations in a Voyage*, 23; Anon., *A Trip to Ireland, Being a Description of the Country, People, and Manners . . .* (London, 1699), 8; William Shaw Mason, ed., *A Statistical Account or Parochial Survey of Ireland, Drawn up from the Communications of the Clergy* (3 vols., Dublin, 1814–19), II:363, III:448–49;

John Loveday, *Diary of a Tour in 1732 Through Parts of England, Wales, Ireland and Scotland* (Edinburgh, 1890), 165; Thomas Somerville quoted in J. G. Fyfe, ed., *Scottish Diaries and Memoirs, 1746–1843* (Stirling, Scotland, 1942), 228. See also A. Young, *Tour in Ireland*, I:249; Cullen, *Life in Ireland*, 53; MacLysaght, *Irish Life*, 71.

in the Southern States," observed a visitor, "prevails to a lamentable extent." Another man claimed that in one southern town with "fifty or sixty houses" there "was but one man . . . that was not in the constant habit of getting drunk."[30]

Drinking patterns in the South differed from those in the North. The average Northerner, like the average Englishman, tended to be a thrifty and a moderate drinker, if he touched alcohol at all. "The greatest vice I knew was drunkeness," claimed an Englishman. "The common drink among the people of the middle and northern region [of the United States] is cyder," reported a visitor. "The use of beer is confined for the most part to the towns, and only in Pennsylvania and Maryland is good domestic beer to be found in the country towns, where the inhabitants are mainly Germans." Much of the liquor produced in the North went elsewhere for consumption; in 1850 Cincinnati alone shipped 14,500,000 gallons of whiskey to the South, and Southerners supplemented such imports with local products. As early as 1810, Kentucky produced enough bourbon to provide every person in the state with 5 gallons a year.[31]

The ordinary Southerner would drink almost anything; he also believed that if something was worth doing, it was worth overdoing. Southerners, claimed a fellow Southerner, drink "alcoholic beverages to excess" but generally were "too lazy" to make their own whiskey; "they prefer to tramp to the nearest groggery with a gallon-jug on their shoulders, which they get filled with 'bust-head,' 'rot-gut,' or some other equally poisonous abomination; and then tramp home again, reeling as they trudge along, and laughing idiotically, or shouting like mad in a glorious state of beastly intoxication."[32]

Not all Southerners drank to excess, but few missed an opportunity to imbibe. "Though they drink on all occassions, whether from sociability or self-indulgence, and at all times, from rosy morn to dewy eve, and long after; though breath and clothes are 'alive' with the odour of alcohol, you will scarcely ever see a . . . [Southerner] drunk," insisted one man. "From morning till night the barrooms of the [South's] hotels are full; the bar, indeed, being the chief source of the hotelkeepers' revenue," a traveler discovered. Another visitor reported that Southerners commonly celebrated the most trivial events with a "drinking session" that lasted all day. "I'm in a tar-

30. M. Hall, *Aristocratic Journey*, 206; Joseph Sturge, *A Visit to the United States in 1841* (Boston, 1842), 173; Adam Hodgson, *Letters from North America* . . . (2 vols., London, 1824), II:249; Olmsted, *Journey through Texas*, 68. See also Francis Asbury, "Bishop Asbury Visits Tennessee, 1788–1815: Extracts from his Journal," ed. Walter B. Posey, *Tennessee Historical Quarterly* 15 (1956), 253–68.

31. Nichols, *Forty Years of American Life*, I:86; Schopf, *Travels in the Confederation*, II:219; James Finlay Weir Johnston, *Notes on North America* . . . (2 vols., Edinburgh and London, 1851), I:276; Paul W. Gates, *The Farmer's Age: Agriculture, 1815–1860* (New York, 1960), 13.

32. Claiborne, "Trip through the Piney Woods," 514; Hundley, *Social Relations*, 268.

SOUTHERNER WITH JUG

From *Harper's New Monthly Magazine* 24 (1861–62), 607.

nation hurry to liquor," exclaimed a Southerner who wanted to settle his business quickly. "The process of *liquoring* is gone through several times before a bargain is struck," explained a traveler in Texas.[33]

Liquor drinking was expected on nearly all occasions. "He made us drink plenty of toddy," explained a visitor at a Southerner's home. A teacher recorded that he was given a bottle of whiskey "which we drank in School in Company," and a southern member of Congress remarked: "no person who is temperate and lives cleanly like a gentleman, and who will not therefore condescend to drink and hurrah with Tom, Dick and Harry, need ever hope for political preferment."[34]

A special fondness for liquor also characterized British Celts. "A love of drinking, which is . . . a prevailing passion with the Irish, may readily be ascribed to . . . a natural fondness of excitement, to convivial feelings, or the extravagant notions too generally encouraged of universal hospitality," asserted an Englishman. "The habit of intemperate drinking had grown to such an excess in Ireland," insisted an onlooker, who believed that "there was something in the people's constitution congenial to the excitement of ardent spirits. The propensity for intoxication among the people has been remarked from the earliest times. . . . No class of society, even the gravest, was exempt from this indulgence. Even judges on the bench were seen inebriated, without much shame, and with little censure." Every occasion seemed to call for a drink, and the numerous Irish holidays were "celebrated . . . by the most disgusting drunkeness and debauchery." In 1717 a friend claimed that the earl of Kenmare, one of Ireland's Catholic gentry, "never drinks between meals, except with company worth while, and that seldom above two bottles at a time."[35]

33. Henry Anthony Murray, *Lands of the Slave and the Free* . . . (2 vols., London, 1855), I:226; A. Mackay, *Western World*, I:182; Philo Tower, *Slavery Unmasked: Being a Truthful Narrative of Three Years' Residence and Journeying in Eleven Southern States* . . . (Rochester, N.Y., 1856), 81; Houstoun, *Texas and the Gulf*, 76. See also Thomas Hamilton, *Men and Manners in America* (2 vols., Philadelphia, 1833), II:198; Aleksandr Borisovich Lakier, *A Russian Looks at America: The Journey of Aleksandr Borisovich Lakier in 1857*, ed. Arnold Schrier and Joyce Story (Chicago, 1979), 222; Everest, *Journey*, 118; Eugene L. Schwaab, ed., *Travels in the Old South: Selected from Periodicals of the Times* (2 vols., Lexington, Ky., 1973), I:185, II:339.
34. Hunter, *Quebec to Carolina*, 220;

Harrower, *Journal*, 115; Hundley, *Social Relations*, 269–70.
35. Thomas Crofton Croker, *Researches in the South of Ireland* . . . (1824; reprint, New York, 1969), 228; John Edward Walsh, *Sketches of Ireland Sixty Years Ago* (Dublin, 1847), 60, 62–63; Mason, *Statistical Account* . . . *of Ireland*, II:403, 181; Edward MacLysaght, ed., *The Kenmare Manuscripts* (Dublin, 1942), 14. See also Giraldus Cambrensis, *The First Version of the Topography of Ireland*, trans. John J. O'Meara (Dundalk, Ireland, 1951), 15; T. Campbell, *Philosophical Survey*, 39; Anon., *Ireland in 1804*, 33; Cullen, *Life in Ireland*, 44–45; MacLysaght, *Irish Life*, 69, 194; Mason, *Statistical Account* . . . *of Ireland*, III:204–05.

The Welsh too were known as heavy drinkers. A visitor suggested that most parties and dances in Wales "conclude in drunkenness, fighting, and seduction." Various sources depict Welsh drovers as "not distinguished for their sobriety" but as "a crowd of brawling, swearing, drink-besotted" men, who went "from one inn to another, with little thought for the welfare of [their] . . . cattle, singing to the harp and with an eye on loose women."[36]

"The inhabitants of Scotland," declared a seventeenth-century traveler, "are a drunken kind of people." Whiskey was forced upon visitors, and even Scottish preachers sometimes admitted that they "drank rather too much." Dr. Alexander Webster, minister of the Tolbooth Church in Edinburgh from 1737 to 1784, could drink his friends "all under the table," for he had the reputation of being "a five-bottle [a day] man." Nearly all Scots, insisted one eighteenth-century wayfarer, "have fallen into habits of intemperance." A native agreed. "By means of hard drinking and its usual consequences," acknowledged John Ramsay, "more estates were impaired [before1745] than by all the other articles of expense in housekeeping put together. And besides plentiful libations in one another's houses, it was very much the fashion to drink to excess . . . in the tavern." Contemporaries reported that eighteenth-century Scots were "much addicted to [the] drinking of whiskey; whence, at their public meetings (such as burials, &c.) squabbles are frequent" and that "inhabitants of all ranks . . . are apt to assemble in the evening at whisky-houses," where they engaged in the "excessive use of . . . liquor." The Reverend Andrew Gallie reported that in his parish of only 2,000 people there were four whiskey stills, "and more are in contemplation. The retailing houses are upwards of 30, [and] . . . seem to be making a rapid progress in debauching the morals . . . of the common people." The Reverend John Fraser, who blamed distilleries in his and neighboring parishes for corrupting the "health, morals and industry of . . . the inhabitants," stated that there were "8 dram-houses in the parish, where spirits are sold at a low price; . . . half the said number would be fully sufficient to accommodate travelers." In his parish, lamented the Reverend Daniel Rose, "nineteen . . . whisky houses . . . endanger[ed] the morals of the people by furnishing secret opportunities of indulging a propensity to drunkenness." The Reverend Harry Robertson confessed that his parish contained "a number of blind whisky houses [where] . . . tipplers, and dram-drinkers . . . sometimes sit up whole nights at their debauch. . . . It is not uncommon to see two mechanics, or day labourers, repairing once or twice a-day to one of these ensnaring

36. Davies and Edwards, *Welsh Life,* 139–40; Anon., *Ireland in 1804,* 33; P. G. Hughes, *Wales and the Drovers:* *The Historic Background of an Epoch* (London, 1943), 24–25.

haunts, and drinking a choppin bottle of unmixed whisky at each time."[37]

Unlike many Englishmen, who denounced "dicing and cards," Celts were as devoted to gambling as they were to drinking. In premodern Wales the most "popular games of chance with the privileged and the disenfranchised classes alike were cards and dice." Even some preachers gambled in Scotland. In 1757 a minister noted in his diary: "procure[d] . . . for . . . myself . . . three tickets in the guinea lottery. Had never opportunity of trying my fortune, as they call it, at so small a risque, and if by the Providence that orders all things I should succeed so far as to be enable[d] to discharge any considerable part or the whole of my debts, it would be a great blessing." A seventeenth-century observer of the Irish reported: "Gameing and laziness they are much addicted to, their chiefest games are five-cards, all-fours &c. . . . At which they will play away all, to their very clokes." In the eighteenth century one man wrote, "They will pawn their last rag for the pleasure of gaming," and another concluded: "The intense passion of the Irish for gambling has often been observed. Campion, writing nearly three hundred years ago, mentions it, and notices a class . . . whose only occupation . . . was playing at cards. He describes them as gambling away their mantles and all their clothes, and then lying down in their bare skins in straw by the road-side, to invite passers by to play with them for their glibbes [hair], their nails, their toes, and even more important parts of their bodies, which they lost or redeemed at the courtesy of the winner. Card-playing is, at this day, indulged in by the Irish peasantry with an eagerness perfectly astonishing, and is often the parent of many vices. It is not uncommon . . . to spend whole days playing. . . . The propensity for gambling exhibits itself at the earliest ages. Boys of ten years old, sent with car-loads of turf to market-towns, commonly gamble on the proceeds of their merchandize."[38]

37. Christopher Lowther, *Our Journall into Scotland Anno Domini 1629 . . .*, ed. W. D. (Edinburgh, 1894), 16; George Ridpath, *Diary of George Ridpath: Minister of Stitchel, 1755–1761*, ed. Sir James Balfour Paul (Edinburgh, 1922), 8; Alexander Carlyle quoted in Fyfe, *Scottish Diaries and Memoirs*, 133; Anon., *Journal of a Tour Through the Northern Counties of Scotland . . . in Autumn 1797* (Edinburgh, 1798), 87; John Ramsay quoted in Fyfe, *Scottish Diaries and Memoirs*, 181–82; Sinclair, *Statistical Account of Scotland*, XVII:4, 33, 509, 518, 193, 492–93. See also John Erskine, *Extracts from the Diary of a Senator of the College of Justice, 1717–1718*, ed. James Maidment (Edinburgh, 1843), 28–31; McLaren, *Understanding the Scots*, 52; Fyfe, *Scottish Diaries and Memoirs*, 228, 552.

38. Valle, *Gentleman's Recreations*, 135; Geraint Dyfnallt Owen, *Elizabethan Wales: The Social Scene* (Cardiff, Wales, 1964), 53; Ridpath, *Diary*, 116–17; Dineley, *Observations in a Voyage*, 19; Edward D. Clarke, *A Tour Through the South of England, Wales, and Part of Ireland, Made During the Summer of 1791* (London, 1793), 326; Walsh, *Sketches*, 66. See also Anon., *Letters from an Armenian in Ireland, to His Friends at Trebisond, &c.*, trans. Edmond S. Pery (London, 1757), 147–48; Cullen, *Life in Ireland*, 101–02; MacLysaght, *Irish Life*, 29–31, 157.

Antebellum Southerners were as devoted as other Celts to gambling. "The inhabitants [of the South] are universally addicted to gambling and drinking," asserted a traveler. "The billiard rooms are crowded from morning to night, and often all night through." An Englishman found "Gambling, in the Middle States, . . . about as common as in England; it is far more so as you proceed to the southward, and dreadfully prevalent in New Orleans." An Englishwoman, who denounced New Orleans "gambling-houses, of which, be it remembered, there are many," soon discovered that other Southerners besides the citizens of New Orleans had a fondness for gambling. "It exists in all shapes," she reported, "and their horse-races are attended more regularly and more energetically even than our own; the betting, too, on these occasions, is most spirited." Southerners were "excessively addicted to gambling," claimed a Yankee. "This horrible vice, so intimately associated with so many others, prevails like an epidemic." Another visitor in the South noted: "Lotteries, expelled from the northern states, still florish here." And still another traveler observed that Southerners habitually spent their evenings drinking and playing games of chance.[39]

Gamblers favored such popular indoor games as cards, dice, and dominoes. One man explained that North Carolinians "are much addicted to gaming, especially at cards and dice, hazard and all-fours, being the common games they use; at which they play very high, nay to such a pitch, that I have seen several hundred pounds won and lost in a short time." A Yankee visitor in the South contended that "a game they call 'poker' appeared to be the game most played. It is said to be a very fascinating game & one which none play well except old players. It is a game which depends on calmness of mind & coolness of nerve. He who can win & not be elated & lose and not be depressed will make the best 'brag' & 'poker' player." Another Northerner described how the Creoles of New Orleans played dominoes: "In every cafe and cabaret, from early in the morning . . . till late at night, devotees to this childish amusement will be found clustered around the tables, with a tonic, often renewed and properly sangareed, at their elbows. Enveloped in dense clouds of tobacco-smoke issuing from their eternal segars . . . they manoeuvre their little dotted, black and white parallelograms with won-

39. Ashe, *Travels in America*, 237; Hodgson, *Letters*, II:258; Houstoun, *Texas and the Gulf*, 170; Flint, *Recollections*, 324; Thomas Ewbank, *Life in Brazil; or a Journal of a Visit to the Land of Cocoa and the Palm* . . . (New York, 1856), 20; Hunter, *Quebec to Carolina*, 236. See also John Benwell, *An Englishman's Travels in America* . . . (London, 1853), 210–11; Pearse, *Narrative*, 90; Houstoun, *Texas and the Gulf*, 221; James Logan, *Notes of a Journey through Canada, the United States of America, and the West Indies* . . . (Edinburgh, 1838), 172; Schwaab, *Travels in the Old South*, I:94, 189–90; Thomas H. Palmer, " 'Observations Made During a Short Residence in Virginia': In a letter from Thomas H. Palmer, May 30, 1814," ed. John Cook Wyllie, *Virginia Magazine of History and Biography* 76 (1968), 387–414.

derful . . . skill." Hundreds of coffeehouses were filled each day with these "thirsty time-killing" Southerners, as this man called them. "As custom authorises this frequenting of these popular places of resort," he declared, "the citizens of New Orleans do not, like those of Boston, attach any disapprobation to the houses or their visitors."[40]

Inveterate gamblers were common in the South. In one hotel a traveler saw men crowded around several tables, "as thick & as busy as bees in a hive, . . . engaged in . . . all the excitements of gambling— the game being faro, & the stakes by no means contemptible." A Northerner told of a Georgian who, "after losing all his money [on a bet], staked [his] six slaves . . . on a game of billiards [and lost]." "Gambling [in the South] is a common mode of amusement," noted another Yankee, "and so great is the passion for it that men have lost in a night their all." This man averred that "not to gamble is considered by these natives as to be rather squeamish." He also related how a Southerner on a riverboat, when told that his wife was ill in her cabin, refused to leave a game of cards. When advised that she was worse, he gambled on. At last, informed that she was dead, he remarked: "Ah, I could not help it."[41]

Gambling was so widespread that many men practiced it as a profession. A traveler on a riverboat en route from Montgomery to Mobile observed that the "professional gamblers, who form so large an ingredient in the population of the South, . . . had the most sinister look about them that I had ever witnessed." Another visitor made a similar report. "Many gamblers [in the South] spend their time in travelling upon boats to catch the unwary & obtain money," he remarked.[42]

Yet the experience of another Yankee suggests that gamblers often were considered respectable members of southern society. When asked to share his bed at a crowded southern tavern with a gentleman, the Northerner replied: "If you *know* him to be in reality a gentleman, sir, I will consent." The landlord stated that he knew the prospective bedfellow "in every respect to be an honorable gentleman." So in came a heavily armed man. When he took off his clothes, he also "detached a bowie knife and pistols,—laying the knife and one pair of the pistols on the table, and placing another pair under his pillow. I shuddered," admitted the Yankee, "having never slept with pistols—but I composed my nerves with the landlord's assurance of a favorable acquaintance, and the historical fact that *Southern* 'gentlemen' sleep with pistols." The two men engaged in polite conversation after the light was extinguished until the

40. Brickell, *Natural History,* 31–32; Whipple, *Southern Diary,* 84; [Joseph Holt Ingraham], *The South-West; by a Yankee . . .* (2 vols., New York, 1835), I:114–15.

41. A. Mackay, *Western World,* I:183; Parsons, *Inside View,* 119; Whipple, *Southern Diary,* 125.

42. A. Mackay, *Western World,* II:267; Whipple, *Southern Diary,* 84.

Southerner mentioned that he was a "gambler *by profession.*" Horrified by this confession, the Northerner announced: "The landlord assured me that you were a *gentleman,* sir, but had he told me of your profession, I would not have consented to share my bed." The gambler, who could not understand such squeamishness, "entered into an elaborate argument to prove that his profession was as honest and honorable as that of the physician."[43]

Gambling was widespread and accepted in a society that revered the racing of horses and other such sensual pleasures. Many Southerners spent as much of their time as they could "drinking, gambling, horse-racing, fox-hunting," and doing what a contemporary called "enjoying life." A Yankee described the activities and the arrangements at a southern "gander pulling" as typical: "The whiskey kegs on the stumps—the gaming tables under the shades—the cock-fights in the pens—the horse-race out in the woods—will amuse the crowd to-morrow. And the fox-chase . . . will close the festivities." A visitor in Natchez noted: "Gambling and horseracing are the prevailing amusements."[44]

Celts delighted in racing horses and betting on the outcome. Scots and Irishmen, in the words of one authority, "have always been at home on horseback." James Logan claimed that "horse racing, now so popular in England, was . . . introduced from Scotland" about 1260. Early in the seventeenth century a visitor to the Hebrides wrote: "The Natives are much addicted to riding. . . . They have Horse-racing for . . . Prizes, for which they contend eagerly. There is an antient Custom, by which it is lawful for any of the Inhabitants to steal his Neighbour's Horse the night before the Race and ride him all next day, provided he delivers him safe and sound to the Owner after the Race." In 1752 a woman wrote from Ireland: "All this neighbourhood are now in an uproar of diversions. They began last Wednesday and are to last till Saturday,—each day a horse-race, assembly and ball."[45]

Horse racing was quite popular in the Old South throughout the antebellum period. A foreign visitor to the United States reported that horse racing "is more prevalent in the southern States" than anywhere else in the country. A Yankee, who objected to racing, wrote from South Carolina: "Curiosity induced me to go once, which will satisfy me for life." "In New England," boasted the

43. Parsons, *Inside View,* 101–02.

44. Hundley, *Social Relations,* 168; Parsons, *Inside View,* 100; Ashe, *Travels in America,* 317.

45. MacLysaght, *Irish Life,* 144–45; James Logan, *The Scottish Gael; or, Celtic Manners, as Preserved Among the Highlanders . . .* (1876; reprint, 2 vols., Edinburgh, 1976), I:366–67; Martin Martin, *A Description of the Western Islands of Scotland* (1716; reprint, Edinburgh, 1981), 79; J. Stevenson, *Two Centuries,* 277. See also Charles Rogers, *Social Life in Scotland: From Early to Recent Times* (1884; reprint, 2 vols., Port Washington, N.Y., 1971), II:307–13; Cullen, *Life in Ireland,* 62.

president of Yale College, "horse racing is almost and cockfighting absolutely unknown." In the South both private and public courses received almost constant use. One man attended a solid week of racing in Virginia, and the visitors frequently commented on the distances people traveled to see horse races and the sizable amounts of money wagered on them. An observer reported a race in which two horses ran "for a purse of 500 Pounds; besides small Betts almost inumerable."[46]

Both long and short races found enthusiastic supporters. Some tracks were a mile in length and circular; others were only a quarter of a mile and straight. One man remarked that North Carolinians were so fond of horse racing that "they have race-paths, near each town, and in many parts of the country. Those paths, seldom exceed a quarter of a mile in length, and only two horses start at a time. . . . These courses being so very short, they use no manner of art, but push on with all the speed imaginable; many of these horses are very fleet." A visitor noted that with Southerners the racing of quarter horses "is a great favorite of the middling and lower classes; and they have a breed of horses to perform it with astonishing velocity, beating every other for that distance with the greatest ease."[47]

Some Southerners were so attached to racing that they devoted nearly all of their time to it. A native of Alabama described a certain type of Southerner who "is great on horse-flesh. His conversation runs chiefly on dogs and horses, horse-trappings and the like; and he himself much affects jockey caps, and other sporting articles of costume, and fills his house with wood-cuts of all the celebrated racers, as well as with whips, saddles, bridles, spurs, etc., etc. Besides, from association so constantly with jockeys and grooms, he soon learns all the slang phrases peculiar to jockeydom, and rattles them off most volubly on all occasions." Robert W. Withers, a planter of Greene County, Alabama, who died in 1854, kept a detailed record of those things that he considered important—the births and deaths of his family, slaves, and racehorses.[48]

Riding and racing horses delighted Southerners, but they cared

46. Hodgson, *Letters*, II:258; Welcome Arnold Green, *The Journal of Welcome Arnold Green: Journeys in the South, 1822–1824*, ed. Alice E. Smith (Madison 1957), 29; Timothy Dwight, *Travels in New England and New York*, ed. Barbara Miller Solomon (4 vols., Cambridge, Mass., 1969), IV:238; Harrower, *Journal*, 65, 40; Hunter, *Quebec to Carolina*, 251–52; Philip Vickers Fithian, *Journal & Letters of Philip Vickers Fithian, 1773–1774: A Plantation Tutor of the Old Dominion*, ed. Hunter Dickinson

Farish (1943; reprint, Charlottesville, 1968), 32.
47. Hunter, *Quebec to Carolina*, 219; Brickell, *Natural History*, 31; Thomas Anburey, *Travels Through the Interior Parts of America . . .* (2 vols., London, 1789), II:349.
48. Hundley, *Social Relations*, 245; Robert W. Withers Papers, Southern Historical Collection, University of North Carolina, Chapel Hill. See also W. Russell, *Diary North and South*, I:414.

little for foot races or walking—those activities were too exhausting. A foreigner reported that in the South he witnessed "Wrestling, leaping, and such activities . . . , yet I never observed any foot races." Southerners could move quickly if they chose to, as "Stonewall" Jackson's foot cavalry demonstrated during the Confederacy's struggle for independence. But most Southerners, a visitor noted, "move at a slow, dragging pace, and are evidently not good marchers naturaly." His observation was confirmed by a Confederate who admitted: "Before this war we were a lazy set of devils; our Negroes worked for us, and none of us ever dreamt of walking, though we all rode a great deal." In their reluctance to run or walk, southern men differed somewhat from traditional Scots, who "go the Highland trot with wonderfull expedition," and Irishmen, who "in swiftness . . . equal and sometimes surpass their horses." But neither southern nor Celtic women were walkers. "Miss Juliet could not walk a mile, [and] says few South state American women can," reported an Englishwoman; "so say all the ladies here in the boat [going down the Mississippi River]." And an eighteenth-century visitor said of Irish women: "It is deemed almost a reproach for a gentlewoman to be seen walking; . . . but, if they walk ill, they certainly dance well."[49]

Southerners never walked where they could ride, even "if only to fetch a prise of snuff from across the way," wrote an observer. No sooner was a young Southerner "rid of his bib and tuckers," insisted a native of the Old South, "[than he was] mounted a-horseback; and this was not a hobby-horse either, . . . but a genuine live pony. . . . By the time he is five years old he rides well." Jefferson Davis's doctor quoted Davis as saying after the Civil War that "his people were better horsemen than those of the North." Various visitors mentioned horseback riding as a "favorite amusement" of Southerners or "a very fashionable pastime," and an Englishwoman stated that in Louisiana "the pleasure-taking citizens," both white and black, rode fast horses everywhere and "thoroughly enjoy[ed] themselves."[50]

49. Brickell, *Natural History*, 31–32; Fremantle, *Diary*, 90, 181; Richard Pococke, *Tours in Scotland 1747, 1750, 1760*, ed. Daniel William Kemp (Edinburgh, 1887), 127; Maxwell, *Irish History*, 320; Bodichon, *American Diary*, 56; T. Campbell, *Philosophical Survey*, 46.

50. Schopf, *Travels in the Confederation*, II:65; Hundley, *Social Relations*, 31; John J. Craven, *Prison Life of Jefferson Davis* . . . (1866; reprint, Biloxi, 1979), 320; [Charles A. Clinton?], *A Winter from Home* (New York, 1852), 24; Whipple, *Southern Diary*, 73; Houstoun, *Texas and the Gulf*, 155–56. During the American Revolution various generals complained about the unwillingness of Southerners "to stir without a horse." General Daniel Morgan, for example, wrote: "We have to feed such a number of horses that the most plentiful country must soon be exhausted. Could the militia be persuaded to change their fatal mode of going to war, much provision might be saved, but the custom has taken such a deep root that it cannot be abolished" (quoted in John Morgan Dederer, *Making Bricks Without Straw: Nathanael Greene's Southern Campaigns and Mao Tse-tung's Mobile War* [Manhattan, Kans., 1983], 45).

Whites and blacks enjoyed two other "universal pastimes," as a contemporary called them—fishing and hunting. "The chiefest diversions here [in the South]," reported a traveler, "are fishing, fowling, and hunting wild beast." All sorts and classes of Southerners fished and hunted, often together, just as had their Celtic ancestors. Few Southerners would allow anything to prevent them from spending a day with gun or fishing pole. One man complained that he disliked work because it interrupted his "hunting and fishing." Premodern Celts were "excellent marksmen," as Daniel Defoe and other travelers noted, and Southerners maintained that reputation. A visitor in the South explained: "the sons of the poorest farmer are often as good shots as Viscount Palmerston, and in many instances are as fond of fox-hunting as the sons of the gentry." Shortly after the typical white Southerner learned to ride, he received a gun and was taught to use it. "When he tires of his gun," recalled an Alabamian, "he takes his fishing rods and other tackle, and goes angling." A sojourner in Mississippi was amazed when his host sent "two of his sons, little fellows that looked almost too small to shoulder a gun," for food. "One went off towards the river and the other struck into the forest, and in a few hours we were feasting on delicious venison, trout and turtle." Blacks hunted and fished just as enthusiastically as whites, if less often.[51]

Many Southerners considered fishing an ideal amusement. If practiced correctly, this comfortable pastime required a minimum expenditure of energy to produce maximum results, but even if few fish were caught, one could always boast of the monster that barely got away. Fishing, as performed by Southerners, exemplified perhaps better than anything else their commitment to a leisure ethic. Putting a worm or some insect under water—a procedure often called "drowning worms"—became an art form in the Old South. Catching a fish was far less important to most anglers than escaping the nagging thoughts of everyday life.

To defend the virtues of fishing was typically southern. Jefferson Davis said that "one of the counts he had against Benjamin Franklin was [his] . . . fierce attack on the gentle fisherman." Davis believed that Franklin's "soul was a true type or incarnation of the New

51. Brickell, *Natural History,* 31; Daniel Defoe, *A Tour through the Whole Island of Great Britain [1724–1726],* ed. Pat Rogers (New York, 1971), 666; Burt, *Letters,* II:221; Gideon Lincecum, "Autobiography of Gideon Lincecum," *Mississippi Historical Society Publications* 8 (1904), 467; Hundley, *Social Relations,* 95–96, 32; Claiborne, "Trip through the Piney Woods," 522; John W. Blassingame, ed., *Slave Testimony: Two*

*Centuries of Letters, Speeches, Interviews, and Autobiographies* (Baton Rouge, 1977), 280–82, 653. On fishing and hunting in premodern Celtic Britain, see Sir Jonah Barrington, *Personal Sketches of His Times,* ed. Townsend Young (3d ed., 2 vols., London, 1869), I:38–43; Burt, *Letters,* II:172; Sinclair, *Statistical Account of Scotland,* XVII:507; MacLysaght, *Irish Life,* 38, 132, 214, 228.

England character—hard, calculating, angular, unable to conceive any higher object than the accumulation of money. He was the most material of great intellects. None of the lighter graces or higher aspirations found favor in his sight. . . . The hard, grasping, money-grubbing, pitiless and domineering spirit of the New England puritan found in Franklin a true exponent." Davis further contended: "His school of common sense was the apotheosis of selfish prudence. He could rarely err, for men err from excess of feeling, and Franklin had none." Another Southerner, who defended the values of fishing and hunting, claimed that in the North these activities and "every species of pastime which hinders the making of money is regarded as sinful."[52]

Southerners considered hunting quite as enjoyable as fishing and no more "sinful." An abundance of game throughout the antebellum South encouraged hunting. An Englishwoman wrote from Louisiana: "game is very plentiful here at all seasons of the year—snipes in abundance, and thousands of wild ducks; . . . plenty of deer, quail, gray squirrel and woodcock." Other visitors reported such additional game as partridges, turkeys, curlews, plovers, blackbirds, hares, and foxes. One man spoke fondly of an elk hunt on horseback in Kentucky. Another traveler explained how black bears were tracked and fought, sometimes with only a bowie knife, in the canebrakes—a "dreadful struggle," he admitted, "in which the bear is sometimes victorious." The hunting of bears with only a butcher knife was reportedly the favorite sport of wealthy South Carolinian Wade Hampton.[53]

"The usual weapon of the Southern" hunter, explained a contemporary, was not the knife but "the deadly rifle, . . . and this he handles with such skill as few [others anywhere] possess." A traveler who watched some Southerners on a boat shooting rifles at various objects reported: "I saw some good specimens of . . . skill. A duck was discovered on the water, at the distance of fifty yards, and a sportsman assured us he would take off the top of its head, at that distance; he quite succeeded, and the poor little bird was brought to us literally scalped." Some Southerners could "bark off" a squirrel by firing a rifle so that the ball struck near the squirrel's head, killing the animal by concussion without inflicting a wound.[54]

Few Southerners, or other Celts, went hunting without their

52. Craven, *Prison Life*, 85; Hundley, *Social Relations*, 35.

53. Houstoun, *Texas and the Gulf*, 63; Hunter, *Quebec to Carolina*, 210, 245; Tixier, *Travels*, 45–46, 69, 84; Hundley, *Social Relations*, 32–33, 37; Hoffman, *Winter in the West*, II:156; John W. Thomason, Jr., *Jeb Stuart* (New York,

1941), 214.

54. Hundley, *Social Relations*, 199; Houstoun, *Texas and the Gulf*, 235; Philip Henry Gosse, *Letters from Alabama* . . . (London, 1859), 131–33. See also Lyell, *Second Visit*, II.88; Houstoun, *Texas and the Gulf*, 63.

horses and dogs. "The Scottish Celts, holding that bodily labour of all sorts was mean and disgraceful, devoted themselves mainly to the chase," wrote an authority. The Irish and Scots kept all sorts of hunting dogs—foxhounds, greyhounds, wolf dogs, and other "fierce dogs." Hunts for large game in the Old South, as one man noted, required "skillful horsemanship, a quick eye and steady aim, [and] thoroughly trained horses and dogs." Travelers observed that dogs in the South participated in nearly every type of hunting. One little dog was even used to swim out in a stream and attract alligators. There were dogs for hunting coon, possum, deer, ducks, quail, and for cows and hogs—for example, the Catahoula hog-dog, a special breed. Travelers discovered that every Southerner owned "dogs, both wild and tame," as an Englishwoman noted, just as an eighteenth-century visitor observed that in Ireland "Every cabbin has a dog regularly," and a sixteenth-century sojourner in Scotland found "barking . . . dogs round about" every home. Southerners often kept packs of dogs that did nothing more than bark at strangers or sleep under the front porch. "Walk up to the planter's gate," wrote a visitor, "and we shall be welcomed by the barking of some twenty dogs—hounds, setters, spaniels, terriers, mongrels and 'curs of low degree.' " All of these dogs were considered valuable and necessary; indeed, dogs were so closely associated with Southerners that criticism of a man's dog—even a flea-bitten, worthless, under-the-porch sleeper—was dangerous. Southerners might well kill anyone who demeaned or stole one of their dogs. "Drink my whiskey, steal my wife, but don't mess with my dog," was an old southern expression.[55]

Southerners and other Celts enjoyed such "blood" sports as cock fighting and bear baiting, and they often combined these and other amusements with drinking. Some sportsmen "not infrequently [had] two bottles of different kinds of liquors, dangling, one on either side, from [their] . . . saddles," recorded an observer, who nevertheless believed that the popularity of outdoor activities kept many Southerners healthy despite their dissipation.[56]

55. Rogers, *Social Life*, II:256 (see also 257–86); Cambrensis, *First Version*, 29; MacLysaght, *Irish Life*, 140, 141, 142; Thomas Bellingham, *Diary of Thomas Bellingham, An Officer under William III*, ed. Anthony Hewitson (Preston, Scotland, 1908), 94; Hundley, *Social Relations*, 39–40; Flint, *Recollections*, 339; Hunter, *Quebec to Carolina*, 220–21; Anon., *A Visit to Texas: Being the Journal of a Traveller . . .* (New York, 1834), 94, 141, 125–26; Captain Flack, *A Hunter's Experiences in the Southern States . . .* (London, 1866), 192; Tixier, *Travels*, 72; Houstoun, *Texas and the Gulf*, 128; A. Young, *Tour in Ireland*, I:150; Peter Hume Brown, ed., *Scotland Before 1700, from Contemporary Documents* (Edinburgh, 1893), 123; Schwaab, *Travels in the Old South*, I:237; Bill AuCoin, *Redneck* (Matteson, Ill., 1977), 48–49.

56. Olmsted, *Journey through Texas*, 14; Brickell, *Natural History*, 31–32; François Jean, Marquis de Chastellux, *Travels in North-America . . .* (2 vols., Dublin, 1787), II:386; Fyfe, *Scottish Diaries and Memoirs*, 293, 427–49; MacLysaght, *Irish Life*, 11, 149; Hundley, *Social Relations*, 245, 40.

A HUNTER

From F. D. Srygley, *Seventy Years in Dixie . . .*
(Nashville, 1891), 58.

Not all Celts lived dissolutely. They may not have played with the "decorum and moderation" of Englishmen and Yankees, but Scots, Irishmen, Welshmen, and Southerners all loved sports and recreation. "Sport in Ireland has been an integral part of the daily round as far back as recorded history goes," wrote an authority. "As long as men have lived in Ireland they have played." Celts enjoyed various games, including "shinny," which I played with a ball and "a bent stick" as a boy in the South. But premodern Celts and antebellum Southerners were not much interested in the popular English games of bowling and tennis; nor did they consider it fun to throw "dead dogs and cats . . . at passers-by on certain festival days," or to ring bells, as did the English. Moreover, said a member of the Irish gentry, "the English . . . are as ignorant of an Irish fair as they are of every other matter respecting the 'sister kingdom,' and that is saying a great deal. John Bull, being the most egotistical animal of the creation, measures every man's coat according to his own cloth, and fancying an Irish mob to be like a London rabble, thinks that Donnybrook fair is composed of all the vice, robbery, swindling, and spectacle—together with still rougher manners of its own—of his dear St. Bartholomew. Never was John more mistaken." Many pious Celts, in the Old South and elsewhere, kept "away from race-courses, cock-pits, groggeries, brothels, and the like," noted a contemporary; they made no bets, played no cards, avoided "profane company," and tried to live by the "admonition of the Lord." They partook of such simple pleasures as telling or listening to ghost stories, quilting, husking corn, pulling candy, and whittling. An Englishwoman reported that Southerners spent a good deal of their time "cutting away" at a stick or any nearby wooden furniture.[57]

One of the most popular of Celtic amusements was eating. Premodern Scots, Irish, and Welsh enjoyed feeding and being fed. "The *English* eat well, but are no great Feasters," explained a Frenchman. "They do not invite their Friends to eat at their Houses so frequently as we do in France: But upon certain solemn Occasions they make sumptuous or rather extravagant Banquets." Celts, when they could

57. Valle, *Gentleman's Recreations*, 3, 4, 8, 100–108; Alan Fitzpatrick, "A Nation of Sportsmen," in *Ireland By the Irish*, ed. Michael Gorman (London, 1963), 69; MacLysaght, *Irish Life*, 131, 155; Davies and Edwards, *Welsh Life*, 46; Anon., *The Present State of Ireland: Together with Some Remarques Upon the Antient State Thereof* (London, 1673), 153; Mason, *Statistical Account . . . of Ireland*, III:207; Cesar de Saussure, *A Foreign View of England in the Reigns of George I & George II: The Letters of* Monsieur Cesar de Saussure to His Family, trans. and ed. Madame Van Muyden (London, 1902), 294–95; Paul Hentzner, *A Journey into England in the Year MDXCVIII*, ed. Horace Walpole (Edinburgh, 1881), 54; Barrington, *Personal Sketches*, II:326–27; Hundley, *Social Relations*, 94, 216–17; Mallory Journal, December 27, 1856; Olmsted, *Journey through Texas*, 16; Boggs, *Alexander Letters*, 127, 141; Schwaab, *Travels in the Old South*, II:355; Houstoun, *Texas and the Gulf*, 217.

afford the expense and all too often when they could not, entertained their friends regularly and lavishly.[58]

Southerners were equally extravagant with food. "Gentlemen, we are a great people," proclaimed a Mississippi host, who offered his guests large quantities of "Beef-steak, with or without onions, roast turkey, pork, hominy, fish, eggs, . . . and . . . various drinkables." A Swedish tutor listed the various items served at a typical southern party: "the table . . . was completely covered with turkey, ducks, ham, chicken, chicken salad, oyster pate, bread and butter, cloudberry jelly, blancmange, ice cream, cakes, and on small silver dishes scattered everywhere on the table, various confections commonly called sugarplums; in addition champagne and other wines. One selects in no special order whatever strikes the fancy, and consequently it happens that many begin with ice cream and end with ham." Outsiders complained about the taste and the sameness of southern food but rarely about the amount served. An Englishwoman declared "that eating was . . . the favourite amusement of the ladies of New Orleans. They breakfasted at nine, then a luncheon was spread at eleven, dinner at four, tea at six, and supper at nine o'clock." She also contended: "It is the want of employment to fill up their long leisure hours, (for though highly gifted . . . [southern] ladies are not studious and literary) which, increases the number of their meals, fosters their love of dress, and creates the tendency to gossip."[59]

The same characteristics were noted in the ladies of premodern Celtic Britain. "An eternal round of cards," lamented an Irish woman in 1783. "I once thought our women were better than common, but I recant . . . ; you may be for months, in what is called our best company, without hearing a book named, an opinion stated, or a sentiment introduced which could give rise to a conversation interesting to anyone above a chambermaid." Another observer complained that Irish women spent too much on clothes, dressed far beyond their means, and were devoted to "show," "style," and "modern fashions." But they compensated for these and other faults, said an onlooker, by being "very comely creatures. . . . They are not so reserved as the English, yett very honest." One continental Eu-

58. Henri Misson, *M. Misson's Memoirs and Observations in His Travels over England, With some Account of Scotland and Ireland*, trans. Mr. Ozell (London, 1719), 77; Fyfe, *Scottish Diaries and Memoirs*, 64; Rogers, *Social Life*, I:231–40; Logan, *Scottish Gael*, II:149–55; MacLysaght, *Irish Life*, 89–91; Daniel Corkery, *The Hidden Ireland: A Study of Gaelic Munster in the Eighteenth Cen-*

tury (1924; reprint, Dublin, 1979), 48–49.

59. Lyell, *Second Visit*, II:160; Roos, *Travels in America*, 105; J. W. Dorr, "A Tourist's Description of Louisiana in 1860," ed. Walter Prichard, *Louisiana Historical Quarterly* 21 (1938), 1180–81; Mallory Journal, May 1, 1860; Houstoun, *Texas and the Gulf*, 82.

# Cracker Culture

ropean viewed Scottish women in much the same way as a Frenchman who found the women of the Old South "charming"; "they please me more than those of the northern states," he admitted. "The Scottish ladies, without possessing, perhaps, in so high a degree, that regular beauty which foreigners are struck with among the English, have more grace and vivacity in their countenances," contended a Swiss. "And, although quite as modest, they are equally removed from that cold reserve, and passion to excel, which is a reproach to the English. . . . It is difficult to meet with ladies more amiable . . . [than those] in Scotland. In like manner, that simplicity, grace, and cheerfulness, which they display in their manner of dancing, renders the balls in Edinburgh extremely animated."[60]

The sensual and leisurely pleasures prevailed in the Old South just as they did in premodern Celtic Britain. The lazy Celtic ways that so infuriated the English infuriated the Yankees as well; neither could understand people who, as one critic charged, spent as much time as they could "in idleness and drinking, to the great injury of . . . both . . . morals and industry." It was hard for good Anglo-Saxons to believe that anyone would rather be idle than working, or that anyone could actually believe as did an Alabamian that "if you tax the mind too greatly, both it and the body must suffer. It is all work and no play, you know, that makes Jack a dull boy." If one complained to a Southerner "for not having a job finished at the time agreed upon," noted a Yankee, "he refers you, complacently, to the time unexpectedly spent in amusements."[61]

The leisurely Celtic lifestyle—one of the keystones of Cracker culture—permeated the poor whites and planters alike. People of varied ranks in premodern British Celtic clans often ate, danced, and hunted together, just as did members of extended families in the antebellum South. The typical planter probably spent about as much of his time in "idle habits—hunting, [fishing], [dancing], gander-pulling, card-playing, and getting drunk"—as did his "poor white" cousin. As a perceptive Yankee said of Southerners: "They are easy and amiable in their intercourse with one another, and excessively attached to balls and parties. They certainly live more

60. Martha McTier to Dr. William Drennan [1783–84, autumn or winter], in *The Drennan Letters, Being a Selection from the Correspondence [of] William Drennan, M.D., . . . during the Years 1776–1819*, ed. D. A. Chart (Belfast, 1931), 21; Mason, *Statistical Account . . . of Ireland*, II:402–03; Gernon, "Discourse of Ireland," 357; Montule, *Travels in America*, 85; L. Saussure, *Travels in Scotland*, 27.

61. John Stevens, *The Journal of John Stevens, Containing a Brief Account of the War in Ireland, 1689–1691*, ed. Robert H. Murray (Oxford, 1912), 140–41; Robert Payne, *A Brief Description of Ireland: Made in the Yeere 1589* (London, 1590), 4; Mason, *Statistical Account . . . of Ireland*, II:363, 165–66; Hundley, *Social Relations*, 43; Parsons, *Inside View*, 130.

in sensation, than in reflection. The past and the future are seasons, with which they seem little concerned. The present is their day, and . . . in other words, 'a short life and a merry one,' their motto. Their feelings are easily excited. Tears flow. The excitement passes away, and another train of sensations is started. In the pulpit they expect an ardour, an appeal to the feelings, which the calmer and more reflecting manner of the North would hardly tolerate."[62]

62. Kirk and Thoresby, *Tours in Scotland*, 5; Ramsay, *Scotland and Scotsmen*, II:394–95; Hundley, *Social Relations*, 174, 162–263; Nuttall, *Journal of Travels*, 88; Flint, *Recollections*, 323–24.

# VI

# *Violence*

VISITORS from Europe and the North to the Old South often described white Southerners as a *"heathen* race" of "barbarians" who were "more savage than the Indians." One foreigner complained that killings in Louisiana, which "would be called murder[s] in France," were as common as "quarrels followed by fist fights." A dispute in Texas between Methodists and Presbyterians became so furious, explained a stranger, that "the president of the Presbyterian University was shot down on the street." Some men in Kentucky reportedly "roasted to death, before a large log fire, one of their friends, because he refused to [take a] drink. They did it thus: Three or four of them shoved and held him up to the fire until they themselves could stand it no longer; and he died in 20 hours after. No legal inquiry took place," claimed a visitor from England; "nor, indeed ever takes place among *Rowdies,* as the Backwoodsmen are called." Travelers elsewhere in the antebellum South were appalled by what they saw. "Horrible," announced a Northerner who witnessed several violent encounters, "I would not live in [the South] . . . for a mine of gold."[1]

Stories of southern exorbitance were commonplace. As a joke, a playful Alabama "boy" bit off a piece of a man's ear. On another occasion, several young Kentuckians rode "down to Savannah, with

1. Charles Fenno Hoffman, *A Winter in the West* (2 vols., New York, 1835), II:231; George Hanger Coleraine, *The Life, Adventures, and Opinions of Col. George Hanger,* ed. William Combe (2 vols., London, 1801), II:404–05; Victor Tixier, *Tixier's Travels . . . [1839–1840],* ed. John Francis McDermott (Norman, Okla., 1940), 40; Frederick Law Olmsted, *A Journey through Texas . . .* (1857; reprint, New York, 1969), 69–70; William Faux, *Memorable Days in America . . .* (London, 1823), 179; Henry Benjamin Whipple, *Bishop Whipple's Southern Diary, 1843–1844,* ed. Lester B. Shippee (Minneapolis, 1937), 40. See also George William Featherstonhaugh, *Excursion through the Slave States . . .* (2 vols., London, 1844), II:42–69; J. B. Dunlop, "The Grand Fabric of Republicanism: A Scotsman Describes South Carolina—1810–1811," ed. Raymond A. Mohl, *South Carolina Historical Magazine* 71 (1970), 170–88.

a drove of horses and mules . . . and, having sold them, they were spending the effects of the sale to suit their taste." These young men attracted attention by throwing "three, heavy, cut-glass tumblers, [a] large platter, [some] plates, and knives and forks, and small articles of furniture" from their hotel room window. When the manager went up to investigate, the roisterers threatened to shoot him if he came into their room. The next morning they uncomplainingly paid seventy dollars in damages in addition to their regular fare. A Yankee who witnessed these events expressed "astonishment that those young men would spend so large a sum of money for such a foolish gratification." He was told "that that was a small amount, compared with what is frequently paid for such 'busts' by young men at the South." More typical, he learned, was a young man from the Georgia backcountry who on a Sunday morning drove his carriage on the sidewalks, creating havoc among the pedestrians, and then rode into the saloon at Savannah's largest hotel, where he shot at the bartender. Captured by the police and fined five hundred dollars, the man replied: "Cheap enough! I have had a good frolic."[2]

Good frolics appealed to Southerners, even such dangerous affairs as the race of two boats down the Mississippi River. On board one boat "was an old lady, who, having bought a winter stock of bacon, pork, &c., was returning to her home on the banks of the Mississippi." Fun lovers on board both boats insisted upon a race; cheers and drawn pistols obliged the captains to cooperate. As the boats struggled to outdistance each other, excited passengers demanded more speed. Despite every effort, the boats raced evenly until the old lady directed her slaves to throw all her casks of bacon into the boilers. Her boat then moved ahead of the other vessel, which suddenly exploded: "clouds of splinters and human limbs darken[ed] the sky." On the undamaged boat passengers shouted their victory. But above their cheers could "be heard the shrill voice of the old lady, crying, 'I did it, I did it—it's all my bacon!' "[3]

Southerners seemed all too addicted to such extravagant and deadly activity. A European visitor reported that it was "absolutely necessary to carry arms in the South." Houses in Grand Gulf, Mississippi, another man claimed, "show the most conclusive proof of outward violence in broken windows, splintered doors, etc. . . . Several suspicious characters have been hanged and 1 whipped to death. Here every man carries a cane that illy conceals a poniard & from

2. W. Stuart Harris, "Rowdyism, Public Drunkenness, and Bloody Encounters in Early Perry County," *Alabama Review* 33 (1980), 19; Charles G. Parsons, *Inside View of Slavery: or,* a *Tour Among the Planters* (Cleveland, 1855), 29–31.

3. Henry Anthony Murray, *Lands of the Slave and the Free . . .* (2 vols., London, 1855), I:227–29.

the bosom of everyone the silver handle of a dagger peeps out." A Texan told a Swiss traveler: "We in Texas don't need so much quiet and orderly people, we need restless minds, men that have a noose around their necks and sparks in their bodies, who don't value their lives more highly than a nutshell and are handy with their rifles." Southerners typically exaggerated their tales and often "put on" outsiders, but a visitor was correct when he said that in the South a "bowie-knife was a universal, and a pistol a not at all unusual, companion." And incidents were bound to occur. "Yesterday a gentleman, drunk, in the stage, drew his dirk," reported a traveler. "He had the stage stopped, jumped out and fought the other passengers, myself excepted. They dressed him soundly, disarmed him, and with the unanimous consent of the screaming ladies, left him behind, on the road, to fight and spit fire at the trees."[4]

One observer mentioned several specific encounters that he claimed were characteristically southern. The first was an enraged diner "deliberately shooting at another in the dining saloon." Next was the case of a man, "hard pressed by creditors, who . . . seized a bowie-knife in each hand, and rushed among them, stabbing and ripping right and left, till checked in his mad career of assassination by a creditor, in self-defence, burying a cleaver in his skull." A third incident involved one Levi Tarver, who met another man on a public road and exchanged "high words" with him; the man "drew a bowie-knife, and completely severed, at one blow, Levi's head from his body." The final affair occurred when two gentlemen began kicking each other at a "respectable evening party" after one stepped on the other's toe; a borrowed bowie knife brought the dispute to a bloody end. The man who reported these events did not consider all Southerners to be "blood-thirsty"; indeed, he thought that many were "the most kind, quiet, and amiable men I have ever met; but, when taken in connexion with the free use of the bowie-knife, they afford strong evidence that there is [in the South] a general and extraordinary recklessness of human life."[5]

The Southerner's propensity to fight surprised and disturbed many observers. "The darkest side of the southerner is his quarrelsomeness, and recklessness of human life," wrote a wayfarer. "The terrible bowie-knife is ever ready to be drawn, and it is drawn and used too, on the slightest provocation. Duels are fought with this

4. William Kingsford, *Impressions of the West and South . . .* (Toronto, 1858), 53; Barton Griffith, *The Diary of Barton Griffith, Covington, Indiana, 1832–34 . . .* (Crawfordsville, Ind., 1932), 13; Charles Sealsfield, *America: Glorious and Chaotic Land . . .*, trans. E. L. Jordan (Englewood Cliffs, N.J., 1969), 151; Olmsted, *Journey through Texas*, 20; Faux, *Memorable Days*, 200. See also J. B. Dunlop, "A Scotsman Visits Georgia in 1811," ed. Raymond A. Mohl, *Georgia Historical Quarterly* 55 (1971), 259–74.

5. H. Murray, *Lands of the Slave and the Free*, I:243–46.

horrible weapon, in which the combatants are almost chopped to pieces; or with the no less fatal, but less shocking rifle, perhaps within pistol-distance." In the matter of duels, one traveler said that a colonel in the South Carolina militia introduced him to several "young gentlemen . . . who, with the young colonel, had all there met as gay proud birds of a feather; men, I mean, who, in duels, had killed their man each!" Some encounters were especially gruesome. A man described what he called "one of the bloodiest duels ever fought in this section of ᴛhe country. The arrangement was that each [antagonist] should be armed with a double barrelled gun loaded with buck shot, with a pair of pistols & a bowie knife. At the word they were to advance towards each other and fire at such time as they pleased. If the guns failed to kill they were to use the pistols & then finish with bowie knives & fight until one or the other was killed. They fought until both were very badly mutilated and then the seconds separated them."[6]

Various writers have attempted to account for southern violence but with little success. The usual explanation that slavery made Southerners violent is far too simplistic; so is the assertion that the antebellum South was a frontier and therefore a violent society. Some of the most violent parts of the South had few slaves; nor were all frontiers in America and abroad tumultuous places. The South was and still is a violent society because violence is one of the cultural traditions that Southerners brought with them to America.[7]

Their Celtic ancestors were, authorities agree, characteristically violent. "Their propensity to fight led them into hostilities on very slight occasions," one writer explained. "The whole race was warlike and fierce, and ready to fight with the greatest ardour . . . but accompanied with a rashness and temerity not very compatible with military discipline." Proud and contentious Scots, Irish, Welsh, and

6. Philip Henry Gosse, *Letters from Alabama* . . . (London, 1859), 250–51; Faux, *Memorable Days*, 45; Whipple, *Southern Diary*, 32–33.

7. The influence of culture on southern violence is noted in such important recent studies as Sheldon Hackney, "Southern Violence," *American Historical Review* 74 (1969), 906–25; Raymond D. Gastil, "Homicide and a Regional Culture of Violence," *American Sociological Review* 36 (1971), 412–27; Dickson D. Bruce, Jr., *Violence and Culture in the Antebellum South* (Austin, 1979); John Shelton Reed, "Below the Smith and Wesson Line: Southern Violence," in *One South: An Ethnic Approach to Regional Culture* (Baton Rouge, 1982), 139–53; Elliott J. Gorn, " 'Gouge and Bite, Pull Hair and Scratch': The Social Significance of Fighting in the Southern Backcountry," *American Historical Review* 90 (1985), 18–43; Bertram Wyatt-Brown, *Southern Honor: Ethics and Behavior in the Old South* (New York, 1982); and Edward L. Ayers, *Vengeance and Justice: Crime and Punishment in the 19th-Century South* (New York, 1984). Wyatt-Brown and Ayers also emphasize the importance of honor as well as cultural continuity, and Wyatt-Brown further recognizes the Celtic influence (among others) in shaping the Old South, but none of these works traces the emphasis on violence and honor in southern culture to its primary source—the South's Celtic heritage.

A DISPUTE AT DINNER

From *Harper's New Monthly Magazine* 13 (1856), 312.

"AN IRISH MODE OF 'CHALLENGING A JURY'"

From *Punch, or the London Charivari* 6 (1844), 80.

other Celtic people—touchy about their honor and dignity—were ever ready for either mass combat or individual duels.[8]

Scotland's history, as an Englishman noted, was "characterised by violence of a scale and of an intensity unknown in England." Clansmen went everywhere armed, and their accoutrements included a knife, pistols, a sword, and often a gun as well. "The Highlanders have been always fond of arms, and handle them with great dexterity," observed a contemporary. "They are accustomed from their infancy to wear them." Moreover, "Highlanders were eternally handling their firearms, and frequently discharging them; no prohibition had . . . been able to prevent that abuse." A Scottish historian noted that the Highlanders "lived in a perpetual state of war . . . ; thus arms were a sort of profession to [them]. . . . They usually despised all peaceful means of subsistence." "Every person wished to be thought a soldier," explained an eighteenth-century Scot, who insisted that the popular poetry of the country "might, with great propriety, be termed pastorals for warriors. And great was their influence upon . . . both sexes, from the highest to the lowest. Their poetical tales, breathing a warlike spirit, were well calculated to inspire the men with an ardent desire of imitating, on some future occasion, their ancient worthies. The women, too, who were passionately fond of them, regarded the martial virtues as essential in a son or a lover."[9]

Conflicts and feuds were customary. "The Highlanders, before they were disarmed," observed Dr. Samuel Johnson, "were so addicted to quarrels, that the boys used to follow any publick procession or ceremony, however festive, or however solemn, in expectation of the battle, which was sure to happen before the company dispersed." An English officer reported that the people of Inverness had small windows with heavy shutters on the ground floor of their houses because "in their Clan-Quarrels, several had been shot from

8. James Logan, *The Scottish Gael; or, Celtic Manners, as Preserved Among the Highlanders* . . . (1876; reprint, 2 vols., Edinburgh, 1976), I:116–17. See also Alwyn Rees and Brinley Rees, *Celtic Heritage: Ancient Tradition in Ireland and Wales* (London, 1961), 122–23; Lloyd Laing, *Celtic Britain* (New York, 1979), 148; Barry Cunliffe, *The Celtic World* (New York, 1979), 42–59; Gerald of Wales, *The Journey Through Wales and The Description of Wales,* trans. Lewis Thorpe (New York, 1978), 233–74; Ann Ross, *Everyday Life of the Pagan Celts* (London, 1970), 56.

9. Walter Allen, *The British Isles* (London, 1965), 21; Thomas Kirk and

Ralph Thoresby, *Tours in Scotland, 1677 & 1681,* ed. Peter Hume Brown (Edinburgh, 1892), 29; James Maxwell, *Narrative of Charles Prince of Wales' Expedition to Scotland in the Year 1745* (Edinburgh, 1841), 27, 110; Robert Chambers, *History of the Rebellion of 1745–1746* (Edinburgh, 1869), 31; John Ramsay, *Scotland and Scotsmen in the Eighteenth Century, from the MSS. of John Ramsay, Esq. of Ochteryre,* ed. Alexander Allardyce (2 vols., Edinburgh, 1888), II:408, 409. See also Logan, *Scottish Gael,* I:328; Eve Begley, *Of Scottish Ways* (New York, 1977), 55–57, 61–62, 100–101.

the opposite Side of the Way, when they were in their Chamber, and by these Shutters they were concealed and in safety."[10]

A careful observer described the Irish as "a barbarous and . . . a warlike people," with a "romantic sense of honour"; inordinately proud; "wild and unruly"; "with passions the most violent and sensitive." Such quarrelsome people were always ready to fight foreigners—or each other. Murder in early seventeenth-century Ireland was punished "only by [a] fine," and in the sixteenth century a visitor claimed that the native Irish left "the right arms of their infant males unchristened . . . [so that they] might give a more ungracious and deadly blow." Travelers agreed that the Irish enjoyed fights and feuds. "It is not unusual with them to meet in clans or factions, for the avowed purpose of a battle," wrote an Englishman. And a German visitor noted "the sudden and continual wild quarrels and national pitched battles with the shillelah (a murderous sort of stick which every man keeps hidden under his rags), in which hundreds take part in a minute, and do not resist till several are left dead or wounded on the field; the frightful war-whoop which they set up on these occasions; the revenge for an affront or injury, which is cherished and inherited by whole villages."[11]

Duels, as late as the eighteenth century, "were an everyday occurrence in their lives," wrote a distinguished Irish historian, "and the results were often fatal." An Irish judge recalled: "Our elections were more prolific in duels than any other public meetings: they very seldom originated at a horse-race, cock-fight, hunt, or at any place of amusement: folks then had pleasure in view, and 'something else to do' than to quarrel; but at all elections, or at assizes, or, in fact, at any place of business, almost every man, without any very particular reason, immediately became a violent partisan, and frequently a furious enemy to somebody else; and gentlemen often got themselves shot before they could tell what they were fighting about." This judge also observed: "It is incredible what a singular

---

10. R.W. Chapman, ed., *Johnson's Journey to the Western Islands of Scotland and Boswell's Journal of a Tour to the Hebrides with Samuel Johnson, LL.D.* (Oxford, 1970), 40; Edward Burt, *Burt's Letters from the North of Scotland*, ed. R. Jamieson (1754; reprint, 2 vols., Edinburgh, 1974), I:61. On Scottish violence, see also John Prebble, *Culloden* (Harmondsworth, England, 1967), 32–53, 300.

11. Thomas Crofton Croker, *Researches in the South of Ireland . . .* (1824; reprint, New York, 1969), 2, 4, 13, 224–25, 231; Constantia Maxwell, ed., *Irish History from Contemporary Sources (1509–1610)* (London, 1923), 352; Edmund Campion, *A Historie of Ireland, Written in the Yeare 1571*, ed. James Ware (1633; reprint, Dublin, 1809), 21; William Shaw Mason, ed., *A Statistical Account or Parochial Survey of Ireland, Drawn up from the Communications of the Clergy* (3 vols., Dublin, 1814–19), III:471; [Hermann Ludwig Heinrich], *Tour in England, Ireland, and France in the Years 1826, 1827, 1828, and 1829* (Philadelphia, 1833), 348–49. See also Mason, *Statistical Account . . . of Ireland*, II:97, 364–65, 455–56, III:72–73.

passion the Irish gentlemen, though in general excellent-tempered fellows, formerly had for fighting each other"—this from a man who remembered 227 "memorable and official duels" fought during what he called "my grand climacteric."[12]

Another Irishman stated that the "universal practice of duelling [in eighteenth-century Ireland] . . . contributed not a little to the disturbed and ferocious state of society." He pointed out that dueling clubs existed throughout the country; in fact, no gentleman could take "his proper station in life till he had 'smelt powder,' as it was called; no barrister could go circuit till he had obtained a reputation in this way; no election, and scarcely an assizes, passed without a number of duels; and many men of the bar . . . owed their eminence, not to powers of eloquence or to legal ability, but to a daring spirit and the number of duels they had fought." A dueling "code of laws and regulations were drawn up as a standard, to refer to on all points of honour." Irish laws prohibited dueling, "but such was the spirit of the times, that they remained a dead letter. No prosecution ensued, or even if it did, no conviction would follow."[13]

When South Carolinians "talked of the duello, and of famous hands with the pistol in these parts," a native of Ireland noted, their "conversation had altogether very much the tone which would have probably characterised the talk of a group of Tory Irish gentlemen over their wine some sixty years ago." Indeed, the eighteenth-century Irish gentlemen who so vigorously favored dueling were known as "Fire-Eaters," and the published *Irish Code of Honor* was the model for South Carolina's own dueling code.[14]

Violence was also a significant part of the culture of the Celtic fringe of England and Wales. The "reiver" tradition of the English-Scottish border country prevailed in Cumberland even into the nineteenth century, and an Englishman noted that many of the "inhabitants . . . are descendants of the borderers, who yet retain much of their native fierceness and savage courage." The Welsh, who loved combat so much that they would "fight without protection against men clad in iron, unarmed against those bearing weap-

---

12. Edward MacLysaght, *Irish Life in the Seventeenth Century* (1939; reprint, Dublin, 1979), 91; Sir Jonah Barrington, *Personal Sketches of His Own Times*, ed. Townsend Young (3d ed., 2 vols., London, 1869), I:285, 272–73. See also Charles Topham Bowden, *A Tour through Ireland* (Dublin, 1791), 25–26; De Latocnaye, *A Frenchman's Walk through Ireland, 1796–7*, trans. and ed. John Stevenson (Belfast, 1917), 120–21.

13. John Edward Walsh, *Sketches of Ireland Sixty Years Ago* (Dublin, 1847),

18, 22–23, 30. See also Daniel Corkery, *The Hidden Ireland: A Study of Gaelic Munster in the Eighteenth Century* (1924; reprint, Dublin, 1979), 57.

14. William Howard Russell, *My Diary North and South* (2 vols., London, 1863), I:188; Barrington, *Personal Sketches*, I:270 (the chapter on dueling is entitled "The Fire-Eaters"); Jack K. Williams, *Dueling in the Old South: Vignettes of Social History* (College Station, Tex., 1980), 40–41, 100.

ons, on foot against mounted cavalry," enjoyed the sport of "purring," in which two opponents grasped each other firmly by the shoulders. At the starting signal, they began kicking each other in the shins (their shoes had toeplates). The first man to release his grip was declared the loser.[15]

In describing the violent ways of antebellum Southerners, observers often used the same terms employed in descriptions of other Celts and sometimes even compared Southerners to Celts. The first trial in Williamsburg County, South Carolina, was held in 1806, and the four men—at least three with Irish surnames—who were charged with assault and battery reportedly said they had "held a good old Irish discussion with sticks, pleaded guilty, paid their fines, and considered the money well spent." In 1861 an observer found Irishmen living in the South as eager as native Southerners to fight Yankees. In fact, an Englishman stated, the Old South "appears to resemble Ireland, or what Ireland was 60 years ago. One hears of bowie-knives and revolvers continually, and I was assured that nine-tenths of the party carried them in their pockets." In a Montgomery, Alabama, hotel in May 1861 William H. Russell noted the same phenomenon: "One of our party comes in to say that he could scarce get down to the [hotel lobby] . . . on account of the crowd, and all the people who passed him had very sharp bones. He remarks thereupon to the clerk at the bar, who tells [him] that the particular projections he alludes to are implements of defence or offence, as the case may be, and adds, 'I suppose you and your [English] friends are the only people in the house who haven't a bowie-knife, or a six-shooter, or Derringer about them.' " Furthermore, Southerners were as willing as any other Celts to use the weapons they carried. One sightseer declared that a Southerner would challenge anyone to a duel, "no matter whether he be his best friend or his worst enemy. He acts on the impulse of the moment, and puts no restraint on his passions. When provoked he gives way to the feeling of revenge, and as all classes go armed, he attacks the object of his hatred. . . . The only security for life . . . is the belief that every one is armed and ready to use his weapons in an instant."[16]

In their violent attitudes and practices Celts and Southerners were

15. George MacDonald Fraser, *The Steel Bonnets* (New York, 1972); James Dugdale, *The New British Traveller; or, Modern Panorama of England and Wales* . . . (4 vols., London, 1819), I:621; Gerald of Wales, *Journey Through Wales,* 234; Bruce Felton and Mark Fowler, *Felton's & Fowler's More Best, Worst and Most Unusual* (New York, 1976), 86.
16. Mary R. Reid, "Williamsburg County [South Carolina] Court House," *Three Rivers Chronicle* 1 (1981), 2; W. Russell, *Diary North and South,* I:411, 238; Robert Everest, *A Journey Through the United States and Part of Canada* (London, 1855), 91; James Logan, *Notes of a Journey through Canada, the United States of America, and the West Indies* . . . (Edinburgh, 1838), 178.

vastly different from the peaceful professions and habits of English-men and Yankees, who boasted that they were and always had been less violent and more civilized than their neighbors. "More robberies and murders are committed in Virginia, than in all England," stated an Englishman visiting the South. "There are fewer capital crimes committed in New England since its settlement than in any other country on the globe . . . in proportion to the number of its inhabitants," claimed the president of Yale College. "During the last fourteen years," he declared shortly before his death in 1817, "I have traveled . . . twelve thousand miles, chiefly in New England and New York, and in this extensive progress have never seen two men employed in fighting. Nor do I remember more than one instance of this nature which fell under my own eye during my life."[17]

Duels, which were so popular with Celts and Southerners, were much rarer in England and in the North. English gentlemen denounced dueling as early as the seventeenth century, and a Frenchman wrote in the eighteenth century: "It may be said with entire justice that Englishmen are very brave [but] . . . very few are partisans of duelling." The English frequently denounced and lampooned dueling. As for New England, Timothy Dwight claimed that, since its settlement, five duels had been fought there and only two involved residents.[18]

Southerners, who scorned such pacifism, considered Yankees and Englishmen too business-minded and dishonorable to fight. An Englishman reported that Southerners held the English in "contempt" because they "believe that we, too [like Yankees], have had the canker of peace upon us. One evidence of this, according to Southern men, is the abolition of duelling. This practice, according to them, is highly wholesome and meritorious." But others regarded these affairs of honor as deplorable atrocities. "Cruel horrid custom thus to butcher & destroy men for the false code of honor," admonished a Yankee. "Honor! It is a vague idea the duelist has of honor." Dr.

17. Faux, *Memorable Days,* 127; Timothy Dwight, *Travels in New England and New York,* ed. Barbara Miller Solomon (4 vols., Cambridge, Mass., 1969), I:123.

18. Donna Andrew, "The Code of Honour and Its Critics: The Opposition to Duelling in England, 1700–1850," *Social History* 5 (1980), 409–34; Marcia Valle, *The Gentleman's Recreations: Accomplishments and Pastimes of the English Gentleman, 1580–1630* (Cambridge, 1977), 65; Cesar de Saussure, *A Foreign View of England in the Reigns of George I & George II: The Letters of Monsieur Cesar de Saussure to His*

*Family,* trans. and ed. Madame Van Muyden (London, 1902), 179; Dwight, *Travels,* I:123. On the lack of violent crime in Puritan New England, see David T. Konig, *Law and Society in Puritan Massachusetts: Essex County, 1629–1692* (Chapel Hill, 1979); David H. Flaherty, "Crime and Social Control in Provincial Massachusetts," *Historical Journal* 24 (1981), 339–60; and Eli Faber, "Puritan Criminals: The Economic, Social, and Intellectual Background of Crime in Seventeenth-Century Massachusetts," *Perspectives in American History* 11 (1977–78), 83–114.

# Cracker Culture

Samuel Johnson, who denounced dueling, insisted that there was never a "case in England [unlike in Celtic areas] where one or other of the combatants *must* die: If you have overcome your adversary by disarming him, that is sufficient[;] . . . you should not kill him; your honour, or the honour of your family, is restored, as much as it can be by a duel." Shocked by bloody southern encounters, an Englishman wrote: "The barbarous baseness and cruelty of public opinion [in the South] dooms young men, when challenged, to fight. They must fight, kill or be killed, and that for some petty offence beneath the notice of the law. Established names only . . . may refuse to fight, but this is rarely done; to refuse is a stain and high dishonor." An Englishwoman stated: "Very often fathers will go . . . with their sons—quite boys—to see them fight. . . . There is a recklessness and carelessness about these Southerners which I did not think the Anglo-Saxon race could attain under any circumstances." Her mistake, of course, was thinking that the South's cultural heritage was Anglo-Saxon.[19]

Southern ways simply were too foreign for most Yankee and English observers to understand or appreciate. One Northerner was appalled that a southern woman would have her brother's marble monument inscribed "Micajah Green Lewis who fell in a duel." But southern women, like traditional Celtic women, often supported dueling. After all, an Englishman acknowledged, the South was a violent place, "the land of Lynch law and bowie knives . . . [as] barbarous as a jungle inhabited by wild beasts." Even the literature written by Southerners, a Northerner declared, was "atrocious"—full of "gouging, biting, and horse-play which form the body of their humour"—and "valuable only to the moralist as expressive of the sort of savage spirit which slavery could breed in people."[20]

To blame southern violence on slavery rather than the South's cultural heritage was typical, even though most Yankees regarded Southerners with fully as much contempt as Englishmen regarded

19. W. Russell, *Diary North and South,* I:93; Whipple, *Southern Diary,* 29; Chapman, *Johnson's Journey,* 313–14; Faux, *Memorable Days,* 187; Barbara Leigh Smith Bodichon, *An American Diary, 1857–8,* ed. Joseph W. Reed, Jr. (London, 1972), 64. See also J. Williams, *Dueling,* 75.

20. Welcome Arnold Green, *The Journal of Welcome Arnold Green: Journeys in the South, 1822–1824,* ed. Alice E. Smith (Madison, 1957), 116–17; J. Williams, *Dueling,* 19; W. Russell, *Diary North and South,* II:9, 11; William Dean Howells, "American Letter: The Southern States in Recent American Litera-ture," *Literature,* no. 47 (London, September 10, 1898), 231. See also Philo Tower, *Slavery Unmasked: Being a Truthful Narrative of Three Years' Residence and Journeying in Eleven Southern States . . .* (Rochester, N.Y., 1856), 386; H. Murray, *Lands of the Slave and the Free,* I:247; John Benwell, *An Englishman's Travels in America . . .* (London, 1853), 106, 115; John Henry Vessey, *Mr. Vessey of England: Being the Incidents and Reminiscences of Travel in a Twelve Weeks' Tour through the United States and Canada in the Year 1859,* ed. Brian Waters (New York, 1956), 103.

Celts. A Northerner advised Yankees to "mingle freely" with Southerners "and . . . strive to bring up their habits, by a successful example, to the New England standard." When that proved impossible, stronger measures were recommended. "I believe," announced a saintly Northerner, "that the great conception of a Christian society, which was in the minds of the Pilgrims of the Mayflower . . . is to displace and blot out the foul [South] . . . with all its heaven-offending enormities." Many Massachusetts soldiers in the Civil War favored a policy of genocide toward Southerners. "I would exterminate them root and branch," wrote one Yankee just after the war. "They have often said they preferred it before subjugation, and, with the help of God, I would give it them. I am only saying what thousands say every day."[21]

In calls to exterminate Southerners and their "odious ways," Northerners sounded much like Englishmen who advocated the obliteration of their "barbarian" Celtic neighbors. It may be no coincidence that the Irish-born reporter William H. Russell described northern Secretary of War Edwin Stanton as "excessively vain . . . a rude, rough, vigorous Oliver Cromwell sort of man." Typically, Yankees referred to Southerners as dirty and ignorant, just as the English had spoken of the Irish, the Welsh, and the Scots. A Connecticut soldier informed his sister that the "Rebels are Barbarians and savages."[22]

In support of these charges of barbarism, several Yanks reported that some Confederates beheaded their enemies. A Massachusetts soldier claimed that in May 1862 he discovered in an abandoned Rebel camp five neatly polished skulls inscribed with the words "Five Zouaves' Coconuts killed at Bull Run by Southern lead." Another Yankee insisted that Confederates had used the skulls of slain Federals as soup bowls, and a Minnesotan reported that he found in an abandoned Confederate campsite the cranium of a Union soldier that had been "used by the Rebs for a soap dish."[23]

Such claims may have been true. Though the practice of decapitating an enemy and saving his head appears to have been uncommon in the Confederacy, it was not unprecedented either in Celtic history or in the Old South. "They cut off the heads of enemies slain in battle and attach them to the necks of their horses," explained Diodorus. "The bloodstained spoils [the ancient Celts] . . . carry off as booty, while striking up a paean and singing a song of victory;

21. Abner D. Jones, *Illinois and the West* (Boston, 1838), 157; Julian M. Sturtevant, *An Address in Behalf of the Society for the Promotion of Theological Education in the West* (New York, 1853), 568–69; Bell I. Wiley, *The Life of Billy Yank: The Common Soldier of the Union* (Indianapolis, 1951), 346.

22. W. Russell, *Diary North and South*, II:433; Prebble, *Culloden*, 231–300; Wiley, *Life of Billy Yank*, 349.

23. Wiley, *Life of Billy Yank*, 347.

and they nail up these first fruits upon their houses." Livy, writing in the third century B.C., mentioned "Gallic horsemen . . . with heads hanging at their horses' breasts, or fixed on their lances, and singing their customary songs of triumph." He also stated that Celts beheaded the Roman consul-elect Lucius Postumius, "cleaned out the head . . . and gilded the skull, which thereafter served them . . . as a drinking cup."[24]

Lest these accounts be dismissed as hyperbole, it should be remembered that beheading enemies is a recurring theme in Irish and Welsh literature. Cu Chulainn, the famous Celtic folk hero, collected many heads; indeed, he once displayed twelve that he had taken in combat. A judge recalled a contest between two Irish gentlemen who "in the presence of the archbishop and all the chief authorities and ladies of rank" fought with broadswords and large knives until one beheaded the other "very expertly with his knife . . . and . . . handed it to the lords-justices . . . by whom the head and neck was most graciously received." Scots often beheaded their enemies, especially those who aroused their hatred, and decapitation also was practiced in the antebellum South. When Kentuckians captured outlaw Micajah Harpe, for example, they not only cut off his head but Squire Silas McBee rode home with it attached to his saddle and stuck the trophy on a tree "as a warning to other outlaws." The actual beheading was done in a gruesome manner by a man who "took Harpe's own butcher knife, . . . and taking Harpe by the hair of the head, drew the knife slowly across the back of his neck, cutting to the bone." While this occurred, Harpe remarked: "You are a God damned rough butcher, but cut on and be damned." The executioner proceeded to cut around Harpe's neck, and "then wrung off his head, in the same manner a butcher would of a hog." A few years later the head of Samuel Mason was exhibited in Natchez, and the heads of Wiley Harpe and James May were stuck on poles by a Mississippi roadside as "warnings to highwaymen." Late in the antebellum period a Yankee visitor in the South saw a sight, he wrote, "which makes my very blood run cold as I think of it . . . a human head stuck on a pole." An outlawed runaway slave had been killed and his severed head "put upon the highway, as a terror to deter other slaves from following in his footsteps."[25]

24. Ross, *Everyday Life of the Pagan Celts*, 73; Cunliffe, *Celtic World*, 83–86.

25. T. G. E. Powell, *The Celts* (New York, 1958), 108; Ross, *Everyday Life of the Pagan Celts*, 72–74; Cunliffe, *Celtic World*, 82–87; Mary McGarry, comp., *Great Folk Tales of Old Ireland* (New York, 1972), 74, 91; Jeremiah Curtin, *Myths and Folk-Lore of Ireland* (New York, 1975), 309–26; Barrington, *Personal Sketches*, I:271; Wallace Notestein, *The Scots in History* (reprint, Westport, Conn., 1970), 36; James Hall, *Letters from the West; Containing Sketches of Scenery, Manners, and Customs . . .* (reprint, Gainesville, 1967), 265–82; Paul I. Wellman, *Spawn of Evil* (New York, 1965), 80–100, 120–35; Tower,

# Violence

Violent deaths were far more frequent in the South than in other parts of the country. In a sparsely populated region of Georgia a visitor learned that "about as many men died by being *killed*, as in any other way; there being a man in jail for murder, in each of five contiguous counties." "The South has the unenviable distinction of having slain a greater number of their fellow men with murderous hands than all the other States ... put together," announced a Mississippi preacher in 1855. During the preceding year, he pointed out, more men died violently in Mississippi alone than in all the six New England states, though those states had an aggregate population five times as great as that of Mississippi. "The reckless manner in which the sixth commandment, which forbids murder, is disregarded in this community, is truly alarming," proclaimed this minister, who insisted that if "these murders were committed by vagabonds and the scum of society ... [the] moral effect would not be so injurious to society. But ... [too often] men of fair standing in society, received and regarded as gentlemen, are the perpetrators of the butcheries!"[26]

Visitors noticed the excessive violence in southern society and how unconcerned most Southerners were about it, as well as how often crimes of violence went unpunished. "The law is not duly enforced," complained an observer, who charged that "legalized duelling ... and deliberate assassination" were all too common. Other peripatetics stated that men literally got away with murder in the Old South. As one Yankee insisted, "The administration of justice throughout the South is far more imperfect and partial than in the North."[27]

Southern courts and lawmen often paid little attention to violence. "Public fights" in the South, where "gentlemen descend to the common bully," remarked a Yankee, were abundant. "Witnessed

---

*Slavery Unmasked*, 144. During the American Revolution, Major Henry ("Light-Horse Harry") Lee, the famous Virginia cavalry leader and father of Robert E. Lee, ordered the head of an executed deserter cut off and placed on the gallows as a warning to others. This, he informed General George Washington, "had a very immediate effect for the better on both troops and inhabitants" (Lee quoted in Charles Royster, *A Revolutionary People at War: The Continental Army and American Character, 1775–1783* [New York, 1979], 81–82).

26. [Jeremiah Evarts], *Through the South and the West with Jeremiah Evarts in 1826*, ed. J. Orin Oliphant (Lewisburg, Pa., 1956), 105; the Reverend James A.

Lyon quoted in the *Columbus* (Mississippi) *Eagle*, June 1, 1855. On the high homicide rate in the Old South, see Robert M. Ireland, "Homicide in Nineteenth Century Kentucky," *Register of the Kentucky Historical Society* 81 (1983), 134–53.

27. William Charles Macready, *The Diaries of William Charles Macready, 1833–1851*, ed. William Toynbee (2 vols., London, 1912), II:246; Whipple, *Southern Diary*, 128–29; Josiah Quincy, "A Journal, 1773," in *Josiah Quincy (1722–1864), Memoir of the Life of Josiah Quincy ...*, ed. Eliza Susan Quincy (3d ed., Boston, 1875), 89, 95; Parsons, *Inside View*, 139.

a laughable trial today of one judge . . . for having whipped another judge," wrote this same observer, who also noted that "there are six indictments against individuals for fights at this session of court." But none of these was regarded as a serious offense. "During the recess of court," explained this Northerner, "one of the . . . jury men came below & found his hopeful son of some 8 or 9 years of age fighting with another boy. The father looked coolly on until it was ended and then said, 'Now you little devil, if you catch him down again bite him, chaw his lip or you never'll be a man.' Really a singular character to guard over the peace & well being of the country but only one of the numerous specimens of this fighting spirit only to be found in the South."[28]

Just how ineffective southern lawmen were in suppressing violence is illustrated in the account of a foreigner who saw two young North Carolinians fighting "in front of the house and in the presence of the Justice of the Peace. Women, children, and blacks gathered around." Several times the justice calmly asked the fighters to stop. When they ignored him, he stepped back to enjoy the combat. His wife, "outraged at the disobedience," rushed up and "repeated the commands of her husband, but was received with derision. Finally, the antagonists cooled, shook hands by the fighting code, and each rode on his way." At that point the puzzled foreigner asked the justice: "By the law, must they not give obedience to your commands, and abstain from their squabbling in your presence?" His answer was: "They should." And when asked if he could not bring the men into court and have them punished for their behavior, he replied: "I could." But it was clear to the foreigner that this "good-natured Justice, who seemed to make far less of the matter than his indignant wife, and was of the opinion that it was more in keeping with his official worth to pass over an apparent slight, instead of taking the proud revenge which an injured self-love might demand."[29]

Another reason why the justice may have been reluctant to enforce the law, which apparently the foreigner failed to perceive, was that it would have been dangerous to do so. A lawman who was too diligent, or who offended the wrong man or family, could get himself injured or killed. Southern families, like those of their Celtic ancestors, were extended and clannish, and family feuds in the Old South were as easy to start and as difficult to stop as they were in premod-

28. Whipple, *Southern Diary*, 24–25. See James W. Ely, Jr., and David J. Bodenhamer, "Regionalism and the Legal History of the South," in *Ambivalent Legacy: A Legal History of the South*, ed. David J. Bodenhamer and James W. Ely, Jr. (Jackson, Miss., 1984), 17–24, for a review of the literature on southern violence and crime.

29. Johann David Schopf, *Travels in the Confederation [1783–1784] . . .*, trans. and ed. Alfred J. Morrison (new ed., 2 vols., New York, 1968), II:123.

A FIST FIGHT

From *Harper's New Monthly Magazine* 24 (1861–62), 282.

ern Scotland and Ireland. Southerners tended to protect family members from the law and to take revenge against family enemies just as their forefathers had done. In 1830, rather than allow a deputy sheriff to serve a writ on one of their kinsmen, some rural Alabamians imprisoned the deputy beneath a grocery store until he promised to leave the area and never come back. When several feuding Kentucky families met at a funeral they opened fire on each other, regardless of the crowd. "These occurrences are so common in this State," claimed an Englishman, "that little excitement was produced, and no attempt was made to arrest the parties."[30]

Such actions had Celtic models. In 1730 an English officer observed that Scots were inclined to excuse the crimes of their fellow clansmen. Jail keepers often allowed "Murderers and other notorious Villains" to escape, insisted an Englishman, who claimed that "the greatest Part of these Escapes have been the Consequences, either of Clan-Interest or Clannish Terror. As for Example, if one of the Magistrates were a Cameron (for the Purpose), the Criminal (Cameron) must not suffer, if the Clan be desirous he should be saved." "If keeping the peace in Scotland had depended on the justices," wrote a scholar, "Scotland would have been overrun with rioters and foreign invaders. It is quite possible to read the justice of the peace minutes and not be aware that general peacekeeping was one of their duties." And in Ireland as late as 1778, a justice of the peace who issued a summons for a gentleman would be virtually forced into a duel because he had insulted that person.[31]

Life for a lawman was as hazardous in the Old South as in Ireland. In 1861 a Southerner admitted to a visitor that "the law is nearly powerless [to stop] shootings and stabbings" because the perpetrators "are so reckless, they have things their own way." A sojourner in South Carolina told of a young colonel, with the Celtic surname of McKinnon, who threatened to kill both a family friend and a hotel owner when neither would extend him additional credit. He tried "to shoot the landlord, and then attempted to shoot himself, but had no prime. He then begged round for prime, but could get none. I endeavoured to reason with him," reported the frightened visitor, "but with as much effect as with a woman possessed with seven devils. 'I have a right, sir,' said he, 'to do as Brutus did. What Cato did, and Addison approved, cannot be wrong.'" This dangerous

30. W. Harris, "Rowdyism," 20; Henry Arthur Bright, *Happy Country This America: The Travel Diary of Henry Arthur Bright [1852]*, ed. Anne Henry Ehrenpreis (Columbus, Ohio, 1978), 236–37. See also William Gilpin, *Observations . . . Made in the Year 1776, on Several Parts of Great Britain . . .* (2 vols., London, 1789), I:211.
31. Burt, *Letters*, I:46–47; Ann E. Whetstone, *Scottish County Government in the Eighteenth and Nineteenth Centuries* (Edinburgh, 1981), 48; Frank O'Connor, ed., *A Book of Ireland* (Glasgow, 1980), 264–65.

and independent-minded young man, described as "naturally witty and highly gifted," at age twenty-two had "abandoned three wives [and] killed several men."[32] An Englishwoman noted that when Southerners "engaged in a dispute, however violent may be the discussion, the courtesy of the 'sir' is never omitted. On the contrary it is repeated at every third word, and mixed up as it is with the oaths and denunciations, with which they always interlard their discourse, the effect is curious enough."[33] Southerners knew that the words they used as well as their tone of voice could prevent or start a fight; they also knew that custom sanctioned their violent ways. Even if they were taken to court, their chances of escaping punishment were excellent. Men often killed and went free in the South just as in earlier times they had in Ireland and Scotland. As one observer in the South noted, enemies would meet, exchange insults, and one would shoot the other down, professing that he had acted in self-defense because he believed the victim was armed. When such a story was told in court, "in a community where it is not a strange thing for men to carry about their persons deadly weapons, [each member of the jury] feels that he would have done the same thing under similar circumstances so that in condemning him they would but condemn themselves." Consequently, they free the slayer, "and a hundred others, our sons and half grown lads amongst them, resolve in their hearts, that since every man may go armed, and every one is therefore justifiable in slaying his enemy, they will do likewise." In Alabama a lawyer reportedly told a visitor: "We have more cases on the docket in this county now, for murder, than can be tried during the next ten years." And a Mississippian complained that "while we were trying a man for murder at the last court at Starkville, the next county seat above, two murders were committed within gunshot of that court house."[34]

The actions of southern courts often amazed outsiders. An Englishman described how in Augusta, Georgia, in 1834 the mayor presided "at a court for the trial of petty offences. . . . The Aldermen sat as a jury & they were trying a man for fighting in the market,

32. W. Russell, *Diary North and South,* II:44; Faux, *Memorable Days,* 47–48.

33. Matilda Charlotte (Jesse) Fraser Houstoun, *Texas and the Gulf . . .* (Philadelphia, 1845), 191.

34. Kevin Danaher, *Gentle Places and Simple Things: Irish Customs and Beliefs* (Dublin, 1979), 31–36; MacLysaght, *Irish Life,* 271–77; L. M. Cullen, *Life in Ireland* (London, 1979), 44, 57, 107–09; Ian Whyte, *Agriculture and Society in Seventeenth-Century Scotland* (Edinburgh, 1979), 14–16; Thomas Pennant, *A Tour in Scotland; MDCCLXIX* (reprint, Perth, Scotland, 1979), 205; Sir John Sinclair, ed., *The Statistical Account of Scotland, 1791–1799* (reprint, 20 vols., East Ardsley, England, 1981), XVII:153, 215; Prebble, *Culloden,* 32–53; the Reverend James A. Lyon quoted in the *Columbus* (Mississippi) *Eagle,* June 1, 1855; Parsons, *Inside View,* 142, 144.

there was as little ceremony or distinction as can be imagined, the offender with his accuser & witnesses stood together side by side, & the Mayor was so polite as to Mister them all, even the dirty scoundrel who had been making a riot." The mayor explained to the anxious Englishman how local justice worked. "There is no apprehending before the trial," said the mayor; "we just serve them with a summons to appear, & if they neglect it we fine them, & should they escape by leaving the state, we are very glad to get rid of them; the principle may be bad, but we cant undertake to prosecute rogues for our neighbours, it is enough if we rid ourselves of them." A Northerner reported that in the South the "classification of crimes is singular. Manslaughter, bigamy and falsely packing cotton are under one head. Murder here costs about 2 years imprisonment or $1000 fine. . . . Such juries as they have here are beyond any man's control."[35]

The meeting of these "uncontrollable" juries on court days in the various county seats often provided entertainment to Southerners. The courtrooms were the stage on which dramas of real life— murder, assault, slander, and other crimes—were played before appreciative audiences. During a single session a Carroll County, Georgia, grand jury indicted one man for keeping drunken and disorderly company about his place and for "menacing voters"; indicted another man "for assaulting and violently beating Absalom Adams on election day [and] for threatening to beat . . . Thomas Wynn and having pistols and rocks to annoy the good people"; required two more men to stand trial "for fire hunting at night to the great annoyance of their neighborhood"; and indicted still another man for keeping "a gambling house at the Villa Rica gold mines."[36]

People sometimes traveled many miles to attend court; to exchange news and gossip; to buy and sell things; and to drink, gamble, dance, and socialize with their friends. A carnival mood often prevailed in ordinarily sleepy county seats on court days, just as had been the custom in Scotland and Ireland. A New Englander reported that Southerners "seem to look upon law as a species of amusement, and to regard 'court-week' [as a festival]." Some Southerners regularly let their children miss school when court was in session, and one judge twice adjourned court to attend horse races at which, said a contemporary, "he officiated with more appropriateness than on the bench."[37]

35. George Townsend Fox American Journal, December 4, 1834, Public Library, South Shields, Durham, England; Whipple, *Southern Diary*, 24.

36. James C. Bonner, *Georgia's Last Frontier: The Development of Carroll County* (Athens, Ga., 1971), 34.

37. Charles S. Sydnor, *The Development of Southern Sectionalism, 1819– 1848* (Baton Rouge, 1948), 34; Eugene L. Schwaab, ed., *Travels in the Old South: Selected from Periodicals of the Times* (2 vols., Lexington, Ky., 1973), II:439. On southern county courts, see Ralph A.

*Violence*

With such a variety of judges in the South, one visitor pointed out, "there is but little certainty of right & justice being properly meted out. . . . The judge has great power & can exercise a great influence," yet his will could be frustrated in various ways. A traveler remarked: "Mrs. Reid told me of an amusing revenge the 'crackers' had on her husband by sending him to Congress to get rid of him as judge."[38]

Other than violent acts, the crime that most often came before judges and juries was theft. Some Southerners, it was charged, would rather steal than work. One man called such people "the poorest and the idlest of the human race—averse to labor, and impatient of the restraints of law and the courtesies of civilized society." A Texan, cursing his neighbors for stealing hogs, told a visitor: "If ever were any hog-thieves anywhere, it's here." He claimed that several families in the county "ostensibly had a little patch of land to attend to, but . . . really . . . derived their whole lazy subsistence from their richer neighbors' hog droves."[39]

What most observers failed to understand was that the stealing of livestock was a long and honored Celtic tradition. The greatest of all Celtic folk tales, *The Cattle-Raid of Cooley*, features the exploits of Cu Chulainn, the heroic Ulster warrior and cattle stealer. Irishmen continued the practice of livestock raids into modern times, as did the Highland Scots. A traveler in eighteenth-century Scotland wrote: "The Highlanders . . . esteemed the open theft of cattle . . . by no means dishonorable." Southerners expected and tolerated a certain amount of livestock stealing, but when it became excessive and blatant they reacted violently. In 1832 a group of Georgians rounded up a gang of horse thieves, whipped them, and ran them

Wooster, *The People in Power: Courthouse and Statehouse in the Lower South* (Knoxville, 1969); idem, *Politicians, Planters, and Plain Folk: Courthouse and Statehouse in the Upper South, 1850–1860* (Knoxville, 1975); Robert M. Ireland, *The County Courts in Antebellum Kentucky* (Lexington, Ky., 1972). On court days in Ireland and Scotland, see Barrington, *Personal Sketches*, I:285; Mason, *Statistical Account . . . of Ireland*, II:82–83, 364–65; Constantia Maxwell, *Country and Town in Ireland Under the Georges* (Dundalk, Ireland, 1949), 48–56, 156–58; Charles Rogers, *Social Life in Scotland: From Early to Recent Times* (1884; reprint, 2 vols., Port Washington, N.Y., 1971), II:308–11, 333–35; Sinclair, *Statistical Account of Scotland*, XVII:4, 273; Edward J. Cowan, ed., *The People's Past* (Edinburgh, 1980), 36–38; Whetstone, *Scottish County Government*, 1–3, 27–31, 116–17; I. F. Grant, *Highland Folk Ways* (London, 1961), 353; Rosalind Mitchison, *Life in Scotland* (London, 1978), 19; Whyte, *Agriculture and Society*, 44–47. On children missing school on court days see Sarah Witherspoon (Ervin) McIver Diary, March 24, 1854, Southern Historical Collection, University of North Carolina, Chapel Hill. On the judge adjourning court for a race see Everett Dick, *The Dixie Frontier: A Social History of the Southern Frontier from the First Transmontane Beginnings to the Civil War* (reprint, New York, 1964), 229.

38. Whipple, *Southern Diary*, 45–56.
39. J. Hall, *Letters from the West*, 271–72; Olmsted, *Journey through Texas*, 66.

out of the county. This appears to have been standard procedure throughout the antebellum South. A visitor recounted that it was customary for notorious livestock thieves to be "tied to a tree, lashed without mercy, and ordered to leave the county within a given time."[40]

Aside from livestock poaching and some minor pilferage, theft probably was as uncommon in the rural South as in the Scottish Highlands. An Englishman reported from the South in 1855: "There is such a sense of security in this country, that doors and windows are as often left open as closed." A wayfarer in Scotland noted in the eighteenth century "that crimes were few, remarkably few, among the Highlanders. That they fought fiercely with men of another sept on occasion; that they 'lifted' cattle from a hostile clan or made a foray on an alien Lowlander with placid conscience is true . . . but it is said that cases of theft from dwelling-houses seldom occurred, highway robberies were unknown, the people lived with their property safe without bolts or bars . . . and in many a mansion not a door was locked." Between 1655 and 1807 the Scottish Baron Court of Stitchill recorded only a single case of housebreaking.[41]

Southerners worried little about burglary, yet the punishment for crimes against property in the Old South was often more severe than that for certain crimes of violence. "A man may, here, murder . . . almost with impunity, or by paying a paltry fine to the state," exclaimed an English visitor in the South, "but if he steals . . . he must be hanged for it." The situation was similar in eighteenth-century Ireland. A traveler remarked that "the criminal law of Ireland is the same as that of England, but in the execution it is so different, as scarcely to be known. I believe it is a fact," he continued, "that no man was ever hanged in Ireland for killing another in a duel: the security is such that nobody ever thought of removing out of the way of justice, yet there have been deaths of that sort, which had no more to do with honour than stabbing in the dark."[42]

Most Southerners believed just as did their Celtic ancestors that

40. MacLysaght, *Irish Life*, 276; Whyte, *Agriculture and Society*, 14; Pennant, *Tour in Scotland*, 205; Bonner, *Georgia's Last Frontier*, 33; J. Hall, *Letters from the West*, 291–92.

41. H. Murray, *Lands of the Slave and the Free*, I:225–26; Henry Grey Graham, *The Social Life of Scotland in the Eighteenth Century* (2 vols., London, 1900), II:235–36; Gunn and Gunn, *Records of the Baron Court*, 215. David J. Bodenhamer, "Law and Disorder in the Old South: The Situation in Georgia, 1830–1860," in *From the Old South to the New: Essays on the Transitional South*,

ed. Walter J. Fraser, Jr., and Winfred B. Moore, Jr. (Westport, Conn., 1981), 109–19, concludes that more crimes, especially violent ones, took place in southern towns than in the countryside but that the "theft of livestock was more common in predominantly rural areas."

42. Faux, *Memorable Days*, 49; Ayers, *Vengeance and Justice*, 111; Arthur Young, "A Tour in Ireland; With General Observations on the Present State of the Kingdom in . . . 1776, 1777, and 1778," in *A General Collection of . . . Voyages and Travels*, ed. John Pinkerton (10 vols., London, 1809), III:875.

under certain circumstances to kill was honorable; to steal, except perhaps a "stray" cow or hog, was dishonorable. William H. Russell found Southerners to be remarkably honest even when they had the need and the opportunity to steal. Another man discovered that numerous Texans "had fled from justice, or as they chose to call it, from law, in their own country." But most of these men had committed only crimes of violence and were thus considered honest citizens. "I saw at the breakfast table one morning, among those who were seated with me, four murderers who had sought safety in this country; and a gentleman assured me, that on one occasion, he had sat down with eleven," claimed this traveler, who nevertheless believed that "from evidence of general honesty and confidence between man and man, I should think money would be as safe here without lock and key as in our own country. I am confident that if stores were left in some part of the United States without a watch and exposed as many are in Texas, they would be robbed one of the first nights."[43]

Southerners and other Celts were also alike in their attitude toward law enforcement and what acts they condoned. They consistently ignored laws designed to control their movement and independent actions, such as legislation regarding the making and drinking of whiskey and traffic regulations. Even today Southerners and Irishmen are partial to what they call moonshine—and the attraction, one suspects, has something to do with its being illegal. The Irish disregard traffic laws; they drive and stop and park and walk anytime and anywhere they please, just as Southerners tend to do. (One indication that Dallas may be losing some of its southernness is the current vigorous enforcement of the city's ordinance against jaywalking.) "Less than ten years ago," a visitor to Ireland wrote in 1972, "there were no speed limits in Dublin, and parking meters, which have been installed only recently, are blatantly ignored." Today Highland Scots are more Anglicized, but they were not always so.[44]

The types of combativeness and selective lawlessness found in the Old South were precisely those found in the premodern Celtic areas of the British Isles, and antebellum Southerners were just as

43. W. Russell, *Diary North and South,* II:47–48; Anon., *Visit to Texas: Being the Journal of a Traveller . . .* (New York, 1834), 214–16.

44. Derek A. C. Davies, *Ireland* (New York, 1972), 9–10; see also MacLysaght, *Irish Life,* 78, 37, 54, 68, 73, 162, 255, 287, 291, 299, 308; L. Cullen, *Life in Ireland,* 44–45, 87, 96–97. On moonshining in the South see William F. Holmes, "Moonshining and Collective Violence: Georgia, 1889–1895," *Journal of American History* 67 (1980), 589–611; idem, "Whitecapping: Agrarian Violence in Mississippi, 1902–1906," *Journal of Southern History* 35 (1969), 165–85; idem, "Whitecapping in Georgia: Carroll and Houston Counties, 1893," *Georgia Historical Quarterly* 64 (1980), 388–404; and Ayers, *Vengeance and Justice,* 260–64.

"THE FIGHTING PARSON"

From F. D. Srygley, *Seventy Years in Dixie . . .*
(Nashville, 1891), 352.

martial and prideful, just as combative and touchy about their honor as were their Celtic ancestors. A Mississippian told a Yankee woman that "he could say what few other Southerners could say, that he, *a native of the South, had never thrown a card, been on a race track, or fought a duel.*" She considered him an "honor to any mother, to any State," but to most Southerners, men and women, he was a "sissy." The culture demanded that "real" southern men be quick to take offense and ready to avenge by physical force any insults or wrongs they suffered. The slightest breach of courtesy or any unfairness in business was sufficient reason for a challenge. Southerners almost never considered duelists as criminals or enforced laws against dueling. Nearly all Southerners were willing to fight to protect their pride and honor, including planters, politicians (the governor of South Carolina wrote a standard text on dueling), and plain folk; even preachers dueled.[45]

It was characteristic of Southerners and other Celts to settle their personal disputes, especially those related to their honor, outside the courtroom. "Questions affecting personal character were rarely referred to courts of law," noted a Tennessee lawyer. "To carry a personal grievance into a court of law degraded the plaintiff in the estimation of his peers and put the whole case beneath the notice of society." Southerners were just as ready to protect their honor or that of their kin as was the Scot who knew no English but, while standing protectively behind his clan chief's chair during a banquet, mistook the whiskey-stimulated conversation for a quarrel between his leader and an English officer. This loyal clansman "took it into his head that his master was insulted, and, without farther ceremony, drawing a pistol from his belt, snapped it at the head of the English officer, who would have been a dead man, if the pistol had not providentially missed fire." The ease with which Southerners justified violence is typified in a letter from an Alabamian to a kinsman in 1834: "Dr Withers shot a Mr Stolingworth . . . who very improperly attempted to horsewhip him in the streets for some remark on his character."[46]

The mother of Andrew Jackson reportedly told her son: "Never tell a lie, nor take what is not your own, nor sue anybody for slander

45. Schwaab, *Travels in the Old South,* II:340; J. Williams, *Dueling,* 13, 23, 60, 66–67, 40, 76, 34; Bodichon, *American Diary,* 97; Henry Herz, *My Travels in America [1846–1851],* trans. Henry Bertram Hill (Madison, 1963), 93; John F. H. Claiborne, "A Trip through the Piney Woods [1841]," *Mississippi Historical Society Publications* 9 (1906), 512; Timothy Flint, *Recollections of the Last Ten Years,* ed. C. Hartley Grattan (1826; reprint, New York, 1932), 324.

46. J. Williams, *Dueling,* 25; Louis Simond, *Journal of a Tour and Residence in Great Britain, During the Years 1810 and 1811* (2 vols., Edinburgh, 1817), I:413–14; George M. Johnston to Charles W. Johnston, August 22, 1834 (copy), George Doherty Johnston Papers, University of Alabama, Tuscaloosa.

or assault and battery. *Always settle them cases yourself!"* Jackson not only followed his mother's advice, he followed his Celtic and southern heritage: he fought several duels and engaged in what a contemporary called another "one hundred fights or *violent and abusive* quarrels."[47]

Whether fights in the Old South were formal duels or simply rough-and-tumble contests, they were an intrinsic part of a culture that was as violent as its Celtic progenitor and—what is highly significant—just as unrepentant of its combativeness. Southerners, like other Celts, were proud of their violent ways. An Irishman might as readily have been describing the antebellum South when he observed that near the end of the eighteenth century "the *Fire-eaters* were in great repute in Ireland. No young fellow could finish his education till he had exchanged shots with some of his acquaintances. The first two questions always asked as to a young man's respectability and qualifications, particularly when he proposed for a lady, were,—'What family is he of?'—'Did he ever blaze [i.e., engage in a duel]?' " It certainly was no coincidence that the Old South's "best-known and most feared duelist" was of Celtic descent—Alexander Keith McClung.[48]

The combative tradition of Celtic Britain and the Old South doubtless encouraged some men to bully others, but Southerners and other Celts believed that it also promoted courtesy and the careful weighing of words before speaking. South Carolinian Benjamin F. Perry, who killed a man in a duel, said: "When a man knows that he is to be held accountable for his want of courtesy, he is not so apt to indulge in abuse. In this way dueling produces a greater courtesy in society and a higher refinement."[49] The rash and the insolent in the Old South as well as in premodern Scotland, Ireland, and Wales rarely died in bed, unless put there by a mortal wound.

47. J. Williams, *Dueling*, 5, 18.
48. Barrington, *Personal Sketches*, I:273; J. Williams, *Dueling*, 37.

49. Lillian A. Kibler, *Benjamin F. Perry, South Carolina Unionist* (Durham, N.C., 1946), 135.

# VII

# *Morals*

"THE state of morals differs so much in different parts of America," proclaimed an Englishman. In the South, he wrote, "the people . . . all seemed degenerate. . . . Their general demeanour [was] . . . more rude and familiar [than in other parts of the country], and their conversations more licentious and profane." Most Englishmen and Northerners agreed that antebellum Southerners were far more immoral than Northerners. After visiting both North and South, a foreigner concluded that New Englanders "appear to me in general, a cleaner people in their morals." A Russian visitor declared: "If the inhabitants of the southern states reproach their northern brothers for their coldness and dryness, the latter reproach the southerners, and quite justifiably it seems to me, for their luxury and immorality, which are not at all the same as gaiety and nonchalance." A New Yorker called Southerners "the greatest criminals of the age," these men of the "*brave* South," who threatened with "bowie knives, and pistols, and bludgeons" the northern preachers who went among them to teach righteousness. "Let us pray for the day when honest [Yankee] wine and oil shall take the place of . . . [southern] barbarous whisky and hog-fat," wrote another Northerner, who exclaimed that any New Yorker would "rather own . . . ten acres on the Hudson [River] than . . . five hundred . . . on the Mississippi."[1]

Such critical observations were made throughout the South. A Northerner announced that Virginians "are profane, and exceeding wicked." Another man declared that North Carolinians "live for the

1. Adam Hodgson, *Letters from North America* . . . (2 vols., London, 1824), II:248, I:37–38; John Griffith, *A Journal of the Life, Travels, and Labours in the Work of the Ministry of John Griffith* (London, 1779), 60; Aleksandr Borisovich Lakier, *A Russian Looks at America: The Journey of Aleksandr Borisovich* *Lakier in 1857*, ed. Arnold Schrier and Joyce Story (Chicago, 1979), 223; Abram Pryne quoted in John Hope Franklin, *A Southern Odyssey: Travelers in the Antebellum North* (Baton Rouge, 1976), 247–48; Frederick Law Olmsted, *A Journey through Texas* . . . (1857; reprint, New York, 1969), 7, 41.

most part after an indolent and luxurious manner; . . . for I have
frequently seen them come to the towns, and there remain drinking
. . . for eight or ten days successively." In South Carolina a Yankee
noticed constant "gambling, . . . much drinking and profane lan-
guage. . . . The picture," he indignantly reported, "was full of disgust.
I desire neither to see it again nor to contemplate it more." In Georgia
another New Englander was "greatly annoyed in the middle of the
night by the swearing & vociferation of a number of young men,
who had been drinking. I do not think I have heard so much swearing,
indicating habits of the grossest profaneness, at any public house
where I have stopped, within the last 20 years. There is great reason
to fear that Georgia is preeminent in this vice." A visitor claimed
that the habits of Alabamians had led "to a gratification of their
worse passions" and had destroyed "the character of the people."
An Englishman, who heard "disgusting" conversations in southern
bars, insisted "that any individual possessing the slightest preten-
sions to the name of gentleman, in any hotel I had visited in England,
on indulging in the indecourous language I heard at these places,
would . . . have met with ejectment, without ceremony. Here, how-
ever, a laxity of moral feeling prevails, that stifles all sense of pro-
priety; and scurrility, obscene language, and filthy jests . . . form
the chief attractions of such places." "I do not know how other
people feel," wrote an Englishwoman, "but I cannot come amongst
these [southern] people without the perception that every standard
of right and wrong is lost,—that they are perverted and degraded."[2]
The wickedness of southern cities and towns rarely escaped the
notice of contemporaries. "The aspect of society, as it presents itself
to the superficial eye of a stranger, is such as might be expected
where public worship is totally disregarded," a visitor wrote of
Mobile. "Profaneness, licentiousness, and ferocity, seemed to be
characteristic of the place." New Orleans, of course, seemed to many
visitors the capital of vice. One man concluded—surely in exagger-
ation—that there were no more than ten moral women in the city.
He insisted that he had met only two of these, and that even they
were "privately talked of." But almost all observers reported im-

2. Philip Vickers Fithian, *Journal &*
*Letters of Philip Vickers Fithian, 1773–*
*1774: A Plantation Tutor of the Old*
*Dominion*, ed. Hunter Dickinson Farish
(1943; reprint, Charlottesville, 1968),
62; John Brickell, *The Natural History of*
*North-Carolina* (Dublin, 1737), 31–34;
Jared Sparks, "Journal of a Southern
Tour in 1826," in Herbert Baxter Adams,
*The Life and Writings of Jared Sparks*
. . . (2 vols., Boston, 1893), I:428; [Jere-
miah Evarts], *Through the South and the*
*West with Jeremiah Evarts in 1826*, ed.
J. Orin Oliphant (Lewisburg, Pa., 1956),
100; James Logan, *Notes of a Journey*
*through Canada, the United States of*
*America, and the West Indies* . . . (Edin-
burgh, 1838), 180, 177; John Benwell,
*An Englishman's Travels in America* . . .
(London, 1853), 212; Barbara Leigh
Smith Bodichon, *An American Diary,*
*1857–8*, ed. Joseph W. Reed, Jr. (London,
1972), 62.

morality to be rampant in New Orleans. A Northerner stated that "there appears to be no such condition known here as adultry, fornication or prostitution. . . . There are hundreds upon the back of hundreds now living in this city like man and wife, with large families round them, and yet they were never married. Connections of this kind though quite too common through the whole south, yet they exist in New Orleans to a fearful extent." A foreigner claimed that "the people here are grosser and more open in their vice than in any other part of the United States. Almost every one, married as well as unmarried, keeps a mistress, on whom he expends large sums of money. It is quite common for a young man to take his mistress to the theatre, and sit with her . . . the whole evening." An Englishman was shocked to hear "a party in the public-room discussing the merits of the different dealers in 'fancy-girls' . . . and their respective stocks, with as much gusto as amateurs of pictures of race-horses would use respecting their favourite articles."[3]

And yet one Yankee argued that slavery in the South was more benign in urban areas and in the border states because there "the slaveholder is surrounded by influences that change the external features of the system, and tend to check its excesses." This was the case, he insisted, because in the towns of the South as well as in southern states bordering the North most of the "men who are prominent in the learned professions, and more successful in business, are . . . from the North. If we inquire of the most enterprising, wealthy merchants in the cities, not only on the coast, but in the interior of the slave States, where they originated, they will point us to their remote country homes in New England, where they first saw the light, where their early years of life were employed in vigorous exercise on the rough farm in summer, and in the common school in winter. These men learned the value of schools and churches before they left their good old puritan homes, and they have struggled manfully to maintain these institutions, in spite of the downward tendencies, and the untoward influences of the slave system." There was all the difference in the world between these noble sons of New England and the " 'live Crackers,' as the inhabitants of those [interior] districts [of the South] are familiarly called. Here," declared this outspoken Yankee, "we behold the native slaveholder alone with his slaves, having no Northern men about him to

3. Hodgson, *Letters,* I:153 (see also 156); Jean Chevalier de Champigny, *The Present State of the Country . . . of Louisiana* (London, 1744), 34; Christian Schultz, *Travels . . . in the Years 1807 and 1808 . . .* (2 vols., New York, 1810), II:195; Philo Tower, *Slavery Unmasked:* *Being a Truthful Narrative of Three Years' Residence and Journeying in Eleven Southern States . . .* (Rochester, N.Y., 1856), 334; Logan, *Notes of a Journey,* 180; Robert Everest, *A Journey Through the United States and Part of Canada* (London,1855), 104.

influence his conduct, to check the full indulgence of his appetites, or restrain his passions."[4]

The criticism Southerners received from outsiders about their morality was the same received from outsiders by premodern British Celts. In Scotland, a visitor charged in 1776, "gross ignorance and wickedness abound"; he also accused the Scots of "scandalous uncleanness of all sorts." Other eighteenth-century observers found "morals corrupted" in Scotland, or they claimed that the Scots "in their morals, . . . are not sufficiently strict." Likewise, the eighteenth-century Irish were accused of being "ignorant of moral duties." A Frenchman declared: "When an Irishman presents himself at the door of [an Englishman] . . . , the latter fears immediately an attack on his purse, his wife, his daughter, or his wine."[5]

Among many Celtic vices, swearing particularly seemed to upset visitors. "Of all the people I ever met, whether educated in the army, the navy, in the universities, or at home," insisted an Englishman, "the Irish are the greatest swearers. Not a word passes without an oath vociferated in the most vehement manner, and horrid imprecations are familiarly delivered upon the most trivial events." "As the Scotch are nasty," wrote a traveler, "so I found them as prophane, and vitious." Another eyewitness noted: "Swearing was thought the right, and the mark, of a [Scottish] gentleman [in the eighteenth century]. And, tried by this test, nobody, who had not seen them, could now be made to believe how many gentlemen there were. . . . The naval chaplain justified his cursing the sailors, because it made them listen to him; and Braxfield [Robert Macqueen (1722–99), who, with the title of Lord Braxfield, became Lord Justice Clerk in 1788] apologized to a lady whom he damned at whist for bad play, by declaring that he had mistaken her for his wife."[6]

Visitors variously accused Celts of "perjury," "promiscuous ways," "whoring," "prostituting their daughters," and "vices too gross to be more than alluded to." Even some clergymen behaved shamefully. In eighteenth-century Ireland—where "the clergy

4. Charles G. Parsons, *Inside View of Slavery: or, a Tour Among the Planters* (Cleveland, 1855), 5–6.

5. John Mill, *The Diary of the Reverend John Mill, Minister of the Parishes of Dunnrossness, Sandwich and Cunningsburgh in Shetland, 1740–1803 . . .* , ed. Gilbert Goudie (Edinburgh, 1889), 47, 24; Sir John Sinclair, ed., *The Statistical Account of Scotland, 1791–1799* (reprint, 20 vols., East Ardsley, England, 1981), XVII:441, 64; William Shaw Mason, ed., *A Statistical Account or Parochial Survey of Ireland, Drawn up from the Communications of the Clergy* (3 vols., Dublin, 1814–19), II:324; De Latocnaye, *A Frenchman's Walk through Ireland, 1796–7*, trans. and ed. John Stevenson (Belfast, 1917), 19.

6. Edward D. Clarke, *A Tour Through the South of England, Wales, and Part of Ireland, Made During the Summer of 1791* (London, 1793), 327; Joseph Taylor, *Journey to Edenborough in Scotland [in the Eighteenth Century]*, ed. William Cowan (Edinburgh, 1903), 136; Henry Thomas Cockburn quoted in J. G. Fyfe, ed., *Scottish Diaries and Memoirs, 1746–1843* (Stirling, Scotland, 1942), 330–31.

might easily be characterized as drunken, disorderly, and immoral, or worse"—priests were convicted of adultery, and the Archbishop of Tuam warned one priest: "I am positively determined not to tolerate any whiskey drinking or other publick irregularities among my clergy. . . . Particularly you must not be known to associate with such persons as Mathw. Martin or Martin's Strumpets; much less should you church such persons." Nor were Scottish preachers always models in their behavior. For example, Roderick Mackenzie (1751–1835), "Parson Rory," as he was called, "was one of the finest looking Highlanders of his day," recalled a contemporary, but "His character as a preacher and minister was much lowered by his . . . habits as a man."[7]

Outsiders always seemed ready to believe the worst about Southerners and their Celtic forebears; indeed, anyone who doubted all "the stories of the general immorality and looseness of living which have been said to characterise the Southerner" was an exception. Few observers disagreed with the Yankee who insisted that Southerners were the most "debased white population in the United States," that there was a justifiably "bad opinion abroad about [them] . . . owing to the wildness of [their] society & the bad state of [their] public morals." Not every Southerner went "about with tobacco in his pocket, a bottle of whiskey in one hand, and his prick in the other," as Andrew Johnson of Tennessee claimed Whig congressional candidate William B. Carter did in 1845, but many travelers in the South were shocked by what they saw and heard.[8]

Interracial sexual relations were of special interest to most visitors. "So general in Kentucky is the intercourse between white men and black and yellow women, that soon it will indeed be difficult to know and distinguish who is who," a visitor reported. Some travelers devoted entire chapters of their books to the "indescribably seductive" octoroons, and the "whole barracoons of beautiful slavewomen . . . let to gentlemen for sleeping companions." Some Northerners, unable to resist temptation, leaped into the fleshpots. Henry Stiles Atwood, a Connecticut-born Yankee who could trace his lineage back to a physician in Oliver Cromwell's army, settled on

7. Edward MacLysaght, *Irish Life in the Seventeenth Century* (1939; reprint, Dublin, 1979), 53, 54, 67, 74; Henry Boswell, *Historical Description of . . . the Antiquities of England and Wales . . . and Other Curiosities in Scotland and Ireland . . .* (London, 1786), unnumbered pages; Emmet Larkin, "The Devotional Revolution in Ireland, 1850–75," *American Historical Review* 77 (1972), 631, 627–28; Donald Sage quoted in Fyfe, *Scottish Diaries and Memoirs*, 471–74.

8. William Kingsford, *Impressions of the West and South during a Six Weeks' Holiday* (Toronto, 1858), 53; Henry Benjamin Whipple, *Bishop Whipple's Southern Diary, 1843–1844*, ed. Lester B. Shippee (Minneapolis, 1937), 44, 190; Andrew Johnson to David T. Patterson, July 10, 1845, in *The Papers of Andrew Johnson*, ed. LeRoy P. Graf, Ralph W. Haskins, and Patricia P. Clark (7 vols. to date, Knoxville, 1967–), I:216–17.

229 acres in Wilcox County, Alabama, in 1821. An unscrupulous and dishonest merchant, he eventually acquired 272 slaves and some 12,700 acres of land worth $100,000. He also became the father of seven mulatto children born to his slaves Candis and Mary. Sexual contact between slaves and native white Southerners was frequent enough for a South Carolina woman to write: "Bad books are not allowed house room, except in the library under lock and key, the key in the master's pocket; but bad women, if they are not white, or serve in a menial capacity, may swarm the house unmolested; the ostrich game is thought a Christian act. Such women are no more regarded as a dangerous contingent than canary birds would be."[9]

Occasionally a sexual relationship with a slave broke up a marriage, as apparently was the case in a Virginia family in 1859. "I infer the adultry [of S. H. Parrott] . . . is with a woman of his own and if so no compromise on any other terms [can be made] but to send her off," wrote the brother of Mrs. Parrott, whose husband denounced his brother-in-law for interfering in family matters. "If other people would attend to their own business and let ours a lone they would have enough to do," announced Parrott; "they [are] trying their best to sepperate us. I think she [his wife] has no such idea of leaving me as they suppose." Yet later letters suggest that Mrs. Parrott did indeed leave her husband. "I regret my sister did not await your advice and have the Settlement you suggested," wrote Mrs. Parrott's brother, "but all things happen possibly for the best and we must be satisfied."[10]

Comments on sexual behavior, though ordinarily omitted from polite conversation, sometimes appeared in the writings of Southerners. In 1845, for example, a man told his kinsman about a Louisville, Kentucky, "widow whom I have, or rather who has been sparking me. . . . She is rich and is engaged to be married but like most widows is fond of flirtation." During the Civil War a Texan claimed that husbandless Arkansas women often acted "without virtue." In 1856 Mrs. Albert Sidney Johnston, wife of the commander of the Second United States Cavalry, noted in her diary that Lieutenant Charles William Field, a native Southerner who would

9. William Faux, *Memorable Days in America* . . . (London, 1823), 171; Charles Sealsfield, *America: Glorious and Chaotic Land* . . . , trans. E. L. Jordan (Englewood Cliffs, N.J., 1969), 96–109; Tower, *Slavery Unmasked*, 316–29; Benwell, *An Englishman's Travels*, 117–18; Daniel Fate Brooks, "Henry Stiles Atwood: Antebellum Eccentric of Wilcox County," *Alabama Review* 34 (1981),

20–30; Mary Boykin Chesnut, *A Diary from Dixie* . . . , ed. Isabella D. Martin and Myrta Lockett Avary (reprint, Gloucester, Mass., 1961), 46.

10. D. J. Hartsook to A. R. Blakey, October 31, 1859, S. H. Parrott to D. J. Hartsook, October 18, 1859, D. J. Hartsook to A. R. Blakey, December 9, 1859, February 22, 1860, Angus R. Blakey Papers, Duke University.

become a major general in the Confederate army, "had taken a woman from her good decent husband in Missouri and brought her here to Texas." Moreover, she had a baby fathered by Field. "Oh! you immoral men," exclaimed Mrs. Johnston; "what should be your fate for all the sorrow you cause in this world. I never can talk to the man with pleasure or patience again & yet he is considered a gentleman and a fine officer."[11]

What often shocked visitors both in premodern Celtic Britain and in the Old South was the uninhibited conduct of the plain folk. Contemporaries noted that Scottish and Irish women often "saluted with a kiss" even strangers and sometimes "were undelicate in their conversation and vulgar in their manners." There is no evidence that chastity was "a virtue much cultivated," acknowledged an authority on Ireland; "adultery, incest and promiscuous sexual intercourse were rife, feminine modesty being a rarity." Observers claimed that rustic Southerners were much the same as British Celts. Charles Woodmason denounced the Crackers of backcountry Carolina for "their gross Licentiousness, Wantonness, Lasciviousness, Rudeness, Lewdness, and Profligacy." He insisted that these people "live in Concubinage—swopping their Wives as Cattle, and living in a State of Nature, more irregularly and unchastely than the Indians." Nor had Crackers changed their ways when a New Englander observed them in the late antebellum period. They still practiced "licentiousness, fornication, and adultery," he declared; "here these giant, horrid evils, . . . appear to be regarded as matters that come as much within the routine of the social relations, and the open and unrestricted indulgence of the citizens, as a general thing, as much so as any of the common civilities of life."[12]

Sleeping arrangements in the backcountry disturbed many visitors. One traveler found himself sharing a bed with a "man and his wife, and one daughter about sixteen years of age." A foreigner and his traveling companions stayed overnight in Tennessee at the cabin of one Captain Chapman where there were only two beds. The visitors spread their blankets on the floor between the two beds and

11. R. S. Ewell to Benjamin S. Ewell, February 28, 1845, Richard Stoddert Ewell Papers, Library of Congress; Robert W. Glover, ed., "The War Letters of a Texas Conscript in Arkansas," *Arkansas Historical Quarterly* 20 (1961), 355–87; Eliza Johnston, "The Diary of Eliza (Mrs. Albert Sidney) Johnston: The Second Cavalry Comes to Texas," ed. Charles P. Roland and Richard C. Robbins, *Southwestern Historical Quarterly* 60 (1957), 493–95.

12. Thomas Somerville and Elizabeth Mure quoted in Fyfe, *Scottish Diaries and Memoirs*, 240, 73; Edward Burt, *Burt's Letters from the North of Scotland*, ed. R. Jamieson (1754; reprint, 2 vols., Edinburgh, 1974), II:112–13; Mac-Lysaght, *Irish Life*, 51, 48 (see also 49–50, 58–59); Charles Woodmason, *The Carolina Backcountry on the Eve of the Revolution: The Journal and Other Writings of Charles Woodmason, Anglican Itinerant*, ed. Richard J. Hooker (Chapel Hill, 1953), 52, 15; Tower, *Slavery Unmasked*, 333.

lay abreast with their feet to the fireplace. "Captain Chapman got into one bed with his wife, which seemed perfectly straightforward to us," reported one of the visitors. "A rather pretty girl who we knew was unmarried got into the other, and that too seemed perfectly straightforward. A strapping young man of about 20 or 22 arrived shortly afterward . . . ; not standing on ceremony, he undressed and plunked himself into the girl's bed; and while that was indubitably natural, it occasioned a certain surprise on our part," admitted the foreigner. "It had no such effect on the captain, who, to relax from the day's fatigues, was enjoying a prose with his wife of which we (though present) were the topic, and in the course of which he found us *odd fellows*, to leave our *home* and undergo all the travail of a painful journey to see deserts, savages, and a thousand other things that a man might reasonably think not worth all the trouble. Nor was he distressed by the young man's intimate manner with his daughter. His other daughter blew out the candle and slipped into the young people's bed, so that the young man was in the middle. That seemed to us even more extraordinary; but the flow of matrimonial conversation abated not a whit. We . . . paid close attention to these goings-on, and saw to our left, by the gleam of the fire, the young man and the first daughter get up and settle again at the foot of the bed; in a word, we saw all that one can see, while the paternal word-mill continued to grind away as before."[13]

Such activities may have encouraged the early marriages that were so typical of premodern British Celts and Southerners alike,[14] just as the observations of such activities may have excited the passions of other visitors. One Northerner confessed that he gave whiskey and food to a simple North Carolina girl whom he met along a mountain road. She was walking to Tennessee to visit relatives and had stopped him to ask directions. He warned her, "if she required further assistance, not to apply to any passing cavalier she might encounter, but to seek it from the hospitable country people around." He then admitted that "as I guarded her against travellers of my own condition in life; . . . somehow,—whether from my saddle

13. Andrew Burnaby, *Travels through the Middle Settlements in North America . . . in the Years 1759 and 1760* (1775; reprint, Ithaca, N.Y., 1960), 102–03; Louis Philippe, *Diary of My Travels in America [1797]*, trans. Stephen Becker (New York, 1977), 113.

14. Thomas Campbell, *A Philosophical Survey of the South of Ireland, in a Series of Letters to John Walkinson, M.D.* (London, 1777), 147; MacLysaght, *Irish Life*, 46; Maire O'Brien and Conor Cruise

O'Brien, *A Concise History of Ireland* (New York, 1972), 106; Sinclair, *Statistical Account of Scotland*, XVII: 324–25; Fyfe, *Scottish Diaries and Memoirs*, 68–69, 75–76; Timothy Flint, *Recollections of the Last Ten Years*, ed. C. Hartley Grattan (1826; reprint, New York, 1932), 325; John F. H. Claiborne, "A Trip through the Piney Woods [1841]," *Mississippi Historical Society Publications* 9 (1906), 524–25.

turning, or from my leaning over too far while making my words as impressive as possible, I really don't know,—but my mouth, before I knew it, came in contact with as sweet a pair of lips—!"[15]

Even more ample proof to many travelers that Southerners were immoral was that they had fun on Sundays. "One of the strangest sights to a New England man, on visiting Southern States, is the desecration of the Sabbath," wrote a Yankee. "In some of the cities, especially if a good number of the business men are from the North, the churches are tolerably well attended,—there being but one service for the day. But even here the afternoon and evening are much devoted to amusements." Another Northerner declared that in the South "there is no Sabbath . . . , they work, run, swear and drink here, on Sundays just as they do on any other day of the week." A New Englander reported that the "first sounds that salute the ear" in the South on Sunday mornings "are the firing of guns, the beating of drums, and the noise of the hunting horn. They have boat parties, riding parties, hunting parties, fishing parties, drinking parties, gaming parties, and dancing parties. And the Sabbath is almost invariably the day for horse races, and military parades." Southerners, recorded a visitor, "are devoted to pleasure, music, dancing, card-playing, and racing. Sundays and weekdays all come alike to them, as far as I can learn." An Englishman was surprised that "the slaves have Sunday for a day of recreation, and upon many plantations they dance for several hours during the afternoon of this day"; another noted that "the slaves on Sunday have the same privileges which their masters enjoy." A Northerner complained that in Texas on Sundays the stores "were all open, and made their best sales." An Englishman observed that "the Sabbath, in the Eastern and Northern States at least, is scrupulously observed," but not in the South. "Saw the Sabbath horribly profaned, both by white and colored people, by walking in whole droves in the fields, along the highways, playing, running, wrestling, jumping, singing, racing horses over the plains, &c," lamented a Yankee visitor in North Carolina; "so unlike a New England Sabbath as to shock the nerves of a descendant of the Puritans." Another Northerner claimed that Sunday in the South "loses the quiet stillness which hallows the day in New England. Here it is a day of leisure not of rest." The Sundays that Southerners spent in "revelry & mirth, feasting & dancing, conviviality & pleasure" outraged this Yankee, who proclaimed: "Little do the denizens of a quiet northern village know of the sin & wickedness committed on this day." An Englishman, equally repelled by

15. Charles Fenno Hoffman, *A Winter in the West* (2 vols., New York, 1835), II:237–40.

the merrymaking he observed, declared: "when I think of the moral pollution which pervades [the South] . . . , the rocky shores of New England have a thousand times more charms to me."[16]

To New Englanders, with their tradition of strict Sabbath observance that featured lengthy services in unheated churches and a long list of forbidden activities, nearly all Southerners seemed to be defilers of the holy day. The Puritan fathers had punished any citizen who fished, hunted, sailed, danced, jumped, rode—except to and from church—or worked on Sunday. And many of these restrictions prevailed until late in the eighteenth century, and in less stringent form much longer. An astonished Frenchman wrote from New England to a friend in 1779: "You may leave home only to go to church. On Sunday they do not cook, sweep, cut the hair, shave, or even make the beds. It is forbidden for a woman to kiss her child on Sunday. . . . The only instruments allowed are the trumpet, the harp, and the drum, and since the best musicians are punished most severely, you would have a bad time here."[17]

Most Southerners would have had "a bad time" in New England too, for on the Sabbath they engaged enthusiastically in all of those activities forbidden to good Yankees. "To show my friends how the day is kept I will note down a few of the violations of the Sabbath," wrote a New England preacher, who then described some twenty sacrilegious activities held on a single Sunday in New Orleans: a military parade, a horse race, a duel with small swords, a fist fight "for a $300 bet between two boxers," a cock fight, a masquerade ball, an exhibition by a German magician, several plays, a "French opera with ballet dancers," two circuses, a showing at the wax works, performances by numerous organ grinders, open stores and grog shops, various types of gaming and gambling, many "parties of pleasure," an "Italian Fantoccini," Kentucky minstrels, an ordinary ball, countless dinner parties, and joyful rides on horseback and in

16. Parsons, *Inside View,* 192; Tower, *Slavery Unmasked,* 261, 79; Everest, *Journey,* 111; Isaac Holmes, *An Account of the United States . . .* (London, 1823), 332; John Henry Vessey, *Mr. Vessey of England: Being the Incidents and Reminiscences of Travel in a Twelve Weeks' Tour through the United States and Canada in the Year 1859,* ed. Brian Waters (New York, 1956), 90; Olmsted, *Journey through Texas,* 84–85; George W. F. Howard, *Travels in America* (New York, 1851), 77; Whipple, *Southern Diary,* 98–99; Hodgson, *Letters,* II:260.

17. Ruth Henshaw Bascom, "A New England Woman's Perspective on Norfolk, Virginia, 1801–1802: Excerpts from the Diary of Ruth Henshaw Bascom," ed. A. G. Roeber, *Proceedings of the American Antiquarian Society* 88 (1978), 277–325; Alice Morse Earle, *Home Life in Colonial Days* (reprint, Middle Village, N.Y., 1975), 376–79; François, Marquis de Barbe-Marbois, *Our Revolutionary Forefathers . . . ,* trans. and ed. Eugene Parker Chase (New York, 1929), 105–06.

carriages. "Oh! when will men learn to look upon the Sabbath as they should, when will they feel that this day is holy & sacred & not a day for dissipation & gaiety," lamented this Yankee divine.[18]

Nor was New Orleans the exception. A "descendant of the Puritans," as he described himself, denounced "the horrible desecration of the Christian Sabbath" by Southerners everywhere; "throughout the entire south, with but few exceptions, the Sabbath, instead of being a day of rest, or of worship, is a holiday—occupied mainly in pleasure-taking and sports." Some Southerners attended church in the morning, "but in the afternoon and evening the Sabbath is more shockingly profanated, especially in Charleston," claimed this man. "It may be safe to say that from three to five thousand persons go out on steam ferries, and other craft, on pleasure excursions to Sullivan's Island, and other places of public resort, every Sunday afternoon, during the spring and summer season, where there are eating and drinking saloons, and other horrible places of abandonment, to which multitudes go and stay until the midnight hour closes in upon their revelry." Slaves also used Sundays as "a sort of holiday to . . . visit each other at their quarters, roam the fields, or what not." Another outraged Northerner averred that "Sabbath evening in the South is a time of unusual dissipation. . . . Theaters and other like places of amusement are open, and thronged more than any other evening; while the drinking saloons, billiard rooms, and other dens of infamy, are frequented by the riotous and noisy crowd." Yet another traveler declared that all over the South the "Sabbath is still dreadfully and generally profaned."[19]

Eighteenth-century Southerners observed the Sabbath no better than those in the late antebellum period. "A Sunday in Virginia dont seem to wear the same Dress as our Sundays in the Northward," wrote a Northerner. "Generally here by five o-Clock on Saturday every Face (especially the Negroes) looks festive & cheerful—All the lower class of People, & the Servants, & the Slaves, consider it as a Day of Pleasure & amusement, & spent it in such Diversions as they severally choose—The Gentlemen go to Church to be sure, but they make that itself a matter of convenience." Anglican itinerant Charles Woodmason declared that backcountry Carolinians "are without any Religion at all. They came to Sermon with Itching Ears only, not with any Disposition of Heart, or Sentiment of Mind—Assemble out of Curiosity, not Devotion, and seem so pleas'd with

18. Whipple, *Southern Diary,* 119–20, 117. See also Tower, *Slavery Unmasked,* 388–89; [Joseph Holt Ingraham], *The South-West; by a Yankee* . . . (2 vols., New York, 1835), I:219.

19. Tower, *Slavery Unmasked,* 387–88; Parsons, *Inside View,* 193; Hodgson, *Letters,* II:232.

SUNDAY IN THE SOUTH
From *Harper's New Monthly Magazine* 11 (1855), 291.

their native Ignorance, as to be offended at any Attempts to rouse them out of it."[20]

Premodern British Celts, most observers agreed, also desecrated the Sabbath. "Instead of listening to tub-preachers on the Sabbath here [in Ireland], as in London, the lower orders, imitating the higher, are gambling at what they call pitch and toss, in the public streets, or boxing . . . , unimpressed with the fears or the hopes which the contemplation of eternity inspires," announced an Englishman in 1791. Anglican ministers in Ireland considered the local practice of fun and games on Sundays outrageous. "They assemble on . . . Sunday evenings and amuse themselves by dancing," lamented the Reverend John Graham. "It is to be regretted, that the Sabbath evening should be spent in this way." From County Wexford the Reverend Thomas Handcock reported that the people "are uncommonly fond of dancing, and the young men of ball playing: for these amusements they assemble in multitudes in the evenings of Sundays and holy days." The Reverend James Neligan wrote from County Sligo: "The Lady Days [religious holidays] are observed with the most scrupulous attention, that is to say, so far as abstaining from all kind of daily labour, or following any trade or calling, although their sanctity does not operate on their minds so as to induce them to refrain from sports and pastimes, cursing or swearing, or frequenting typling houses, and drinking to excess. At the same time it is not unusual to see them actively employed on sundays at their usual labour, without seeming to think that they are transgressing a positive command of God, or doing an act either sinful or indecent." An English preacher visiting Ireland could not believe what he witnessed on Sundays—"drunkenness, noise, beating of drums and fifes at the doors of alehouses, and low gambling in the streets." In the countryside he saw "about one hundred and fifty peasants, who were playing at a game called hurl, which consists in striking a ball high in the air with wooden clubs like flattened spoons. Others were rolling a large stone; a bagpiper was enlivening the scene with his music; and the women, who were spectators, were dealing out porter to the parties."[21]

Visitors in Scotland and Wales reported similar profanation of the Sabbath. Daniel Defoe claimed that many Scots seemed "not to know a Sunday or Sabbath, from a working day." Frequently Scots

20. Fithian, *Journal*, 137; Woodmason, *Carolina Backcountry*, 13. See also Josiah Quincy, "A Journal, 1773," in *Josiah Quincy (1772–1864), Memoir of the Life of Josiah Quincy . . .*, ed. Eliza Susan Quincy (3d ed., Boston, 1875), 94; Whipple, *Southern Diary*, 21.

21. Charles Topham Bowden, *A Tour through Ireland* (Dublin, 1791), 26–27; Mason, *Statistical Account . . . of Ireland*, III:346, II:544, 364; Anon., *Ireland in 1804*, ed. Seamus Grimes (1806; reprint, Dublin, 1980), 28, 56. See also MacLysaght, *Irish Life*, 36, 153, 154.

spent Sundays sobering up from what one visitor called their usual "*Saturday* Night haunt of the Alehouses." Sunday services in Scotland and Wales often were marred by noises from inside or outside the churches. A Scot recalled that at times certain "drawbacks to the solemnity of the service arose"—for example, when a "number of collies, which came with their masters, chased each other [through the church] or quarrelled with each other as the spirit moved them," or when horses were raced around the churchyard. On Sundays in Wales "crowds of countryfolk, including some squires," danced to the "music of pipe, *creoth* [fiddle] and harp," and in one town "the gay ladies . . . would hire a piper every Sunday to play for them during divine service."²²

Sundays in England were quite different. "There is no kingdom wherein Sunday is better observed than in England," wrote a seventeenth-century eyewitness, "for, so far from selling things on that day, even the carrying of water for the houses is not permitted; nor can anyone play at bowls, or any other game, or even touch a musical instrument, or sing aloud in his own house, without incurring the penalty of a fine." "The *English* of all Sects . . . make Profession of being very strict observers of the Sabbath Day," wrote a French visitor in the eighteenth century. "I believe their Doctrine . . . does not differ from ours, but most assuredly our Scruples are much less great than theirs." An authority on eighteenth-century England acknowledged that "Sunday was a day apart. A vestige of the Puritan day of enforced godliness, it was still a time of enforced inactivity. Even before the Evangelical sabbatarian crusade late in the century, most trading, work, and entertainment were banned." In 1791 a German discovered that the London "public houses are on Sunday very full indeed; but the ear of the passengers is not struck with music and dancing, as is too much the case abroad; nor is there cardplaying." Nor did the situation change much in the nineteenth century. "Sunday, in England, being a day of funereal gloom, and not a holiday," wrote a tourist, "Children must not play on Sundays. I once saw two little creatures of six or seven playing with oranges in the street. A gentleman went up to them and gave them a severe reprimanding for their naughtiness." In 1835 a German traveler claimed that the English "lower classes, who often have to toil wearily through every other day, find Sunday the weariest of all.

22. Daniel Defoe, *A Tour through the Whole Island of Great Britain* [1724–1726], ed. Pat Rogers (New York, 1971), 671; Anon., *The Comical Pilgrim; or, Travels of a Cynick Philosopher, Thro' the Most Wicked Parts of the World, Namely England, Wales, Scotland, Ireland, and Holland* (London, 1723), 54; James Russell quoted in Fyfe, *Scottish Diaries and Memoirs,* 559; Geraint Dyfnallt Owen, *Elizabethan Wales: The Social Scene* (Cardiff, Wales, 1964), 57–58. See also Sir Leonard Twiston Davies and Averyl Edwards, *Welsh Life in the Eighteenth Century* (London, 1939), 116–17.

Often, after serving an austere master, they are made to see in the Father of Love an austerer [master] still. Singing, music, dancing, the drama, and all amusements . . . are forbidden, and denounced as schools of the devil."[23]

Accustomed as Northerners and Englishmen were to such compulsory and solemn religious practices, it is easy to understand why Celtic ways so offended them. They complained that few Southerners, for example, attended church regularly. "With Religion they have nothing to do," charged a New Yorker. "It is lamentable to see the destitute situation of this country," reported a minister from the backcountry South. "No part of the United States is so destitute of preaching. . . . In this part of the country there are many, who have lived so long without any religious privileges, that they have become almost entirely indifferent concerning them." In 1854 a colporteur of the American Tract Society reported that where he traveled in the South "*three-fourths* of the people are destitute of public services on the Sabbath." Another seller of religious books stated: "I visited [in the South] 60 families, numbering 221 souls over ten years of age; only 23 could read, and 17 write; 41 were destitute of the Bible; the average of their going to church was once in 7 years. Several between 30 and 45 years old had heard but one or two sermons in their lives. Some grown up youths had never heard a sermon or a prayer until my visit." "All over the planting districts," insisted a Northerner who visited the South in the 1850s, "very few attend church, and very few of the churches have constant preaching." He noted that in Albany, Georgia, a town of some twenty stores that exported annually "12,000 bales of cotton," only thirty-nine people (including three blacks) attended the Methodist church, the only one open on "a beautiful Christmas Sabbath. . . . There were three thousand souls within sound of a church-going bell, had there been one. Where were they?" This same man charged that only forty-eight people attended the Presbyterian church, the only one in Dublin, Georgia, a town of some two thousand inhabitants, and that at Oglethorpe, "a smart young city at the termination of the South-western railroad, where there was a population of over three thou-

---

23. Jorevin de Rocheford, "Description of England and Ireland in the 17th Century," in *The Antiquarian Repertory: A Miscellaneous Assemblage of Topography, History, Biography, Customs, and Manners,* comp. Francis Grose (4 vols., London, 1807–09), IV:573; Henri Misson, *M. Misson's Memoirs and Observations in His Travels over England, With some Account of Scotland and Ireland,* trans. Mr. Ozell (London, 1719), 310– 11; Roy Porter, *English Society in the Eighteenth Century* (London, 1982), 169; Frederick August Wendeborn, *A View of England Towards the Close of the Eighteenth Century* (2 vols., London, 1791), II:269–70; [Raul Blouet], *John Bull and His Island* (New York, 1884), 92, 194; Frederick von Raumer quoted in Edward Smith, *Foreign Visitors in England, and What They Have Thought of Us . . .* (London, 1889), 153.

sand, there was no church service during the Sabbath I spent there."[24]

Visitors offered various explanation for the Southerner's impiety. One traveler remarked that Sunday in the South "seemed a day on which people loved to get drunk." Another found "that many of the people were accustomed to be intoxicated Saturday night, and therefore, were unable to attend church on the Sabbath." Some observers simply considered Southerners to be profane people. "Were I asked what is the national religion of the Texan people," wrote an Englishwoman, "I should answer none. It is true . . . that the religious observance of the Sabbath is not more neglected than it is in catholic countries in Europe. On the other hand, the feeling of devotion, respectful upholding of religion is apparently absent." Another English traveler insisted that "profane language . . . prevails to an awful degree on the shores of the Gulf of Mexico." A Northerner reported that Southerners were so undevout and addicted to frolics that a group of them, returning from a visit to the county seat and forced by a heavy rainstorm to take shelter in a church, "sent a nigger off after a fiddler, and some whiskey," and spent the rest of the night and early the following Sunday morning "drinking and dancing." As still another Northerner pointed out: "The Sabbath [in the South] is rather a day of recreation and pastime with the slaves, . . . in which they visit each other, and spend the day in a very unbecoming manner—following closely the example of their masters."[25]

A major reason why Southerners appeared so irreligious to Northerners and Englishmen had to do with the early decline of the established Anglican (Episcopal) church. Anglicanism was never strong outside the tidewater South, even in the colonial period; long before the American Revolution, Episcopalianism lost out in the southern backcountry to Presbyterian, Baptist, and Methodist denominations that Celts either brought with them from Britain or infiltrated and captured after arriving in the Old South. During the late antebellum period the Episcopal church could claim only a handful of members in the Old South, and these were concentrated in the eastern states. In Charleston, the wealthiest Southerners reportedly were Episcopalians—whom one traveler called "the most bigotted, sectarian, and illiberal [people] in the United States"—but fewer than 5 percent of the South's Episcopalians resided in the

24. Schultz, *Travels*, II:134; Eugene L. Schwaab, ed., *Travels in the Old South: Selected from Periodicals of the Times* (2 vols., Lexington, Ky., 1973), I:198, 199; Parsons, *Inside View*, 196, 195.

25. Anon., *An Immigrant of a Hundred Years Ago* . . . (Hattiesburg, Miss., 1941), 15; Parsons, *Inside View*, 195, 198–99;

Matilda Charlotte (Jesse) Fraser Houstoun, *Texas and the Gulf* . . . (Philadelphia, 1845), 192; Hodgson, *Letters*, II:259; Tower, *Slavery Unmasked*, 79. See also Marion Alexander Boggs, ed., *The Alexander Letters, 1787–1900* (Athens, Ga., 1980), 69; Schwaab, *Travels in the Old South*, I:190.

A SOUTHERN DISTILLERY

From *Harper's New Monthly Magazine* 15 (1857), 733.

backcountry. Beyond the Atlantic seaboard there were only little islands of them surrounded by a sea of Celts, who dominated the South's principal denominations—Baptist, Methodist, Presbyterian, and Christian (Disciples of Christ). Even in the Alabama Black Belt, a major plantation region, the overwhelming majority of church members were Baptists, Presbyterians, or Methodists. In 1856, for example, Greene County, Alabama, had thirty-eight congregations—eleven Presbyterian, ten Methodist, ten Missionary Baptist, four Primitive Baptist, and three Episcopal—with a total of 4,150 members, but only 2 percent of these were Episcopalians. In other words, some 98 percent of the churched residents of a plantation county in the Deep South in the late antebellum period were Baptists, Presbyterians, or Methodists.[26]

British Celts, before they migrated to the American South, generally had been Presbyterians, unchurched, or nominal Catholics; most of those who settled in the Old South, if they joined any church at all, became some sort of Baptists, Methodists, Presbyterians, or Disciples of Christ. Preliminary investigation of church membership rolls in antebellum Texas indicates that 70 percent of the members of Baptist, Methodist, Presbyterian, and Disciples of Christ churches were of Celtic background. These denominations not only spread Celtic ways across the South; they helped Celticize (i.e., southernize) outsiders who settled in the region and joined local churches. In 1859 an Englishman noted that at a church he attended in the South "the service was the same as the Presbyterian Churches in Scotland," and in 1981, after visiting churches of various denominations in the South, a Scot declared that she recognized many of the hymns sung in these churches as those her grandmother, a Highland Scot, used to sing.[27]

Southerners were not so much irreligious as they were careless

26. Thomas Gage, "Episcopal Church," in *The Encyclopedia of Southern History,* ed. David C. Roller and Robert W. Twyman (Baton Rouge, 1979), 409–10; Walter B. Posey, "The Protestant Episcopal Church: An American Adaptation," *Journal of Southern History* 25 (1959), 23, 29–30; [Evarts], *Through the South,* 80; Rosalie Roos, *Travels in America, 1851–1855,* ed. Carl L. Anderson (Carbondale, Ill., 1982), 18; Benwell, *An Englishman's Travels,* 181; George Townsend Fox American Journal, December 15, 1834, Public Library, South Shields, Durham, England; V. Gayle Snedecor, *A Directory of Greene County [Alabama] For 1855–6 . . .* (Mobile, 1856), 54–58.

27. Donald G. Mathews, "Religion," in Roller and Twyman, *Encyclopedia of*

*Southern History,* 1046–47; Rufus B. Spain, "Baptist Churches," ibid., 102–04; Myron J. Fogde, "Methodist Church," ibid., 814–15; Robert D. Mitchell, "The Presbyterian Church as an Indicator of Westward Expansion in 18th Century America," *Professional Geographer* 18 (1966), 293–99; Robert Strange, "Religious Movements in the South," in *The South in the Building of the Nation,* ed. Samuel C. Mitchell (12 vols., Richmond, 1909), X:460; Roos, *Travels in America,* 117; Susan Hammack, "Name Analysis of Texas Protestant Church Membership Rolls, 1836–1865" (unpublished seminar paper in possession of the author); Harvey Hughey and William Law to Whom It Might Concern, February 16, 1801, Love Family Papers, Winthrop College, Rock

about church attendance; after all, none of the popular denominations of the South prescribed especially demanding dogma. The way to heaven, as explained by most preachers and accepted by most Southerners, was simple enough—one only had to believe in the divinity of Jesus and to be baptized. The reward was an everlasting life of comfort and leisure in a heaven of many mansions.[28]

Such beliefs fostered a more tolerant and relaxed set of religious practices than those found in New England. Most Southerners were compelled by neither conscience nor community pressure to be especially pious. They attended church or stayed home at their own convenience and pleasure. Bad weather would sometimes prevent as devout a Baptist as James Mallory from attending service. "No preaching near, and churches are so open and the cold so intence that it would not be prudent to attend them," he wrote on one occasion. Another time he noted: "rained until ten oclock, prevented our going to preaching." And later: "was at preaching near us, a light rain prevented a good turn out." A Georgia woman recalled: "We went very little to Sunday School; mother taught us at home. My brother Porter came out from Sunday School one afternoon and said, 'he didn't think Heaven was such a great place nohow, . . . because the Bible said it flowed with milk and honey.' He had such a hatred to milk that he never would eat anything that even looked as though it had milk in it."[29]

When Southerners attended church they frequently displayed manners that offended Yankees and Englishmen. Anglican Charles Woodmason admonished backcountry Southerners to arrive at church on time, to "Bring no Dogs with You—they are very troublesome," to refrain from the "indecent Custom of Chewing or of spitting" during the service, and to "Keep your Children as quiet as possible." He also told them not to "whisper, talk, gaze about—shew light Airs, or Behaviour," and to "Pray drink before you enter or before Service begins, not to go out in midst of Prayer, nor be

Hill, South Carolina; Anon., *An Historical Sketch of Indiantown Presbyterian Church in Williamsburg County, S.C., 1757–1957* (n.p., 1957), iii–iv, 5–6, 20–21, 24, 49, 52–55; Vessey, *Mr. Vessey of England,* 59–60; Fay MacDonald Young to Dr. Jerry C. Oldshue, April 11, 1981 (copy in possession of the author). Leroy V. Eid, "The Scotch-Irish as Celtic Christians" (MS in possession of the author), observes that "the Scotch-Irish evolved from Gaelic peoples (from both sides of the North Channel) that were primarily pastoral [and] . . . secular. . . . Because many of the Ulster Scots had Gaelic backgrounds, because many of the native Irish converted in Ireland to Protestantism before emigrating, because the Irish medieval church had never been oriented toward the papacy, the South became Protestant even though Celtic."

28. Anne C. Loveland, *Southern Evangelicals and the Social Order, 1800–1860* (Baton Rouge, 1980), 4–13, describes the conversion experience of several southern ministers.

29. James Mallory Journal, January 10, 1864, November 12, 1854, October 21, 1855 (original owned by Edgar A. Stewart of Selma, Alabama), microfilm copy, University of Alabama, Tuscaloosa; Boggs, *Alexander Letters,* 128.

running too and fro like Jews in their Synagogues." A later observer claimed that during church services Southerners "often talked, and sometimes even laughed as loud, as to be distinctly heard by those who wished to give all attention to the solemnities of the occasion." "I must say what struck me most [at a southern church service] was the extremely irreverent manner in which people continued coming in during the whole time of the prayers being read, creaking the doors and walking, not with the air of persons accidentally too late but as if it was a habitual practice, as I suppose it is," remarked an Englishwoman. "It is not the Custom for Gentlemen to go into Church til Service is beginning, when they enter in a Body, in the same manner as they come out," noted a Northerner teaching in the South. (A tourist in seventeenth-century Scotland recorded the same complaint.) It appalled a Yankee to hear a southern "clergyman read prayers with the most gay, indifferent, and gallant air imaginable." Southerners might have put more money in the collection plates—they had "always been more ready to give their five and ten dollars, than northern people," as one observer put it—but even their openhandedness seemed sinful to thrifty Northerners.[30]

Equally reprehensible to numerous travelers was both the lack of bookishness and theological sophistication and the general ignorance and emotionalism of most Southerners and other Celts, who freely expressed their emotions, sometimes shouting wildly and singing at religious gatherings.[31] (Even today the exuberance of southern "gospel music" offends certain people, especially non-Southerners and sophisticates.) A Yankee living in the Old South noted that good Englishmen and Northerners scorned southern

30. Woodmason, *Carolina Backcountry*, 88–89; Schwaab, *Travels in the Old South*, I:191; Margaret (Hunter) Hall, *The Aristocratic Journey; Being the Outspoken Letters of Mrs. Basil Hall Written During a Fourteen Months' Sojourn in America, 1827–1828*, ed. Una Pope-Hennessy (New York, 1931), 198; Fithian, *Journal*, 38; Christopher Lowther, *Our Journall into Scotland Anno Domini 1629 . . .*, ed. W. D. (Edinburgh, 1894), 16; Quincy, "Journal," 75; [Evarts], *Through the South*, 80.

31. John Ramsay, *Scotland and Scotsmen in the Eighteenth Century, from the MSS. of John Ramsay, Esq. of Ochteryre*, ed. Alexander Allardyce (2 vols., Edinburgh, 1888), II:417, 428–29; Richard Pococke, *Tours in Scotland 1747, 1750, 1760*, ed. Daniel William Kemp (Edinburgh, 1887), 88; Burt, *Letters*, II:207–12; Alexander Campbell, *A Journey from Edinburgh through Parts of North Britain . . .* (2 vols., London, 1802), I:259;

Thomas Crofton Croker, *Researches in the South of Ireland . . .* (1824; reprint, New York, 1969), 78–99, 223, 234; MacLysaght, *Irish Life*, 178; Mason, *Statistical Account . . . of Ireland*, I:318, III:27, 72, 130, 208, 491; Martin Martin, *A Voyage to St. Kilda* (London, 1753), 721; Sinclair, *Statistical Account of Scotland*, XVII:324, 561–62; Robert Hunter, Jr., *Quebec to Carolina in 1785–1786 . . .*, ed. Louis B. Wright and Marion Tinling (San Marino, Calif., 1943), 214; Whipple, *Southern Diary*, 77, 84–85; Charles Lanman, *Adventures in the Wilds . . .* (2 vols., Philadelphia, 1856), I:457; Sir Charles Lyell, *A Second Visit to the United States . . .* (2 vols., New York, 1849), I:270; Tower, *Slavery Unmasked*, 77; B. A. Botkin, ed., *A Treasury of Southern Folklore . . .* (reprint, New York, 1980), 469–70, 527–48; Lauren C. Post, *Cajun Sketches From the Prairies of Southwest Louisiana* (Baton Rouge, 1962), 172–73.

religious practices "with a self righteousness which will never take them to Heaven." They viewed with contempt people who whooped and hollered, chewed and spit tobacco in church, and were not "influenced by reasonable motives only." "I was altogether surprised and shocked to find [at a southern Methodist service]," reported a Northerner, "that the greater part of the audience evidently came together for purposes of levity, or something worse; if any thing can be worse than to go to the house of God for the deliberate purpose of merriment. I should think three quarters of the persons present were young fellows and young girls, gaily dressed, whispering, laughing, and prepared to leave the house with far other emotions than the preaching of the gospel was intended to produce."[32]

Southerners seemed to devote little attention to theological questions, church dogma, or denominational disputes. A visitor admitted that Southerners would listen to any good preacher, regardless of his church. Another sojourner mentioned a Southerner who "was not a member of any church, but a regular attendant at the Baptist or Presbyterian meeting." Baptists, Methodists, and Presbyterians often attended the church of whatever denomination happened to have a preacher that particular Sunday. "The communicants belong to several denominations," reported a witness, "and seemed on the occasion to forget their little differences." When a traveler asked the denomination of the only church in a southern town, he was told: "Oh, none in particular. They let anybody preach that comes along." Few Southerners were as faithful as an old Negro Baptist who refused to have anything to do with other sects. When asked why, he replied: "You've read [in the Bible] about John de Baptis', haint you?" With this confirmed, the old man declared: "Well, you never read 'bout any *John de Methodis'*, did you?" Southerners frequently switched denominations for reasons that had little or nothing to do with dogma. A person or a whole family might simply find it more convenient to change churches. Often a spouse would join the church of his wife or her husband.[33]

32. David G. Sherman to his sister, July 31, 1851, MS privately owned (copy in possession of the author); [John Shebbeare], *Letters on the English Nation: By . . . a Jesuit, who Resided Many Years in London* (2 vols., London, 1755), I:196; Henry Arthur Bright, *Happy Country This America: The Travel Diary of Henry Arthur Bright [1852]*, ed. Anne Henry Ehrenpreis (Columbus, Ohio, 1978), 161–62; [Evarts], *Through the South*, 88.

33. [Evarts], *Through the South*, 103; Lyell, *Second Visit*, II:73; Mallory Journal, August 20, December 3, 1854, September 9, 1855, January 11, 1863;

Schwaab, *Travels in the Old South*, I:191; Olmsted, *Journey through Texas*, 84–85, 77; Andrew Leary O'Brien, *The Journal of Andrew Leary O'Brien . . .* (Athens, Ga., 1946), 40. A minister living in Ulster at the beginning of the nineteenth century claimed that in twenty-four years he had not "perceived the least animosity between the different denominations of Christians on account of their religious opinions, and their clergy live freely together on a friendly footing." Mason, *Statistical Account . . . of Ireland*, III:447.

What outsiders often misunderstood was that southern religious practices made good sense to Southerners and mirrored their beliefs and leisurely ways. "The Sabbath [in the South] . . . is not observed as in the estimation of New-Englanders it should be," noted a traveler, who explained that Southerners "defend the custom of crowding their theatres, attending military parades, assembling in ball-rooms, and mingling . . . on this day, by wielding the scriptual weapon—'the Sabbath was made for man—not man for the Sabbath'; and then making their own inductions they argue that the Sabbath is, literally, as the term imports, a day of rest, not a day of religious labour. [*Shabath*, in Hebrew, means "to rest."] They further argue, that religion was bestowed upon man, not to lessen, but to augment his happiness—and that it ought therefore to infuse a spirit of cheerfulness and hilarity into the mind—for cheerfulness is the twin-sister of religion."[34]

The argument that the Sabbath ought to be a day of leisure and enjoyment made little headway with outsiders or with some of the South's own Yankeefied ministers.[35] Most Northerners agreed with the visiting sailor who tried to attend church one Sunday in Edenton, North Carolina, only to discover that the preacher, along with most of the church members, had gone fishing for herring. The enraged visitor left his views in verse on the door of the empty church:

"A Broken-windowed church,
"An Unfinished steeple,
"A herring-catching parson,
"And a damned set of people."[36]

34. [Ingraham], *The South-West*, I:219–20. See also Lyell, *Second Visit*, II:95.

35. Loveland, *Southern Evangelicals*, ix–x, 91–158, points out that southern ministers often "set themselves against popular opinion" by favoring Sabbath observance and temperance and by opposing dueling.

36. Hunter, *Quebec to Carolina*, 271.

# VIII

# *Education*

"I have always been cheated most by men who could write," ex-
plained a Southerner, who owned forty slaves and considerable
landed property but could not read or write; nor could his nine
grown sons. "Send my sons to school to learn to read and write? No
Sir," he informed a visitor. "It would make just such devils out of
them as you Yankees are!"

To prove his point this Cracker told how a Connecticut drummer
had sold him a clock for ten dollars that was "warranted to last
ninety-nine years." When a forty-dollar clock arrived, instead of
what the old man had ordered, he refused to pay for it and was sued.
He got no satisfaction in court: the judge insisted that the written
order called for a forty-dollar clock; furthermore, the paper that
supposedly guaranteed the clock for ninety-nine years (the clock
had stopped running within a week) only warranted it to *last* ninety-
nine years, not to keep time. "Now," asked the old man, "do you
suppose I am fool enough, since that, to believe there is any benefit
in learning to write?"[1]

Most Southerners, whether or not they considered literacy com-
patible with honesty, had far less regard for formal education than
did the average Northerner. As early as 1753 the governor of South
Carolina observed that the people of the upcountry "abound in
Children, but none of them bestow the least Education on them,
they take so much care in raising a Litter of Piggs, their Children
are equally naked and full as Nasty." On the eve of the American
Revolution the Reverend Charles Woodmason described backcoun-
try Carolinians as being ignorant and impudent. "Very few can
read—fewer write," he noted. "Few or no Books are to be found in
all this vast Country. . . . Nor do they delight in Historical Books or

1. Charles G. Parsons, *Inside View of*     (Cleveland, 1855), 180–85.
*Slavery: or, a Tour Among the Planters*

193

in having them read to them, as do our Vulgar in England for these People despise Knowledge, and instead of honouring a Learned Person, or any one of Wit or Knowledge be it in the Arts, Sciences, or Languages, they despise and Ill treat them—And this Spirit prevails even among the Principals of this Province."[2]

Formal education enjoyed scarcely more respect among plain Southerners at the end of the antebellum period than it had in colonial times. In 1834 a Virginian reported that fewer than half of his neighbors ever looked at a newspaper, and about this same time a South Carolinian confessed that more than a third of the white people in his state were illiterate. Some scholars have argued that the white folk of the Old South received relatively more schooling than is often acknowledged, and it is true that by 1861 there were more children in school in the South than at any previous time, but most of these schools were privately and inadequately supported. Rarely did they provide quality or effective instruction. For example, Georgia had a state university as well as academies in each county, but some of these were as poorly conducted as the elementary schools, over which the state exercised no control. A school could be started by anyone inspired to teach and able to find an empty building and enough paying pupils. One such instructor, a deserter from the British navy, established military discipline and whipped accordingly, but he did not last long. In his unheated school, he would place students in a circle and make them dance around the room to keep warm, and he would encourage the boys to wrestle so their blood would circulate faster. He was replaced by a "wandering, drunken Irishman," who "knocked, kicked, cuffed, and whipped at a great rate." He, in turn, was followed by two other drunks who frequently dismissed classes so they could go on binges.[3]

Most southern schools were primitive compared to those in the North. "A majority of our farmers' daughters," boasted a Yankee, "can walk from their dwellings to schools of a quality such as at the South can be maintained not twice in five hundred square miles." "The standard of education in [southern] . . . academies has always been far below that of the common schools in the New England States," stated another Northerner. "I visited several acad-

2. Governor James Glen quoted in Mary Katerine Davis, "The Feather Bed Aristocracy: Abbeville District in the 1790s," *South Carolina Historical Magazine* 80 (1979), 146; Charles Woodmason, *The Carolina Backcountry on the Eve of the Revolution: The Journal and Other Writings of Charles Woodmason, Anglican Itinerant*, ed. Richard J. Hooker (Chapel Hill, 1953), 52–53.

3. Quoted in John Hope Franklin, *A*

*Southern Odyssey: Travelers in the Antebellum North* (Baton Rouge, 1976), 195–96; Frank L. Owsley, *Plain Folk of the Old South* (1949; new ed., Baton Rouge, 1982), 145–49; Avery O. Craven, *The Growth of Southern Nationalism, 1848–1861* (Baton Rouge, 1953), 167, 271–73; E. Merton Coulter, *Old Petersburg and the Broad River Valley of Georgia: Their Rise and Decline* (Athens, Ga., 1965), 27–28.

"A SOUTHERN SCHOOL-HOUSE"

From North Carolina Collection, UNC Library at
Chapel Hill

emies, and in none of them were reading, writing and arithmetic so thoroughly taught as they are in the common schools of Maine and New Hampshire." "Education is not extended to the masses here as at the North," concluded a woman who made several trips through the South between 1853 and 1859.[4]

Northern schools impressed most visitors. Foreigners agreed, as one of them expressed it, that in "the northern States, education . . . may be considered as universal." The New England school system received special praise from Europeans and Americans alike. "The Public institutions of Boston are admirably conducted," announced an Englishman.[5] A Southerner, after visiting the North, acknowledged that "there is no other region inhabited by the Anglo-Saxon race . . . where national education has been carried so far." Northerners even educated their womenfolk, not just in literature and the polite arts but in Latin and mathematics, because these subjects reputedly developed their "mental strength and acuteness." "The Yankees are too shrewd, and too habitually observant of practical utility, not to perceive this truth, and act accordingly," observed another Southerner.[6]

On the other hand, various evidence suggests that support for formal education in the Old South was less than enthusiastic. In 1850 the federal census reported that more than 20 percent of the South's native whites could neither read nor write, compared with only 0.42 percent of New England's. A Maine physician, who had traveled in the South, contended that there were many more illiterate Southerners than the census indicated. He found not only the "non-slaveholders . . . ignorant and degraded, but . . . the slaveholders in the planting districts . . . quite as destitute of learning as the poor whites," and he reported that a friend once "called on 21 families of slaveholders, and found only two—a man and his wife—who could read." A visiting foreigner claimed that in the South "the general ignorance of the parents . . . makes them attach no value to the education of their children." In the 1850s another traveler discovered not a single bookstore in Austin, Texas, and only one in

4. Frederick Law Olmsted, *The Cotton Kingdom: A Traveller's Observations on Cotton and Slavery . . .* , ed. Arthur M. Schlesinger (new ed., New York, 1953), 560; Parsons, *Inside View*, 178; Lillian Foster, *Way-Side Glimpses, North and South* (New York, 1860), 108. See also Charles Fenno Hoffman, *A Winter in the West* (2 vols., New York, 1835), II:192.

5. Joseph Sturge, *A Visit to the United States in 1841* (Boston, 1842), 171; George W. F. Howard, *Travels in America* (New York, 1851), 13. See also Michel Chevalier, *Society, Manners and Politics in the United States . . .* , trans. Thomas Gamaliel Bradford (Boston, 1839), 334; Adam Hodgson, *Letters from North America . . .* (2 vols., London, 1824), II:3.

6. J. C. Myers, *Sketches on a Tour Through the Northern and Eastern States, the Canadas and Nova Scotia* (Harrisonburg, Va., 1849), 364; Anon., "Letters from New England—4," *Southern Literary Messenger* 1 (1835), 274–75.

# Education

Nashville. Southerners, reported still another tourist, had no respect for knowledge or for academics.[7]

Despite the efforts of such idealists as Thomas Jefferson and Archibald D. Murphey, the only southern states to adopt systems of free public education prior to the Civil War were Kentucky and North Carolina. German-born Christopher G. Memminger tried unsuccessfully in South Carolina to secure statewide public schools similar to those in Charleston. School laws in Louisiana looked impressive but were rarely enforced; one teacher's certificate bore the *marks*, rather than the signatures, of twelve parish school directors. Late in the antebellum period the state school superintendent recommended to the Louisiana legislature that at least two of the state's three directors of common schools should be required by law to know how to read and write. Even in North Carolina, which boasted the most educationally advanced common school system in the Old South, classes met only four months a year.[8]

There was much opposition to North Carolina's public school system, which developed slowly and imperfectly. In 1800 a newspaper reported that nine-tenths of the North Carolinians were illiterate. Twenty-nine years later Tryam McFarland explained that his senate committee had reported unfavorably on a "bill for the education of poor children" because "the vast expenditure required" for such a program would necessitate additional taxes, which the people would resist; moreover, the "equal contribution of all for the benefit of some [would] be equally irreconcilable with strict justice and the sentiments of the Community at large." A careful scholar doubts that the North Carolina legislature would have adopted a public school system had not Congress voted in 1836 to distribute the United States Treasury's surplus revenue among the states. North Carolina's share—$1,433,757.39—became in effect the public school fund. The school act of 1839 was more form than fact, however, because it required neither the erection of schoolhouses nor the support of the schools by county taxation. There was no way to punish counties for deciding, as the Cumberland County Court did in 1855, that "the school tax is for the present dispensed with." Edgecombe County did not levy its first school tax until 1853, and in many counties the amount of the school tax levied varied consid-

7. Bureau of the Census, *Compendium of the Seventh Census: 1850* (Washington, D.C., 1851), 153; Parsons, *Inside View,* 177–78; Robert Russell, *North America, Its Agriculture and Climate* (Edinburgh, 1857), 301–02; Frederick Law Olmsted, *A Journey through Texas* . . . (1857; reprint, New York, 1969),111, 36; [Joseph Holt Ingraham], *The South-West; by a Yankee* . . . (2 vols., New York, 1835), I:233–34.

8. Clement Eaton, *A History of the Old South: The Emergence of a Reluctant Nation* (3d ed., New York, 1975), 436–39; J. H. Franklin, *Southern Odyssey,* 56; Olmsted, *Journey through Texas,* 52–53.

erably from year to year. Teachers of any kind were difficult to find, and county courts frequently appointed "one of the most illiterate . . . citizens" as chairman of the board of superintendents. The many problems and defects in the system led A. W. Brandon, chairman of the Rowan County supervisors, to declare in 1854: "I do not think the Public Schools will ever prosper and work well."[9]

There were, of course, well-educated people in the Old South. Some of them could match knowledge and pens with the best of northern scholars. Frank L. Owsley has pointed out that "if college attendance is any test of an educated people, the South had more educated men and women in proportion to population than the North, or any other part of the world." In 1860, 1 out of every 247 whites in the South was attending college, compared with only 1 out of every 703 in the North. What Owsley fails to reveal is how poor were some of the colleges Southerners attended and how little was learned by some students. The records of student life at many southern colleges reveal that drinking, gambling, and carousing were the rule rather than the exception.[10]

A few Southerners read and collected books, but usually they were considered curiosities by their neighbors. In colonial Virginia two of the most prominent book collectors were William Byrd II, who, besides reading Greek, Latin, and Hebrew, had a library of more than 3,600 volumes when he died in 1744, and Robert "King" Carter, who owned some 1,500 volumes by 1774. The South Carolina novelist, William Gilmore Simms, had amassed a library of 10,700 volumes when Yankee troops burned it in 1864. Alabama planter Hugh Davis had a collection of 631 books at the time of his death in 1862.[11]

The library of John D. Ashmore of Anderson District, South Carolina, itemized by its owner in 1856, reveals what kind of books one educated southern planter collected. Ashmore owned 1,475 titles— 320 on literature, 171 on philosophy or politics, 66 on travel, history, or biography, 56 on religion, 24 on military affairs, and 838 reference

9. Guion Griffis Johnson, "Public Schools," in *The Southern Common People: Studies in Nineteenth Century Social History*, ed. Edward Magdol and Jon L. Wakelyn (Westport, Conn., 1980), 55–73.

10. Owsley, *Plain Folk*, 147–48; James B. Sellers, *History of the University of Alabama, 1818–1902* (University, Ala., 1953), 197–257. See also E. Merton Coulter, *College Life in the Old South* (New York, 1928); Philip A. Bruce, *History of the University of Virginia, 1819–1919* (5 vols., New York, 1922); D. V. Hollis, *The University of South Carolina* (2 vols., Columbia, S.C., 1951–56); and James F. Hopkins, *The University of Kentucky: Origins and Early Years* (Lexington, Ky., 1951).

11. Louis B. Wright, *The Cultural Life of the American Colonies, 1607–1763* (New York, 1957), 145; Louis Morton, *Robert Carter of Nomini Hall: A Virginia Tobacco Planter of the Eighteenth Century* (Charlottesville, 1964), 214; Clement Eaton, *The Mind of the Old South* (rev. ed., Baton Rouge, 1967), 262; Weymouth T. Jordan, *Hugh Davis and His Alabama Plantation* (University, Ala., 1948), 18.

works or unclassified items. He listed among his holdings such titles as *Shakespeare* (two volumes); *The Christian Library* (six volumes); *McCauley's Miscellanies* (two volumes); *Elements of Moral Philosophy*; *Works of Calhoun*; *Scott's Works*; *Napoleon and His Marshalls* (two volumes); *Washington and His Generals* (two volumes); *Scott's Campaign in Mexico*; *Militia Tactics*; *Jefferson's Writings*; *Helper's Impending Crisis*; *Helper's Impending Crisis Dissected*; *Lincoln & Douglas Debates*; *Patent Office Reports*; *Compendium of the Seventh Census*; *Penal Codes in Europe*; *Course of Latin Studies*; *Columbian Orator*; *Accounts of Irish Heirs*; *Religious Instructions for Negroes*; *Brittons & Saxons*; *High Life in New York*; *Dickens' Works*; *Scott's Poetry*; *Burns' Poetical Works*; *Family Preacher*; *The Victims of Gaming*; *Mothers of the Bible*; *The Young Mother's Guide*; *The Young Bride*; *Conversational Philosophy*; *Geography of the Heavens*; *Murray's English Grammar*; *Dictionary of Congress*; *Niles Register*; biographies of Henry Clay, John C. Calhoun, Zachary Taylor, Daniel Webster, and Alexander H. Stephens; and more than 700 public documents on agriculture.[12]

Ashmore was a literate and ambitious planter but withal enough of a Southerner to reveal how much he hated the materialism he practiced. On December 20, 1853, he wrote in his farm journal: "My provision crop this year is abundantly sufficient I think for the next years support . . . provided it is used with care and economy—Damn such a word."[13]

The better-educated Southerners—usually the well off and the ambitious—were often sufficiently "Yankeefied" to want their children educated by Northerners. Consequently, they either brought in tutors from the North or sent their sons and daughters to northern schools. A woman whose father had migrated to Georgia from the North recalled: "There were no public schools in those days [the 1840s], and good private schools were few and far between, so when my father's four oldest children, who were girls, were old enough to begin their education, he went on to East Hampton in Massachusetts and brought back a teacher, and built a little school-house in the grove where she took a limited number of scholars." When his boys were old enough to start school, he went to Massachusetts for a male tutor. A visitor to Natchez observed: "The principal persons of wealth send their children for instruction . . . to the New England states—a distance of three thousand miles. There is an academy here, but it is neglected."[14]

12. Schedule of Books Owned, May 1856, John D. Ashmore Papers, Southern Historical Collection, University of North Carolina, Chapel Hill.

13. John D. Ashmore Farm Journal, December 20, 1853, Ashmore Papers.

14. Marion Alexander Boggs, ed., *The Alexander Letters, 1787–1900* (Athens, Ga., 1980), 122; Thomas Ashe, *Travels in America . . .* (3 vols., London, 1808), I:317.

Various reasons were given for sending children to the North, but most of them were designed to protect young Southerners from their cultural traditions. "*Our* boys & girls at home are too apt to take things carelessly all the time . . . without ever feeling themselves called upon for any great excitement to ambition, energy or reflection," stated a South Carolinian. A Louisianian believed there were too many corrupting influences in the South. "The more you see of our society, especially our young men," he told a friend, "the more you will be impressed with the importance of a change in our system of education if we expect the next generation to be anything more than a mere aggregation of loafers charged with the duty of squandering their fathers' legacies and disgracing their names." Frederick Law Olmsted claimed that many planters sent their sons to northern schools to prevent them from having sexual relations with slaves. One planter told him that there was "no possibility" of children "being brought up in decency at home."[15]

Though there was no guarantee that Southerners exposed to a northern education would become "Yankeefied," people who feared that their children would learn alien ways and ideals in the North had good reason to be concerned. Northern teachers often tried to blot out as much of a student's southernism as possible. One young man explained to his father how the "solemn class smoke" at Yale College was supposed to bury "all sectional and personal animosities and unite us as brothers." But for such a ceremony to be effective, all participants had to accept the Yankee version of truth.[16]

Frequently Southerners brought back from northern colleges what Virginian R. H. Garnett called "their second-hand history and shallow philosophy." At home these brainwashed youngsters "joined the place-hunting politicians in an outcry against Southern indolence, and its fancied cause, Southern slavery; they pointed us to Northern opulence and the growth of Northern cities, not as what they really are, . . . but as examples of their superior enterprise and industry until at last we began to believe, what was so often dinned into our ears, that slavery was the moral, social and political evil they pretended."[17]

Antisouthern teaching was so persistent in northern institutions that a traveler in the late antebellum period noted that South Carolinians no longer sent their children to college outside the South,

15. Charles Manigault quoted in Michael P. Johnson, "Planters and Patriarchy: Charleston, 1800–1860," *Journal of Southern History* 46 (1980), 65; Braxton Bragg to G. Mason Graham, June 27, 1860, David F. Boyd Family Papers, Walter L. Fleming Collection, Louisiana State University, Baton Rouge; Olmsted, *Cotton Kingdom*, 240.

16. J. H. Franklin, *Southern Odyssey*, 71; Boggs, *Alexander Letters*, 152.

17. Anon., "Education at the South," *De Bow's Review* 10 (1851), 476.

as "was formerly the custom," because the "students returning from the North so often came home 'tainted with Abolitionism.' " In 1855 Mississippian C. K. Marshall concluded that it was now impossible "for southerners to be safely educated at the north. They cannot come back with proper feelings towards their families and their people."[18]

Marshall was right; northern schooling did not always destroy the traditional values of Southerners, but it did so often enough to justify concerns. For example, of the approximately 350 Southerners who had been graduated from the United States Military Academy and were in the military service at the outbreak of the War for Southern Independence, only 168 of them joined the Confederate army. Their West Point education, though far less "Yankee" in content than at most northern schools, and the service that followed it kept 162 Southerners in the Federal army and willing to fight against their own kin.[19]

Southerners awoke relatively late to the dangers of northern schooling. It was not until the 1850s that James De Bow announced: "It is time to call home our youth from north of Mason and Dixon's line. Subject them no more to the poison of Yale and Amherst, and . . . Harvard." Why, asked another man, should Southerners continue to lavish "their wealth . . . upon [Yankee] institutions and faculties who esteem it a condescension to teach Southern pupils, and spurn their parents and guardians as graceless barbarians?"[20]

Most Southerners resented what a group of Georgians called the hypocritical northern "Reverend professors and Clergymen" who used the lectern and the pulpit to denounce the people of the South. Such antisouthernism was widespread. It was typified by young Henry Adams of Massachusetts, who in his autobiography characterized his classmate at Harvard, William H. F. ("Rooney") Lee, the son of Robert E. Lee, as "simple beyond analysis; so simple that even the simple New England student could not realize him. No one knew enough to know how ignorant he was; how childlike; how helpless before the relative complexity of a school. As an animal, the Southerner seemed to have every advantage, but even as an animal he steadily lost ground." Adams concluded that "the Southerner had no mind; he had temperament. He was not a scholar; he had no intellectual training; he could not analyze an idea, and he

---

18. James Silk Buckingham, *The Slave States of America* (2 vols., London, 1842), I:54; C. K. Marshall, "Home Education at the South," *De Bow's Review* 18 (1855), 430–31.

19. Ellsworth Eliot, Jr., *West Point in*

the Confederacy (New York, 1941), xv; E. B. Long with Barbara Long, *The Civil War Day By Day: An Almanac, 1861–1865* (Garden City, N.Y., 1971), 709.

20. *De Bow's Review* 21 (1856), 440–41; ibid. 22 (1857), 312.

could not even conceive of admitting two; but in life one could get along very well without ideas, if one only had the social instinct."[21]

Though never completely successful in their efforts to keep southern students at home, the advocates of "a southern education for Southrons" continually denounced Yankee institutions. De Bow wrote: "better would it be for us that our sons remained in honest ignorance and at the plough-handle than that their plastic minds be imbued with doctrines subversive to their country's peace and honor, and at war with the very fundamental principles upon which the whole superstructure of the society they find at home is based." De Bow was delighted in 1860 by what he called the "exodus of Southern students recently from Colleges of the North," and Edmund Ruffin of Virginia, who assailed Yankee "hostility & malignity," was ecstatic when he learned that "267 of the southern medical students at the two colleges in Philadelphia, have, by agreement left those institutions."[22]

Many Southerners not only agreed with De Bow that it would be better for their children to remain "in honest ignorance" than to become "imbued with doctrines subversive" to southern society, but they objected when certain subjects were neglected or emphasized at northern schools. One man denounced the instruction at Harvard because he heard twenty-six members of the graduating class speak at commencement and all "their speeches were poorly written and worse spoken." In the opinion of this Southerner any school that failed to teach oratory was worthless. Another Southerner claimed that to get along with the Yale faculty, a "diminutive and low-minded set," one must be "a dull plodding mathematician." He insisted that the "best passport to Yale College is a New England appearance and a knowledge of mathematics."[23] Inasmuch as most Southerners loved oratory and disliked mathematics, Yale and Harvard were good places to avoid.

Southerners frequently objected also to the importation of Yankees to teach in the South. Parson William G. Brownlow of Tennessee castigated Memphis school officials for bringing "a gang of low-flung nutmeg dealers" from Connecticut to instruct southern children. Humorist Joseph G. Baldwin of Alabama pictured a fic-

21. Ibid. 21 (1856), 552–53; Henry Adams, *The Education of Henry Adams: An Autobiography* (Boston, 1918), 56–59.

22. *De Bow's Review* 10 (1851), 362; ibid. 28 (1860), 243; Edmund Ruffin, *The Diary of Edmund Ruffin: Volume I, Toward Independence, October, 1856–April, 1861*, ed. William K. Scarborough (2 vols. to date, Baton Rouge, 1972–), I:377, 384. See also John S. Ezell, "A Southern Education for Southrons," *Journal of Southern History* 17 (1951), 303–27.

23. Hugh Blair Grigsby quoted in Fitzgerald Flourney, "Hugh Blair Grigsby at Yale," *Virginia Magazine of History and Biography* 62 (1954), 166–90; A. F. Rightor to Andrew McCollam, July 25, 1851, Andrew McCollam Papers, Southern Historical Collection, University of North Carolina, Chapel Hill.

tional Miss Charity Woodey, "a new importation from Yankeedom," as "one of the 'strong-minded women of New England' who exchange all the tenderness of the feminine for an impotent attempt to gain the efficiency of the masculine nature." Such women, he noted, in "trying to *double-sex* themselves, *unsex* themselves, losing all that is lovable in woman and getting most of what is odious in man. . . . She had come out as a missionary light to the children of the South, who dwell in the darkness of Heatheness," and was quick "in delivering her enlightened sentiments upon the subject of matters and things about her." After barricading the door to the room of an unpopular Yankee professor, students at the University of Alabama "put a blower on top of the chimney to smoke him out. When, red-eyed and shaking, he found that he could not open his door he raised a window to get aid and the boys threw rocks at him."[24]

The dislike of Yankee professors may only have been an excuse for misbehavior, which was common among southern students. A general lack of self-discipline coupled with a high sense of honor and a propensity for violence hampered their scholarly pursuits. "There is not that substantial family discipline maintained, and the salutary home influence in the South, that are every where seen in New England," observed a Yankee. "The child of the slaveholder is taught to resist every insult, every aggression upon his rights, with physical force, and, if need be, with a fatal weapon. He is instructed to regard a 'coward' as the meanest, most odious character in the world, and he shuns no danger to avoid such an opprobrious epithet. Thus the son is often the first sent to the pistol gallery, before he is taught to read."[25]

Two Northerners once watched five Georgia boys throwing knives at a tree. Two of the boys, George and John, quarreled and George threw a rock at John, who avoided it by jumping behind a tree. "John, you mean coward," roared George; "dodge behind a tree, eh! You mean dog! I'll have nothing more to say to you." The other boys joined George in denouncing John as a "mean coward" who was afraid of a little rock. "We'll never play with you again," they exclaimed as they left disconsolate John standing disgraced behind the tree. "Let that scene be repeated the next day," noted one of the Northerners, "and Johnny would not dodge the stone. He would not endure another frown of public opinion like that, and thus lose the confidence and companionship of all his little comrades. He will

24. Brownlow quoted in Bell I. Wiley, "The Spurned Schoolteachers from Yankeedom," *American History Illustrated* 14, no. 10 (February 1980), 15; Joseph G. Baldwin, *The Flush Times of Alabama and Mississippi: A Series of Sketches* (reprint, New York, 1957), 212–13; Sellers, *History of the University of Alabama*, 210.

25. Parsons, *Inside View*, 179.

'stand his ground' the next time—and then, as he advances in years, he will take the knife, and, at last, the bullet, preferring *death* to the name and disgrace of a *coward*."[26]

Schooling often clashed with the values and unrestrained habits of young Southerners. When a female teacher scolded a boy of eight, he "drew his knife, and defied her to punish him." She managed by a ruse to disarm him, but his brother, age ten, pulled a pistol from his jacket and forced the teacher to dismiss school for the day. When she informed the father of these boys what they had done and told him that they would be spanked upon their return to school, he replied: "I can beat my boys enough at home, madam." A graduate of Maine's Bowdoin College teaching in Tennessee complained that twice in one term when he tried "to punish boys belonging to his academy, they had drawn pistols upon him, and he was unable to inflict the punishment." In Pontotoc, Mississippi, a young man, who objected to his younger brother's being punished, killed the principal of the male academy with a bowie knife.[27]

One man refused to let his undisciplined son attend school because he feared the boy would kill his classmates and the teacher. It was necessary to keep the lad away from school, said one of his brothers, "unless there's some way of getting the devil out of him." Another brother announced: "he'll get shot before he's eighteen. He *drawed* his knife twice on me already; and unless we keep him at home, young as he is, a rope or a rifle will soon be the finishing of him."[28]

Southern youths frequently continued their violent ways in college. On numerous occasions Southerners assaulted their classmates or professors. After whiskey was discovered in his room at the University of Alabama, George Lister "assaulted a professor with a deadly weapon." A few years later Thomas Jefferson Gordon was expelled from the same institution for attacking a professor. A South Carolinian admitted that he was dismissed from the United States Military Academy for two offenses: "One for having used a dagger too freely in a *personal* contest; and the other for having made an *unprovoked* attempt to shoot a man, who had let fall some unguarded words, hostile to my feelings." A Mississippian also was expelled from the academy for wounding another cadet in a duel. After the Mississippian left West Point a classmate wrote him: "Perry has nearly recovered [I believe], he *Limps* considerably yet from the wound he received in his *seat of honor*. You will receive in a few days a letter signed by the whole corps save seven or eight *Damned Yankees* . . . commending your conduct &c." More than once South Carolina College students threatened professors and

26. Ibid., 179–80.
27. Ibid., 180–82.

28. Hoffman, *Winter in the West*, II:192.

fired weapons at them. The president of the school complained that "the windows under my bedroom have been repeatedly shattered at various hours of the night and guns fired under my window." At the University of Virginia students horsewhipped one professor and murdered another; at Oakland College in Mississippi a drunken student stabbed the school's president to death.[29]

Southerners were not just violent and undisciplined students; they displayed a contempt for formal education that went beyond mere rowdiness. A foreigner who visited South Carolina College found the students "very disorderly, frequently disturbing congregations on . . . Sunday, because the . . . [president of the college] is too idle to preach, and thereby keep them together. Saw several of these learned young gentlemen stretched on a table, with their learned legs carelessly hanging out of their chamber windows, which seemed nearly all broken. Want of discipline is here too palpable, but there is no lack of whiskey." A schoolmistress admitted that her pupils dispersed in the spring because they were "disinclined for study as soon as the weather became oppressive." A schoolmaster in backcountry Georgia found his forty-five pupils—"fifteen grown young men, five of them married, five grown young ladies, and boys and girls of all sizes and ages"—unteachable. "These children had been born and raised to the age I found them among the cows and drunken cowdrivers on the outer borders of the State, and they were positively the coarsest specimens of the human family I had ever seen. . . . In the course of the first day they had half a dozen fights in the house; talking and laughing went on incessantly. . . . Those married and grown up young men participated in the devilment and seemed to enjoy it hugely."[30]

Witnesses repeatedly told of the difficulties of teaching southern children. A visitor at a Georgia academy noted that while "the teacher was demonstrating a sum on the board, two lads had a misunderstanding, and one of them knocked the other down. The noise attracted the attention of the teacher, who looked around before the boy had time to get up; but he took no notice of it. The recitations in reading and arithmetic—writing was inadmissible for want of writing desks—were far inferior to those in the common schools of New England." A teacher from New Hampshire told a fellow Yankee that he could not confine southern boys long enough,

29. Sellers, *History of the University of Alabama*, 209–10, 224–25; Arney Robinson Childs, *Planters and Business-men: The Guignard Family of South Carolina, 1795–1830* (Columbia, S.C., 1957), 67; Ripley A. Arnold to St. John R. Liddell, March 21, 1835, Moses, St. John R. Liddell and Family Papers, Louisiana State University, Baton Rouge.

30. William Faux, *Memorable Days in America* . . . (London, 1823), 53; Catherine C. Hopley, *Life in the South From the . . . Spring of 1860 to August 1862* (1863; reprint, 2 vols., New York, 1974), I:110; Gideon Lincecum, "Autobiography of Gideon Lincecum," *Mississippi Historical Society Publications* 8 (1904), 459.

without interruption, to teach them anything. "There," he said, pointing to a bright ten-year-old, "is a boy that has been here the most of a whole term,—but he has not learned all his letters. His father will permit no restraint upon him when he wishes for any amusement,—such as gaming and fishing,—and it is useless for me to try to teach him to read."[31]

Southerners generally cared little for reading. The southern woman described by a traveler as "sitting with a pipe in her mouth, doing no work and reading no books" would doubtless have agreed with the southern man who, when asked by a Yankee if he liked to read, replied: "No, it's damned tiresome." It has often been said, only partly in jest, that more Southerners wrote books than read them. "You know," a North Carolinian informed a visitor, "we people . . . do not like books so well, but we like to remember and memorize many things that we do love." A Virginian told Yankee tourist Jared Sparks that "there will be no such thing as book-making in Virginia for a century to come. People here prefer talking to reading, as Mr. Houston said of those in Tennessee." Another Yankee, who was surprised "to find the houses of slaveholders so generally destitute of books," believed "there were more books, and more men of liberal education . . . in the State of Maine, with her half a million inhabitants, than in all the slave States!"[32]

The aversion to reading extended to reading music. A New Englander, who visited a southern "singing school," wondered "how music could be taught, where so many of the people could not read." He discovered that the teacher used no books; sixty pupils were "taught by rote," and they sang "Remarkably well," admitted the visitor, who "was indeed surprised to hear them sing so well." When he asked why no books were used, the teacher replied "in a tone of decided prejudice against *book* knowledge: 'We don't believe in this blind note-singing here.' "[33] In contrast to the practice in the North, singing in southern churches was often done without hymnbooks. Few southern musicians could read music, and, as was indicated earlier, even in the late twentieth century the best southern country and bluegrass instrumentalists played and composed by ear.

Because so many Southerners deprecated formal education, outsiders usually considered them benighted. An Englishwoman who taught in the South thought Southerners "easy contented beings; unsullied by contact with the world, simple-minded and guileless more than any other people under the sun; and if not over-much

31. Parsons, *Inside View,* 182–83.

32. Sir Charles Lyell, *A Second Visit to the United States* . . . (2 vols., New York, 1849), II:73; Olmsted, *Cotton Kingdom,* 301; B. A. Botkin, ed., *A Treasury of Southern Folklore* . . . (reprint, New York, 1980), 306; Jared Sparks, "Journal of a Southern Tour in 1826," in Herbert Baxter Adams, *The Life and Writings of Jared Sparks* . . . (2 vols., Boston, 1893), I:417; Parsons, *Inside View,* 182.

33. Parsons, *Inside View,* 186–87.

given to intellectual pursuits, they win esteem by more lovable qualities." Less charitable observers called them empty-headed and superstitious. "In no part of the Union," said a New Yorker, "will you find so many current superstitions as among Southerners." These superstitions and customs, which critics generally considered absurd, included many traditional beliefs that Southerners shared with their Celtic ancestors. For example, they believed that if salt was spilled, a little should be thrown over the shoulder to save luck; that clothes should be washed on Mondays; that a garment put on inside out should be left unchanged; that it was bad luck to walk under a ladder or to break a mirror; that one should count to ten before starting back for something that had been forgotten; that the crowing of a cock at midnight meant that someone who heard it would die before dawn; that nailing a horseshoe over the doorway or finding a four-leaf clover brought good luck; that the dead should be attended by wakes; that bodies should be buried facing toward the east; that graves should be "dressed with flowers and evergreens," for which plastic flowers often have been substituted in recent years; and that it sometimes rained fish and frogs.[34]

34. John Ramsay, *Scotland and Scotsmen in the Eighteenth Century, from the MSS. of John Ramsay, Esq. of Ochteryre*, ed. Alexander Allardyce (2 vols., Edinburgh, 1888), II:417, 428–29; Richard Pococke, *Tours in Scotland 1747, 1750, 1760*, ed. Daniel William Kemp (Edinburgh, 1887), 88; Edward Burt, *Burt's Letters from the North of Scotland*, ed. R. Jamieson (1754; reprint, 2 vols., Edinburgh, 1974), II:207–12; Alexander Campbell, *A Journey from Edinburgh through Parts of North Britain . . .* (2 vols., London, 1802), I:259; Thomas Crofton Croker, *Researches in the South of Ireland . . .* (1824; reprint, New York, 1969), 78–99, 223, 234; Edward MacLysaght, *Irish Life in the Seventeenth Century* (1939; reprint, Dublin, 1979), 178; William Shaw Mason, ed., *A Statistical Account or Parochial Survey of Ireland, Drawn up from the Communications of the Clergy* (3 vols., Dublin, 1814–19), I:318, III:27, 72, 130, 208, 491; Martin Martin, *A Voyage to St. Kilda* (London, 1753), 721; Sir John Sinclair, ed., *The Statistical Account of Scotland, 1791–1799* (reprint, 20 vols., East Ardsley, England, 1981), XVII:324, 561–62; Robert Hunter, Jr., *Quebec to Carolina in 1785–1786 . . .*, ed. Louis B. Wright and Marion Tinling (San Marino, Calif., 1943), 214; Hopley, *Life in the South*, I:90; Hoffman, *Winter in the West*, II:291; Frederick Hall, *Letters from the East and from the West* (Washington, D.C., 1840), 338–39; Johann David Schopf, *Travels in the Confederation [1783–1784] . . .*, trans. and ed. Alfred J. Morrison (new ed., 2 vols., New York, 1968), II:135; Henry Benjamin Whipple, *Bishop Whipple's Southern Diary, 1843–1844*, ed. Lester B. Shippee (Minneapolis, 1937), 77, 84–85; Charles Lanman, *Adventures in the Wilds . . .* (2 vols., Philadelphia, 1856), I:457; Lyell, *Second Visit*, I:270; Philo Tower, *Slavery Unmasked: Being a Truthful Narrative of Three Years' Residence and Journeying in Eleven Southern States . . .* (Rochester, N.Y., 1856), 77; Botkin, *Treasury of Southern Folklore*, 469–70, 527–48; Lauren C. Post, *Cajun Sketches From the Prairies of Southwest Louisiana* (Baton Rouge, 1962), 172–73; Norbert F. Reidl and Carol K. Buckles, "House Customs and Beliefs in East Tennessee," *Tennessee Folklore Society Bulletin* 41 (1975), 49, 52, 54; Brid Mahon, "Beliefs and Customs Associated with Dress in Ireland," in *Folklore Studies in the Twentieth Century: Proceedings of the Centenary Conference of the Folklore Society*, ed. Venetia J. Newall (Totowa, N.J., 1980), 284; Donald G. Jeane, "The Traditional Upland South Cemetery," *Landscape* 18 (1969), 40; Sarah Evelyn Jackson, "Unusual Words, Expressions, and Pronunciations in a North Carolina Mountain Community," *Appalachian*

Visitors often reported, usually critically, other practices and sayings that Southerners adopted from their Celtic ancestors. It was customary, for example, in Ireland, Scotland, and the Old South to call sour milk "bonny clabber" and to call married women "Miss"; to hard-boil, dye, and abuse Easter eggs—either by rolling them or cracking them against each other in competition. John Morgan Dederer notes that "jumping the broomstick," frequently described as a marriage ceremony brought from Africa by slaves, was actually a Celtic custom transferred to the Old South but still practiced "in the North of Britain and by Scottish railroad navvies in the mid-nineteenth century." "Sik," a common southern word "for setting on a dog," is Scottish in origin; so are the southern words "biddable," meaning obedient or subservient, "bed-fast," meaning confined to bed, and "right hurtful." An old southern saying about the weather—"Evening red and morning gray, Sets a traveler on his way. But evening gray and morning red, Pour down rain upon your head."—appears to be a variation of the Scottish version—"Evening red and morning gray, Is a sure sign of a beautiful day. But evening gray and morning red, Put on your hat or you'll wet your head." The southern call or shout "spboi," which was used in managing swine, foxhounds, and other animals, reportedly is of Irish origins, and the southern adage "Devil take the hindmost" probably derived from the Welsh admonition: "Home, home, let each try to be first, And may the Tailless Sow [symbol of the Devil] take the hindermost."[35]

The famous traveler, Frederick Law Olmsted, found many Southerners to be remarkably ignorant by his standards. Of some Tennesseans, he reported: "Their notions of geography were amusing. . . . They thought Virginia lay to the southward, and was a cotton-growing State. . . . New York, they thought, lay west of Georgia, and between them and Texas."

*Journal* 2 (1975), 156–57; Estelle D. Broadrick, "Old Folk Sayings and Home-Cures," *Tennessee Folklore Society Bulletin* 44 (1978), 35; T. J. Farr, "Riddles and Superstitions of Middle Tennessee," *Journal of American Folk-lore* 48 (1935), 331.

35. Frederick Law Olmsted, *A Journey in the Back Country* . . . (1856; reprint, New York, 1970), 240; Eve Begley, *Of Scottish Ways* (New York, 1977), 104–07; Padraic O'Farrell, *Superstitions of the Irish Country People* (Dublin, 1978), 9, 42, 61–62; Hector Boece, *History of Scotland* (London, 1527), 83; Arthur Young, *Arthur Young's Tour in Ireland (1776–1779)*, ed. Arthur W. Hutton (2 vols., London, 1892), I:258; Mason,

*Statistical Account . . . of Ireland*, I:48, 123, III:491, 207–08; John Morgan Dederer, "Afro-Southern and Celtic-Southern Cultural Adaptation in the Old South" (MS in possession of the author); J. W. Pearce, "Notes from Louisiana," *Dialect Notes* 1 (1890–96), 69; W. H. Carruth, "The Language Used to Domestic Animals," ibid., 263–68; C. R. Gaston, "Notes on 'Stubboy,' " ibid. 2 (1900–1904), 347–48; John F. H. Claiborne, "A Trip through the Piney Woods [1841]," *Mississippi Historical Society Publications* 9 (1906), 537; Mary Corbett Harris, *Crafts, Customs and Legends of Wales* (Newton Abbot, England, 1980), 27.

But about some things Southerners displayed remarkable understanding. They knew, for example, that the North was where the "Yankees came from—'the people that used to come peddling.' " An untutored Virginia woman shrewdly observed: "I reckon all cities are pretty much alike." A Tar Heel, told that New York City contained some 700,000 people, offered a perceptive comment on city life: "I suppose there's some people been living there all their lives that don't know each other, and never spoke to one another once yet in their lives, ain't there?" Assured that such was the case, he remarked: "'Tain't so here, people's more friendly, this country." And when Olmsted informed another North Carolinian, who had his geography somewhat confused, that Charleston was not near New York, the man replied with a shrug: "Ain't it? well, 't was Charleston . . . or New York, or some place out there."[36]

These rustic Southerners, who were by no means dissatisfied with their condition, repeatedly made it clear that they could do without instruction. Indeed, most of them wanted no more than they already had. Olmsted stayed overnight with some relatively well-off North Carolinians whom he described as "good-natured, intelligent people, but very ignorant." "The man told me that he had over a thousand acres of rich tillable land, besides a large extent of mountain range," reported Olmsted. "I did not see a single book in the house, nor do I think that any of the family could read." When Olmsted took out a map to explain his route, the man "said he 'wasn't scollar'd enough' to understand it, and I could not induce him to look at it." Yet this man lived comfortably and was thoroughly content in his ignorance. "He reckoned he's got enough to make him a living for the rest of his life," Olmsted declared, "and he didn't know any use a man had for more'n that." A determined Yankee book drummer once told a Southerner that "a set of books on scientific agriculture" would teach him to "farm twice as good as you do." To which the Southerner replied: "Hell, son, I don't farm half as good as I know how now."[37]

Even their critics admitted that not all Southerners were stupid. The Yankee prison physician who attended Jefferson Davis during his incarceration after the war was impressed by his "large, varied, and practical education; the geology, botany, and all products of his section appearing to have in turn claimed his attention. Not the superficial study of a pedant, but the practical acquaintance of a man who has turned every day's fighting, shooting, riding, or picnicking, to scientific account." A New Hampshire schoolmistress

36. Hopley, *Life in the South*, I:91; Olmsted, *Journey in the Back Country*, 240, 250–51, 249.

37. Olmsted, *Journey in the Back Country*, 258–59; Jonathan Daniels, *A Southerner Discovers the South* (New York, 1938), 163–64.

who taught in the South was even more emphatic about the native intelligence of Southerners. "As a general thing, pupils at the South are not as far advanced in intellectual attainments at the ages of ten and twelve as the same class of students in the North," stated Emily P. Burke, "but as far as my experience goes, when they are brought under good intellectual culture their minds are more vigorous, and intellectual development more rapid, than has been the case with children of the same age I ever had the care of at the North." Crackers were "not so well educated as the rest of the Americans," admitted a Frenchman; "however, nature has endowed them with that quickness of comprehension which is characteristic of southern people." Most plain Southerners "are ignorant, so far as book-learning is concerned," acknowledged a wanderer, "but they are well supplied with common sense." "They have a high estimation of their own qualities & look on book learning as all superfluous," observed another visitor; "many of them are ... sharp witted & very intelligent."[38]

What soon became obvious to most observers was that the ordinary Southerner's notion of what was worth learning varied sharply from their own views. The Cracker curriculum was far different from the standard Yankee curriculum. The skills of the scribbler, reader, and figurer—so necessary to trade and industry—were of small concern to the average Southerner; he admired more the skills of the hunter, fisher, fighter, and fiddler. These and other leisurely activities were considered by him to be natural and worthwhile, fun to learn and to practice, and consistent with honesty and honor. He had not the slightest desire to be schooled in the "system of education in New England," which, a foreign visitor claimed, "makes the most knavish 'tricky' set of fellows."[39]

A visitor at an Alabama school noted that "the pupils are, mostly, as rude as the house—real young hunters, who handle the long rifle with more ease and dexterity than the goosequill, and who are incomparably more at home in 'twisting a rabbit,' or 'treeing a possum,' than in conjugating a verb." He concluded that the "long rifle is familiar to every hand; skill in the use of it is the highest accomplishment which a southern gentleman glories in; even the children acquire an astonishing expertness in handling this deadly weapon at a very early age."[40]

38. John J. Craven, *Prison Life of Jefferson Davis* ... (1866; reprint, Biloxi, 1979), 95–96; Emily P. Burke, *Reminiscences of Georgia* (Oberlin, Ohio, 1850), 195–204; Edouard de Montule, *Travels in America, 1816–1817*, trans. Edward D. Seeber (Bloomington, 1951), 86; Lanman, *Adventures in the Wilds*, I:500; Whipple, *Southern Diary*, 77.

39. Henry Arthur Bright, *Happy Country This America: The Travel Diary of Henry Arthur Bright [1852]*, ed. Anne Henry Ehrenpreis (Columbus, Ohio, 1978), 101.

40. Philip Henry Gosse, *Letters from Alabama* ... (London, 1859), 44, 140.

"NO USE FUR THE INFERNAL TOWN"

From F. D. Srygley, *Seventy Years in Dixie* . . .
(Nashville, 1891), 64.

A wealthy Southerner recalled how her father tried but failed to make a scholar of her brother, "who was more interested in his hunting and traps than in his studies." One day when the boy came home late for dinner he gave his usual explanation that he had been in the woods looking at his traps. "Did you catch anything?" asked his father. To the reply of "no, sir," the father, who had covertly placed a book in the trap, insisted: "Why, wasn't your trap down?" To which his son admitted that it was, but said there was nothing in it "but a Davies' Arithmetic." The boy, explained his sister, "was a very matter-of-fact youth and took it as quietly as though it was the most natural thing in the world to catch a Davies' Arithmetic in a trap in the woods." The boy continued to hunt.[41]

The attitude of the unsophisticated Southerner toward education was the same as that of his Celtic forebears, whom English observers consistently described not merely as unschooled but uninterested in being schooled. "At the English Conquest," wrote Thomas Croker in the early nineteenth century, "Ireland was unquestionably in a state of profound ignorance; . . . and 'to the present day,' says Sir Richard Cox, 'very few of the Irish aim at any more than a little Latin, which every cow-boy pretends to, and a smattering of logic, which very few of them know the use of.' " Sorley Boy MacDonnell, a major figure in sixteenth-century Ulster, could neither read nor write, as is attested by several of his letters preserved in the Irish State Papers. He legitimized his signature by touching the pen as his secretary wrote his name for him. At the end of the eighteenth century numerous Anglican ministers reported on what they considered the deplorable state of schooling in Ireland. Two preachers from County Cork declared that the "children here are very indifferently educated" and that many citizens suffer from "their inability to read." There were no public schools or public libraries in County King, stated the Reverend Patrick Fitzgerald; "the parish clerk keeps a licensed Protestant school, which is very badly attended." In County Kilkenny, the Reverend James A. Ker announced, "Education is at a very low ebb." "The education of the children here is irregular and imperfect," admitted a minister from County Clare. "The hedge schools are as miserable, and the books read in them as worthless as they have been observed to be in other parts of Ireland." The situation was the same in County Wexford. "Nothing can be more deplorable," claimed the Reverend Edward Barton; "the people have no place to resort to, but a few miserable hedge-schools where the teachers are almost in as great need of instruction as themselves." The greatest need throughout Ireland, insisted the Reverend John Graham of County Londonderry, "is school-houses

41. Boggs, *Alexander Letters*, 127–28.

and teachers. . . . The school-houses are in general wretched huts, built of sods in the highway ditches, from which circumstances they are denominated hedge-schools. They have neither door, window, nor chimney; a large hole in the roof serving to admit light, and let out the smoke, which issues from a fire in the middle of the house. A low narrow hole cut in the mud wall on the south side of the hut, affords ingress and egress to its inhabitants. These schools are fully attended in summer—half empty in spring and harvest, and from the cold and damp, utterly deserted in winter; so that the children, who periodically resort to them for instruction, usually forget in one part of the year, what they have learned in the other." Mr. Graham believed that the instruction at these hedge-schools was dangerous and subversive. When the students "have learned to read," he charged, "their attention is directed to the biographies of robbers, thieves, and prostitutes, the reveries of knights errant and crusaders, a seditious history of Ireland, tales of apparitions, witches and fairies, and a new system of boxing."[42]

Various reasons were offered by preachers and others why education was so badly neglected in Ireland. The Reverend James Farrell of County Longford reported that "there does not appear a wish or desire for education here"; the Reverend Edward Bayly of County Kilkenny believed it was because the people "are almost universally idle." In County Tyrone, averred the Reverend John Groves, the people "seem unwilling to make those sacrifices of expense, or of the children's time, that is necessary for this purpose." The citizens of County Cork displayed "shrewdness"—one of their "national characteristics"—"in no ordinary degree," wrote the Reverend William A. Evanson. "They are, however, too indolent to cultivate their minds." It was obvious to more perceptive observers that the Irish resisted English efforts to educate them because they realized that such instruction was designed to Anglicize them and thus to destroy their culture. A seventeenth-century traveler explained that although the Irish appeared to reject schooling "through Laziness, and want of Industry," the real reason was "their innate Pride, and Self conceitedness, which make them disdain to be taught by Foreigners."[43]

The Scots and Welsh resisted English education for the same reason the Irish did. Early in the eighteenth century a traveler noted

42. Croker, *Researches*, 325; State Papers, Ireland, Elizabeth, 63/23/10, iii, v, 63/24/4, i, Public Records Office, London; Mason, *Statistical Account . . . of Ireland*, III:116, 374, II:147, III:246, II:465, I:5, 597–99 (see also I:450, II:45–46, 199, III:473).

43. Mason, *Statistical Account . . . of Ireland*, III:291, I:420, III:165–66, 471; Anon., *A Trip to Ireland, Being a Description of the Country, People, and Manners . . .* (London, 1699), 4. See also Mason, *Statistical Account . . . of Ireland*, I:157, 529; Croker, *Researches*, 78–79, 232, 234–35.

that the Scots of the Highlands and Western Isles suffered from "the want of knowledge of letters, and other useful arts and sciences" but that this might be an advantage, for "they are to this day happily ignorant of many Vices that are practised in the Learned and Polite World." His conclusion that the Scots "are generally a very sagacious People, quick of Apprehension," was echoed by another observer, who explained that they were by no means "destitute of good understandings." Highlanders were particularly aware that formal education threatened their traditional pastoral and warrior ways; they recognized that reading and writing and commerce and industry would undermine their "passionate love and genius for music, as well as the kindred strains of moving, though simple poetry"; they fully understood how English schooling endangered those clannish values that repudiated labor and striving for wealth but revered leisure and "the exposure & hardness which their ancestors boasted they were able to endure."[44]

Men who were reluctant to become part of an industrial society understandably rejected the arts and sciences needed to maintain such a society. Neither southern Crackers nor their Celtic ancestors abjured education, but what they favored were skills that would sustain, not help to destroy, their culture. Somehow they seemed to understand, just as American Indians often understood, that Yankee or English education was as dangerous to them and to their culture as Yankee or English bullets. "Tell our Great Father at Washington," some Indian leaders informed a government agent, "that we are very sorry we cannot receive teachers among us, for reading and writing . . . is very bad for Indians. Some of the Creeks and Cherokees learnt to read and write, and they are the greatest rascals among all Indians."[45]

What outsiders taught, under the guise of enlightenment and knowledge, was merely subservience to alien ways and values. Many Southerners saw formal education as an insidious way to acculturate and enslave them. Learning to read and to write would, rather than free them, put them even more at the Yankees' mercy by making

44. Martin Martin, *A Description of the Western Islands of Scotland* (1716; reprint, Edinburgh, 1981), 199–201; [William Thomson], *A Tour in England and Scotland, in 1785* (London, 1788), 222; Joseph Farington, *The Farington Diary*, ed. James Grieg (3d ed., 2 vols., New York, 1923), I:330. See also Sir Leonard Twiston Davies and Averyl Edwards, *Welsh Life in the Eighteenth Century* (London, 1939), 124–25; Ramsay, *Scotland and Scotsmen*, II:406–08; Alwyn Rees and Brinley Rees, *Celtic Heritage: Ancient Tradition in Ireland and Wales* (London, 1961), 83–84, 89–90. Recent scholarship has shown that even among Lowlanders the literacy of Scots has been overstated. Rob Houston, *Scottish Literacy and Scottish Identity: Illiteracy and Society in Scotland and Northern England, 1600–1800* (New York, 1986).

45. Washington Irving, *Wolfert's Roost and Other Papers* (rev. ed., New York, 1865), 332–33.

them mere cogs in the northern machine. They could remain free only by perfecting the skills that reinforced their own traditions. In argument against the establishment of a public school system in North Carolina, one man stated that it was unnecessary as well as undesirable "that *everybody* should be able to read and cipher. If one is to keep a store or a school, or to be a lawyer or physician, such branches may, *perhaps*, be taught him; though I do not look upon them as by any means indispensable; but if he is to be a plain farmer, or a mechanic, they are of no manner of use, rather a determent."[46]

Two things must be remembered about education in the Old South. First, only a small minority of antebellum Southerners could both read and write and often did so. As exceptions to the prevailing social pattern, they were more Yankeefied in outlook and actions than their neighbors or kinsmen who, even if they could read and write, rarely took up pen or paper.

Aleksandr I. Solzhenitsyn, the traditionalist and Nobel laureate, has pointed out that when writers leave the Soviet Union and attempt to write for an international audience they often can no longer produce true Russian literature. Because it is so difficult, perhaps impossible, to translate the richness of the Russian language, the works of émigré writers usually fail to present the real "Russian consciousness." An excellent example is Vladimir Nabokov. "To reach Western readers," observed Solzhenitsyn, "Nabokov was obliged to use his brilliant knowledge of English. This meant breaking with the past. He was born anew, with a new soul, but he lost his Russian roots."[47]

Something similar happened to many of the Southerners who were exposed to Yankee education. Not all of them were influenced equally, and several managed to overcome their northern education and become ardent southern nationalists—John C. Calhoun and William Lowndes Yancey, for example—but nearly all adopted certain nonsouthern views and ways that weakened or destroyed their native values and traditions. Historians, willing captives of their own educational biases, too rarely have recognized the significance of this acculturation process. All too frequently they have assumed that the better-educated Southerners—those who habitually wrote letters or kept diaries—represented the views and experiences of the majority, and the historians have based their works mainly upon such sources. But the records kept by literate and Yankeefied Southerners reflect less the doings and beliefs of the majority than the acts and thoughts of a small though admittedly influential minority; used for generalizations about the whole of southern society, these

46. G. Johnson, "Public Schools," 57.
47. Hilton Kramer, "A Talk with Solzhenitsyn," *New York Times Book* *Review* 85, no. 9 (May 11, 1980), 3, 30–32.

documents distort more than they clarify because they represent what Solzhenitsyn defined as "works not very deeply rooted in the consciousness or experience of the people."

The second thing to remember is that most Southerners simply embraced their cultural traditions when they spent their time hunting rather than reading, fishing rather than writing. To them hunting and fishing were as natural and as pleasant as loafing; reading and writing were as unnatural and as unpleasant as studying. The average Southerner learned only what he needed to learn, and sometimes not even that; generally he studied only that which was enjoyable, for pleasure meant more to him than profit. His knowledge might be considered useful, but that was incidental. The skills he admired most were those that allowed him to live in accord with yet also to dominate his environment. Most Crackers seemed reasonably content with their place in this world and with what they might expect in the next. Unburdened by a work ethic and unhurried by driving ambition, they treasured the ways of their forefathers and were satisfied to live out their lives innocent of different skills. "The great excuse that the ignorant [Southerners] have for remaining so," complained a Northerner, "is that they can be as happy and virtuous without education as with it."[48]

Some doubtless knew that many things threatened their culture—including machines and profits, increased cotton production, progress, and formal education. Had Crackers been readers, they might have perceived that what was happening to them and their traditional ways in the late antebellum period had happened to their Highland ancestors only a century or so earlier. Thomas Pennant, who visited Scotland after the final defeat of the Highlanders by the English and the destruction of the clans, vividly described the changes that had taken place. Traditionally, said Pennant, "the native Highlander . . . was indolent to a high degree, unless roused to war, or to any animating amusement; . . . hospitable . . . , and full of generosity . . . , much affected with the civility of strangers, [imbued with] . . . a natural politeness and address . . . much pride, and consequently are impatient of affronts, and revengefull of injuries." They were "decent in . . . general behaviour; inclined to superstition, yet attentive to the duties of religion. . . . But in many parts of the Highlands," reported Pennant, "their character begins to be more faintly marked; they mix more with the world, and become daily less attached to their chiefs: the clans begin to disperse . . . through different parts of the country . . . ; and the chieftain tasting the sweets of advanced rents, and the benefits of industry,

48. James Champlin, *Early Biography,*
*Travels and Adventures of Rev. James*
*Champlin, who was Born Blind . . .*
(Columbus, Ohio, 1842), 78.

dismisses . . . the crowds of retainers." Without their traditional clan structure to sustain them, Highlanders were forced either to become tenant farmers or to migrate—often to one of Britain's industrial cities. Ill equipped to survive such cultural uprooting— even "the antient sports of the Highlanders, such as . . . hunting, fowling and fishing, are now disused," acknowledged Pennant[49]— Highlanders, along with the Welsh and the Irish, joined the mudsills of industrial Britain. Those Celts who escaped the traps of tenancy, mining, and factories often found a place in the British army, for from the late eighteenth through the twentieth centuries, meaningless pageants and games aside, only on battlefields selected by the English were Celts allowed to be what their ancestors had been; there they were welcome to die bravely fighting England's wars.

Perhaps it was fortunate for Crackers that they were not readers; had they been able to infer from a perusal of Celtic history what was in store for them, it would have broken their hearts—but probably not their spirits. Like their Celtic ancestors, Crackers would fight, even if beforehand they knew that their cause was lost.

49. Thomas Pennant, *A Tour in Scotland; MDCCLXIX* (reprint, Perth, Scotland, 1979), 193–94.

# IX

# *Progress*

VISITORS who complained about the nature of education in premodern Scotland, Wales, and Ireland, and in the Old South rarely had anything more favorable to say about the conditions of travel in these areas. First of all, travelers, especially those from England and the North, were not used to the roads they encountered. English roads, wrote an eighteenth-century tourist, "are always kept in good order with coarse or fine gravel or sand, and the slightest unevenness is mended at once." Roads in the northern United States also generally received praise from voyagers, but not those of the South. "We pursued our journey southward by the public stages, and found both the roads, the vehicles, and every arrangement in connection with them, very inferior to those of the North," stated a nineteenth-century visitor.[1]

Travelers had similar things to say about Irish roads. "The roads of this kingdom are . . . by no means equal to the English [roads]," reported an eighteenth-century tripper in Ireland. At about the same time, Arthur Young complained of "a vile stoney road" in one part of Ireland and in another of a road constructed over "quaking bogs, that . . . move under the carriage." Because roads were so bad in eighteenth-century Ireland, admitted a native, there was "very little travelling . . . and if there had been much, the ruts and holes would have rendered thirty miles a-day a good journey."[2]

1. Frederick Kielmansegge, *Diary of a Journey to England in the Years 1761–1762*, trans. Philippa Kielmansegge (London, 1902), 19; Charles Joseph Latrobe, *The Rambler in North America . . .* (2 vols., London, 1835), II:5.
   2. John Bush, *Hibernia Curiosa: A Letter . . . Giving a General View of the Manners, Customs, Dispositions, &c. of the Inhabitants of Ireland* (London, 1769), 41; Arthur Young, *Arthur Young's Tour in Ireland (1776–1779)*, ed. Arthur W. Hutton (2 vols., London, 1892), I:249, 177; Sir Jonah Barrington, *Personal Sketches of His Own Times*, ed. Townsend Young (3d ed., 2 vols., London, 1869), I:85. See also Edward MacLysaght, *Irish Life in the Seventeenth Century* (1939; reprint, Dublin, 1979), 242, 244–46, 250–51.

ROAD IN EIGHTEENTH-CENTURY SCOTLAND

From Edward Burt, *Burt's Letters from the North of Scot-
land* (2 vols., London, 1754), II:130.

Conditions were equally poor in Wales and Scotland through the eighteenth century. In the words of one trekker, "Bad was the road and dreary was the way." Even at the beginning of the eighteenth century, recalled George Robertson, "the common carrier from Selkirk to Edinburgh, thirty-eight miles distant, required two weeks to make out his journey betwixt the two towns, going and returning," and as late as the 1760s "it still took a day and a half for the stage coach to travel between Edinburgh and Glasgow. This was by the only road passable. . . . It was an arduous undertaking."³

Touring the antebellum South was no easier. "On the whole, the road from Charles Town [South Carolina] to Wilmington [North Carolina] is certainly the most tedious and disagreeable of any on the Continent of North America," declared a pilgrim in 1773; "it is through a poor, sandy, barren, gloomy country without accommodations for travellers. . . . Neither man nor beast can stand a long journey thro' so bad a country where there's much fatigue and no refreshment." More than a decade later one traveler stated that southern "roads were awful," and another claimed that the main road through the southern states "was so extremely bad in many places that we twice were obliged [within a few miles] to get out and clap our shoulders to the wheels, to assist a restive horse in drawing the stage up two hills; otherwise we must have remained there all night."⁴

Southern roads were just as defective throughout the later antebellum period as they had been in the eighteenth century. A Frenchman complained in 1816 of "traveling over dreadful roads in which, in France, one would certainly expose neither travelers nor coaches." In the 1820s an excursionist called southern roads "proverbially bad." During the next two decades visitors described the South's roads as "wretched indeed," "dreadful," "execrable and often dangerous." Frequently, there were no roads at all, only "the path of former travellers," insisted an Englishwoman: "Stumps of trees were left in the middle of the path, which lies through a thick forest." Nor had the situation changed appreciably in the 1850s. An

3. Edward D. Clarke, *A Tour Through the South of England, Wales, and Part of Ireland, Made During the Summer of 1791* (London, 1793), 256; Charles Cordiner, *Antiquities & Scenery of the North of Scotland, in a Series of Letters to Thomas Pennant, Esq.* (London, 1780), 89, 97, 102; R. L. Willis, *Journal of a Tour from London to Elgin made About 1790 . . .* (Edinburgh, 1897), 61; George Robertson quoted in J. G. Fyfe, ed., *Scottish Diaries and Memoirs, 1746–*

*1843* (Stirling, Scotland, 1942), 257–59.

4. Hugh Finlay, *Journal Kept by Hugh Finlay, Surveyor of the Post Roads on the Continent of North America . . .* , ed. Frank H. Norton (Brooklyn, 1867), 67; Louis Philippe, *Diary of My Travels in America [1797]*, trans. Stephen Becker (New York, 1977), 35; Robert Hunter, Jr., *Quebec to Carolina in 1785–1786 . . .* , ed. Louis B. Wright and Marion Tinling (San Marino, Calif., 1943), 262.

Englishman called his route across Georgia and Alabama "the very worst road I have travelled on," and a Southerner admitted that throughout the South "roads [were] in bad order." A woman avowed that the roads were in such a sorry condition one simply could not travel when it rained. "The roads leading into the state [of Texas] through Louisiana, south of Natchitoches," noted an itinerant, "are scarcely used, except by residents along them and herdsmen bringing cattle to the New Orleans market." He observed that travel was especially difficult because the "ferries across the numerous rivers and bayous are so costly and ill tended, [and] the roads so wet and bad."[5]

Not only were ferries poorly tended in the Old South, but bridges were few and often rickety, just as they were in premodern Celtic Britain. Travelers frequently complained of "the scarcity of bridges" in Ireland, and an authority noted that in 1630 "there were only some 220 fair-sized bridges in the whole country [of Scotland]." Late in the eighteenth century a native Scot concluded: "No country is more neglected in respect of roads. . . . The bridges . . . in like manner have been neglected." For centuries Scots drowned trying to ford rivers where there were no bridges. In 1834 an Englishman journeying through the South feared the same would happen to him crossing a river: "with a strong tide against us & a heavy rain in front we crossed very unpleasantly in an open boat." Had he crossed on a bridge, he might have been in just as much danger. Earlier another

5. Edouard de Montule, *Travels in America, 1816–1817*, trans. Edward D. Seeber (Bloomington, 1951), 132; Margaret (Hunter) Hall, *The Aristocratic Journey; Being the Outspoken Letters of Mrs. Basil Hall Written During a Fourteen Months' Sojourn in America, 1827–1828*, ed. Una Pope-Hennessy (New York, 1931), 195; Henry Benjamin Whipple, *Bishop Whipple's Southern Diary, 1843–1844*, ed. Lester B. Shippee (Minneapolis, 1937), 78; George Townsend Fox American Journal, December 10, 1834, Public Library, South Shields, Durham, England; Sir Charles Lyell, *A Second Visit to the United States . . .* (2 vols., New York, 1849), II:70; Matilda Charlotte (Jesse) Fraser Houstoun, *Texas and the Gulf . . .* (Philadelphia, 1845), 224; Anon., *The English Party's Excursion to Paris . . . to which is Added, a Trip to America . . .* (London, 1850), 342; James Mallory Journal, December 16, 1850, January 10, 1851 (original owned by Edgar A. Stewart of Selma, Alabama),

microfilm copy, University of Alabama, Tuscaloosa; Sara Witherspoon (Ervin) McIver Diary, April 18, 1854, Southern Historical Collection, University of North Carolina, Chapel Hill; Frederick Law Olmsted, *A Journey through Texas . . .* (1857; reprint, New York, 1969), 43. See also Robert Everest, *A Journey Through the United States and Part of Canada* (London, 1855), 115; John Henry Vessey, *Mr. Vessey of England: Being the Incidents and Reminiscences of Travel in a Twelve Weeks' Tour through the United States and Canada in the Year 1859*, ed. Brian Waters (New York, 1956), 78–79, 81; Olmsted, *Journey through Texas*, 27–28; Elijah Swift, "Elijah Swift's Travel Journal from Massachusetts to Florida, 1857," ed. Virginia Steel Wood, *Florida Historical Quarterly* 55 (1976), 181–88; Royce Gordon Shingleton, "Stages, Steamers, and Stations in the Ante-Bellum South: A British View," *Georgia Historical Quarterly* 56 (1972), 243–58.

FORDING A SOUTHERN STREAM

From *Harper's New Monthly Magazine* 11 (1855), 299.

English tourist in the South complained: "Some of the bridges are exceedingly dangerous crossing them, many of them being loose and partly carried away with the late rain."[6]

One reason why roads and bridges in Celtic areas were bad was because Celts had an outright prejudice against them. Highland Scots "had a strong aversion to roads," noted an observer. "In 1761," recalled a Scot, "I was in company with Peter Graham. ... The conversation turning on roads, he said he saw no use of them but to let burghers and red-coats into the Highlands, none of whom, in his father's time, durst venture beyond the Pass of Aberfoyle." Other Scots, who considered roads uncomfortable for them or their cattle to walk on, preferred "to go without the Road, and ride or walk in very incommodious Ways," observed an Englishman. Still other Celts objected to having "a public road close in upon any man's private residence." The same desire to preserve individual freedom even at the cost of discomfort prevailed in the Old South. One eyewitness noted "an extraordinary indifference to practical internal improvements" among antebellum Southerners; another wrote: "The internal improvements [in the South] ... are advancing, though slowly in comparison with those of the northern sections of the Union."[7]

Not only was travel in Celtic areas slow, but often it was disagreeable and dangerous. "Ireland ... lagged far behind England as regards travelling facilities," noted an authority. "The Irish stage-coaches are a most uneasy and unsafe mode of conveyance," wrote a late-eighteenth-century traveler. "The mail-coaches do not keep the same regular pace which distinguishes them in England. ... In England, except to change horses, the mail-coach never stops. ... In Ireland, on the other hand, the coach has frequently to wait a quarter of a hour or more, at petty villages, until the letters are assorted and stamped." Travel was equally slow and uncomfortable in the Old South. "It took, in those days, about five or six days to go to New York," recalled a rural Georgian. "Part of the way was by railroad, part by stage, and part by water. There were no checks for your baggage and whenever you changed you had to go and see your

6. MacLysaght, *Irish Life*, 248; W. R. Kermack, *Historical Geography of Scotland* (Edinburgh, 1926), 109; Sir John Sinclair, ed., *The Statistical Account of Scotland, 1791–1799* (reprint, 20 vols., East Ardsley, England, 1981), XVII:410–11, 366; Fox Journal, November 29, 1834; Hunter, *Quebec to Carolina*, 162.

7. Sinclair, *Statistical Account of Scotland*, XVII:521–22; John Ramsay quoted in Fyfe, *Scottish Diaries and Memoirs*, 187; Edward Burt, *Burt's Letters from the North of Scotland*, ed. R. Jamieson (1754; reprint, 2 vols., Edinburgh, 1974), II:333–34; George Robertson quoted in Fyfe, *Scottish Diaries and Memoirs*, 260; John F. H. Claiborne, "A Trip through the Piney Woods [1841]," *Mississippi Historical Society Publications* 9 (1906), 510; James Silk Buckingham, *The Slave States of America* (2 vols., London, 1842), I:44.

baggage transferred from one railroad to another, or from one stage to another. There were no sleeping cars, and if you traveled at night, you had to sit up all night, so ladies could not travel alone then as they do now." Stages frequently were crowded and rarely ran on time. An Englishman, traveling with his wife and baby, objected to the two A.M. departure time from Richmond, Virginia; he got "the stage proprietor . . . to accommodate us as far as he could by delaying the carriage three hours," but then the foreigners found themselves "packed up together" in the stage with nine people. Another Englishman complained because he was forced to travel through much of Georgia in "a common waggon without springs, in which we were jolted beyond any thing I ever experienced before." A wayfarer stated that his trip through the southern states in 1786 was "the most tiresome and disagreeable journey I ever in my life experienced." Some sixty years later another tourist announced: "All traveling in the South is more perilous than it is any where else. The 'reason why' is . . . that the climate is too relaxing to the body and too stimulating to the brain of the Anglo-Saxon races, and that they become reckless and careless in consequence."[8]

Recklessness was often thrust upon travelers. A woman journeying through southwestern Virginia in 1855 reported: "Our carriage was much tried; the horses floundered along the brink of a precipice, our driver calling to us to throw our weight now upon one side, now on the other, to keep a balance. At one time within half a foot of deep water, where, in case of being overturned, we must have been drowned, if we had escaped being smashed in the fall; at another, with a descent of three hundred feet, without the smallest guard [rail] upon our right. But our Irish coachman was civil and expert; he assured me he would not have anything happen to us for fifty dollars." Nevertheless, one Englishman contended that southern stage "drivers . . . were very inferior to those of the Northern States"; and another Englishman wrote: "The stage was overset last week, an occurrence which happens, on an average about six times a-year."[9]

Some adventurers deemed other forms of transportation to be

8. Sinclair, *Statistical Account of Scotland*, XVII:81, 154; Fynes Moryson, *An Itinerary: Containing His Ten Yeeres Travell* . . . (4 vols., Glasgow, 1617–18), III:482; MacLysaght, *Irish Life*, 240–41; Anon., *Ireland in 1804*, ed. Seamus Grimes (1806; reprint, Dublin, 1980), 37, 48–49; Marion Alexander Boggs, ed., *The Alexander Letters, 1787–1900* (Athens, Ga., 1980), 124; M. Hall, *Aristocratic Journey*, 195–96; Fox Journal, December 4, 1834; Hunter, *Quebec to* *Carolina*, 280; Charles Mackay, *Life and Liberty in America* . . . (New York, 1859), 188. See also Eugene Alvarez, *Travel on Southern Antebellum Railroads, 1820–1860* (University, Ala., 1974), 150–96.

9. Amelia Matilda Murray, *Letters from the United States, Cuba and Canada* (New York, 1856), 190–91; Buckingham, *Slave States*, I:234; Anon., *English Party's Excursion*, 243.

superior to southern stages. South Carolina railroads received praise from some travelers, but others complained that most railroads in the South charged exorbitant fares compared to those in the North and that the cars were uncomfortable and "miserably constructed." One Yankee toured Georgia on what he called "the worst railroad ever invented. Our northern corduroys are safe compared to this. The passengers were amused on this road by running off the track, sending rails up through the bottom of the cars and other amusements of the kind calculated to make one's hair stand on end. We only ran off the track once and that was in running backwards. I never have seen so wretched management. At one of the stations . . . we were detained 25 minutes for the men to chop wood for the engine. This is the first railroad I have ever seen where the cars were stopped to cut fuel. We were seven & a half hours running . . . a distance of forty miles—at the enormous rate of five miles an hour. Bah! Stage coaches can well laugh at such railroads."[10]

Many travelers considered southern steamboats as unimpressive and as uncomfortable as southern railroads. "Generally speaking," reported an Englishman, "we . . . found steam-boat travelling extremely disagreeable." Steamboats in the South often were faster and cheaper than other means of transportation, but in the eyes of some excursionists these advantages were offset by the reputed dangers of river travel. Southern vessels not merely suffered a high number of accidents, but all too frequently they broke down. "Like the greater number of . . . [southern] boats I had the fortune to travel upon," a man wrote of one vessel, "some part of her machinery was 'out of order.' " Furthermore, travelers on steamboats usually had the unpleasant experience of mixing closely with plain Southerners, or as one fastidious sightseer called them, " 'raal green ones,' men 'who had never travelled'—and perhaps 'had worn all the hair off their breast climbing persimmon trees.' "[11]

Some people believed that the only thing worse than traveling through the Old South was stopping there overnight. There were

10. Lillian Foster, *Way-Side Glimpses, North and South* (New York, 1860), 89; Boggs, *Alexander Letters*, 114; Philo Tower, *Slavery Unmasked: Being a Truthful Narrative of Three Years' Residence and Journeying in Eleven Southern States . . .* (Rochester, N.Y., 1856), 159; Whipple, *Southern Diary*, 74, 76. See also Everest, *Journey*, 115; [Charles A. Clinton?], *A Winter from Home* (New York, 1852), 40; Vessey, *Mr. Vessey of England*, 93–94.

11. Captain Basil Hall, *Travels in North America in the Years 1827 and* *1828* (3 vols., Edinburgh and London, 1829), III:309; Olmsted, *Journey through Texas*, 37; Whipple, *Southern Diary*, 94. See also Lyell, *Second Visit*, II:48, 49, 52–53; M. Hall, *Aristocratic Journey*, 200; Charles Lanman, *Adventures in the Wilds . . .* (2 vols., Philadelphia, 1856), II:169; Victor Tixier, *Tixier's Travels . . . [1839–1840]*, ed. John Francis McDermott (Norman, Okla., 1940), 43–45; Whipple, *Southern Diary*, 131, 138–39; Olmsted, *Journey through Texas*, 37–38, 44; Vessey, *Mr. Vessey of England*, 102.

some excellent southern hotels, but nearly all of them were in Charleston, New Orleans, Mobile, Savannah, and a few other places.[12] In 1861 a man noted that Montgomery, Alabama, had only two hotels: "Montgomery Hall, of bitter memory—like the much-sung 'Raven of Zurich,' for uncleanliness of nest and length of bill— had been the resort of country merchants, horse and cattle-men. . . . The Exchange—of rather more pretentions and vastly more comfort—was at that time in the hands of a northern firm, who 'could keep a hotel.' " Away from the larger towns, where there were no Northerners to "keep a hotel," visitors had little hope of finding anything in the South approaching the inns that were so plentiful in New England and that received so much praise from foreigners who found them remarkably like English inns—comfortable, cheap, and full of reading material.[13]

Travelers often complained that in the Old South most hotels and inns were awful and that the accommodations provided by private individuals were often worse. "The Hotels [in the South]," wrote an Englishman, "are generally badly kept, and in several indescribable ways uncomfortable." One pilgrim called a Richmond, Virginia, hotel "a vilely dirty place." Another pronounced a North Carolina inn the worst in America. "We made a halt at Captain Bartley's inn, a real hovel," wrote a tourist in Virginia, who two days before had declared: "Put up at the Red Lion, a beggerly inn." A rambler through Arkansas believed that it required "more than the usual amount of patriotism, or desire for destinction," for state legislators to spend three months of the year in any Little Rock hotel. He stayed in what he called an awful "Irish hole, dignified with the appellation of hotel," and run by an "officious son of the Emerald Isle." Rarely did journeyers display the wit of the Yankee who concluded: "Of one thing I am certain, the inn keeper wisely concluded no man ever stopped at his house twice & so he made the most of his charge." More often complaints were made without humor in the manner of

12. [Clinton?], *Winter from Home,* 4, 6; Houstoun, *Texas and the Gulf,* 83; A. Murray, *Letters from the United States,* 189, 201–02, 309; Whipple, *Southern Diary,* 14, 195–97, 200–201; Tower, *Slavery Unmasked,* 159; M. Hall, *Aristocratic Journey,* 266.

13. Thomas C. DeLeon, *Four Years in Rebel Capitals . . . ,* ed. E. B. Long (new ed., New York, 1962), 40. See also Lanman, *Adventures in the Wilds,* II:189. On the high quality of English and northern hotels and inns, see Pierre J. Grosley, *A Tour to London [in 1765]; or, New Observations on England, and Its Inhabitants* (2 vols., London, 1772), I:19; A. Murray, *Letters from the United States,* 190; Adam Hodgson, *Letters from North America . . .* (2 vols., London, 1824), II:120; Thomas Hamilton, *Men and Manners in America* (2 vols., Philadelphia, 1833), I:156; Philippe, *Diary of My Travels,* 15, 44; Alice Morse Earle, *Home Life in Colonial Days* (reprint, Middle Village, N.Y., 1975), 357, 360; Johann David Schopf, *Travels in the Confederation [1783–1784] . . . ,* trans. and ed. Alfred J. Morrison (new ed., 2 vols., New York, 1968), II:35; Montule, *Travels in America,* 26, 138.

the traveler who stayed overnight in backcountry North Carolina in what he described as "a most wretched tavern (though it scarce deserves the name of one)."[14]

Private homes seldom offered travelers greater comforts. "Every shanty sells spirits and takes in travelers," reported a visitor. "In [the South] . . . , where there is no regular travelling, and indeed little travelling of any kind, no taverns, properly so called, are kept up," explained a more understanding wayfarer. "But in their stead, some houses near the road are always open to any one who calls, and the best fare the inhabitants have, is cheerfully set before the guests. Of course, a charge is made, which varies, as might be expected, inversely as the quality of the entertainment." That the quality was usually low is indicated by the common notation in the journals of those who traveled through the antebellum South. "We put up at this miserable hut," was a typical comment.[15]

There were quite as many complaints about accommodations in premodern Celtic Britain as about those in the Old South. "An Irish inn has been an eternal subject of ridicule," admitted an Irishman. "It is true that in [the eighteenth century] . . . most of the inns in Ireland were nearly of the same quality—a composition of slovenliness, bad meat, worse cooking, and few vegetables save the royal Irish potato." "There is not absolutely one good inn in [Dublin]," insisted a stranger in the 1760s; "not one, upon my honour, in which an Englishman of any sense of decency would be satisfied with his quarters, and not above two or three in the whole city that he could bear to be in." Other writers damned all Irish accommodations. After spending a night "in a cabbin, called an inn," Arthur Young prayed: "Preserve me, fates! from such another." He also considered himself fortunate indeed to have "escaped without a cold, or the itch" from another "miserable cabbin," which he "had been assured was an exceeding good inn." The experience of a German visitor in Ireland—having to repair "the broken windows of my [bed] chamber

14. Henry Arthur Bright, *Happy Country This America: The Travel Diary of Henry Arthur Bright [1852]*, ed. Anne Henry Ehrenpreis (Columbus, Ohio, 1978), 182; M. Hall, *Aristocratic Journey*, 198; Hodgson, *Letters*, II:131; Philippe, *Diary of My Travels*, 45–46; Gilbert Hathaway, *Travels in the Two Hemispheres* . . . (Detroit, 1858), 236, 187; Whipple, *Southern Diary*, 70; Hunter, *Quebec to Carolina*, 281. See also Anon., *A Visit to Texas: Being the Journal of a Traveller* . . . (New York, 1834), 31–32; Olmsted, *Journey through Texas*, 103; Lyell, *Second Visit*, II:172–73; Ebenezer Davies, *American Scenes—and Christian Slavery: A Recent Tour of Four Thousand Miles in the United States* (London, 1849), 77–79; Schopf, *Travels in the Confederation*, II:156; Whipple, *Southern Diary*, 79; Houstoun, *Texas and the Gulf*, 217–18; Eugene L. Schwaab, ed., *Travels in the Old South: Selected from Periodicals of the Times* (2 vols., Lexington, Ky., 1973), I:56.

15. Olmsted, *Journey through Texas*, 62; B. Hall, *Travels*, III:272; Finlay, *Journal*, 54.

... with pillows"—paralleled that of a guest at a southern inn, who "slept ... with a broken window at the head of our bed, and another at our side."[16]

Reports were no more favorable on accommodations in Scotland and Wales. "They have no such Innes [in Scotland] as bee in England," lamented a seventeenth-century Englishman. "Few inns were then to be met with on the most frequented roads, in which the traveller could either eat or sleep with comfort," admitted an eighteenth-century Scot. "They were so ill provided with the most necessary articles, that on a journey people used to carry a knife and fork." A Frenchman discovered in Scotland "the worst and dirtiest inn" he ever encountered, and a Swiss claimed it "well required the fatigue of the day to be able to sleep in the miserable beds which were prepared for us" in Scottish inns. Englishmen reported Welsh inns to be equally as bad. One tourist recalled staying in a "miserable hole," where he and his traveling companions had to "break the windows in our bed rooms to let in the fresh air."[17]

Complaints centered on what travelers considered the slatternliness of Celts, whose houses as well as sleeping arrangements shocked visitors. Travelers referred to "the despicable huts, or cabbins" of the Irish. "Their dwellings are usually very indifferent," explained a viewer, "and even devoid of necessaries. Many sleep on the damp floor. Their clothing for day or night is often very scanty." "Here [in a Scottish inn] had we a choking smoky Chamber, and drunken unruly company thrust in upon us," grumbled an Englishman; another reported "sad Entertainment" at what reportedly was an inn, where he and his companions "were put into such a dismall hole of a room." Still another visitor wrote, "Scots villages are ... mere collections of hovels." People in Scotland lived far "less comfortable than [people] in England," claimed a tourist, and Scottish houses, "with [their] thatched roofs and chimneys of mud," were

16. Barrington, *Personal Sketches,* I:85; Bush, *Hibernia Curiosa,* 19; A. Young, *Tour in Ireland,* I:105, 177; [Herman Ludwig Heinrich], *Tour in England, Ireland, and France in the Years 1826, 1827, 1828, and 1829* (Philadelphia, 1833), 333; Olmsted, *Journey through Texas,* 107. See also William Shaw Mason, ed., *A Statistical Account or Parochial Survey of Ireland, Drawn up from the Communications of the Clergy* (3 vols., Dublin, 1814–19), III:53; J. Bennett Nolan, *Benjamin Franklin in Scotland and Ireland, 1759 and 1771* (Philadelphia, 1938), 165; Anon., *Ireland in 1804,* 55; MacLysaght, *Irish Life,* 253.
17. Moryson, *Itinerary,* III:482;

Thomas Somerville quoted in Fyfe, *Scottish Diaries and Memoirs,* 234; Louis Simond, *Journal of a Tour and Residence in Great Britain, During the Years 1810 and 1811* (2 vols., Edinburgh, 1817), II:396; L. A. Necker de Saussure, *Travels in Scotland: Descriptive of the State of Manners, Literature, and Science* (London, 1821), 67; [Richard Fenton], *A Tour in Quest of Genealogy, through Several Parts of Wales, Somersetshire, and Wiltshire ...* (London, 1811), 21; Joseph Hucks, *A Pedestrian Tour through North Wales, in a Series of Letters [1795],* ed. Alun R. Jones and William Tydeman (Cardiff, Wales, 1979), 12, 36, 55.

"very dirty." A witness referred to the "usually very humble Cottages" of Wales. "I was not so vain as to expect very splendid Furniture in such contemptible Huts," he wrote. "I found no Apartments in these . . . Habitations, every Edifice being a *Noah's Ark*, where a promiscuous Family, a miscellaneous Heap of all Kinds of Creatures did converse together in one Room; the Pigs and the Pullen, and other Brutes either truckling under, or lying at the Bed's-Feet of the little more refin'd, yet their Brother Animals."[18]

Visitors often found inns and houses that took guests in the Old South just as disgusting. A Northerner insisted that the typical southern cabins in which he stayed had several windowpanes "broken, and the outside door could not be closed from without; and when closed, was generally pried open with a pocket-knife by those who wished to go out. A great part of the time it was left open. Supper was served in another room, in which there was no fire, and the outside door was left open for the convenience of the servants in passing to and from the kitchen, which as usual here at large houses, was in a detached building. Supper was, however, eaten with such rapidity that nothing had time to freeze on the table." Putting five or six persons in one small bedroom was common. "Three gentlemen and myself were crammed into a filthy room which already contained two strangers," reported an Englishman, who at another inn was quite disturbed when a "woman very coolly inquired whether I had any objection to allow a passenger to divide my bed, and seemed very much displeased at my refusal." Another foreigner complained that in one house "we slept nine in a small room. We were fortunate enough to get the best bed. . . . There were three men in one of the beds. It was curious to hear them disputing who should sleep in the middle. Their conversation in the night was truly laughable."[19]

Dirty accommodations and uncomfortable beds were less funny.

---

18. Bush, *Hibernia Curiosa*, 45; Mason, *Statistical Account . . . of Ireland*, II:324; Christopher Lowther, *Our Journall into Scotland Anno Domini 1629 . . .*, ed. W. D. (Edinburgh, 1894), 16–17; Joseph Taylor, *Journey to Edenborough in Scotland [in the Eighteenth Century]*, ed. William Cowan (Edinburgh, 1903), 98; Washington Irving, *Tour in Scotland, 1817, and Other Manuscript Notes*, ed. Stanley T. Williams (New Haven, Conn., 1927), 66; [Benjamin Silliman], *A Journal of Travels in England, Holland and Scotland . . .* (2 vols., New York, 1810), II:299; Anon., *The Comical Pilgrim; or, Travels of a Cynick Philosopher, Thro' the Most Wicked Parts of the World, Namely England, Wales, Scotland, Ireland, and Holland* (London, 1723), 47.

19. Olmsted, *Journey through Texas*, 103; Fox Journal, December 10, 1834; William Faux, *Memorable Days in America . . .* (London, 1823), 201; Lucius Verus Bierce, *Travels in the Southland, 1822–1823: The Journal of Lucius Verus Bierce*, ed. George W. Knepper (Columbus, Ohio, 1966), 53; Everest, *Journey*, 101; George William Featherstonhaugh, *Excursion through the Slave States . . .* (2 vols., London, 1844), II:42–69; William Howard Russell, *My Diary North and South* (2 vols., London, 1863), I:237, 137; Hunter, *Quebec to Carolina*, 227.

"I think pretty nearly the greatest hardship we encountered on our journey [through the South]," wrote an Englishman, "was the impossibility of getting any thing to lie upon but feather beds, made of ill-cured materials, scantily bestowed in a flaccid bag, laid on rumbly, uneven cross-planking." A Northerner visiting in Mississippi had to sleep "upon some boards in a windowless . . . room [where] . . . at dead of night we were suddenly awakened by the loud and dreadful howling of a dog, [who] . . . we found directly under our rude bed, which was his accustomed lair." Englishmen and Yankees were used to having comfortable beds with "two sheets" on them, but most Celts managed "with one sheet . . . [or with] only their clothes and blanket to cover them"; consequently, a common complaint by travelers in Celtic regions was that they were expected to sleep with scant or dirty bedding. "At night we retired to very disagreeable beds and dirty linen," wrote one man. Another discovered that the bed assigned to him at one place "had been already slept in several nights." Travelers in premodern Ireland regularly made the same complaint.[20]

Bugs bothered many tourists. "I passed the night [in an Irish inn] defending myself from the monsters who regarded me as their lawful prey, and when the sun rose it was on a bloody scene," reported a French wayfarer in 1796. Englishman William Howard Russell, like many other travelers in the antebellum South, spent many uncomfortable nights in southern inns. At one, where he was accused by natives of "miserable aristocratic fastidiousness" because he demanded a mattress to sleep on, he was nearly devoured by bugs. "Had it not been for the flies, the fleas would have been intolerable," he wrote. "I found that my bed was alive with bugs, fleas, and other vermin," complained William Faux; "rose at two A.M., to shake myself and enjoy a respite from these creeping, tormenting bedfellows." "My accommodations this evening were extremely bad," bewailed another traveler in the South. "I threw myself down upon my mattress, but suffered so much from cold, and was so infested with insects and vermin, that I could not close my eyes." Still another visitor lamented: "After eating a little supper I retired to a most disagreeable bed, where I got no sleep for the bugs and mosquitoes."[21]

20. B. Hall, *Travels*, III:271; Lanman, *Adventures in the Wilds*, II:196; Charles P. Moritz, *Travels, Chiefly on Foot, through Several Parts of England, in 1782* (London, 1795), 34; L. M. Cullen, *Life in Ireland* (London, 1979), 62; Olmsted, *Journey through Texas*, 25; Hunter, *Quebec to Carolina*, 280; Fox Journal, December 10, 1834; Barrington, *Personal Sketches*, I:85–86.

21. De Latocnaye, *A Frenchman's Walk through Ireland, 1796–7*, trans. and ed. John Stevenson (Belfast, 1917), 115; W. Russell, *Diary North and South*, I:237; Faux, *Memorable Days*, 70; Andrew Burnaby, *Travels through the Middle Settlements in North America . . . in the Years 1759 and 1760* (1775; reprint, Ithaca, N.Y., 1960), 44–45; Hunter, *Quebec to Carolina*, 274, 278.

Just as disturbing to many guests were the unsanitary ways of Celts. Critics emphasized "the sluttish and uncleanly" habits of the Irish. "The dirt of the streets [in Cork] . . . is shameful," wrote a Frenchman, and an Englishman described eighteenth-century Dublin as "one great stink." In Ireland, contended an eyewitness, "nastiness is in perfection, if perfection can be in vice, and the great cause of it, laziness, is most predominant. . . . All the kingdom, especially in the north, is infected with the perpetual plague of the itch." Other critics charged that the Irish were "defective in cleanliness," rarely changed or washed clothing, and allowed "heaps of filth" in their cabins; moreover, they seemed content "to acquiesce in that wretchedness" and had "no idea of English cleanliness, either in apartments, persons or cookery."[22]

Scots received similar criticism. A foreigner claimed that it was easy for him to tell that he was in a "country very different from England" because in Scotland the houses were "miserably dirty." An eighteenth-century visitor, who reported that Scots "never wash yir rooms," often saw "large heaps of nastiness swept into one corner, or . . . more commonly under ye beds." "The great objection to the Scotch is their want of cleanliness, of this they seem to have no feeling beyond what is forced upon them," stated an Englishman; "they live in a state of disorder, smoke & filth, most disgusting to those who are accustomed to the polished neatness and regularity which is so generally found in England." Even more scathing was another traveler who insisted that one thing "which makes this Country so much despis'd by the English . . . [is that] every street shows the nastiness of the Inhabitants, the excrements lye in heaps. . . . In a Morning the Scent was so offensive, that we were forc't to hold our Noses as we past the streets, and take care where we trod for fear of disobliging our shoes, and to walk in the middle at night, for fear of an accident on our heads. The Lodgings are as nasty as the streets, and wash't so seldom, that the dirt is thick eno' to be par'd off with a Shovell, Every room is well scented with a close stoole, and the Master, Mistress, and Servants lye all on a floor, like so many Swine in a Hogsty; this with the rest of their Sluttishness, is no doubt the occasion of the Itch, which is so common amongst them." Nor had much changed in the early nineteenth century when a New Englander visiting Edinburgh complained about what he

22. Barnaby Rich, *A New Description of Ireland: Wherein is Described the Disposition of the Irish* . . . (London, 1610), 24; Latocnaye, *Frenchman's Walk,* 74; Joseph Farington, *The Farington Diary,* ed. James Greig (3d ed., 2 vols., New York, 1923), I:107; John Stevens, *The Journal of John Stevens, Containing a* *Brief Account of the War in Ireland, 1689–1691,* ed. Robert H. Murray (Oxford, 1912), 140; Mason, *Statistical Account . . . of Ireland,* II:402, III:302, II:156; Barrington, *Personal Sketches,* I:85–86; Anon., *Ireland in 1804,* 35; Cullen, *Life in Ireland,* 79.

called the "most shameful deficiency in the accommodations of the town, which renders the environs at all times offensive; in the morning the nuisance exists in the streets, it is not removed till a late hour in the forenoon; I can hardly write upon the subject without offence, nor think of it without disgust; and the circumstance is the more surprising, as the contiguous, sister country [England] is distinguished for a punctilious attention to every point of comfort and decency." In the eighteenth century an English officer recalled "a Mischance that happened" after spending the night in the home of a Highlander: "rising early, and getting out of my [bed] . . . pretty hastily, I unluckly set my Foot in the Chamber-Pot, a Hole in the Ground by the Bed-side, which was made to serve for that Use in case of Occasion."[23]

"Dirty" was a term frequently applied by travelers to things they encountered in the Old South—a "dirty tavern," a "dirty cabin," a "dirty cloth," a "dirty cook," a "dirty-looking wife." An Englishwoman called New Orleans "the dirtiest town without any exception that I ever saw. There seems to be no attempt at public cleanliness and private houses follow the public street." Southern towns generally, said a visitor, "are miserable little dilapidated places"; another traveler complained that even the capitol of Mississippi had "ragged carpet; . . . windows cracked and broken; the walls and ceiling discoloured by mildew"; and yet another critic claimed that every edifice in Lexington, Kentucky, "seems filthy, neglected, and in ruins, particularly the court-house, . . . which, with its broken windows, rotten window-frames, rotten broken doors, all ruined and spoiled for lack of paint and a nail, looks like an old abandoned bagnio, not fit to be compared with any workhouse in England." One tourist from England said that Southerners "look as if their clothes had never been taken off, their faces washed, or their hair combed"; another concluded that Southerners "are not clean people." A Yankee described southern boardinghouses as "filth, filth."[24]

23. Simond, *Journal of a Tour,* I:344–45; John Loveday, *Diary of a Tour in 1732 Through Parts of England, Wales, Ireland and Scotland* (Edinburgh, 1890), 163; Farington, *Diary,* I:330; J. Taylor, *Journey to Edenborough,* 134; [Silliman], *Journal of Travels,* II:299; Edward Burt, *Burt's Letters from the North of Scotland,* ed. R. Jamieson (1754; reprint, 2 vols., Edinburgh, 1974), II:65.

24. Hodgson, *Letters,* I:152; Olmsted, *Journey through Texas,* 68; W. Russell, *Diary North and South,* I:136; Frederick Hall, *Letters from the East and from* the West (Washington, D.C., 1840), 48–49; Jacob Young, *Autobiography of a Pioneer; or, the Nativity, Experience, Travels, and Ministerial Labors of Rev. Jacob Young . . .* (Cincinnati, 1857), 223; Featherstonhaugh, *Excursion,* II:82; Vessey, *Mr. Vessey of England,* 70; Bodichon, *American Diary,* 111; Fox Journal, November 29, 1834; W. Russell, *Diary North and South,* II:6–7; Faux, *Memorable Days,* 191; [Sarah] Mendell and [Charlotte] Hosmer, *Notes of Travel and Life* (New York, 1854), 128.

Even today Southerners, in comparison to more disciplined Northerners, continue to scatter garbage along streets and highways despite laws prohibiting such practices. Professor John D. W. Guice of the University of Southern Mississippi stated in a letter to me: "One can encounter more trash [in Mississippi] between Purvis and Hattiesburg (a twenty-minute ride) than one could in a year of riding in Nebraska." He also noted "the common practice of throwing everything from garbage to abandoned appliances to worn-out cars along the edge of Southern rural roads." In Ireland and Scotland just as in the South, I have noticed numerous instances of one or more inoperable automobiles or rusting farm machines parked in a householder's front yard.

Few visitors to the Old South were as adaptable as the man who decided "to adopt the customs of the country" when confronted with a "common lavabo, and why not? One rain bathes the just and the unjust, why not one wash-bowl! Not twice in the next six months, away from cities or from residences we pitched for ourselves, did we find any other than this equal and democratic arrangement." Most travelers in the South were more fastidious. One man reported: "there was but one washbasin, as they called it, in the house; only one towel; and every thing looked and felt damp and dirty." What bothered another man was the numerous "accommodations of another kind, to which it is impossible more particularly to refer, of the most filthy description." A foreigner declared that he and his traveling companions, having spent the night in the loft of a house, were unable to find "a window or opening that should do service for a chamber pot, . . . so we insisted on some sort of receptacle; they brought us a kitchen kettle!" Yet another wayfarer recorded: "I rose this morning at six, not being able to sleep for the confounded noise of talking that three men . . . kept up during the whole night. One of them was very anxious to get a draft of water and was just going to apply his mouth to a mug that had been made use of by another as a *pot de chambre*. What curious scenes and adventures one meets with in traveling!"[25]

Contemporaries agreed that most Celtic architecture was as unimpressive as Celtic accommodations. To be sure, some of the dwellings of premodern Celtic Britain were substantial and elaborate, and so were certain houses in the Old South; indeed, a few were, as one writer called them, "romantic and elegant." One such dwelling was described by its owner, who wished to sell it, as "a very fine large and genteel brick house, two story high, with four rooms above and four below with a fireplace to each room, a large passage, [and] four

25. Olmsted, *Journey through Texas*, 26; B. Hall, *Travels*, III:263; Everest, *Journey*, 87; Philippe, *Diary of My Travels*, 60–61; Hunter, *Quebec to Carolina*, 227–28.

fine cellars." Other houses were appropriately designated "beautiful," "handsome," "graceful," and "stately." Every southern state had a number of residences that justly could be called mansions, and many of these fine old houses have been preserved or restored. But neither antebellum southern mansions nor the houses of the premodern Celtic gentry were as numerous as romantic chronicles and Hollywood legends suggest or as large and costly as certain English mansions and some of those built in the late nineteenth century by Yankee "robber barons" and their descendants.[26]

Most Southerners, even planters, resided not in mansions but in unpretentious abodes. "I was much surprised, on considering the richness of the soil," wrote a northern visitor to the South, "that the houses and barns were so thriftless and wretched in aspect. They were so, in fact, to one coming from the North." A sojourner in Georgia, who described a plantation worth $125,000, asked: "And in what kind of house does my reader imagine this wealthy man resided? In a miserable log hovel, a decayed and windowless one, which a respectable member of the swine family would hardly deign to occupy." Of a cotton planter who owned some thirty slaves, another traveler declared: "We found his house like most southern plantation houses . . . , merely a good frame boarded up and floors laid with lath partitions without plastering." A foreigner, invited to a planter's home, had expected to "find a large, costly residence or palace, but found instead a little house made of wood, set on four blocks several feet above the sandy ground, with a cramped sitting room and a bedroom on the first floor, under which geese, etc. have their abode." Still another traveler spoke of a certain southern log house that took "high rank for comfort" because it was "the first we had met having glass windows, and the second, I think with any windows at all."[27]

Even the better southern cabins offered few luxuries. "We stopped for the night at a remarkably comfortable house," wrote a traveler, "but could look out, as usual, at the stars between the logs. There

26. MacLysaght, *Irish Life*, 93–99; Daniel Corkery, *The Hidden Ireland: A Study of Gaelic Munster in the Eighteenth Century* (1924; reprint, Dublin, 1979), 42–67; Ian Whyte, *Agriculture and Society in Seventeenth-Century Scotland* (Edinburgh, 1979), 114–19; James Logan, *The Scottish Gael; or, Celtic Manners, as Preserved Among the Highlanders* . . . (1876; reprint, 2 vols., Edinburgh, 1976), II:3–5; Burnaby, *Travels through the Middle Settlements*, 9; *Virginia Gazette*, February 5, 1767; Archibald Taylor, "Plantation Life in Tidewater Virginia in Ante-Bellum Days," *Industrial South* 6, no. 6 (February 11, 1886), 61–62; James C. Bonner, "Plantation Architecture of the Lower South on the Eve of the Civil War," *Journal of Southern History* 11 (1945), 370–88.

27. Olmsted, *Journey through Texas*, 14–15; Lanman, *Adventures in the Wilds*, I:384; Whipple, *Southern Diary*, 35; Henry Melchior Muhlenberg, *The Journals of . . . Henry Melchior Muhlenberg*, trans. Theodore G. Tappert and John W. Doberstein (2 vols., Philadelphia, 1942), II:607; Olmsted, *Journey through Texas*, 65.

A CRACKER HOME

From *Harper's New Monthly Magazine* 8 (1853–54), 21.

being but one bed, B. lay upon the floor with his feet to the fire." Another visitor, who traveled from Virginia through Louisiana, repeatedly slept in "log huts, . . . through sides and roofs of which the stars twinkled upon us as we lay on the floor." Even in a large southern farmhouse, stated yet another observer, the rooms "were separated from each other by a board partition only; and every thing said or done within the outer walls was distinctly audible through the flimsy wainscot." The better-furnished cabins, wrote one man, contained "a couple of bedsteads, . . . an oaken table or two, half a dozen rush-bottomed chairs, and a couple of long rifles with powder-horn and bullet-pouch, suspended upon a buck's antlers over a large fireplace."[28]

Most structures were comparatively primitive. They usually consisted of one or two rectangular rooms: either a single-pen log house with a rock chimney or a dogtrot log cabin of two rooms separated by a central passage. Other types of construction included double-pen cabins, a simple way to enlarge a house, and saddlebag houses with central chimneys.[29] "Almost all these forest houses in the interior," wrote a traveler in the South, "consist of two divisions, separated by a wide, open passage, which extends from the front to the back of the building. They are generally made of logs, covered with a very steep roof, I suppose to carry off the heavy rains. The apartments, at the ends of these dwellings, are entered from the open passage which divides the house in two, the floor of which is raised generally two to three feet from the ground." An English-woman explained that in the South most houses were "raised a foot or two from the ground, by means of small, but solid blocks of wood, one of which is placed at either of the four corners. This is ingenious," she declared; "it raised the house out of the road, and in the summer keeps out the snakes, &c., to say nothing of the pigs."[30]

Writers almost invariably considered most southern houses shabby and frequently contrasted them with the "beauty, neatness, and simplicity" of the "pretty hamlets of New England," New York,

28. Olmsted, *Journey through Texas,* 76 (see also 68); Hodgson, *Letters,* II:58; Charles Fenno Hoffman, *A Winter in the West* (2 vols., New York, 1835), II:307–08, 189–90.

29. Fred B. Kniffen, "Folk Housing: Key to Diffusion," *Annals of the Association of American Geographers* 55 (1965), 549–77; Fred B. Kniffen and Henry Glassie, "Building in Wood in the Eastern United States: A Time-Place Perspective," *Geographical Review* 56 (1966), 40–66; Henry Glassie, *Pattern in the Material Folk Culture of the Eastern United States* (Philadelphia, 1968),

64–124; Milton B. Newton, Jr., *Louisiana House Types: A Field Guide* (Baton Rouge, 1971); Fred B. Kniffen, *Folk Houses of Louisiana* (Baton Rouge, 1942); Eugene M. Wilson, *Alabama Folk Houses* (Montgomery, 1975); D. Gregory Jeane and Douglas Clare Purcell, eds., *The Architectural Legacy of the Lower Chattahoochee Valley in Alabama and Georgia* (University, Ala., 1978); Terry G. Jordan, *Texas Log Buildings: A Folk Architecture* (Austin, 1978).

30. B. Hall, *Travels,* III:271–72; Houstoun, *Texas and the Gulf,* 123.

and Pennsylvania. One observer deemed even the best dwellings of the South inferior to the "handsome houses [that] are very much the fashion of Boston"; and another stated: "I have no doubt the county of Worcester, Massachussetts, contains more good houses than the whole cotton growing country of the United States." Foreigners also noted the similarities between New England structures and those in England and Germany.[31]

Many southern abodes seemed so deplorable that visitors compared them to the huts of Ireland. Southerners "live in . . . the most wretched hovels I ever saw in my life," announced an Englishwoman; "I am sure no Irish cabin can be poorer, and the people themselves look squalid and miserable." At best, said a Yankee, the average Southerner lived much like the "Irishman, who has just separated himself, for the first time in his life, from the same apartment with his pig."[32]

Such comparisons were appropriate, for many antebellum structures were similar to those in premodern Ireland, Scotland, and Wales.[33] Most observers agreed that Celtic houses tended to be sim-

31. W. Russell, *Diary North and South*, I:232; Hoffman, *Winter in the West*, I:3; F. Hall, *Letters from the East and West*, 93; [Jeremiah Evarts], *Through the South and the West with Jeremiah Evarts in 1826*, ed. J. Orin Oliphant (Lewisburg, Pa., 1956), 93; John E. E. D. Acton, *Acton in America: The American Journal of Sir John Acton, 1853*, ed. S. W. Jackman (Shepherdstown, Pa., 1979), 39; Montule, *Travels in America*, 21; Shirreff, *A Tour through North America . . . as Adapted for Agricultural Emigration* (Edinburgh, 1835), 40, 52. On the beauty and neatness of English houses and their similarities with New England dwellings, see Abbott L. Cummings, *The Framed Houses of Massachusetts Bay, 1625–1755* (Cambridge, Mass., 1979), esp. chaps. 1 and 2; Ralph Nevill, *Old Cottage and Domestic Architecture of South-West Surry, and Notes on the Early History of the Division* (Guildford, England, 1889), 12–14, 58; Harry Forrester, *The Timber-Framed Houses of Essex: A Short Review of Their Types and Details, 14th to 18th Centuries* (Clelmsford, England, 1959), 14–20; J. Frederick Kelly, *The Early Domestic Architecture of Connecticut* (New York, 1963), 6–19; Anthony N. B. Garvan, *Architecture and Town Planning in Colonial Connecticut* (New Haven, Conn., 1951), chap. 5; Allen Connally, "The Cape Cod House: An Introductory Study," *Journal of the Society of Architectural Historians* 19 (1960), 47–56; Henry Glassie, *Passing the Time in Ballymenone: Culture and History of an Ulster Community* (Philadelphia, 1982), 404, 767; P. Eden, "Smaller Post-medieval Houses in Eastern England," in *East Anglian Studies*, ed. Leonel Munby (Cambridge, 1968), 71–93; Moritz, *Travels*, 31, 114; Paul Hentzner, *A Journey into England in the Year MDXCVIII*, ed. Horace Walpole (Edinburgh, 1881), 29, 34–35; Hugh Miller, *First Impressions of England and Its People* (Boston, 1852), 196.

32. M. Hall, *Aristocratic Journey*, 204; Samuel W. Judson to Henry Watson, Jr., December 8, 1832, Henry Watson, Jr., Papers, Duke University.

33. On the similarities between Celtic housing in Britain and in the Old South, see Henry Glassie, *Folk Housing in Middle Virginia: A Structural Analysis of Historic Artifacts* (Knoxville, 1975), 75, 95, 130, 132, 133, 137, 140, 145–46, 165–66, 179; idem, "The Types of the Southern Mountain Cabin," in *Study of American Folklore*, ed. Jan Harold Brunvand (New York, 1968), 338–70; idem, *Passing the Time*, 768; Alexander Fenton, "Material Culture as an Aid to Local History Studies in Scotland," *Journal of the Folklore Institute* 2 (1965), 334; R. W. Brunskill, *Vernacular Architecture of the Lake Counties* (London, 1974), 70–

ple, dirty, and poorly constructed. Folk houses, which were called cabins in Celtic Britain and the Old South, were called cottages in England and New England. Most premodern Celts lived in houses that were described as "wretched"—often without windows, flooring, or chimney—"the door serving for that and the window too." In the eighteenth century Arthur Young found scarcely "ten dwellings in the kingdom [of Ireland] . . . that were fit for an English pig to live in." Early in the nineteenth century Thomas Croker observed: "The cabins of the [Irish] peasantry are most deplorable; and the state of filth in which the owners live, inconceivable to an Englishman." In the Old South the "houses are poorly constructed," stated a Yankee visitor. "The habitations we have met with," reported a tourist in Alabama, "have been for the most part nothing but boarded sheds." A pilgrim in 1861 reported that the "huts [of the South] were all alike windowless." Another man admitted that windowless cabins, "perforated with numerous doors, are well enough suited for a summer shelter, but totally destitute of comfort in the winter." It was not unusual for Southerners to leave their log cabins "partly . . . unchinked at all seasons of the year," reported a voyager. "The common log-house is almost the only kind of habitation here met with," announced a traveler in the southern backcountry, "and the majority of these are poorly and carelessly built."³⁴

Few Celtic houses were airtight and waterproof. In Ireland and Scotland travelers reported that the "common-place accounts of . . . holes in the wall for windows are all true"; indeed, most Celtic cabins had "Gaps" in the walls and openings "in the roof which answers both for the window and the chimney." Charles Lanman

---

71; M. W. Barley, *The House and Home: A Review of 900 Years of House Planning and Furnishing in Britain* (Greenwich, Conn., 1963), 53; I. F. Grant, *Highland Folk Ways* (London, 1961), 153–54; Colin Sinclair, *The Thatched Houses of the Old Highlands* (Edinburgh, 1953), 67, 71; Alan J. Gailey, "The Scotch-Irish Contribution to American Architecture," in *Selected Proceedings of the Scotch-Irish Heritage Festival, II at Winthrop College,* ed. Jack W. Weaver (Baton Rouge, 1983), 53–69; Iorwerth C. Peate, *The Welsh House: A Study in Folk Culture* (London, 1940), esp. chap. 5; T. Jordan, *Texas Log Buildings,* 81, 106–23, 133.

34. A. Young, *Tour in Ireland,* II:151, I:35, 462; Thomas Crofton Croker, *Researches in the South of Ireland . . .* (1824; reprint, New York, 1969), 61; Mason, *Statistical Account . . . of Ireland,*

III:24–25, II:246–47; Anon., *Comical Pilgrim,* 83; Daniel Defoe, *A Tour through the Whole Island of Great Britain [1724–1726],* ed. Pat Rogers (New York, 1971), 600; Burt, *Letters,* II:59, 61, 63–64, 80; J. Taylor, *Journey to Edenborough,* 145; Robert Forbes, *Journals of the Episcopal Visitations of the Right Rev. Robert Forbes, M. A., of the Dioceses of Ross and Caithness, . . . 1762 & 1770 . . . ,* ed. J. B. Craven (London, 1886), 143; Willis, *Journal of a Tour,* 63; Whipple, *Southern Diary,* 39; Everest, *Journey,* 116; W. Russell, *Diary North and South,* I:212; Thomas Nuttall, *A Journal of Travels into the Arkansas Territory During the Year 1819,* ed. Savoie Lottinville (1821; new ed., Norman, Okla., 1979), 88; Claiborne, "Trip through the Piney Woods," 515; Lanman, *Adventures in the Wilds,* I:500.

stayed in a similar structure in Mississippi: "our bed-room was ventilated on an entirely new principle; that is to say, by wide cracks in the floor, broad spaces between the logs that composed the walls, huge openings in the roof, and a window with a shutter that could not be closed." Another visitor in the Old South complained of "the houses not being calculated for winter—the windows and doors loose and opening in every direction for the admission of the cold air; and the fireplaces wide and deep, consuming a great deal of wood and emitting but little heat; the chill penetrates to the marrow." A foreigner who stayed in one of the oldest houses in Knoxville, Tennessee, reported that "laziness has so pervaded the way of life that they have not yet plugged up the holes in the outer walls cut for scaffolding when they built the house. There are five of these openings in our room, and scarcely a whole pane in the windows." In December 1841 the wife of a wealthy Southerner admitted, "We are all shivering over the fire morning and night, though it is pleasant enough in the middle of the day," and the wife of a physician and planter noted in her diary in September 1856 that her "house leaked much" after heavy rains.[35]

Only rarely was much time or money expended on southern houses. In 1852 an Alabamian and his slaves built and furnished a large two-story house in a few weeks at a cost of $950. A woman claimed that ordinarily in Texas a "six-roomed house is raised, from floor to ceiling, and rendered fit for habitation in a week. I do not mean to say that they are remarkably air-tight, or particularly well-arranged; but to build any house in so short a time is worthy to remark." A Southerner told a traveler "that when he first began farming in the woods, he had lived in the small log-house which I saw in the back court adjoining the kitchen. In the course of time, as more land was cleared, and his means were thereby increased, he had been enabled to build the new house which we were in, close to the roadside." The traveler asked why there were no windows in the new house. "Oh," said the farmer, "we never make the windows in the first instance, but build up the walls with the logs, and then cut out the windows. Now, I have not yet money enough to enable me to go into the matter; but I hope, in the course of the year, to put in a couple of glazed windows. After which, I shall go on gradually till I make it all comfortable."[36]

Most Southerners intended, in that vague sort of way, to add various comforts to their houses someday, provided they could do

35. Anon., *Ireland in 1804*, 36–37; Burt, *Letters*, II:80; Cordiner, *Antiquities & Scenery*, 114; Lanman, *Adventures in the Wilds*, II:191; [Clinton?], *Winter from Home*, 16; Philippe, *Diary of My Travels*, 63; Boggs, *Alexander Letters*, 75; McIver Diary, September 5, 1856.

36. Mallory Journal, February 28, 1852; Houstoun, *Texas and the Gulf*, 124; B. Hall, *Travels*, III:272–73.

so without too much trouble or effort. "They are fond of good living, and their chief business is to make themselves as comfortable as possible," explained a visitor to the South. "They esteem solid enjoyment more than display." Another observer noted that "private residences are arranged with an air of comfort" in the South. "The village is every bit a Southern one," reported a traveler; "all the houses being one story in height, and having an open verandah before them." Rich and poor Southerners wanted houses with plenty of cool places to sit. A sojourner pointed out that even the unpretentious dogtrot cabin had a breezeway that "answers in this mild climate the purpose of a verandah, or sitting room, during the day." A planter's residence, declared a writer, usually was "protected by a wide gallery which is built around it. Large hallways, on which the doors of the apartments look, allow drafts, and gigantic acacias present to the rays of the sun an impenetrable barrier which keeps the house cool."[37]

The unfavorable reactions of many visitors to southern housing revealed as much about their tastes and backgrounds as it did about the cultural values of antebellum Southerners. The simple and often dilapidated cabins of Southerners, sparsely furnished and set in unlandscaped surroundings, represented yet another example of the South's barbarism to critical outsiders. Witnesses invariably used terms of disdain in describing the southern environment, dwellings, and the people who inhabited them: "small and dingy"; "miserable"; "everything very slovenly and dirty"; "holes, having one room only, and in that . . . all cook, eat, sleep, breed, and die, male and females, all together"; "swine, hounds, and black and white children, are commonly lying very promiscuously together"; "black and white, slave and freeman, camping out together, living sometimes in the same tent or temporary pine-pole cabin; drinking . . . out of the same tin dipper or long-handled gourd . . . ; dining on the same homely . . . fare, and sharing one bed in common, *videlicit*, the cabin floor." "All the livelong day you travel through pine woods of fifty and sixty miles without meeting a human being or passing a hut—I cannot call them houses," lamented an Englishman. Another man who crossed the southern backcountry from Mississippi to Virginia reported that he never saw in a home "a thermometer, nor a book of Shakespeare, nor a piano-forte or sheet of music; nor the light of a carcel or other good center-table or reading-lamp, nor an engraving, or a copy of any kind, or a work of art of the slightest merit." Still another wayfarer was upset by the southern habit of never closing

---

37. Lanman, *Adventures in the Wilds*, I:458; Foster, *Way-Side Glimpses*, 92; Olmsted, *Journey through Texas*, 44; B. Hall, *Travels*, III:272; Tixier, *Travels*, 46.

doors, while others complained that Southerners rarely planted flower gardens or trees as Englishmen and Yankees did.[38]

The same contempt expressed by outsiders for southern living habits permeates descriptions of premodern British Celtic living habits. Even the phrases used are similar: "their cabins are very miserable"; "they have seldom any floor but the earth"; "badly built and proportioned"; "a cave of poverty"; "the field of the slothful"; "awful Huts"; "thatched roofs, grossly put together, covers these poor huts"; "children, and even many of the men and women, without either shoes or stockings"; "miserable huts, made of mud, . . . and covered with turf"; "extremely wretched miserable hovels." "In those parts of England . . . which are purely agricultural," wrote a critic of Irish ways, "we roam with pleasure . . . in the midst of orchards; we wander from cottage to cottage, welcomed by the smile of cheerfulness, and gratified by the comfort of their habitations; the women and children are well fed, nor are any to be found absolutely so poor as to compare with the Irish peasantry." In 1752 an Englishman said of the Irish: "these proud people are more destitute than *savages,* and more abject than *negroes.* The *negroes* in our plantations have a saying, *If negro was not negro, Irishman would be negro.*" A shocked visitor complained that not only did most Irish sleep without sheets but "to tell the *naked Truth* . . . they *live* together like *Adam* and *Eve* before the *Fall,* not a *Rag* to cover them [at night] but themselves. . . . They seldom have any *Partitions* or several Rooms, but sleep in common with their *Swine* and *Poultry.* . . . *Windows* would discover their *Poverty* and *Sluttery* too much, and a *Chimney* is reckoned as *superfluous.* . . . The *Door* . . . serving both to let in the *Light,* and let out the Smoak; so that you may guess their Abodes are pleasant and airy as a *Dungeon.*" "We saw houses . . . put together without mortar,—thatched with rushes or coarse grass,—the floor, earth," wrote a traveler in the Scottish Highlands; "women and children barefooted amidst all this. . . . The bodies of the men wrapped up in their national plaid . . . ; in their

38. Lanman, *Adventures in the Wilds,* II:125; Caroline B. Poole, "A Yankee School Teacher in Louisiana, 1835–1837: The Diary of Caroline B. Poole," ed. James A. Padgett, *Louisiana Historical Quarterly* 20 (1937), 653–54; Faux, *Memorable Days,* 187; Frederick Law Olmsted, *The Cotton Kingdom: A Traveller's Observations on Cotton and Slavery . . . ,* ed. Arthur M. Schlesinger (new ed., New York, 1953), 31; Daniel R. Hundley, *Social Relations in Our South-* *ern States,* ed. William J. Cooper, Jr. (1860; new ed., Baton Rouge, 1979), 196–97; Hunter, *Quebec to Carolina,* 282; Frederick Law Olmsted, *A Journey in the Back Country . . .* (1856; reprint, New York, 1970), 395 (see also 259); Featherstonhaugh, *Excursion,* II:58; Fox Journal, November 29, 1834; A. Murray, *Letters from the United States,* 188; Stanley Koch to his mother [1853?], Christian Koch Papers, Mississippi Department of Archives and History, Jackson.

looks they recalled the . . . American savages; the same proud indolence,—the same carelessness,—the same superiority to want,—the same courage,—the same hospitality,—and unfortunately, I hear, the same liking for spirituous liquors."[39]

Like his Celtic ancestors, the Southerner cared little for what outsiders thought of him; he was pleased enough with where and how he lived. Though he was perhaps not as opulent as he might have liked, his condition represented a compromise between the comforts desired and his unwillingness to work especially hard to obtain them. His rural and pastoral traditions shaped his needs and wants in housing as it did in other things. He still tried to live as his Celtic forefathers had without "cities, or large towns, [but where] each clan . . . had a certain portion of land for culture and pasturage [and] . . . the occupiers lived apart; near enough to assist, not too near to incommode one another." The Celtic tradition, as practiced by premodern Scots, Irish, and Welsh, was to live comfortably but unpretentiously. Their "household furniture was simple and inexpensive," and they did little to improve either "houses or grounds." An eighteenth-century Scot admitted that Highlanders made little effort to "better [their] condition; so long as they can . . . pay their rent and their debts, they appear contented"; at about the same time, an Irish woman remarked: "the people of this country don't seem solicitous of having good dwellings or more furniture than is absolutely necessary." This "survival of traditional standards," as one authority called it, continued in the antebellum South, where Crackers practiced the old Celtic ways. "The houses in Kentucky," wrote a Yankee, "are scarcely deserving of the name. . . . A temporary hut is at first erected, at least as open as a New-England corn crib; yet in those miserable habitations are seen Ladies neatly dressed, who are, as yet, obliged to reside therein for want of better houses." "The Southern gentleman does not live in very grand style—his house is not always showy, nor his furniture elegant,"

39. Mason, *Statistical Account . . . of Ireland*, III:159; Stevens, *Journal*, 139–40; Stephen Perlin, "A Description of England and Scotland," in *The Antiquarian Repertory: A Miscellaneous Assemblage of Topography, History, Biography, Customs, and Manners*, comp. Francis Grose (4 vols., London, 1807–09), IV:516; Burt, *Letters*, II:61; L. Saussure, *Travels in Scotland*, 57; [William Thomson], *A Tour in England and Scotland, in 1785* (London, 1788), 70; Dennis Sullivan, *A Picturesque Tour Through Ireland* (London, 1824), 1; George Berkeley, *A Word to the Wise: or, An Exhortation to the Roman Catholic Clergy* (Dublin, 1752), 6–7; Anon., *A Trip to Ireland, Being a Description of the Country, People, and Manners . . .* (London, 1699), 5; Simond, *Journal of a Tour*, II:395. See also Fynes Moryson, *An Itinerary: Containing His Ten Yeeres Travell . . .* (4 vols., Glasgow, 1617–18), III:318; MacLysaght, *Irish Life*, 66, 107–08.

explained an observer. "The city-bred gentleman from the North will not always find in the planter's home the rich curtains, the sumptuous sofas, the gorgeous picture-frames, or the thousand and one other dainty household goods, so carefully gathered and treasured in his own house." What the Northerner would discover was "that on the Southern plantations the people *'live out of doors'*; that their very houses, ever wide open, are themselves 'out of doors,' and consequently but little more cared for than are the self-caring lawns and woods around them." Charles Latrobe, like many other foreign visitors, commented on the "singularly hap-hazard and disorderly way of living. . . on the [South's] farms and plantations"; and Yankee Joseph Ingraham stated that "planters are not a showy and stylish class, but a plain . . . body of men, who . . . regard comfort, and conformity to old habits, rather than display and fashionable innovations."[40]

Three eyewitness accounts—considered together—graphically reveal the continuity in Celtic domestic habits. A traveler in eighteenth-century Ireland noted that there even the wealthy often lived a rustic life: "I slept at a man's house who had a hundred head of black cattle and two hundred sheep, and there was not a single chair or stool in his house but one three-legged one—no bed but rushes, no vessels for boiling their meals but one, nor any for drinking milk out of but one, which was handed round indiscriminately to all . . . ; yet, this man was said to be very rich." From antebellum Georgia, a businessman wrote: "There are some instances of men of respectable characters, worth 40 or 50,000 dollars, living in houses formed principally of logs, without being either ceiled, plastered or glazed." Charles Lanman described staying overnight in the 1850s at a "cabin in the [Mississippi] pine woods, belonging to an . . . obliging man [whose] estate numbered a thousand acres. . . . It was evident that this family was well enough off to live in comfort," observed Lanman, "but, true to habits which prevail among a large class in the South," they lived quite rudely. Slaves of all ages, with a market value that Lanman estimated at "not less than ten thousand dollars," roamed about the dwelling, "yet . . . wooden benches were used in the place of chairs, one iron spoon answered for the whole

40. Charles O'Conor, *Dissertations on the History of Ireland . . .* (Dublin, 1812), 115; Fyfe, *Scottish Diaries and Memoirs*, 228–29; William Gilpin, *Observations . . . Made in the Year 1776, on Several Parts of Great Britain . . .* (2 vols., London, 1789), II:141–42; MacLysaght, *Irish Life*, 106; Sinclair, *Statistical Account of Scotland*, XVII:323–24; Cullen, *Life in Ireland*, 102, 61; Schwaab, *Travels in the Old South*, I:56; Hundley, *Social Relations*, 57–58; Latrobe, *Rambler in North America*, II:32; [Joseph Holt Ingraham], *The South-West; by a Yankee . . .* (2 vols., New York, 1835), II:102.

family, and the mother added the sugar . . . to the coffee with her fingers, and tasted each cup before sending it round to ascertain if it was right. Such things as andirons, tongs, and wash-basins were considered useless; and the bedstead upon which we slept was a mere board. . . . All [twenty members of] the family, excepting the parents and two sons, were barefooted, and yet the girls sported large finger rings in abundance, and wore basque dresses of calico."[41]

41. Constantia Maxwell, *Country and Town in Ireland Under the Georges* (Dundalk, Ireland, 1949), 139; Schwaab, *Travels in the Old South*, I:144–45; Lanman, *Adventures in the Wilds*, II:196, 192–93.

# X

# *Worth*

THE values of Southerners and Yankees, like those of Celts and Englishmen, were not just different—they were antagonistic.[1] Observers from the 1600s through the 1800s agreed that as a rule Northerners and Englishmen were industrious and business-minded farmers, traders, and manufacturers who were persevering, profit oriented, enterprising, often cold and stiff, sometimes rude and greedy.[2] One Yankee boasted, "We're born to whip universal nature"; another proclaimed, "it has become proverbial, that a Yankee may live where another man would starve." And that model of Yankee virtues, Benjamin Franklin, despite his reputation for in-

1. On the differences between English and Celtic values, see Richard Ned Lebow, *White Britain and Black Ireland: The Influence of Stereotypes on Colonial Policy* (Philadelphia, 1976), 39–40, 46–48; Phillip Luckombe, *A Tour Through Ireland* . . . (London, 1783), 19; Thomas Crofton Croker, *Researches in the South of Ireland* . . . (1824; reprint, New York, 1969), 2, 4, 167; Sir John Sinclair, ed., *The Statistical Account of Scotland, 1791–1799* (reprint, 20 vols., East Ardsley, England, 1981), XVII:573; Daniel Defoe, *A Tour through the Whole Island of Great Britain [1724–1726]*, ed. Pat Rogers (New York, 1971), 660–79.

2. On English characteristics, see Robert Payne, *A Brief Description of Ireland: Made in the Yeere 1589* (London, 1590), 13–14; Thomas Fuller, *The Worthies of England*, ed. John Freeman (1662; reprint, London, 1952), 543; Margaret Hoby, *Diary of Lady Margaret Hoby, 1599–1605*, ed. Dorothy M. Meads (London, 1930), 166, 168; Nicholas Blundell, *Blundell's Diary and Letters Book, 1702–1728*, ed. Margaret Blundell

(Liverpool, 1952), 55; Samuel Sorbiere, *A Voyage to England, Containing Many Things Relating to that . . . Kingdom* (London, 1709), 8–9; Henri Misson, *M. Misson's Memoirs and Observations in His Travels over England, With some Account of Scotland and Ireland*, trans. Mr. Ozell (London, 1719), 2, 190; [Beat Louis Muralt], *Letters Describing the Character and Customs of the English and French Nations* . . . (London, 1726), 12–13, 15–17; Dr. William Drennan to Mrs. Martha McTier, April 17, 1810, *The Drennan Letters: Being a Selection from the Correspondence [of] . . . William Drennan, M.D., . . . during the Years 1776–1819*, ed. D. A. Chart (Belfast, 1931), 384–85; Cesar de Saussure, *A Foreign View of England in the Reigns of George I & George II: The Letters of Monsieur Cesar de Saussure to His Family*, trans. and ed. Madame Van Muyden (London, 1902), 193–94; George Berkeley, *A Word to the Wise: or, An Exhortation to the Roman Catholic Clergy* (Dublin, 1752), 8; [John Shebbeare], *Letters on the English Nation: By*

quisitiveness, spent more of his time while visiting in Ireland and Scotland conducting some of his "ill-starred business ventures" than in observing the conditions and customs of the people.[3] Observers were equally impressed by English success and purposefulness. A Swiss claimed that even English whorehouses were sober and businesslike. A German visitor admired English accomplishments but questioned "the spiritual state of a country which . . . estimates a man's value in terms of his income, as witness the expression: *he is worth a hundred thousand pounds!"*[4]

Just as good Englishmen looked down upon the unacquisitive and improvident Celts, so good Northerners despised the unacquisitive and improvident Southerners. "The anxious, economical, persevering farmer of New England, still in advanced life anxiously toiling, . . . regards with no friendly eye the liberal, careless, high-

---

*. . . a Jesuit, who Resided Many Years in London* (2 vols., London, 1755), I:45; Pierre J. Grosley, *A Tour to London [in 1765]; or, New Observations on England, and Its Inhabitants* (2 vols., London, 1772), I:141–42; [William Thomson], *A Tour in England and Scotland, in 1785* (London, 1788), 16–17; [Benjamin Silliman], *A Journal of Travels in England, Holland and Scotland . . .* (2 vols., New York, 1810), I:284; Ellen Weeton, *Miss Weeton's Journal of a Governess [1807–1825]* (1936; reprint, 2 vols., New York, 1969), II:22; Louis Simond, *Journal of a Tour and Residence in Great Britain, During the Years 1810 and 1811* (2 vols., Edinburgh, 1817), II:391–94; Ralph Waldo Emerson, *English Traits* (Boston, 1856), 156, 158; James M. Hoppin, *Old England; Its Scenery, Art, and People* (1867; reprint, Boston, 1900), 100–104; [Raul Blouet], *John Bull and His Island* (New York, 1884), 13, 47, 49, 237, 239. On northern characteristics, see Isaac Weld, *Travels Through the States of North America . . . during the Years 1795, 1796, and 1797* (5th ed., 2 vols., London, 1807), I:21–22; Timothy Dwight, *Travels in New England and New York*, ed. Barbara Miller Solomon (4 vols., Cambridge, Mass., 1969), IV:225; Edouard de Montule, *Travels in America, 1816–1817*, trans. Edward D. Seeber (Bloomington, 1951), 22, 26, 27, 172, 179–81; Lorenzo de Zavala, *Journey to the United States of North America [1829]*, trans. Wallace Woolsey (Austin, 1980), 191–92; Francis J. Grund, *The Americans in Their Moral, Social and Political Relations* (2 vols., London, 1837), II:1–2;

Frederick Hall, *Letters from the East and from the West* (Washington, D.C., 1840), 241; Henri Herz, *My Travels in America [1846–1851]*, trans. Henry Bertram Hill (Madison, 1963), 47–49; John Benwell, *An Englishman's Travels in America . . .* (London, 1853), 15–16, 62; Aleksandr Borisovich Lakier, *A Russian Looks at America: The Journey of Aleksandr Borisovich Lakier in 1857*, ed. Arnold Schrier and Joyce Story (Chicago, 1979), 29; John Henry Vessey, *Mr. Vessey of England: Being the Incidents and Reminiscences of Travel in a Twelve Weeks' Tour through the United States and Canada in the Year 1859*, ed. Brian Waters (New York, 1956), 43; Anthony Trollope, *North America*, ed. Donald Smalley and Bradford Allen Booth (New York, 1951), 191–92, 193–94; Esther Singleton, *Social New York Under the Georges, 1714–1776* (New York, 1902), 375; John Hope Franklin, *A Southern Odyssey: Travelers in the Antebellum North* (Baton Rouge, 1976), 83, 86, 87, 194.

3. Alexander Mackay, *The Western World . . .* (3 vols., London, 1849), I:46; F. Hall, *Letters from the East and West*, 241; J. Bennett Nolan, *Benjamin Franklin in Scotland and Ireland, 1759 and 1771* (Philadelphia, 1938), 47–49, 64, 161.

4. Henry Meister, *Letters Written During a Residence in England . . .* (London, 1799), 57–58; Johann G. Busch quoted in William D. Robson-Scott, *German Travellers in England, 1400–1800* (Oxford, 1953), 203–04.

spirited Southerner, so different from himself in disposition," observed Englishman David W. Mitchell. " 'Take no thought of the morrow' [is] . . . the motto of . . . the southern population," chided a disciplined Northerner, who charged that the "energies of the South . . . either lie dormant in idleness . . . or [they] . . . are expended in visionary [and reckless] projects . . . for useless luxuries & foolish dissipation." Another Northerner denounced southern wastefulness. "In New-England," he boasted, "a man may put a hundred dollars in a bridge, a turnpike, a rail-road, a bank, an insurance company, or a mill-dam, and thus blend his private advantage with the public good." But in the South even the small planters squandered more money every year than most New England farmers saved in a "life[time] of toil and close economy." He insisted that any Southerner could learn invaluable lessons by attending "a council at a [Yankee] farmer's fireside, on the profitable investment of twenty dollars."[5]

An excellent example of the diligent Yankee was Henry V. Poor, who was born in Maine in 1812. To this Anglo-Saxon Protestant, work and the accumulation of money were paramount. He worked, in fact, almost all the time. Away from home early each morning, he was never back until seven or eight in the evening. "What a foe to love is business," complained his bride, who noted that Henry worked "dreadfully hard—till he [almost] kills himself." Leisure, to him, was a sinful waste of effort. Rarely did he have time for his wife and children and never for friends; even at home in the evenings he continued to work. He excused himself from joining his family on their summer vacations because he "could hardly afford to lose the opportunity to make a little money." When he was not working, he was "as nervous as a fish out of water." Why did he work so hard? Because that was what he had been taught was worthwhile; it was the way of his society. He considered success in business to be "a demonstration of Yankee strength of character." Once he boasted to his wife after an especially profitable venture: "see what a Yankee can do."[6]

Henry Poor was no exception; devotion to hard work and to the accumulation of wealth were long-standing and widespread Yankee commitments. Northerners in general were concerned with "those material cares which are disdained by the white population of the South," concluded Alexis de Tocqueville. "They are taught from

5. David W. Mitchell, *Ten Years in the United States* . . . (London, 1862), 185; Henry Benjamin Whipple, *Bishop Whipple's Southern Diary, 1843–1844*, ed. Lester B. Shippee (Minneapolis, 1937), 61; Eugene L. Schwaab, ed., *Travels in the Old South: Selected from Periodicals of the Times* (2 vols., Lexington, Ky., 1973), I:235. See also J. H. Franklin, *Southern Odyssey*, 44, 165.

6. James R. McGovern, *Yankee Family* (New Orleans, 1975), 79, 84, 99–100.

AGENT OF HUMANE SOCIETY.

VILLAGE LAWYER.

RAILROAD PRESIDENT

WORTH A MILLION.

THE APPLE-PEELER.

NEW ENGLANDERS

From *Harper's New Monthly Magazine* 21 (1860), 760
[upper three figures]; ibid. 22 (1860–61), 723, 733 [lower
two figures].

infancy . . . to place wealth above all the pleasures." In 1837 the New Yorker Washington Irving coined the phrase "the Almighty Dollar" and announced that money was the "great object of universal devotion" among the people he knew. Throughout the North, reported a contemporary, "wealth is the key to respect, honor, and esteem. Almost every man is therefore constrained to become a merchant, a banker, a speculator, or a manufacturer, to secure a position that will bring a sizeable income." Yet to most Northerners a business was more than a source of wealth; it was a veritable ministry, which they followed with the devotion of a pastor. An observer claimed that thousands of Yankees were like the merchant whose energies originally "were directed toward one single end, to make himself rich," but who continued to work hard long after he had made his fortune.[7]

As a rule, Northerners found Southerners scarcely more interested in money than they were in work. Southerners enjoyed what money could buy, but they disdained people who devoted their lives to the making of money. An eighteenth-century traveler claimed that Southerners "are content if they can but live from day to day; . . . and if they have but enough . . . to pay their merchants . . . and to provide for their pleasures; they are satisfied, and desire nothing more." New Englander Timothy Flint, noting in the nineteenth century that money would not buy respect in the South, said that Southerners were "more reckless of the value of money, than any people that I have seen." An Englishman stated that there was "no part of the world where great wealth confers so little rank, or is attended with so few advantages," as in the South. An Englishwoman claimed that Texan hero General Sam Houston, "during his public career, . . . has neither saved nor made a dollar; on the contrary, he is said to be often in pecuniary difficulties." One Yankee believed that Southerners actually "despise money"; another reported that Southerners valued dogs more than wealth.[8]

Southerners acknowledged that they were unskilled in money

7. Alexis de Tocqueville, *Democracy in America* . . . , ed. Phillips Bradley (2 vols., New York, 1945), I:411; Washington Irving, *Wolfert's Roost and Other Papers, Now First Collected* (Philadelphia, 1872), 40; Grady McWhiney, *Southerners and Other Americans* (New York, 1973), 17, 20–22; Freeman Hunt, *Worth and Wealth: A Collection of Maxims, Morals and Miscellanies for Merchants and Men of Business* (New York, 1856), 82–83, 103–05, 120, 503–04.

8. Andrew Burnaby, *Travels through the Middle Settlements in North America* . . . *in the Years 1759 and 1760* (1775; reprint, Ithaca, N.Y., 1960), 27–28; Timothy Flint, *Recollections of the Last Ten Years*, ed. C. Hartley Grattan (1826; reprint, New York, 1932), 327–28, 323; John Dix, *Transatlantic Tracings; or, Sketches of Persons and Scenes in America* (London, 1853), 230; Matilda Charlotte (Jesse) Fraser Houstoun, *Texas and the Gulf* . . . (Philadelphia, 1845), 216; F. Hall, *Letters from the East and West*, 243–44; Charles Lanman, *Adventures in the Wilds* . . . (2 vols., Philadelphia, 1856), I:400.

matters. According to a traditional proverb, Southerners never sold what they could eat and Northerners never ate what they could sell. "We are bad managers," admitted Mary B. Chesnut. A plain Southerner stated that she and her people had no regard for money. "We are a primary people," explained an upcountryman. "We do not understand shares and stocks, the use of money to make money."⁹

Many observers claimed that the North and the South were so different because Northerners revered urban life while Southerners favored rural society and values. "A native of the southern states when he comes to the North finds all his habits violated," noted the president of Yale College, "and would scarcely for any consideration be induced to take up his residence here. A northern man inverts these facts, and would with as much difficulty be persuaded to continue in the South." By the capitalistic standards of the age, nearly all antebellum Southerners were hopelessly backward. They often opposed such "modern improvements" as railroads and banks, and they ranked even middling planters higher on the social scale than the richest merchants and manufacturers. "In a social point of view," wrote a European, "there is this difference in America between the north & the south; that in the former, society, in its narrower sense, takes its chief development in towns, whereas, in the latter, it is more generally confined to the rural districts." Another visitor concluded: "The greatest distinction between the Northern and Southern States [is] . . . the tendency of the population of the former to [move to] the towns and cities, from the meagerness and unattractiveness of life in the country. . . . Generally speaking, the North, as to healthiness and scenery, has considerably the advantage; and yet the natives don't seem to enjoy rural life: they neither talk nor look as if they did; and those are considered, and consider themselves, fortunate, who abandon it to go and push their fortunes in town." The Southerner, on the other hand, had more the "manner and modes of intercourse" of a "country gentleman than any other class of his countrymen; he is more easy, companionable, fond of country life, and out-of-door pursuits," claimed an English traveler. After witnessing the activities at a county seat in the South, including "a speech remarkable for its egotistical nonsense & high flown crackerisms," a Northerner commented: "I never laughed more. It was so rich, so new, so unlike anything we have at the north." Southerners, reported an Englishman, preferred to spend their time at home on their farms. "In this respect," he wrote, "it

9. Owen S. Adams, "Traditional Proverbs and Sayings from California," *Western Folklore* 6 (1947), 63; Mary B. Chesnut, *Mary Chesnut's Civil War*, ed. C. Vann Woodward (New Haven, Conn., 1981), 246, 810; Verna Mae Slone, *What My Heart Wants to Tell* (New York, 1980), xi; Ben Robertson, *Red Hills and Cotton, an Upcountry Memoir* (New York, 1942), 106.

is very different in the North, where rural life seems to be a life of repulsive drudgery, and the towns are looked to for pleasure, ambition, refinement, and social intercourse."[10]

Two antebellum observers summed up how preferences for urban and rural values separated Northerners and Southerners. "The Northern People have interested themselves chiefly in commerce, manufactures, literature, and the like," wrote Daniel R. Hundley, "and we behold the result in the ships, the steamers, telegraphs, the thousand practical inventions, the works of art and genius they have already furnished the world. On the other hand, the South has interested herself in agriculture mainly, political economy, and the nurture of an adventurous and military race." Southerners, as Hundley pointed out, were "enamoured of . . . the Army" and were more warlike than Northerners, who were "not so military in their habits," contended Frederick Hall, "because, though equally brave [as Southerners] and enterprising, they were more industrious, more frugal, and less mercurial in their temperament. Religion was with them a powerful spring of action, and discouraged all wars except those of self-defence. The social and moral virtues, the sciences and arts, were cherished and respected; and there were many roads to office and to eminence [in the North], which were safer and more certain, and not less honourable, than the bloody path of warlike achievement."[11]

Statistics indicate the extent of urban-rural disparity. In 1860 fewer than 10 percent of all Southerners lived in urban places (2,500 or more people). By contrast, nearly 36 percent of all Northeasterners and 16 percent of all Westerners lived in towns or cities. What urbanization the antebellum South experienced was characterized more by the development of market towns and county seats with fewer than 3,000 people than by any increase in the number of cities. Of the sixteen cities in the United States in 1860 with populations of more than 50,000, only New Orleans was in a state that would belong to the southern Confederacy. Besides New Orleans, the Old South could claim only five communities with more than 20,000

---

10. Dwight, *Travels*, IV:248; A. Mackay, *Western World*, I:204; D. Mitchell, *Ten Years in the United States*, 192, 30; George W. F. Howard, *Travels in America* (New York, 1851), 52; Whipple, *Southern Diary*, 38. On the South's rural ways, see also James Mallory Journal, July 15, 1856 (original owned by Edgar A. Stewart of Selma, Alabama), microfilm copy, University of Alabama, Tuscaloosa; George Townsend Fox American Journal, November 1834, Public Library, South Shields, Durham, England; John F. H. Claiborne, "A Trip through the Piney Woods [1841]," *Mississippi Historical Society Publications* 9 (1906), 510; James Crawford King, Jr., " 'Content with Being': Nineteenth-Century Southern Attitudes Toward Economic Development" (Ph.D. diss., University of Alabama, 1985), 4–188.

11. Daniel R. Hundley, *Social Relations in Our Southern States*, ed. William J. Cooper, Jr. (1860; new ed., Baton Rouge, 1979), 50, 49; F. Hall, *Letters from the East and West*, 287–88.

inhabitants—Charleston (40,578), Richmond (37,910), Mobile (29,508), Memphis (22,623), and Savannah (22,292)—and all were ports. What is even more significant, rural values predominated in southern towns and cities. New residents from the rural South who settled in urban areas generally did not become citified; they countryfied the towns.[12]

Another significant difference between Northerners and Southerners was their attitudes toward technology and the concept of progress. Henry V. Poor was a good example of Tocqueville's observation that the Yankee "values science not as an enjoyment, but as a means, and is only anxious to seize its useful applications." In 1849 Poor decided to give up his law practice and lumber business in Bangor, Maine, and to seek his fortune in New York City. At one time Poor had thought of becoming a minister, but now he had discovered a way to preach and to get rich at the same time: he would become the editor and part owner of the *American Railroad Journal*. In his view the railroad was "the great apostle of human progress." He expected it and the industrial developments it supported to change the world for the better, and those who accumulated knowledge and goods would advance as well. "By the new application of the powers of steam and electro-magnetism to the arts of life," he announced, "the present age will be signalized by a more rapid change in [the] order of society, and the progress of the race, than any former one." This was ordained by Poor's Unitarian diety, "the guarantor of the rationality of the universe and its unfolding perfection," who would admit to heaven only those who tried to perfect their lives and to improve the world. Like most Yankees, Poor believed wholeheartedly in material and social progress as well as in the perfectibility of man. He and many of his countrymen were confident that they had not only the wisdom to recognize the world's problems but also the ability to solve them. Their faith in a machine-dominated utopia made them certain that Yankee inventiveness and applied technology could eliminate poverty, ignorance, and isolation.[13] Few worried that their attempts to solve problems might create even greater ones.

12. Cities in the United States in 1860 with more than 50,000 inhabitants were New York, Philadelphia, Brooklyn, Baltimore, Boston, New Orleans, Cincinnati, St. Louis, Chicago, Buffalo, Newark, Louisville, Albany, Washington, San Francisco, and Providence. Anon., *National Almanac and Annual Record for the Year 1863* (Philadelphia, 1863), 310; Bureau of the Census, *Historical Statistics of the United States, 1789–1945* . . . (Washington, D.C., 1949), 29; Blaine A. Brownell and David R. Goldfield, eds., *The City in Southern History: The Growth of Urban Civilization in the South* (Port Washington, N.Y., 1977), 93; David R. Goldfield, *Cotton Fields and Skyscrapers: Southern City and Region, 1607–1980* (Baton Rouge, 1982), 4 and passim.

13. Tocqueville, *Democracy in America*, I:411; McGovern, *Yankee Family*, 79, 81–84, 99–101.

In contrast to the Yankee ideals advocated and practiced by the Henry V. Poors of the North, Southerners usually exerted less effort to make money, to acquire material things, or to improve themselves and the whole world. A Southerner told a traveler that he and his neighbors "try to enjoy what they've got, while they ken. . . . Now, I never calculate to save any thing; I tell my wife . . . I mean to enjoy what I earn as fast as it comes." Nor did Southerners display any special aptitude for inventing gadgets and machines. For example, only 8 percent of the patents issued in 1851 were to residents of southern states. Even in agricultural innovations, Southerners lagged far behind Northerners—only nine of the sixty-two patents classified as agricultural instruments in 1851 were issued to residents of southern states. Southerners generally doubted that much could, or should, be done to improve things in this world. They looked more to the next world, where they believed life would be all leisure and comfort. Contemporaries claimed that Southerners were neither introspective nor much concerned with social betterment. Many, it is true, were outright romantic reactionaries, but they, more than most Northerners, were willing to tolerate the irregularities in man and nature. As one Alabamian said, when pressed by a Yankee for an explanation of why the state capital had been moved from Tuscaloosa to Montgomery, "The fact is, sir, the people here are not like you northern people; they don't reason out every thing so."[14]

In their rural ways and attitudes toward business and money matters, Southerners and premodern British Celts were exactly alike. Celts favored fighting rather than business and looked down on townspeople and tradesmen. In the sixteenth century John Major explained that the Scots "do not bring up their sons to any handicraft. Shoemakers, tailors, and all such craftsmen they reckon as contemptible and unfit for war. . . . Even dwellers in towns they hold as unfit for war." Almost all Highlanders and many Lowlanders continued to denounce trade and to despise businessmen. "There was no class of the community so little thought of at this time [about 1800] as the mercantile," recalled a Scot. As late as the end of the eighteenth century many Highland areas contained, as a local minister explained, "no towns, villages, nor manufactories of any kind. All the inhabitants are employed . . . in tending their cattle, excepting a few artificers." Other observers reported either the absence or the scarcity of manufacturers, banks, and even money lenders. Scots unquestionably favored rural over urban life. "The

14. U.S. Patent Office, *Report of the Commissioner of Patents for the Year 1851*, pt.1: *Arts and Manufactures* (Washington, D.C., 1852), 25, 47–48; Frederick Law Olmsted, *A Journey in the Back Country . . .* (1856; reprint, New York, 1970), 211, 206.

inhabitants of Edinburgh are [so] fond of the country . . . [that] most of those for whom we had letters [of introduction] . . . are absent," lamented a visitor. English Captain Edward Burt reported in the eighteenth century that some rustic Highlanders scorned the handsome monetary offer made by an English officer to transport his pack of hunting hounds across a body of water, because the Scots "entertain a Kind of Pride which is, I think, peculiar to themselves"—they simply refused "to freight their Boats with Dogs." Not even the poorest Highlanders would skin dead horses, which they regarded as "an Employment only *fit for the Hangman*." Scots sold their dead horses for three pence to English soldiers who in turn got six pence for the skinned carcass and another two shillings for the hide.[15]

Traditionally the Irish and the Welsh were just as opposed to trade and the making of money as the Scots. They had no native trading class and few towns of any size or significance. Several distinguished seventeenth-century Englishmen described the Irish as "a Slothful People, . . . bred to no Trades, Manufactures, or other civil Industry." In the eighteenth century Charles Bowden charged that the children of the Irish "semigentry" idle "away their time in barren amusements, ignorant of any business. . . . Too proud to train up their children to business, and too poor to afford them the means of decent subsistence, those semigentry, rear them in habits of sloth. . . . For their offspring, trade is too vile an employment, too grovelling an idea." An eighteenth-century traveler noted that the Welsh had little concern with "the cares of the world" because they were "free from those occupations . . . which engross the attention of a commercial people." "[The Irish] have neither the sturdy tradesmen, nor . . . the shrewd farmers of England," observed Leitch Ritchie at the close of the eighteenth century. Nor were the Irish accomplished at handling money. "Money is rarely used [in Ireland] . . . , and purchases are for the most part made by exchange of goods," reported a sixteenth-century traveler. The Irish gentry was always short of funds, recalled Sir Jonah Barrington, and for many eighteenth-century Irish landowning families "indebtedness was a serious matter." By 1719, for example, Lord Kenmare had so completely mishandled his estate that he was on the verge of being imprisoned and dishonored. A

15. John Major, *A History of Greater Britain* . . . (Edinburgh, 1892), 47; Defoe, *Tour*, 596, 606, 663; Henry Thomas Cockburn quoted in J. G. Fyfe, ed., *Scottish Diaries and Memoirs, 1746–1843* (Stirling, Scotland, 1942), 346; Sinclair, *Statistical Account of Scotland*, XVII:235, 334; Thomas Somerville quoted in Fyfe, *Scottish Diaries and Memoirs*, 232–33; Simond, *Journal of a Tour*, I:348; Edward Burt, *Burt's Letters from the North of Scotland*, ed. R. Jamieson (1754; reprint, 2 vols., Edinburgh, 1974), I:113–15.

friend reported that Kenmare was sober at the moment, "but it is not safe to let him handle money."[16]

Most antebellum Southerners and premodern Celts seemed unburdened by those skills required of good businessmen. A Yankee claimed that the only "excellent business men in the South" were Northerners and foreigners; "the truth compels me," he added, "to say that the standard of business morality in the slave States is very far below what it is in New England." In marked contrast to Northerners, Southerners reportedly broke both verbal and written contracts. Not only would "the lawless Cracker" sell "his corn . . . or his cotton" in violation of his contracted obligation, but the injured party almost never received "redress . . . through the [southern] courts." One observer noted that Irishmen also tended to be "regardless of their oaths," and another stated that Highlanders could not "be depended on for the sincerity of their professions."[17]

What Yankees and Englishmen considered the duplicity of Southerners and Celts probably was nothing more than a careless and a nonbusinesslike attitude—and an unwillingness to be disagreeable by refusing a request—rather than outright dishonesty. After failing to receive some corn that a Southerner had contracted in writing to deliver but ultimately sold to someone else, a frustrated New Englander asked a southern merchant "why . . . so little reliance could be placed upon the integrity of the Crackers." "I know not," replied the merchant, "except that it is the habit of the people. Any man will promise you any thing you want, and engage to do any thing you desire, without the least intention of fulfilling his word."[18]

16. R. A. Butlin, ed., *The Development of the Irish Town* (Totowa, N.J., 1977), 61–100; Letter from ten English Lords, Justices, and Council of Ireland to King Charles I, March 16, 1642, quoted in Richard Cox, *Hibernia Anglicana: or, the History of Ireland* . . . (2 vols., London, 1689), II:app. IV, 11; Charles Topham Bowden, *A Tour through Ireland* (Dublin, 1791), 191; Joseph Hucks, *A Pedestrian Tour through North Wales, in a Series of Letters [1795]*, ed. Alun R. Jones and William Tydeman (Cardiff, Wales, 1979), 61; Leitch Ritchie, *Ireland Picturesque and Romantic* (London, 1838), 32; Constantia Maxwell, ed., *Irish History from Contemporary Sources (1509–1610)* (London, 1923), 320; Thomas Dineley, *Observations in a Voyage through the Kingdom of Ireland . . . in the Year 1681* (Dublin, 1870), 35–36; Sir Jonah Barrington, *Personal Sketches of His Own Times*, ed. Townsend Young (3d ed., 2 vols., London, 1869), I:80; David Large, "The Wealth of the Greater Irish Landowners, 1750–1815," *Irish Historical Studies* 15 (1966–67), 44; Edward MacLysaght, ed., *The Kenmare Manuscripts* (Dublin, 1942), 14, 18. See also Richard Twiss, *A Tour in Ireland in 1775* (London, 1776), 31.

17. Charles G. Parsons, *Inside View of Slavery: or, a Tour Among the Planters* (Cleveland, 1855), 90–91; Edward MacLysaght, *Irish Life in the Seventeenth Century* (1939; reprint, Dublin, 1979), 74; Sinclair, *Statistical Account of Scotland*, XVII:203. See also Giraldus Cambrensis, *The First Version of the Topography of Ireland*, trans. John J. O'Meara (Dundalk, Ireland, 1951), 90–91.

18. Parsons, *Inside View*, 92.

A Northerner suggested that Southerners often failed to fulfill their "business contracts" because they spent too much time in amusements. "No business," he claimed, "is so important at any time as to prevent them from attending the horse-race, the cock-fight, or any other kind of sport." To illustrate, he described how a clergyman, who was waiting for a train, made the mistake of taking a small item to a blacksmith for repair; the blacksmith, while repairing the item, twice stopped to go watch a cock fight. Not surprisingly, the clergyman missed his train.[19]

"In traveling in the South," observed another Northerner, "you become astonished at the little attention men pay to their business. The idea appears to be very prevalent, that if a business is once started, it must take care of itself." This man had to visit the only two stables in Pine Bluff, Arkansas, several times before he could find either of the proprietors. "One of them had gone into the 'bottom,' on the opposite side of the river, hunting wild turkies; while the other was enjoying a social glass at a saloon." "Tuscaloosa [Alabama] ought to be a gem of a place," reported Charles Lanman, "if its men of property would . . . do a little more with their perpetually gloved hands. . . . By way of depicting the peculiar business traits of the modern Tuscaloosians, it has been stated to me that while an extensive bed of coal is known to exist within a mile of the town, it is customary to order, even from Philadelphia the needed supply; and that while the country affords a beautiful quality of marble, the tombstones of the place are all imported from Italy."[20]

Southerners often seemed to be the most casual businessmen. A Texan, headed east with his company to fight Yankees in 1861, wrote: "we have not had to pay for anything scarcely, that we bought on the road." A traveler watched some of Natchez's merchants "spending their time . . . very idly, talking politics and smoking in their stores"; another visitor heard a New Orleans watchmaker tell a customer not to bother him, "as I'm eating my dinner," he said; "s'pose you call again, and see if I've done."[21]

Southern artisans were no more diligent. "The indolence and churlishness of the workingmen around here are unparalleled,"

19. Ibid., 93.
20. Gilbert Hathaway, "Travels in the South-West," *Magazine of Travel* 1 (1857), 231; Lanman, *Adventures in the Wilds*, II:277–78.
21. Robert H. Gaston quoted in Harold B. Simpson, *Hood's Texas Brigade: Lee's Grenadier Guard* (Waco, 1970), 47; George Lewis, *Impressions of America* . . . (Edinburgh, 1845), 231–32; Houstoun, *Texas and the Gulf*, 90–91. On the unbusinesslike ways of Southerners,

see also Catherine C. Hopley, *Life in the South From the . . . Spring of 1860 to August 1862* (1863; reprint, 2 vols., New York, 1974), 111; John D. Ashmore Diary, December 20, 1853, John D. Ashmore Papers, Southern Historical Collection, University of North Carolina, Chapel Hill; Noah K. Davis to Henry G. Jones, August 31, 1865, Walter A. Griess Collection, University of Alabama, Tuscaloosa.

complained a visitor. "If the least thing goes wrong with a saddle, or clothes, or a boot, you cannot find a soul to make repairs, and the other day a cobbler answered us, '*Yes, that's right, I'm a shoemaker, and sometimes I work, but I'm not in the mood right now.*' " Another traveler insisted that Southerners "never enter upon any occupation unless . . . they are compelled to do so." When Frederick Law Olmsted took his horse to a Texas blacksmith, the man said it "was too d——d cold to work, . . . and he was going to shoot some geese." Indolent and unhurried ferrymen were the subjects of almost identical tales told by frustrated travelers in Scotland and the Old South.[22]

When an exasperated Yankee complained that some job had not been finished at the time agreed upon, a complacent Southerner would explain that a "fox[-hunting] party came along, and he had to join that,—or the military paraded, which every body must see." A New Englander wrote: "I was employed to superintend the building of a mill [in the South], and fourteen hands were engaged six days in raising it, after it was framed. The dimensions of the building were only 40 by 70 feet, and the same number of hands at the North would have raised it in half a day; but the master workman took two of the hands and went off fishing a part of two days. The crew rested while they were absent. A squirrel ran by one day, and all the men left the mill, and chased him half a mile before they treed him. In this way was much of the time spent. Some of the owners of the property were on the ground, but I heard no complaint."[23]

To complain too strongly about southern ways could be danger-ous, just as could complaints about local ways in Ireland and Scot-land.[24] The owner of a southern hotel told an Englishwoman that his business was "a losing concern altogether; more went out than came in, and only that morning, having asked a gentleman to pay his bill, the reply was, 'If you come to insult me again sir, by —— I'll shoot you sir.' " When an Englishman, tired of waiting for a Southerner to start working on a house he had contracted to build, hired another man to do the job, the enraged Southerner, who con-sidered himself dishonored, vowed: "to-morrow morn, I will come with men, and twenty rifles, and I will have your life, or you shall have mine."[25]

22. Louis Philippe, *Diary of My Travels in America* [1797], trans. Stephen Becker (New York, 1977), 60; George William Featherstonhaugh, *Excursion through the Slave States* . . . (2 vols., London, 1844), II:30; Frederick Law Olmsted, *A Journey through Texas* . . . (1857; reprint, New York, 1969), 107; *Edinburgh Review* 66 (1820), 445; Philippe, *Diary of My Trav-els*, 58; Olmsted, *Journey through Texas*, 110.

23. Parsons, *Inside View*, 94.

24. On the violent ways of the Celts, see MacLysaght, *Irish Life*, 42, 90–91; Sinclair, *Statistical Account of Scotland*, XVII:473–74.

25. Houstoun, *Texas and the Gulf*, 223; William Faux, *Memorable Days in America* . . . (London, 1823), 161.

Their disinterest in business and money put both Celts and Southerners at the mercy of outsiders. Throughout the seventeenth and eighteenth centuries few of the merchants in Ireland, Wales, or the Highlands were Celts; indeed, nearly all of the most successful businessmen were foreigners.[26]

Usually some combination of Yankees, Englishmen, Germans, Jews, Lowland Scots, or the southern-born sons of Northerners or foreigners dominated business affairs in the antebellum South.[27] "The New Englanders are in general active and . . . full of enterprise," noted a traveler in the South. "Here [in the major southern ports], as well as in most of the small towns, . . . the greater part of the produce is taken out by the New Englanders. . . . The planters . . . are generally in debt to the merchants." Another visitor noted that there were "many northerners located here [in the South] who have been successfully engaged in business for many years." A Yankee who had recently arrived in upcountry Georgia reported to her father: "It's a good place for business and . . . we will make money here." Charles Lanman stated that in Florida "those engaged in the lumbering business . . . are chiefly Northerners, and they of course are thinking more of dollars than of nature." Daniel Hundley believed that nearly all of the Old South's successful storekeepers were either Yankees or Yankee-trained Southerners. Yankees reportedly ran the cotton and paper mills of Virginia and Alabama. "I cannot make money where Northern people are," a Northerner complained. "Only with lazy easygoing Southerners can I make a fortune." Anne Royall claimed that Yankees controlled most of the businesses of Charleston; Frederick Law Olmsted pointed out that the merchants of Norfolk were almost all from New Jersey. He also noted that the Savannah and Macon Railroad, which he praised, was built and managed by Northerners. "I am told that most of the mechanics and . . . successful merchants and tradesmen of Savannah came originally from the North, or are the sons of Northern men," he boasted. A Frenchman insisted that the success of Yankees in the South was not restricted to business: "If you pass a plantation . . . in better order than the others, with finer avenues, with the Negroes'

26. MacLysaght, *Irish Life*, 233–34; Defoe, *Tour*, 380, 606; Sinclair, *Statistical Account of Scotland*, XVII:4–5, 371, 376, 391, 536–37, 558, 622.

27. On the control of southern business by Northerners, see J. H. Franklin, *Southern Odyssey*, 39, 111–12; Lanman, *Adventures in the Wilds*, II:123, 189; Lillian Foster, *Way-Side Glimpses, North and South* (New York, 1860), 80; Charles Mackay, *Life and Liberty in America . . .* (New York, 1859), 176, 180. On the prominence of German and Jewish businessmen in the Old South, see Amelia Matilda Murray, *Letters from the United States, Cuba and Canada* (New York, 1856), 291; Benwell, *An Englishman's Travels*, 205–06.

cabins better arranged and more comfortable, you will be told, 'Oh! that is a Yankee's; he is a smart man!' "[28]

A look at the occupations of people born outside the South but who in 1850 were living in Lowndes County, Mississippi, reveals some significant differences between Celts, on one hand, and Northerners, Englishmen, and Germans, on the other. Of the Celts (Irish and Scots), 35 percent were employed in agriculture, 30 percent were artisans, 15 percent were unskilled laborers, 5 percent were in politics, fewer than 10 percent were in business, and only 5 percent were professionals. Of the Yankees, Germans, and Englishmen, more than 50 percent were in business, nearly 30 percent were artisans, 14 percent were professionals, less than 7 percent were engaged in agriculture, and none was an unskilled laborer.[29]

Southerners were aware that by the late antebellum period the Old South was in danger of becoming an economic colony of the North. In 1847 a resident of Mobile complained that the South's "whole commerce except a small fraction is in the hands of Northern men. 7/8 of our Bank Stock is owned by Northern men. . . . Our wholesale and retail business—everything in short worth mentioning is in the hands of [Yankees]. . . . Financially we are more enslaved than our negroes."[30] Jefferson Davis did not mistake the intentions

28. Johann David Schopf, *Travels in the Confederation [1783–1784]* . . . , trans. and ed. Alfred J. Morrison (new ed., 2 vols., New York, 1968), II:125–26, 131; Whipple, *Southern Diary*, 73, 104–05; Mrs. David Hillhouse to her father, January 26, 1787, in *The Alexander Letters, 1787–1900*, ed. Marion Alexander Boggs (Athens, Ga., 1980), 16–17; Lanman, *Adventures in the Wilds*, II:109; Hundley, *Social Relations*, 98–116; [Sarah] Mendell and [Charlotte] Hosmer, *Notes of Travel and Life* (New York, 1854), 178; Lanman, *Adventures in the Wilds*, II:176; quoted in Chesnut, *Mary Chesnut's Civil War*, 810; Anne Newport Royall, *Mrs. Royall's Southern Tour* . . . (3 vols., Washington, D.C., 1830–31), II:23; Frederick Law Olmsted, *The Cotton Kingdom: A Traveller's Observations on Cotton and Slavery* . . . , ed. Arthur M. Schlesinger (New York, 1953), 120, 212, 220; Michel Chevalier, *Society, Manners and Politics in the United States* . . . , trans. Thomas Gamaliel Bradford (Boston, 1839), 106.

29. Calculated from data in Betty Wood Thomas, comp., *1850 Census, Lowndes County, Mississippi* (Columbus, Miss., 1978), 5–172. My conclusions are supported by the unpublished research of Daniel Pierce, one of my former graduate students, on the ethnic backgrounds of businessmen in interior antebellum Alabama towns. See also Timothy C. Frazer, "Isoglasses and Place Names in Historical Context," *Names: Journal of the American Name Society* 33 (1985), 227–28, who stated: "A common tendency in the settlement of the lower Middle West . . . was for Northerners to gravitate to the towns, sometimes simply transplanting entire communities." Settlers from the South, on the other hand, tended to favor rural areas. "In Sangamon County, Illinois, Southerners made up 57 percent of the 1850 adult rural population, but only 30 percent of the population of Springfield, the state capital."

30. Quoted in J. Mills Thornton, *Politics and Power in a Slave Society: Alabama, 1800–1860* (Baton Rouge, 1978), 255. See also Robert R. Russel, *Economic Aspects of Southern Sectionalism, 1840–1861* (Urbana, Ill., 1924), 48.

of Yankees when he expressed his fear that they would overrun a defeated South, bringing with them what he called "New England's grasping avarice and evil passions"; scarcely had the war ended when the *Nation* announced that Northerners must "colonize and Yankeeize the South, . . . in short to turn the slothful, shiftless Southern world upside down." The antebellum Southerner's distrust of Northerners is revealed in the question a rustic asked a traveler from New York: "Are there any gentlemen, sir, among the Yankees?" Told that there were some, the curious Southerner replied: "Well, you see, stranger, I thought they were all peddlers."[31]

Southerners regarded peddlers and merchants with mixed sentiments throughout the antebellum period. In the South, said Henry A. Bright, "the phrase 'to Yankee' is [the] . . . equivalent with 'to do,' 'to cheat.' 'They'd Yankee you finely,' I heard a man say one day. Sundry hampers of wooden nutmegs, wooden hams covered with canvass, &c. have occasioned this calumny on New England States." Southerners, it should be pointed out, were not always ideal customers. A traveler noted that Southerners, "disposed to idleness and goodliving, commonly buy more of the merchants, and in advance, than their labor amounts to. The merchants are therefore obliged, and it is their custom, to sell on long credit, but they are in consequence involved in continual processes at law and suits for debt."[32]

Justly or otherwise, Southerners displayed a strong antipathy toward Yankees and their business methods. Timothy Flint heard throughout the South "stories about Yankee tricks, and Yankee finesse, and wooden nutmegs, and pit-coal indigo, and gin made by putting pinetops in the whiskey." He acknowledged that he could "relate a score of Yankee tricks, that different people assured us had been played off upon them. I will only remark, that wherever we stopped at night and requested lodgings, we were constantly asked if we were Yankees; and when we answered that we were, we constantly saw a lengthening of visage ensue, but were generally complimented in the end with granting our request. . . . We were then compelled to hear of impositions and petty tricks, and small thefts, and more than all, departure without paying off bills, which, they alleged, had been practised upon them by Yankees. . . . The common reply of the [Ohio River] boatmen to those who ask them what is their lading, is, 'Pit-coal indigo, wooden nutmegs, straw baskets, and [other] Yankee notions.' " Englishman Robert Russell men-

31. John J. Craven, *Prison Life of Jefferson Davis* . . . (1866; reprint, Biloxi, 1979), 100; *Nation* 1 (1865), 67; Charles Fenno Hoffman, *A Winter in the West* (2 vols., New York, 1835), II:197, 244–46.
32. Schopf, *Travels in the Confederation*, II:131; Henry Arthur Bright, *Happy Country This America: The Travel Diary of Henry Arthur Bright [1852]*, ed. Anne Henry Ehrenpreis (Columbus, Ohio, 1978), 240.

tioned a salesman who pretended to be a Southerner "for the purpose of ingratiating himself with his customers; for had he told them he was from the North, he would have . . . done no business." On a visit to Scotland, Washington Irving heard a story of a Yankee clock peddler who cheated Southerners by repairing clocks with broken parts.[33]

After years of being overcharged and cheated, Southerners finally passed laws in some states that banned or severely restricted peddling.[34] In 1859, for example, Alabama required that "hereafter all licenses to peddle goods, wares or merchandise of any description, for which a license is now required by law, shall be charged as follows, viz: To peddle in a wagon, for each wagon in a county, seven hundred and fifty dollars; on a horse, for each horse in a county, five hundred dollars; on foot, in each county, three hundred dollars for each person; which license must be obtained from the Judge of Probate of the county in which such peddling is to take place." The penalty for violating this law was a fine of five hundred dollars plus six months in jail.[35]

Such laws represented an attempt by antebellum Southerners to protect themselves as well as their culture. They believed Dr. William Ellery Channing of Boston's Federal Street Church when he said of Yankees: "Prosperity is the goal for which they toil perseveringly from morning until night." Southerners also believed the *Atlantic Monthly* when it admitted: "Our [northern] soil is sterile, . . . and under the circumstances,—with the Yankee notion that the getting of money is the chief end of man,—exclusive devotion to labor has been deemed indispensable to success. The maxims of Franklin have been literally received and adopted as divine truth. We have believed that to labor is to be thrifty, that to be thrifty is to be respectable, that to be respectable is to afford facilities for being still more thrifty; and our experience is, that with increased thrift comes increased labor. This is the circle of our ambitions and rewards. All begins and ends in labor." The fear of Southerners that

33. Flint, *Recollections*, 32–33; Robert Russell, *North America, Its Agriculture and Climate* (Edinburgh, 1857), 301; Washington Irving, *Tour in Scotland, 1817, and Other Manuscript Notes*, ed. Stanley T. Williams (New Haven, Conn., 1927), 88. On the sharp practices of Yankee businessmen, see also Montule, *Travels in America*, 157, 181; John E. E. D. Acton, *Acton in America: The American Journal of Sir John Acton, 1853*, ed. S. W. Jackman (Shepherdstown, Pa., 1979), 39–40; Benwell, *An Englishman's Travels*, 14–15; Faux, *Memorable Days*, 37, 106; Thomas Colley Grattan, *Civilized America* (2 vols., London, 1859), I:70; Whipple, *Southern Diary*, 22; J. H. Franklin, *Southern Odyssey*, 7, 39, 91.

34. Schwaab, *Travels in the Old South*, II:330.

35. *Acts of Alabama, 1859* (Montgomery, 1860), 8–9. It should be added that some of the Middle Atlantic states also restricted Yankee peddlers to prevent them from swindling and from underselling local merchants.

Yankees living among them would corrupt southern ways and values produced a popular saying: "The difference between a Yankee and a damnyankee is that the Yankee has sense enough to stay where he belongs." A major reason why the editor of the *Charleston Mercury* opposed any restoration of the Union even in 1864 was his belief that Yankee avarice would just lead to another war.[36]

Nothing revealed the Celtic heritage of Southerners more than their concept of worth—what they considered important, valuable, virtuous, estimable. The most apparent characteristic of Southerners, who enjoyed the reputation of being more generous than Northerners, was that they were sensualists. The lives of most Southerners, in the harsh words of a disapproving Northerner, were "filled up with sensual gratifications; consequently, they find ample leisure to qualify themselves—not for the practical purposes of life, but for these, their imaginary positions of refinement and honor, in which the practical world finds them mere drones,—in some instances pests of society, and an incubus upon progress." Other observers spoke of the "Pleasures of every kind [that] are known, loved, and enjoyed here"; of the absence of "frugality"; and of the "indolent repose" that pervaded the Old South. "Idleness is the order of the day here," a planter's wife wrote from Charleston. "There is William Heyward, with a fine disposition, and an excellent capacity—lounging away his mornings—smoking and drinking away his afternoons—and his Evenings the only part of his existence which can be said to be employed are passed very unprofitably in company." A Southerner confessed that he had no desire to work: "I returned, after eight months' absence, to my home. . . . I found my wife working and scuffling and fighting poverty as well as she could. She had been spinning and weaving and had the children well clothed, and they had not consumed the corn and hogs I had provided for them before I went off. . . . I was strong enough to work some, but the time for planting a crop had passed, and I could think of nothing to do. . . . I felt no inclination to work. Indeed I felt more like I needed quiet rest. Accordingly I took my rifle and retired to the canebrake and the . . . forests."[37]

36. William E. Channing quoted in D. H. Hill, "The Old South," *Southern Historical Society Papers* 16 (1888), 436; Anon., "Farming Life in New England," *Atlantic Monthly* 2 (1858), 335–36; Boyce House, *Texas-Proud and Loud* (San Antonio, 1945), 5; *Charleston Mercury,* August 15, 1864. See also Adam Hodgson, *Letters from North America* . . . (2 vols., London, 1824), II:262; Chesnut, *Mary Chesnut's Civil War,* 251.

37. Barbara Leigh Smith Bodichon, *An American Diary, 1857–8,* ed. Joseph W. Reed, Jr. (London, 1972), 64; Philo Tower, *Slavery Unmasked: Being a Truthful Narrative of Three Years' Residence and Journeying in Eleven Southern States* . . . (Rochester, N.Y., 1856), 140; Hoffman, *Winter in the West,* II:220; Schopf, *Travels in the Confederation,* II:164; M. I. Manigault to Gabriel Henry Manigault, December 6, 1808, quoted in Michael P. Johnson, "Planters and Patriarchy: Charleston, 1800–1860," *Journal of Southern History* 46 (1980), 57; Gideon Lincecum, "Autobiography of Gideon Lincecum," *Mississippi Historical Society Publications* 8 (1904), 485.

A SOUTHERNER AND HIS DOGS

From *Harper's New Monthly Magazine* 15 (1857), 735.

Celts, but not Englishmen or Yankees, could appreciate such actions. Englishman Arthur Young, writing of eighteenth-century Ireland, described "the class of little country gentlemen . . . who hunt in the day, get drunk in the evening, and fight the next morning." Young regarded these people and their ways as "perfectly disagreeable." Another Englishman denounced the Irish as only interested in "cock-fighting, horse-racing, hunting, or the ruin of female innocence! Upon an income of two or three hundred [pounds] a year, it is not at all uncommon to see six or seven *gentlemen* reared; and when the little patrimony comes to be divided between them, it will just afford perhaps to each as much as will enable him to exist without labour, to get drunk, insult those whom he pleases, and fight duels. Instead of this class in England," he boasted, "there is a yeomanry, useful, hardy, and industrious."[38]

This Englishman was correct in pointing out that Celts were not yeomen; neither were Southerners. Indeed, they never came close to that English model. "Yeomen," stated an early authority, "are . . . by our law . . . free men borne English, and may dispend of their owne free land in yearelie revenue. . . . [Yeoman] is derived from the Saxon terme Zeoman or Geoman, which signifieth . . . a settled or staid man, such I meane as being maried and of some yeares, betaketh himselfe to staie in the place of his abode for the better maintenance of himselfe and his familie, where of the single sort have no regard, but are likelie to be still fleeting now hither now thither, which argueth want of stabilitie in determination and resolution of judgement, for the execution of things of anie importance."[39]

Celts and Southerners were simply too lazy, too unstable, too migratory, and too committed to sensual pleasures to be yeomen. Indeed, the desire to enjoy a leisurely life and all the pleasures possible, without laboring, were characteristic of both Celts and Southerners and set them apart from most Englishmen and Yankees. A Yankee teacher claimed that Irishmen migrated to the American South because there they hoped "to find all the luxuries of life in abundance without labor." The contentment of Southerners with their lot and their lack of concern for improvement baffled most Northerners. One described visiting a backcountry Southerner who owned "5,000 acres of land, 20 or 30 negroes, 100 head of cattle— & yet lives in a log-house of two rooms, in one of which all his family sleep, & in the other all his company, of both sexes & all

38. Arthur Young, *Arthur Young's Tour in Ireland (1776–1779)*, ed. Arthur W. Hutton (2 vols., London, 1892), I:155; Bowden, *Tour through Ireland*, 192. On the Celtic lack of materialism, see Twiss, *Tour in Ireland*, 31; Dineley, *Observations in a Voyage*, 35–36; Defoe, *Tour*, 596, 663; Thomas Somerville

quoted in Fyfe, *Scottish Diaries and Memoirs*, 233; Derek A.C. Davies, *Ireland* (New York, 1972), 48.

39. Raphaell Holinshed, comp., *Holinshed's Chronicles of England, Scotland, and Ireland* (6 vols., London, 1807–08), I:275.

ages." This man appeared "perfectly easy & contented, & satisfied with himself and all about him. With property enough to educate his sons at college, & his daughters at expensive schools, he does not in fact have them taught to read." This rustic simply enjoyed his leisurely life and taught his children to do the same. Another Southerner told a traveler: *"there's luck in leisure."*[40]

Such carelessness and lack of ambition revealed the values and the Celtic heritage of the antebellum Southerner just as surely as did the assortment he kept in his desk. "There," noted a perceptive observer, "you will find his bonds, accounts, receipts, and even his will, jabbed into pigeon-holes or lying about loose in the midst of a museum of powder-horns, shot-gourds, turkey-yelpers, flints, screws, popcorn, old horseshoes and watermelon seed."[41]

Orderliness, personal ambition, trying to make and to save money all ranked low on the Celtic and southern scales of creditable activities. Southerners were, as John Ramsay said of eighteenth-century Scots, too proud and unbusinesslike to be successful in service or trade; they shared with their Celtic ancestors a desire to "be accounted a Martial People, rather than submit themselves to low and mercenary Employments"; they were as disdainful of money as the old Scottish lady who "lighted her pipe with the note . . . for the money owed her."[42]

If contemporaries were correct, Celts and Southerners were less likely to judge people by their wealth than were Englishmen and Northerners. An eighteenth-century visitor remarked of the western Scots: "they covet no Wealth." "In Charleston wealth does not smooth the way to 'the best society' as it does in Europe or in the northern states," wrote a Swedish tutor, who reported that her employer "takes the greatest pains in selecting the company his daughters keep: his criteria are, first, spotless morals; second, education; third, refined manners. He does not, however, think that all this can be found in every individual but in the individual's family; 'it's in the blood,' he says." Such clannishness, of course, was typically Celtic.[43] Acquiring wealth was unimportant, said one planter;

40. Emily P. Burke, *Reminiscences of Georgia* (Oberlin, Ohio, 1850), 8; [Jeremiah Evarts], *Through the South and the West with Jeremiah Evarts in 1826*, ed. J. Orin Oliphant (Lewisburg, Pa., 1956), 104; F. Hall, *Letters from the East and West*, 140.

41. George W. Bagby, *The Old Virginia Gentleman and Other Sketches*, ed. Ellen M. Bagby (Richmond, 1943), 187.

42. John Ramsay, *Scotland and Scotsmen in the Eighteenth Century, from the MSS. of John Ramsay, Esq. of Ochteryre*, ed. Alexander Allardyce (2 vols., Edin-

burgh, 1888), II:401–02; Burt, *Letters*, I:50–51; George Ridpath quoted in Fyfe, *Scottish Diaries and Memoirs*, 119.

43. Martin Martin, *A Description of the Western Islands of Scotland* (1716; reprint, Edinburgh, 1981), 22; Rosalie Roos, *Travels in America, 1851–1855*, ed. Carl L. Anderson (Carbondale, Ill., 1982), 120; Barrington, *Personal Sketches*, I:80; Raphaell Holinshed, *Holinshed's Irish Chronicle . . .*, ed. Liam Miller and Eileen Power (1577; reprint, Dublin, 1979), 112–13; Maxwell, *Irish History*, 314–15; Sinclair,

"his income was sufficient; . . . moreover, having no children, he was more content to live thus than by wearing out himself and his Negroes." Southerners never let business interfere with their pleasures. A native of the South claimed that the typical Southerner, "whatever may be his engagements, . . . seems never to have any thing to do but to amuse himself and his family and the stranger within his gates."[44]

One Southerner revealed not only his own values but contrasted them with those of Northerners when he wrote: "Yankees are a 'go-ahead,' energetic, enterprising people, full of vim and vigor, and shrewd, smart, and calculating, the very sort of people to get along in this world, the way it is 'put up' at present; but it seems to me they lack a something that the Southerners have, that is necessary in the making up of a number-one gentleman. . . . I don't say this out of prejudice to the Northern people, for we have our faults as well. . . . That the Yankees are an ingenious people, I know all will admit at once. Give one of them a Barlow knife and a piece of white pine for his stock in trade, and he'll make money out of it; if he can't do anything else, he'll whittle it up in wooden nutmegs, that will be better than the imported ones, only they won't flavor a toddy or mince-pie quite so well!"[45]

Making money was not the primary aim of Celts and Southerners; typically, they disbelieved in progress, despised haste, and distrusted machines. After struggling with a recalcitrant fertilizer-spreader, a Southerner lost his temper, denounced the machine as a "dirty low-down evil contraption," and smashed it to pieces with a rock. Traces of such Celtic ways can still be found in recent times in such remote places as the Inner Hebrides. "Ours is a simple culture," insists Angus Macintyre. "Incomers do not change us; no, it is they who are changed. Their pace slows, and they come to feel that there is no need for hurry. That is the philosophy of the Gael, and that is why industry will not succeed here. The islandman has no industrial tradition, except the making of whisky." The old Irish lady may have said it best—"he who made time made plenty of it"—but a modern southern journalist conveyed the same sentiment that Celts and Southerners have shared over the years when he wrote: "my daddy always said, 'Speed kills.' "[46]

*Statistical Account of Scotland,* XVII:155, 203; A. Young, *Tour in Ireland,* II:872–73; Croker, *Researches,* 12–13.

44. Montule, *Travels in America,* 89; Hundley, *Social Relations,* 58, 174, 262–63.

45. John C. Duval, *The Adventures of Big-Foot Wallace, the Texas Ranger and Hunter* (Philadelphia, 1871), 264–65.

46. Robertson, *Red Hills and Cotton,* 210–11; Kenneth MacLeish, "Scotland's Inner Hebrides: Isles of the Western Sea," *National Geographic* 146, no. 5 (November 1974), 708; D. Davies, *Ireland,* 59; Lewis Grizzard, *Kathy Sue Loudermilk, I Love You* (Atlanta, 1979), 58.

"We are a peculiar people, sir!" southern secessionist Louis T. Wigfall told an English reporter in 1861. "We are an agricultural people; we are a primitive . . . people. We have no cities—we don't want them. We have no literature—we don't need any yet. We have no press—we are glad of it. We do not require a press, because we go out and discuss all public questions from the stump with our people. We have no commercial marine—no navy—we don't want them. We are better without them. Your ships carry our produce, and you can protect your own vessels. We want no manufactures: we desire no trading, no mechanical or manufacturing classes."[47]

47. Louis T. Wigfall quoted in William   *South* (2 vols., London, 1863), I:258–59. Howard Russell, *My Diary North and*

# XI

# *Collision*

To bring all this to a conclusion and a focus, it is clear that eyewitness accounts of life in the United States before the 1860s reveal vast and important differences between Southerners and Northerners. Throughout the antebellum period a wide range of observers generally characterized Southerners as more hospitable, generous, frank, courteous, spontaneous, lazy, lawless, militaristic, wasteful, impractical, and reckless than Northerners, who were in turn more reserved, shrewd, disciplined, gauche, enterprising, acquisitive, careful, frugal, ambitious, pacific, and practical than Southerners. The Old South was a leisure-oriented society that fostered idleness and gaiety, where people favored the spoken word over the written and enjoyed their sensual pleasures. Family ties reportedly were stronger in the South than in the North; Southerners, whose values were more agrarian than those of Northerners, wasted more time and consumed more tobacco and liquor and were less concerned with the useful and the material. Yankees, on the other hand, were cleaner, neater, more puritanical, less mercurial, better educated, more orderly and progressive, worked harder, and kept the Sabbath better than Southerners.

Many an observer also recorded that Northerners and Southerners tended to retain their old ways when they moved westward. The Yankee preacher Timothy Flint, for example, noted that Ohio was called a "Yankee state" because of the New England institutions that prevailed in the northern three-quarters of its territory. "The prevalent modes of living, of society, of instruction, of associating for any public object, of thinking, and enjoying," which Flint found there "to be copies of the New England pattern," were as solidly entrenched in the upper Midwest as southern ways were along and below the Ohio River. Flint and others recognized that New Englanders and denizens of the upper Midwest shared fundamental beliefs and habits: "[They] naturally unite themselves into corporate unions, and concentre their strength for public works and purposes. They have the same desire for keeping up schools, for cultivating psalmody, for settling ministers, and attending upon religious worship; and unfortunately the same disposition to dogmatize, to settle, not only their own faith, but that of their neighbour, and to stand resolutely, and dispute fiercely, for the slightest shade of difference of religious opinion. In short, in the tone of conversation, the ways of thinking and expressing thought upon all subjects, in the strong exercise of social inclination, expressing itself in habits of neighbourhood, to form villages, and live in them, in preference to that sequestered and isolated condition, which a Kentuckian, under the name of 'range,' considers as one of the desirable circumstances of existence; in the thousand slight shades of manner, and union of which so strongly marks one people from another, and the details of which are too minute to be described, by most of these things, this is properly designated 'the Yankee state.' "[1]

What antebellum observers described were more than trivial variations between the inhabitants of different areas of the United States; they were deep cultural contrarieties between two distinct peoples who not only disagreed in their ways and values but by 1861 were ready to meet each other in mortal combat. The Southerner who wrote *Sociology for the South* and Abraham Lincoln's law partner probably agreed on very few things, but one of them was that the North and South were discordant cultures. In 1860 George Fitzhugh announced that the division between Southerners and Northerners was more than a "sectional issue"—it was a clash "between conservatives and revolutionaries; . . . between those who believe in the past, in history, in human experience, . . . and those who . . . foolishly, rashly, and profanely attempt to 'expel human nature,' to bring about a millennium, and inaugurate a future wholly unlike anything that has preceded it." That same year William H. Herndon proclaimed that "Civilization and barbarism are absolute antagonisms. One or the other must perish on this Continent. . . . There is no dodging the question. Let the natural struggle, heaven high and 'hell' deep, go on. . . . I am thoroughly convinced that two such civilizations as the North and the South can-not co-exist on the same soil. . . . To expect otherwise would be to expect the Absolute to sleep with and tolerate 'hell.' "[2]

Nor were these exceptional views. Of Southerners, a Northerner

1. Timothy Flint, *Recollections of the Last Ten Years,* ed. C. Hartley Grattan (1826; reprint, New York, 1932), 45.

2. Fitzhugh quoted in Jan C. Dawson, "The Puritan and the Cavalier: The South's Perception of Contrasting Traditions," *Journal of Southern History* 44, (1978), 600; William H. Herndon to Charles Sumner, December 10, 1860, Charles Sumner Papers, Harvard University.

admitted, "there is no sett of People on Gods Earth that I despise and hold in such utter contempt." An Englishman reported that there was nothing Northerners "hate with so deep a hatred" as Southerners. Northern journalists spoke of the South as the home of the "ignorant, illiterate, and barbarian"—a region that "has already sunk three centuries back toward the age of barbarism." Just before the War for Southern Independence, Georgian Alfred Iverson confessed: "there is an enmity between the northern and southern people that is deep and enduring, and you never can eradicate it—never! We are enemies as much as if we were hostile States. I believe that the northern people hate the South worse than ever the English people hated France." In 1860 a southern editor asked: "how can two such antagonistic nationalities dwell together in fraternal concord under the same government? Is not the thing clearly impossible? Has not the experiment been tried . . . , and have not the final results demonstrated its failure? The feelings, customs, mode of thought and education of the two sections, are discrepant and often antagonistic. The North and South are heterogeneous and are better apart. . . . While the South continues a part of the American confederacy, there is no power which can prevent her progressive degradation, humiliation and spoilation by the victorious North. We are doomed if we proclaim not our political independence."[3]

Nothing suggests that cultural differences "caused" the southern states to secede from the Union in the winter of 1860–61. Secession was a series of concrete responses by individual human beings to a set of events that most Southerners perceived as provocations. But the Southerners' cultural heritage conditioned those responses and perceptions and made them all but certain. The nation had long been a house divided against itself, and it could no longer stand.

One last point wants making. If, given the course of events, secession was inevitable, so too was war. In March 1861 Louis T. Wigfall of Texas promised his northern colleagues in the United States Senate: "if the Republican Senators . . . can get the backbone . . . into their President elect . . . we shall . . . fight." Historian Bell I. Wiley, who understood plain Southerners, declared that no "people ever went to war with greater enthusiasm than did Confederates in

3. Franklin Livingston to A. Burnham, March 16, 1861, Zachariah Chandler Papers, Library of Congress; Anthony Trollope, *North America*, ed. Donald Smalley and Bradford Allen Booth (New York, 1951), 20 (on the similar feelings of Yankees toward Southerners some forty years earlier see Lucius Verus Bierce, *Travels in the Southland, 1822–1823: The Journal of Lucius Verus Bierce*, ed. George W. Knepper [Columbus, Ohio, 1966], 51); *Atlantic Monthly* 1 (1857), 22; *Milwaukee Sentinel*, April 15, 1861, quoted in *The Causes of the Civil War*, ed. Kenneth M. Stampp (Englewood, N.J., 1965), 184; *Congressional Globe*, 36th Cong. (1860–61), 2d sess., 12; *New Orleans Bee*, December 14, 1860.

1861." And for four years they fought and died with the same reckless abandon, using the same assault tactics, that had characterized their Celtic ancestors for centuries. Crackers could scarcely have done otherwise. As products of a distinctive culture, they believed— as did all other Celts—that combat was the surest and the best way to protect their rights and their honor. "Turn peace away," wrote a Welsh poet, who revered this deadly but valorous conviction, "for honour perishes with peace."[4]

4. *Congressional Globe*, 36th Cong. (1860–61), 2d sess., 1399; Bell I. Wiley, *The Road to Appomattox* (Memphis, 1956), 43; Grady McWhiney and Perry D. Jamieson, *Attack and Die: Civil War Military Tactics and the Southern Heritage* (University, Ala., 1982), especially 170–91; James Michael Hill, *Celtic Warfare, 1595–1763* (Edinburgh, 1986); Gerald of Wales, *The Journey Through Wales and The Description of Wales*, trans. Lewis Thorpe (New York, 1978), 233.

# Appendix

## SOURCES ON THE
## ORIGINS OF SURNAMES

Sources used to help determine whether the surnames of antebellum Southerners were of English, Scottish, Scotch-Irish, Irish, or Welsh origins: George F. Black, *The Surnames of Scotland: Their Origin, Meaning, and History* (New York, 1946); Sir Robert Matheson, *Special Report on Surnames in Ireland* . . . (Dublin, 1909); idem, *Varieties and Synonymes of Surnames and Christian Names in Ireland* . . . (Dublin, 1901); Edward MacLysaght, *The Surnames of Ireland* (5th ed., Dublin 1980); Charles Wareing Bardsley, *A Dictionary of English and Welsh Surnames* . . . (1901; new ed., Baltimore, 1960); Henry Brougham Guppy, *Homes of Family Names in Great Britain* (1890; reprint, Baltimore, 1968); Sir William Addison, *Understanding English Surnames* (London, 1978); Henry Barber, *British Family Names: Their Origin and Meaning* . . . (1903; reprint, Baltimore, 1968); C. L'Estrange Ewen, *A History of Surnames of the British Isles* . . . (1931; reprint, Baltimore, 1968); Harriet Sutton Rankin, comp., *History of First Presbyterian Church, Fayetteville, North Carolina: From Old Manuscripts and Addresses* (Fayetteville, N.C., 1928), 5–9; Louise Barber Matthews, *A History of Providence Presbyterian Church, Mecklenburg County, North Carolina* (Charlotte, N.C., 1967), 257–309; S. M. Rankin, *History of Buffalo Presbyterian Church and Her People, Greensboro, N.C.* (Greensboro, N.C., 1934), 164–69, 188–200; John Wells Simpson, *History of the First Presbyterian Church of Greensboro, North Carolina, 1828–1945* (n.p., n.d.), 15; Charles William Sommerville, *The History of Hopewell Presbyterian Church for 175 Years from the Assigned Date of Its Organization, 1762* (Charlotte, N.C., 1939), 287–313; Jerry S. Nix, *One Hundred Sixty Years History of Bethel Presbyterian Church, 1812–1972 [Guilford County, N.C.]* (n.p.,

# Appendix

1972), 34–45; Neill Roderick McGeachy, *A History of the Sugaw Creek Presbyterian Church, Mecklenburg Presbytery, Charlotte, North Carolina* (Rock Hill, S.C., 1954), 175–79; Colonial Dames of America (Iredell County, N.C., Committee), comp., *Fourth Creek Memorial Burying Ground, 1756, Statesville, N.C.: History, Legends, Inscriptions* (Statesville, N.C., 1967); Mrs. Robert McDowell, comp., *A List of Those Buried in Historic Steele Creek Burying Grounds, Mecklenburg County, Charlotte, North Carolina* (Charlotte, N.C., 1953); Thomas Hugh Spence, Jr., *The Presbyterian Congregation of Rocky River* (Concord, N.C., 1954), 173–79; George W. McCoy, *The First Presbyterian Church, Asheville, N.C., 1794–1951* (Asheville, N.C., 1951), 11, 20, 21; Herbert Snipes Turner, *Church in the Old Fields: Hawfields Presbyterian Church and Community in North Carolina* (Chapel Hill, N.C., 1962), 250–54; J. G. Ramsay, *Historical Sketch of Third Creek [Presbyterian] Church in Rowan County, N.C.* (Statesville, N.C., 1937), 27–28; Robert Hamlin Stone, *A History of Orange Presbytery, 1770–1970* (Charlotte, N.C., 1970), 347–401; William Henry Foote, *Sketches of North Carolina, Historical and Biographical, Illustrative of the Principles of a Portion of Her Early Settlers* (New York, 1846), 77–136; Anon., *Hillsborough Presbyterian Church: One Hundred and Fifty Years of Service, 1816–1966* (Hillsborough, N.C., 1966), 3–17; List of Scotch-Irish Names, H. E. C. Bryant Papers, Southern Historical Collection, University of North Carolina, Chapel Hill; Session Book of Bethany Church from its Organization in 1775, James King Hall Papers, ibid.; Session Book and Register of Members, Chapel Hill Presbyterian Church Records, ibid.; Cub Creek "Scotch Irish Colony" Papers, Charlotte County, Va., ibid.; Gravestones, McPherson Presbyterian Churchyard, Fayetteville, N.C.; Gravestones, Bethel Presbyterian Churchyard, Hoke County, N.C.; Gravestones, Hillsborough Presbyterian Churchyard, Orange County, N.C.; A Record of the Inscriptions Found on the Gravestones in the Second Graveyard of Sugaw Creek Presbyterian Church, Charlotte, N.C., The Historical Foundation of the Presbyterian and Reformed Churches, Inc., Montreat, N.C.; George Howe, *History of the Presbyterian Church in South Carolina* (2 vols., Columbia, S.C., 1883), II:222–23, 597–98, 660–61; Bullock Creek Cemetery Association, comp., *Roster of Cemetery and Historical Sketch of Bullock Creek [South Carolina] Church* (n.p., 1962); Paul Quattlebaum, "Presbyterian Church on the Waccamaw," *South Carolina Historical Magazine* 54 (1953), 1–9; James M. Readling, *History of Hopewell Presbyterian Church, Claussen, South Carolina, 1770–1970* (Columbia, S.C., 1970), 85–92; Dudley Jones, *History of Purity Presbyterian Church of Chester, South Carolina, 1787–1937* (Charlotte, N.C., 1938), 111–13; James Maxwell Dallas,

*Historic Greenvale "Old Greenville [Presbyterian] Church"* (Abbeville, S.C., 1925), 25, 34–35; John H. Leith, *Greenville Presbyterian Church: The Story of a People, 1765–1973* (Greenwood County, S.C., 1973), 125–28; Mt. Zion Presbyterian Churchyard, Sandy Springs, S.C., Caroliniana Library, University of South Carolina, Columbia; Presbyterian Church Cemetery, Pendleton, S.C., ibid.; Old Concord Presbyterian Churchyard, Anderson, S.C., ibid.; Midway Presbyterian Churchyard, Anderson, S.C., ibid.; First Presbyterian Cemetery, Anderson County, S.C., ibid.; Bethany Presbyterian Church Cemetery, Laurens County, S.C., ibid.; Dorroh Presbyterian Church Cemetery, Laurens County, S.C., ibid.; Little River Dominick Presbyterian Church Cemetery, Laurens County, S.C., ibid.; First (Scots) Presbyterian Church Cemetery, Charleston, S.C., ibid.; Presbyterian Churchyard, Pickens, S.C., ibid.; Old Presbyterian Cemetery, Lancaster, S.C., ibid.; Bethel Presbyterian Cemetery, Walhalla, S.C., ibid.; Rocky Springs Presbyterian Church Cemetery, Laurens County, S.C., ibid.; New Harmony Presbyterian Church Cemetery, Laurens County, S.C., ibid.; Liberty Springs Presbyterian Church Cemetery, Laurens County, S.C., ibid.; Kingston Presbyterian Churchyard, Conway, S.C., ibid.; Mt. Tabar Presbyterian Church, Union County, S.C., ibid.; Old Black Mingo Presbyterian Cemetery, Williamsburg County, S.C., ibid.; Presbyterian Churchyard, Hartsville, S.C., ibid.; Duncan Creek Presbyterian Church Cemetery, Laurens County, S.C., ibid.; Friendship Presbyterian Church, Laurens County, S.C., ibid.; Head Springs Church, Laurens County, S.C., ibid.; Little River Presbyterian Church Cemetery, Laurens County, S.C., ibid.; Old Fields Presbyterian Church Cemetery, Laurens County, S.C., ibid.; Old Presbyterian Cemetery, Lancaster County, S.C., ibid.; Providence [Presbyterian] Church Cemetery, Laurens County, S.C., ibid.; Midway Presbyterian Churchyard, Williamsburg, S.C., ibid.; Presbyterian Churchyard, James Island, S.C., ibid.; Presbyterian Churchyard, Edisto Island, S.C., ibid.; Presbyterian Cemetery, Darlington County, S.C., ibid.; Presbyterian Cemetery, Fairfield County, S.C., ibid.; Union Presbyterian Church, Williamsburg County, S.C., ibid.; Presbyterian Cemetery, Union County, S.C., ibid.; Fair Forest Presbyterian Church, Union County, S.C., ibid.; Tombstones, First Presbyterian Churchyard, Columbia, S.C.; Scotch Cemetery, Kershaw County, S.C.; Robert G. Stephens, *A History of the Washington [Georgia] Presbyterian Church* (n.p., 1980), 1–3; James Stacy, *A History of the Presbyterian Church in Georgia* (Elberton, Ga., 1912), 330–54; James J. Gilbert, *A History of the First Presbyterian Church of Columbus, Georgia* (Columbus, Ga., 1930), 19–20; E. P. Rogers, *A Brief History of the First Presbyterian Church, in Augusta, Geo., with a Catalogue of its Officers and Members* (Charleston, S.C.,

1851), 28–45; Alton H. Glasure, "History of Hebron Church and Community" (M.A. thesis, University of Georgia, 1933), app.; Caroline McKinney Clarke, *The Story of the Decatur Presbyterian Church, 1825–1975* (Decatur, Ga., 1975); Charlotte F. Shenk and Donald H. Shenk, *History of the First Presbyterian Church, Huntsville, Alabama, . . . 1818–1968* (n.p., 1968), 33; Mrs. Thurman M. Kelso, *A History of the First Presbyterian Church, Florence, Alabama, . . . 1818–1968* (Florence, Ala., 1968), 16, 64–74; William E. McIlwain, *The Early Planting of Presbyterianism in West Florida* (Pensacola, Fla., 1926), 7–10; John M. Wilson, "Monroe Presbyterian Church and Cemetery, Algoma, Mississippi, 1821–1823," Presbyterian Historical Foundation, Montreat, N.C.; Virginia L. Jennings, *By These Stones: A Narrative History of the First Presbyterian Church of Baton Rouge, Louisiana* (Baton Rouge, 1977), 171–73; Tombstones, Smyrna Churchyard, near Washington, Ga.; Harry S. Hassall, *A History of Concord Presbyterian Church, Concord, Tennessee* (Knoxville, 1963), 91–93; Ben M. Barrus, Milton L. Baugh, and Thomas H. Campbell, *A People Called Cumberland Presbyterians* (Memphis, 1972), 517–18; J. G. M. Ramsey, *History of Lebanon Presbyterian Church, 1791, "In the Fork," Five Miles East of Knoxville, Tenn.* (Knoxville, 1918), 37–50; Robert L. Bachman, *Historical Sermon, Preached by the Pastor, Rev. Robert L. Bachman, D.D., In the Second Presbyterian Church, Knoxville, Tennessee, September 23, 1906* (n.p., n.d.); Calvin Morgan Fackler, *A Chronicle of the Old First (Presbyterian Church, Danville, Kentucky), 1784–1948* (Louisville, Ky., 1946), 89–94; Robert Davidson, *History of the Presbyterian Church in the State of Kentucky . . .* (New York, 1847), 369–71; Robert Stuart Sanders, *Presbyterianism in Paris and Bourbon County, Kentucky, 1786–1961* (Louisville, Ky., 1961), 5–31; W. H. Averill, *A History of the First Presbyterian Church, Frankfort, Kentucky, Together with the Churches in Franklin County* (Cincinnati, 1902), 240–48; Robert Stuart Sanders, *History of Walnut Hill Presbyterian Church (Fayette County, Kentucky)* (Frankfort, Ky., 1956), 18–28; E. N. Sawtell, *A Manual for the Members of the Second Presbyterian Church in the City of Louisville, Kentucky* (Louisville, Ky., 1833), 10–15; Anon., *History of the Second Presbyterian Church of Louisville, Kentucky, 1820–1930* (n.p., 1930), 26–27; Robert Stuart Sanders, *Annals of the First Presbyterian Church, Lexington, Kentucky, 1784–1959* (Louisville, Ky., 1957), 8–47; Robert Bell Woodworth, *A History of the Presbytery of Winchester (Synod of Virginia) . . . ,1719–1945* (Staunton, Va., 1947), 46–55; Howard McKnight Wilson, *The Tinkling Spring, Headwater of Freedom: A Study of the Church [Tinkling Spring and Hermitage Presbyterian Churches, Fisheville, Virginia] and Her People, 1732–1952* (2d ed., Verona, Va., 1974), 430–36; idem, ed., *Records of the*

*Synod of Virginia, Presbyterian Church in the United States: The Official Records and Relevant Historical Material of the Synod and Its Constituent Presbyteries and Churches on Microfilm* (Richmond, 1970), 54–55; idem, *The Lexington Presbytery Heritage: the Presbytery of Lexington and Its Churches in the Synod of Virginia, Presbyterian Church in the United States* (Verona, Va., 1971), 177–397; Elizabeth V. Gaines, *Cub Creek Church and Congregation [Charlotte County, Va.], 1738–1838* (Richmond, 1931), 73–75; James R. Graham, *The Planting of the Presbyterian Church in Northern Virginia Prior to the Organization of Winchester Presbytery, December 4, 1794* (Winchester, Va., 1904), 140–59; Edward Alvey, Jr., *History of the Presbyterian Church of Fredericksburg, Virginia, 1808–1976* (Fredericksburg, Va., 1976), 174–75; Mary Elizabeth K. Bratton, *Our Goodly Heritage: A History of the First Presbyterian Church of Lynchburg, Virginia, 1815–1940* (Lynchburg, Va., 1940), 12, 24; Sarah M. G. Gordon, *The History of the Presbyterian Church . . . of Gerrardtown, West Virginia* (Ann Arbor, Mich., 1939), 33–37, 60–69.

# Index

# Index

# About the Author

Grady McWhiney is Lyndon Baines Johnson Professor of American History, Texas Christian University. He received his B.S. from Centenary College of Louisiana, his M.A. from Louisiana State University, and his Ph.D. from Columbia University. He is author of *Southerners and Other Americans, Braxton Bragg and Confederate Defeat*, co-author of *Attack and Die: Civil War Military Tactics and the Southern Heritage* (with Perry D. Jamieson), general editor of *Primary Sources of American History*, editor of *Grant, Lee, Lincoln and the Radicals: Essays on Civil War Leadership, Reconstruction and the Freedmen*, and co-editor of *To Mexico with Taylor and Scott, 1845–1847* (with Sue B. McWhiney), *Historical Vistas: Reading in United States History* (with Robert Wiebe), and *Robert E. Lee's Dispatches to Jefferson Davis, 1862–1865* (with Douglas S. Freeman).